Facets of

WUTHERING

HEIGHTS

Selected Essays

Graeme Tytler

Matador
9 Priory Business Park,
Wistow Road, Kibworth Beauchamp,
Leicestershire. LE8 0RX
Tel: 0116 279 2299
Email: books@troubador.co.uk
Web: www.troubador.co.uk/matador
Twitter: @matadorbooks

ISBN 978 1789016 239

British Library Cataloguing in Publication Data.
A catalogue record for this book is available from the British Library.

Printed and bound in Great Britain by 4edge Limited
Typeset in 11pt Aldine401 BT by Troubador Publishing Ltd, Leicester, UK

Matador is an imprint of Troubador Publishing Ltd

For Sachiko

Contents

Acknowledgements

Since all these essays originally appeared in *Brontë Society Transactions* and *Brontë Studies*, I should like to take this opportunity to thank once again the following editors of both journals for accepting the earliest of them for publication: Mark Seaward, Edward Chitham and Robert Duckett. Special thanks are due to Amber Adams, the current editor of *Brontë Studies*, for the immense help and encouragement she has invariably given me in respect of various essays I have in recent years had published in her journal on the novels of all three Brontë sisters. I am deeply grateful to the staff of Matador, Hannah Dakin, Fern Bushnell and Emily Castledine in particular, for efficiently shepherding this collection through to its present format. Nor should I forget to convey my warm appreciation of the interest my sister and brother-in-law, Ruth and Michael Kaye, have shown in my research on Emily Brontë's masterpiece during the past three or four decades. Finally, I must express my infinite gratitude to my wife Sachiko, not only for the superb dexterity with which she has typed my manuscripts, but also for the consummate editorial skills which she has ever brought to bear on each and every one of these essays; to her I gladly dedicate this book.

Preface

These fifteen essays on *Wuthering Heights*, which have been assembled here partly in honour of this the bicentenary year of the birth of Emily Brontë, are, except for some minor changes here and there, substantially the same as those originally published in *Brontë Society Transactions* and *Brontë Studies*. Not the least important function of this collection is to suggest that the love relationship between Catherine and Heathcliff and their presentation as characters need to be viewed rather more dispassionately than has all too often been the case over the years. Further, it is hoped that readers who look upon the second half of the narrative after Catherine's death as something of a let-down may by dint of these essays be encouraged to acknowledge that it is nevertheless integral to the overall structure of the novel. These and other standpoints of mine have for the most part been gradually arrived at through repeated readings of the text during the past three decades. And though I have spent some of that time studying and writing about other great works of fiction, notably those of Charlotte and Anne Brontë, I have focused my research principally on *Wuthering Heights*, and in so doing come to realize more and more not only that, owing to the unwonted richness of its content, it is a book that repays constant, not to say endless, perusal and analysis, but that there is surely a good deal more of critical interest still to be said about this wonderful literary masterpiece.

Wuthering Heights: An Amoral Novel?

*W*uthering Heights has been pronounced an amoral or a non-moral novel, a novel without a moral centre.[1] Of sundry reasons lying behind such designations the most important undoubtedly have to do with the presentation of Catherine and Heathcliff. Thus statements have been made to the effect that both protagonists are above and beyond the confines of ordinary human society and hence not to be judged by its values and principles.[2] Catherine and Heathcliff are, moreover, not seldom esteemed transcendental creatures, whose destiny is to be ultimately reunited in death. In much the same vein are claims that the effusions of these two characters are what alone make the book worth reading, and that the second half of the novel, with its portrayal of Cathy and Hareton, is something of a let-down for the reader.[3] Further support for the idea of the amorality of the novel might even be sought in, say, the apparent indifference to moral questions in those making feminist and psychoanalytical interpretations of the text; in the (formerly common) opinion that the characters have no counterparts in the real world; and in the claim that the two main narrators are not altogether reliable.[4]

It is true that a number of scholars have over the years scrupulously exposed the moral defects of some of the main characters. Thus, as well as speaking of violence, cruelty, uncharitableness and the like, they have summarily condemned particular figures. For example, one scholar has declared Hindley to be 'the villain of *Wuthering Heights*', another scholar has devoted an entire essay to demonstrating that Nelly Dean is 'The Villain in *Wuthering Heights*', while a third scholar has gone so far as to deem Heathcliff 'the greatest villain in fiction'.[5] Yet even though Heathcliff's villainy has been time and again acknowledged, it seems to have detracted from his heroic stature as little as Catherine's untoward deeds have detracted from hers. This may have been due in part to the influence some critics have exerted through their use of the term 'moral' and its cognates in evaluations of the principal hero and heroine. Thus Catherine has been adjudged 'the real moral centre of the book' and even labelled 'absolument morale'; Catherine and Heathcliff's humanity has been said to be 'finer and more morally profound than the standards of the Lintons and the Earnshaws'; Lockwood is understood as someone instructed in 'the moral significance of [Heathcliff and Catherine's] immoral passion'.[6] Clearly, 'moral' and 'morally' in such contexts suggest the grandiose metaphysics of the moralist rather than the more humble ethics of the moral philosopher. Yet to overlook what is fundamentally ethical about *Wuthering Heights* is to miss an important element in the book. My concern here, then, will be to draw attention to an aspect that has hardly figured in criticism on the novel hitherto, namely, the way in which the author, as it were, puts all her main characters, including Lockwood and Nelly Dean, through a rigorous moral test to show how they relate to certain fundamental aspects of truth. By passing judgement on her characters from this standpoint, we are, then, in a better position not only to discern the essence of each of the characters, but to distinguish between them with perhaps greater objectivity.

Let me begin my discussion by considering the role of secretiveness in the plot (or plots) of *Wuthering Heights*. Secretiveness is, of course, a device used by Heathcliff in his bid to deceive Edgar on two counts: first, in order to arrange his tryst with Catherine at the Grange; secondly, in order to bring about the marriage of his son Linton to Cathy. If, however, Heathcliff's secretiveness succeeds well enough in the former case, in the latter case his twofold attempts to exhort Cathy, at the time of her first reunion with Linton, not to tell her father about her intended visits to the Heights, prove to be of no avail, thanks to the girl's frank account to Edgar of her unexpected meeting with Linton. That is why Heathcliff's secretiveness is ultimately dependent for its success on Nelly's own practice of secretiveness. In this connection, it is interesting to note the extent to which secretiveness seems to have been a habit with Nelly throughout her career as housekeeper and nanny to sundry masters and mistresses. One early instance is evident when she tells of 'not daring to speak a syllable' to Hindley about Catherine and Heathcliff's reckless behaviour 'for fear of losing the small power [she] still retained over the unfriended creatures' (*WH*, p. 40).[7] The fact that the ostensible motive for Nelly's secrecy here is power rather than, say, sympathy for two children maltreated by a vicious master does not, however, blind us to the notion that fear is the real motive for her silence. Indeed, it is fear, and usually a quite unfounded fear, that needlessly prevents Nelly from speaking out when she could have done so with impunity. Examples of this may be noted when she fails to report Heathcliff's disappearance in Chapter 9; when she announces Heathcliff's unexpected arrival at the Grange in Chapter 10 without mentioning him by name; and when, in Chapter 12, she sees 'nothing for it but to hold [her] tongue' (*WH*, p. 116) on inferring from the sight of her empty room that Isabella has indeed eloped with Heathcliff.

The last example is one of several by which Nelly makes secretiveness a norm in her dealings with Edgar, and that nowhere more blatantly than when she is stage-managing Heathcliff's tryst with Catherine. But why Nelly should be at all secretive with Edgar is puzzling when we reflect how much she is trusted, and how well she is treated, by him. Certainly, the reader can find no worthy reason behind Nelly's unwillingness to keep Edgar fully apprised of the vexed relationship between Cathy and Linton. This is obvious enough when referring, for example, to the first official meeting between the cousins, at which Linton has exhibited strange behaviour, Nelly says this about her own answer to questions Edgar put to her and Cathy about that meeting: 'I, also, threw little light on his inquiries, for I hardly knew what to hide, and what to reveal' (*WH*, p. 133). We also note how Nelly tries to play down another needless example of secretiveness as 'pardonable weakness' (*WH*, p. 234) when she refrains from correcting Edgar's assumption that Linton resembles him mentally because they are physically alike, just as she will later decline to say anything to Edgar about Cathy's sufferings at the Heights because she wishes to 'add no bitterness [...] to his already overflowing cup' (*WH*, p. 249). Yet Nelly's endeavour to 'please' her master in the latter context, noble as she makes it sound, is, in fact, little more than a papering over of the cracks. Moreover, through her reluctance to speak out truthfully in good time, Nelly may be said to have inadvertently paved the way not only for Cathy's ill-fated marriage to Linton, but also for the girl's subsequent sufferings at the hands of Heathcliff.

Nelly's secretiveness seems in some measure to be motivated in much the same ways as the white lies to which she is equally prone. We think, for instance, of the occasion when, in order to help maintain peace at the Heights, she prevents Heathcliff from reporting Hindley to Mr. Earnshaw for injuring him with an iron weight by 'easily persuading him to let [her] lay the blame of the bruise on the horse' (*WH*, p. 34). This intended lie might seem as venial as, say, the prevarications with which Nelly deigns to alleviate Linton Heathcliff's apprehensiveness on their journey to the Heights in Chapter 20. To be sure, one senses in the latter case the well-intentioned pity of someone who knows that in her position she can do nothing to remedy this painful state of affairs. At the same time, both instances amply illustrate how reluctant Nelly is in general to accept unpleasant human situations, especially those for which she is in no way responsible, and how disposed she is to pretend to herself that things are not as bad as they are in reality. A notable example can be seen when she deceives Edgar into believing that Isabella's letter to her has included 'a wish that he would transmit to her, as early as possible, some token of forgiveness by [Nelly]' (*WH*, p. 129); and, another, when she imparts to Isabella, on visiting her at the Heights, practically the opposite of what Edgar has said in response to the garbled version of the letter: '[My master] sends his love, ma'am, and his wishes for your happiness, and his pardon for the guilt you have occasioned' (*WH*, p. 130). From both references to forgiveness, it would appear that, intent as she is on basking in the momentary gratification she believes she has afforded both her superiors, Nelly seems to delude herself into thinking that she is also doing something commendably moral, and possibly Christian.

But although Nelly is no less apt to tell lies in other contexts, and that sometimes in order to assert her authority in the name of the master she happens to be serving, she is none the less aware of the wrongness of lying.[8] This we see when, with reference to Cathy's first (official) reunion with Linton, she recalls telling Edgar that Heathcliff 'forced [her] to go [into the Heights]', adding, 'which was not quite true' (*WH*, p. 249); or when, earlier, she has told Heathcliff that Edgar is not coming into the kitchen with some servants to evict him from the Grange, she admits to thereby 'framing a bit of a lie' (*WH*, p. 103). Yet by confessing to both these untruths, Nelly makes it abundantly clear that truthfulness for her is at best a convenience or an expedient rather than a habit to be strictly adhered to at all times. On the other hand, when it is a question of truthfulness in general, Nelly seems to have no doubt whatever that it should be sedulously observed by everyone else. This is ironically evident most of all through her continual disbelief of Heathcliff's utterances in the period between his return to Gimmerton and the death of Edgar. That is why there is perhaps nothing surprising about the hypocrisy she sentimentally displays when she has seen through Cathy's attempt to conceal her illicit visits to Linton: 'Oh, Catherine, [...]. You know you have been doing wrong, or you wouldn't be driven to uttering an untruth to me. That does grieve me. I'd rather be three months ill, than hear you frame a deliberate lie' (*WH*, p. 217).

The alacrity with which Emily's characters suspect or accuse one another of lying indicates some awareness on their part of the fundamental immorality of lies.[9] This is plain enough when, at his final meeting with Catherine, Heathcliff taunts her thus: 'You know you lie to say I have killed you' (*WH*, p. 140); and again when, on hearing that Catherine did not mention his name on her deathbed, he exclaims: 'Why, she's a liar to the end!' (*WH*, p. 147). Yet, not unlike Nelly Dean, Heathcliff has a propensity to lie when it suits his particular aims, a notable instance being when, in order to sustain Cathy's sympathy for him during their first encounter, he gives this specious reason for the cessation of communication between the two households: '[Your father] thought me too poor to wed his sister' (*WH*, p. 191). Not unrelated to this are the assertions Heathcliff occasionally makes on oath, as if he already knew that his words might otherwise be disbelieved. Thus in a bid to persuade Nelly to arrange a meeting between himself and Catherine at the Grange, he says: 'I swear that I meditate no harm' (*WH*, p. 134), just as in an endeavour to get Cathy to resume relations with his son, he says: 'I swear Linton is dying, […]' (*WH*, p. 206). As events later disclose, Heathcliff's affirmations on oath fail to guarantee either execution of intention or confirmation of statement.

Catherine, too, is quick to fall back on lies, especially when she finds herself on the horns of a dilemma in her quest to retain Edgar Linton's early interest in her without forfeiting Heathcliff's friendship. Consider, for instance, the lie with which, on the afternoon she expects Edgar's visit, she answers Heathcliff's enquiry as to whether anybody is coming to the Heights: 'Not that I know of' (*WH*, p. 60). That there is something quite pathological about Catherine's lies is suggested when Edgar later accuses her of telling 'a deliberate untruth' in denying that she pinched Nelly's arm. Indeed, as Nelly recalls, Edgar was 'greatly shocked at the double fault of falsehood and violence which his idol had committed' (*WH*, pp. 62-63). One may, therefore, wonder how things would have turned out had Catherine been utterly truthful to both Heathcliff and Edgar on that fateful afternoon.

Being truthful is, however, hardly less problematic in the novel than being deceitful. To be sure, the characters generally seem to consider truthfulness to be a moral desideratum, as is already implicit in their most casual mention of 'truth' and its cognates. Even habitual liars expect others to speak or observe the truth; but, because they are often dissatisfied with mere assertions or asseverations, they are likely to ask someone whether they are 'speaking the truth' or to tell them to 'speak the truth', however unbearable that truth may be.[10] It is interesting to note some of the ways in which Nelly, as well as making pleonastic use of 'true', 'in truth', 'the truth', etc., can be strangely zealous about telling the truth, and sometimes, too, without being consistently truthful.[11] Thus, referring to her visit at the Heights, in response to Isabella's letter, and to her assuring Heathcliff on arriving there that she has brought nothing with her from the Grange, she adds, 'thinking it best to speak the truth at once' (*WH*, p. 130), in spite of the fact that she will presently misrepresent the content of Edgar's message to his sister. Again, Nelly can be oddly strait-laced about truthfulness. Thus it seems surprising that, as someone who has fostered Heathcliff's illicit relations with Catherine and who, as we have seen, is much disposed to white lies, Nelly should tell the former the very opposite of what he has been hoping to hear, namely, that Catherine did not mention his name on her deathbed—perhaps because, ironically enough, Heathcliff has asked Nelly to give him 'a true history of the event' (*WH*, p. 147).

Noteworthy, too, are some of the ways in which Heathcliff seems to pride himself on being truthful. This is evident when, for example, having told Nelly that 'it wounds [Isabella's] vanity to have the truth exposed', he goes on to say this: 'But I don't care who knows that the passion was wholly on one side, and I never told a lie about it. She cannot accuse me of showing a bit of deceitful softness' (*WH*, p. 133). By saying all this, Heathcliff thinks himself absolved of all moral responsibility to his bride. Yet such truthfulness is hardly less base than that with which he hopes to persuade Cathy to visit the Heights and resume relations with his son by saying this to her: 'As true as I live, he's dying for you—' (*WH*, p. 205); or when, having assured Cathy presently that he will be away from the Heights, he adds: '[…] go and see if I have not spoken truth' (*WH*, p. 206). For though Heathcliff will have certainly 'spoken truth' in the latter respect, it is a truth of little ethical value, and the less so as it marks an early stage of that cunning form of deceit by which he will eventually bring about Linton's marriage to Cathy. Heathcliff's tendency to take advantage of the truth is evident when he seeks to justify his having trapped Nelly and Cathy in the Heights by saying this to the latter: 'You cannot deny that you entered my house of your own accord, in contempt of [your father's] injunctions to the contrary' (*WH*, p. 242). Such a fastidious concern with factual exactitude helps us to understand why Heathcliff is so skilled at interpreting various 'truths' of the law to his own benefit.[12]

Like Heathcliff, Catherine can be as blunt with the truth as she is sometimes afraid of it. For example, when Heathcliff has asked her if she is 'speaking the truth' about Isabella's love for him, it is, indeed, 'the truth', as Nelly's narrative corroborates, but a truth intended to cause trouble. That Catherine is, however, by no means concerned to stick to the truth may be gathered when, after she has given Heathcliff a distorted version of what her sister-in-law has actually said about her feelings for him, Isabella reproaches her as follows: 'I'd thank you to adhere to the truth and not slander me, even in joke!' (*WH*, p. 93). It is, moreover, interesting to note Catherine altering Isabella's claim to love Heathcliff 'more than ever [Catherine] loved Edgar' (*WH*, p. 90) by saying this to Heathcliff: 'Isabella swears that the love Edgar has for me is nothing to that she entertains for you' (*WH*, p. 93). But if Catherine's words are clearly meant to enable her to save face, they are nevertheless characteristic of her chronic lapses of memory, one psychologically significant example of which may be noted when, soon after consulting Nelly about whether or not to marry Edgar, she expresses anxiety lest Heathcliff may have overheard their talk by exclaiming: 'What did I say, Nelly? I've forgotten' (*WH*, p. 74). Such forgetfulness is, however, part and parcel of Catherine's general unawareness of the feelings of those closest to her—an unawareness that is signally obvious when, in the same dialogue with Nelly, she presently says: 'Was he vexed at my bad humour this afternoon? Dear! tell me what I've said to grieve him?' (*WH*, p. 74). Catherine's forgetfulness is perhaps much more disturbing when a statement she makes about Heathcliff is in flagrant contradiction with what she has previously said about him. For example, despite having complained to Nelly about Edgar's 'melting into tears' because she said that the newly-returned Heathcliff was 'worthy of any one's regard, and [that] it would honour the first gentleman in the country to be his friend' (*WH*, p. 87), she subsequently tries her utmost, probably out of jealousy, to put Isabella off Heathcliff by painting a most terrible portrait of his character, and that with some rather insensate metaphors and hyperboles.

The failure to be mindful of one's words, as illustrated in the foregoing, is just as noticeable with respect to the making of resolutions. Consider, for instance, how Catherine, in spite of telling Nelly, amid her joy in Heathcliff's unexpected return, that '[t]he event of this evening has reconciled [her] to God and humanity' (*WH*, p. 88), and that henceforth she will be a sort of Christian towards others, she will in effect have ignored that resolution shortly afterwards through her callous treatment of Isabella. Resolutions are, indeed, soon forgotten by some characters, as is evident when, having been lectured by Mr. Linton about Catherine and Heathcliff's intrusion at the Grange, Hindley warns the latter that 'the first word he spoke to Miss Catherine should ensure a dismissal' (*WH*, p. 45), even though, on Catherine's return home after her five-week sojourn at the Grange, he will sardonically tell Heathcliff that he may 'come and wish Miss Catherine welcome, like the other servants' (*WH*, p. 47). Hindley's resolutions or intentions are usually expressed with threats of extreme violence, childish examples of which occur in his drunken behaviour towards Nelly and Hareton in Chapter 9. Equally childish, though much more dangerous, is Hindley's telling Isabella of his determination, despite previous failed attempts, to kill her husband, and that in language at once solemn and superstitious: 'I've formed my resolution, and by God, I'll execute it!' (*WH*, p. 155).

Hindley's inability to act on his violent resolutions ironically reminds us that Heathcliff, in turn, does not kill Hindley, even though he has resolved to do so on his return to Gimmerton. It is true that Heathcliff does keep the resolution with which, in Chapter 11, he taunts Catherine as follows: '[…] thank you for telling me your sister-in-law's secret—I swear I'll make the most of it—and stand you aside!' (*WH*, pp. 99-100), just as he will keep his resolution to marry his son and Cathy. Yet both resolutions, though carried out, are nevertheless nefarious ones. Heathcliff's resolutions to commit violence, however, are generally as futile as Hindley's. Thus we may think of Heathcliff's physical threats against Edgar, especially as imparted to Catherine after the quarrel between the two men in the Grange kitchen: 'I'll crush his ribs in like a rotten hazel-nut, before I cross the threshold! If I don't floor him now, I shall murder him some time, [...]' (*WH*, p. 103). Of similar futility are those vicious resolutions he will later make in reaction to Cathy's defiance of him in Chapter 33.

Nelly's resolutions are many of them expressions of her somewhat overweening sense of responsibility to her superiors. Consider, for example, the fact that she is so uneasy about Heathcliff's influence on the Heights household since his return to Gimmerton, notably with respect to Hareton's upbringing, that, as she tells Lockwood: '[...] it urged me to resolve further on mounting vigilant guard, and doing my utmost to check the spread of such bad influence at the Grange [...]' (*WH*, p. 98). As the word 'further' confirms, Nelly has by then made a resolution to avert the possible consequences of Isabella's infatuation with Heathcliff by saying that she 'determined to watch [the latter's] movements' (*WH*, p. 94). Nelly's failure or inability to act on such noble resolutions is to be sure one of the ironies of her narrative. Again, as with the characters discussed above, some of Nelly's resolutions remain unfulfilled probably because they have been made in the heat of the moment. For example, on finding Cathy at the Heights after a long search for her, Nelly exclaims: 'This is your last ride, till papa comes back. I'll not trust you over the threshold again, you naughty, naughty girl' (*WH*, p. 171). How different events might have turned out to be, had Nelly kept to the latter resolution!

The comic irony of Nelly's words reminds us that she has some years earlier resisted Heathcliff's intention to visit Catherine at the Grange by saying: '—you never shall through my means' (*WH*, p. 131). Indeed, such words could be regarded as 'famous last words', rather like those with which she will later try to prevent Heathcliff from coaxing Cathy into the Heights: 'No, she's not going to any such place' (*WH*, p. 189); or, again, those with which she presently answers Heathcliff's expressed intention to marry his son to Cathy: 'And I'm resolved she shall never approach your house with me again' (*WH*, p. 190). All such statements also have an unmistakably ironic bearing on those with which Nelly shows a dogged determination to thwart Linton's relationship with Cathy. Much more important from a moral viewpoint, however, are the resolutions that Nelly makes about matters of which she has full control. Consider, for instance, the fact that, with respect to the secret meeting she has agreed to arrange between Heathcliff and Catherine at the Grange, she tells of 'affirming, with frequent iteration, that that betrayal of trust, if it merited so harsh an appellation, should be the last' (*WH*, p. 136). That 'that betrayal of trust' will be by no means the last is indirectly underlined with no little irony when, in answer to Cathy's talk about her selfless devotion to her sick father and her claim that she would never 'do an act or say a word to vex him', and only moments before another ill-fated encounter with Heathcliff, Nelly replies: 'Good words [...]. But deeds must prove it also; and after he is well, remember you don't forget resolutions formed in the hour of fear' (*WH*, p. 204).[13]

Nelly's pompous words just quoted are matched by the solemnity of her attitude to promises, as strikingly manifest at first when, on hearing that Catherine has already accepted Edgar's proposal of marriage, she exclaims: '[...] then, what good is it discussing the matter? You have pledged your word, and cannot retract' (*WH*, p. 68). Certainly it is through such words that we may be forcibly put in mind of the importance that many a moral philosopher down the ages has attached to the observance of one's promises. In this connection, it is noteworthy that the characters in general recognize the seriousness of making and keeping promises, particularly the promises they solicit of their interlocutors.[14] That keeping a promise, or claiming to have done so, may however not necessarily be a virtuous or moral act is here and there made plain in the narrative. Consider, for example, the fact that, despite having written of his decision, at the end of Chapter 1, to visit the Heights again 'to-morrow' (*WH*, p. 5), Lockwood tells of having 'half a mind to spend [the afternoon] by [his] study fire' (*WH*, p. 6), and is prompted to carry out his original plan only because he finds a maid putting out that study fire. Yet when, on observing Heathcliff enter 'the house', Lockwood says: 'You see, sir, I am come according to promise!' (*WH*, p. 8), we already know from his preceding diary entries that he is, in fact, telling a lie, at the same time as he is hoping, with his bland use of the term 'promise', to justify his unexpected visit to the Heights. Another trivialization of the promise may be noted when, to Catherine's rebuking him, in the wake of the apple-sauce tureen incident, for speaking to Heathcliff in the first place, Edgar retorts: 'I didn't […]. I promised mamma that I wouldn't say one word to him, and I didn't!' (*WH*, p. 52). Thus Edgar thinks himself exempted from blame simply because what he said about Heathcliff's long hair, though said well within the latter's hearing, was meant only for Hindley's ears. A third heinous example is Hindley's own eagerness to 'keep his promise to Mrs. Linton' (*WH*, p. 51), namely, to ensure that 'her darlings might be kept carefully apart from that "naughty, swearing boy"' (*WH*, p. 48) on Christmas Day. No doubt, such an uncharitable promise also helps to explain why, on his return from church that morning, Hindley pushes Heathcliff back on meeting him halfway between 'the house' and the kitchen. But whether it is a matter of keeping a promise or asking someone to make one,

Hindley is apt to abuse this bond of trust for violent ends. This is starkly exemplified when, during Heathcliff's struggles to get into the Heights through a narrow window, he assures Isabella of his resolve to kill him: 'Promise to hold your tongue, and before that clock strikes—it wants three minutes of one—you're a free woman!' (*WH*, p. 155). That is why it redounds to Isabella's credit that, in spite of yearning for Heathcliff's death, she is not to be coerced into making any such promise.

Like Hindley, Heathcliff, too, is inclined to take advantage of the promise for violent ends. One early instance occurs when, in answer to Nelly's question whether he is being taught by the local curate, young Hareton replies: 'No, I was told the curate should have his — teeth dashed down his — throat, if he stepped over the threshold— Heathcliff had promised that!' (*WH*, p. 98). As in the case of some of Heathcliff's aggressively voiced resolutions mentioned above, such an improbable threat is a gross perversion of the principle of being true to one's word. Again, when, in her letter to Nelly, Isabella tells of Heathcliff's accusing her brother of 'causing' Catherine's illness and of 'promising that [she] should be Edgar's proxy in suffering, till he could get a hold of him' (*WH*, p. 128), it is clear from Nelly's account of her subsequent visit to the Heights that Heathcliff has indeed largely kept that promise. Noteworthy, too, is Heathcliff's tendency to demand promises for selfish reasons. This can be seen when, for example, in her reluctance to elope with Heathcliff the first time he asks her to do so, Isabella is only able to put him off by 'pledging her word of honour to be prepared on their first meeting after that' (*WH*, p. 115); and again, when he succeeds in his bid to 'exact a promise' from Nelly that she will 'get [him] an interview with [Catherine]' (*WH*, p. 131) at the Grange.

That keeping one's promise is, as we saw above, by no means always a good thing may be apparent when we reflect that, not unlike Isabella's 'word of honour' to Heathcliff, Nelly's promise here is part of an act of deceit. And yet, because she has been browbeaten into making that promise, she could have justly broken it by simply reporting the matter to Edgar on her return to the Grange. Further, promises may sometimes be practically indistinguishable from lies, especially promises by which adults deign to placate children. A shameful example may be seen in the ruses that Nelly (with Edgar's collusion) falls back on in order to get Linton Heathcliff started on his journey to the Heights and to keep up his spirits on their way there: 'The poor thing was finally got off with several delusive assurances that his absence should be short; that Mr. Edgar and Cathy would visit him; and other promises, equally ill-founded, which I invented and reiterated, at intervals, throughout the way' (*WH*, p. 181).

In view of Nelly's reverential talk about promises in Chapter 9, her words just quoted may seem anomalous. And yet they may also be thought perfectly consonant with some of her earliest experiences at the Heights. Thus we think of the 'pocketful of apples and pears' which Mr. Earnshaw 'promised to bring [Nelly]' (*WH*, p. 31) on his return from Liverpool, but of which, perhaps significantly, no mention is later made, as if his promise had been but a mere formality. This then helps us to understand why, despite being 'sent out of the house' (*WH*, p. 32) by Mr. Earnshaw for mistreating Heathcliff on his first night at the Heights, Nelly comes back 'a few days afterwards' because, as she adds, she 'did not consider [her] banishment perpetual' (*WH*, p. 32). Clearly, Nelly has by then perforce become accustomed to the idea that giving or keeping one's word is sometimes just a matter of expediency. This, in turn, may explain why, in later years, Nelly is sometimes strangely assiduous in soliciting or observing certain promises by which to reassert her authority over Cathy. For example, despite having just colluded with the latter in paying an illicit visit to Linton, Nelly nevertheless vows to 'keep [her] word', that is, to 'inform Mr. Linton' as she warns the girl, 'if you attempt going to Wuthering Heights again, with or without me' (*WH*, p. 214)—a vow that she will scarcely hesitate to fulfil once she has heard Cathy's confession about her secret meetings with her cousin. Nelly's peremptory language here reminds us of the manner in which, not long before, she has taken the moral high ground as to Linton's letters through her following words to Cathy: 'If I consent to burn them, will you promise faithfully, neither to send nor receive a letter again, nor a book [...], nor locks of hair, nor rings, nor playthings?' (*WH*, p. 200). With this somewhat absurd enumeration of items, Nelly cannot but give the impression of being hypocritically anxious to make up for the shortcomings and inconsistencies that she herself has been liable to in making or keeping promises of her own.

Cathy's solemn answer, 'I promise, Ellen!' (*WH*, p. 200) to the above-quoted request ironically marks the end of an episode that began with an act of deceit. Yet those three words also remind us that, though forbidden by her father on the day after her first illicit reunion with Linton Heathcliff to visit the Heights again, Cathy was none the less anxious to send her cousin a note because, as she tearfully said to Nelly: 'He expected to see me again to-morrow, and there, he'll be so disappointed—and he'll wait for me, and I shan't come!' (*WH*, p. 197). But in spite of Nelly's flatly refusing to let her send either a note or the books she 'promised to lend him' (*WH*, p. 197), Cathy still manages to send a note, impelled to do so in part perhaps by the carking thought of having long been deceived by Nelly and Edgar as to Linton's whereabouts. Again, notwithstanding Nelly's warning her against continuing relations with Linton after her second (illicit) reunion with him, Cathy is able after all, as she tells Nelly in her long confession in Chapter 24, to take advantage of the latter's illness to 'keep [her] word' to Linton, adding, 'for [she] had engaged to call again next day, when [they] quitted him' (*WH*, p. 218). In this connection, one cannnot help noticing that Linton is very much his father's son in his determination to have promises made and kept for his own sake. At the same time, Linton's certainty that a promise for Cathy is absolutely binding is amply confirmed when the latter recalls his saying this to her on her third illicit visit to him: '—I was sure you wouldn't break your word, and I'll make you promise again, before you go' (*WH*, pp. 220-221). Indeed, once Cathy has given her word to someone she always keeps it, or endeavours to do so. We see this not only in her relations with Linton and Nelly Dean, but in those with her father and, later, with Hareton.[15] And if, as we have noted, a promise for Cathy sometimes entails disobedience to her elders, that is because the promise is kept out of compassion for the person to whom it has been given. The importance of the promise for Cathy is nowhere better exemplified than when, puzzled by Linton's strange behaviour at their second (authorized) meeting, Cathy says this to him: 'My father *is* very ill [...] and why am I called from his bedside—why didn't you send to absolve me from my promise, when you wished I wouldn't keep it?' (*WH*, p. 235). Cathy's wholesome attitude to promises stands out more especially when it is contrasted with Heathcliff's somewhat cynical attitude to them, as we may gather from the words he utters to her not long after he has trapped her in the Heights with Nelly: 'As to your promise to marry Linton, I'll take care you shall keep it; for you shall not quit the place till it is fulfilled' (*WH*, p. 242). As events will show, Heathcliff does not quite adhere to the words after the semi-colon, doubtless because, unlike Cathy, he only takes seriously those that will answer to his own needs.

That Cathy must have expected Heathcliff to keep his word is due to her taking it for granted that people usually speak the truth when they make statements of this kind. We recall, for example, her believing everything Heathcliff tells her at their first meeting at the Heights in Chapter 21, no doubt because, as well as being trustful by nature, she has by then discovered Edgar's (and Nelly's) deception of her as to Linton's actual situation. Nevertheless, Edgar's own account of Heathcliff's relationship with Isabella succeeds in counteracting her uncle's influence, as is later confirmed when, in her quarrel with Linton over their respective mothers in Chapter 23, she retails the import of that account, adding, 'Papa told me; and papa does not tell falsehoods!' (*WH*, p. 210). If such words seem to smack of excessive filial loyalty, given that Edgar has been secretive and evasive with her about Linton, they also seem sincere enough to suggest that she has never been told an outright lie by her father. It is this familiarity with truthfulness, as already hinted at when, about to make her confession to Nelly concerning her secret visits to the Heights, she says, 'I hate to hide [the truth]' (*WH*, p. 217), that may explain Cathy's inclination, at her chance encounter with Heathcliff outside Thrushcross park, to believe him when he assures her that Linton is pining to death for love of her, and the more so as he begins two assertions to that effect with 'I swear' (*WH*, p. 206) and challenges her possible disbelief by saying, 'Go and see if I have not spoken truth' (*WH*, p. 206).[16] Nelly's recalling that Cathy regarded what she had heard 'as every syllable true' (*WH*, p. 206), while herself imputing 'silly credulity' (*WH*, p. 207) to the girl, is none the less a sign not only of Cathy's compassion for Linton but, more importantly, of her essential truthfulness. Moreover, in complete contrast to Nelly, Heathcliff and Catherine, for whom lying is, as we have seen, a subterfuge to be readily resorted to, she takes it for granted that people mean what they say simply because she is herself truthful to others.

Yet naive as Cathy may seem to be about human nature, it would be a mistake to dismiss her integrity as a kind of rigid self-righteousness, for there are occasions when she is clearly induced by thoughtfulness to collude with some of Nelly's dishonesties. Consider, for instance, the fact that, though Nelly, significantly enough, had 'hard work [...] to obtain a promise that [Cathy] would not lay the grievance [about Hareton's insulting language] before her father', it is in part owing to Nelly's warning her that she might otherwise be dismissed, that Cathy 'pledged her word, and kept it, for [Nelly's] sake' (*WH*, p. 175). Similarly, when, despite what the reader already knows of Linton's cruelty to Cathy since their marriage, Nelly implores the latter to say, 'she should be happy with young Heathcliff' in order to console her dying father, Cathy avoids falling into the trap of a white lie thus: 'She stared, but soon comprehending why I counselled her to utter the falsehood, she assured me she would not complain' (*WH*, p. 283). As is self-evident, Cathy's silence in that respect does nothing to corrode her moral integrity.

It would, no doubt, be idle to deny or overlook Cathy's various childish faults and foibles—her snobbishness, her clannishness, her priggishness, her presumptuousness, her petulance, even her cruelty. And whereas all such failings are due in part to her sheltered and privileged upbringing, they are surely to be allowed for as readily as those shown by the other major characters during childhood. That Cathy has, nevertheless, already begun to grow out of her childishness soon after her father's death is evident from her commitment to Hareton's education. In this connection, it is important to stress that, whatever may be said to Hareton's disadvantage on account of his acts of violence, for which, at all events, he invariably expresses contrition in some form or other, nowhere in the narrative does he exhibit any form of deceit or dishonesty. Indeed, it is probably Cathy's shrewd awareness of Hareton's inherent probity that may be at the root of the love and respect she comes to show him. That is why it is fitting that two people, who combine moral integrity with considerateness rather better than almost all the other characters, should achieve heroic stature in the end; for otherwise the story of their love relationship might have indeed been the 'sugary romance' it has sometimes been wrongly assumed to be.[17]

It could be argued that this 'happy ending' would not have been possible but for the amoral (and immoral) deeds that preceded it. Such an argument is reinforced by our knowledge that, notwithstanding her many acts of deceit and duplicity, Nelly Dean enjoys something of a triumphant survival at the end of the novel. Yet it is in part through our study of Nelly's words and deeds above that I hope to have shown that propositions as to the amorality of *Wuthering Heights* are none the less unsatisfactory. And though nothing would seem more mistaken than to postulate that the author wished her readers to look upon her book as a kind of moral tract, or even as a testimony to Christian beliefs, it would appear that she was nevertheless intent both on making us aware of the significance of her characters' respective attitudes to facets of the truth, and on encouraging us to judge such attitudes according to traditional ethical values. We have seen how, in this novel of limited settings and restricted movements, deceit plays a conspicuous part in relations between the characters. Also implicit throughout the narrative is the idea of the primacy of mutual trust, as is also the idea of the difficulty of achieving or sustaining it. Accordingly, I have, for example, drawn attention in my discussion to the follies and dangers of being secretive and telling lies. We have seen, too, that making and keeping resolutions or promises are practices to be evaluated in large measure by the motives underlying them. At the same time, Emily seems to be suggesting that morality is not simply a question of being respectably conscious of the dichotomy between virtue and vice, as Nelly so often prides herself on being, but of sometimes being prepared to go beyond this dichotomy when there is a need to act on behalf of others in the right way at the right time. This is made especially palpable for us through Cathy's readiness, as it were, to sacrifice her moral integrity now and again, whether to benefit Linton Heathcliff or to gratify Nelly Dean, as it is also in that touching moment when, despite having forbidden Cathy to read the note Lockwood has brought her from Nelly until Heathcliff has seen it, Hareton is quick to forgo his unswerving loyalty to the latter out of compassion for the girl's feelings. It is through such minor episodes as much as through the more important ones discussed earlier in this essay that Emily Brontë manifests her remarkably perspicacious understanding of human nature, thereby enabling us to see, in ways not often enough recognized hitherto, that *Wuthering Heights* is an intrinsically moral novel.

Brontë Studies, 35/3 (2010)

Notes

1   See, for example, Halliwell Sutcliffe, 'The Spirit of the Moors',
    Brontë Society Transactions, 2 (1903), 176; Emily Brontë, *Wuthering
    Heights*, ed. Philip Henderson & introd. Margaret Lane (London: J.
    M. Dent, 1963), p. viii; C. Day Lewis, 'Emily Brontë and Freedom'
    in Emily Brontë, *Wuthering Heights*, ed. William M. Sale, Jr. (New
    York: Norton, 1963), p. 367; Claire Rosenfeld, 'The Shadow
    Within: The Conscious and Unconscious Use of the Double',
    Daedalus, 92 (1963), 330; L. P. Hartley, 'Emily Brontë in Gondal and
    Gaaldine', *Brontë Society Transactions*, 14 (1965), 7; Wendy A. Craik,
    The Brontë Novels (London: Methuen, 1968), passim; John Hewish,
    Emily Brontë: A Critical and Biographical Study (London: Macmillan,
    1969), p. 140; David Sonstroem, '*Wuthering Heights* and the Limits
    of Vision', *Publications of the Modern Language Association of America*, 86
    (1971), 57; Emily Brontë, *Wuthering Heights*, ed. Graham Handley
    (London: Macmillan Education Ltd., 1983), p. xiii; Frank Goodridge,
    Emily Brontë: Wuthering Heights (London: Edward Arnold, 1985),
    p. 28; Graham Holderness, *Wuthering Heights* (Milton Keynes and
    Philadelphia: Open University Press, 1985), p. 3; Muriel Spark and
    Derek Stanford, *Emily Brontë. Her Life and Works* (London: Arrow
    Books Ltd., 1985), p. 266; Cates Baldridge, 'Voyeuristic Rebellion:
    Lockwood's Dreams and the Reader of *Wuthering Heights*', *Studies in
    the Novel*, 20 (1988), 286; Victoria Moreland, '"It has devoured my
    existence": Emotion and Personality in *Wuthering Heights*', *Brontë
    Society Transactions*, 19 (1988), 263; Emily Brontë, *Wuthering Heights*,
    introd. Katherine Frank (London: J. M. Dent, 1991), p. xvi; Linda
    H. Peterson, *Emily Brontë: Wuthering Heights* (Boston, MA: Bedford
    Books, 1992), p. 10; Robert Barnard, 'What Does *Wuthering Heights*
    Mean?', *Brontë Society Transactions*, 23 (1998), 112; Stevie Davies,
    Emily Brontë (Plymouth: Northcote House Publishers Ltd., 1998),
    p. 39; *Emily Brontë. Wuthering Heights. A Reader's Guide to Essential*

Criticism, ed. Patsy Stoneman (Cambridge: Icon Books Ltd., 2000), p. 55; Emily Brontë, *Wuthering Heights*, ed. Ian Jack and introd. Helen Small (Oxford: Oxford University Press, 2009), p. ix.

2   See, among numerous examples, Emily Jane Brontë, *Wuthering Heights*, introd. Alan Hodge (London: Hamish Hamilton, 1950), p. v; Dorothy Van Ghent, *The English Novel: Form and Function* (New York: Holt, Reinhart & Winston, 1953), p. 164; Mary Visick, 'The Genesis of *Wuthering Heights*', in *Emily Brontë: A Critical Anthology*, ed. Jean-Pierre Petit (Harmondsworth: Penguin Books, 1973), p. 174; Rod Mengham, *Wuthering Heights* (Harmondsworth: Penguin Books, 1989), p. 101.

3   For the references to Catherine and Heathcliff, see G. D. Klingopoulos, 'The Novel as Dramatic Poem (II): *Wuthering Heights*', *Scrutiny*, 14 (1947), 269, 282. For negative criticism of Hareton and Cathy, see especially Laura L. Hinkley, *The Brontës: Charlotte and Emily* (London: Hammond, Hammond & Co. Ltd., 1947), p. 261; Robin Grove, '*Wuthering Heights*', *The Critical Review*, 8 (1965), 75; Craik, *The Brontë Novels*, p. 32; Alan Gardiner, 'Does the Novel Deteriorate After the Death of Catherine?', in *Critical Essays on Wuthering Heights*, eds. Linda Cookson and Brian Loughrey (London: Longman, 1988), p. 92.

4   See, for example, Sandra Gilbert and Susan Gubar, *The Madwoman in the Attic: The Woman Writer and the Nineteenth-Century Literary Imagination* (New York and London: Yale University Press, 1979), pp. 223-285; James Kavanagh, *Emily Brontë* (Oxford: Basil Blackwell, 1985), passim. For comments (among several) asserting the unwontedness of Emily's characters, see, for example, Virginia Woolf, '*Jane Eyre*' and '*Wuthering Heights*' in *The Common Reader* (London: Hogarth Press, 1929), p. 203; and Emily

Brontë, *Wuthering Heights*, introd. by Elizabeth Jennings and notes
by Phyllis Bentley (London: Pan Books Ltd., 1972), p. 6. For
some references (among several) to the unreliable narratives,
see, for example, Irene Cooper Willis, 'The Style of *Wuthering
Heights*', in *Wuthering Heights. An Anthology of Criticism*, ed. Alastair
Everitt (London: Frank Cass, 1967), p. 185; Esther Schönberger-
Schleicher, *Charlotte and Emily Brontë. A Narrative Analysis of Jane
Eyre and Wuthering Heights* (Berne: Peter Lang, 1998), p. 199.

5   See respectively Millicent Collard, *Wuthering Heights—The Revelation.
A Psychical Study of Emily Brontë* (London and New York: Regency
Press Ltd., 1960), p. 13; James Hafley, 'The Villain in *Wuthering
Heights*', *Nineteenth-Century Fiction*, 13 (1958-59), 199-215; T. W.
Reid, '*Wuthering Heights*', in *The Brontës: The Critical Heritage*, ed.
Miriam Allott (London and New York: Routledge, 1974), p. 401.

6   For these quotations, see respectively Q. D. Leavis, 'A Fresh
Approach to *Wuthering Heights*', in *Emily Brontë*, ed. Patsy
Stoneman, p. 58; Georges Bataille, *La Littérature et le Mal* (Paris:
Gallimard, 1957), p. 15; Arnold Kettle, 'Emily Brontë: *Wuthering
Heights*', in *Wuthering Heights. Texts, Sources, Criticism*, ed. Thomas
Moser (New York, Chicago, San Francisco and Atlanta: Harcourt
Brace & World Inc., 1962), p. 193; Mark Schorer, 'Introduction
to *Wuthering Heights*', in *Wuthering Heights*, ed. Moser, p. 185.

7   For quotations from the novel, see Emily Brontë, *Wuthering
Heights*, eds. Ian Jack and Patsy Stoneman (Oxford: Oxford
University Press, 1998). For the sake of convenience, the first
Catherine will be referred to as 'Catherine', the second as 'Cathy'.

8   For some of Nelly's outright lies, see *Wuthering Heights*, pp. 165,
171, 293.

9 For accusations of others for lying, or suspicions that someone is lying, see *Wuthering Heights*, pp. 134, 205, 206, 223, 231, 278.

10 See, for example, *Wuthering Heights*, pp. 77, 94, 99, 107, 213.

11 For Nelly's (and Lockwood's) more or less pleonastic use of 'truth' or 'true', see *Wuthering Heights*, pp. 32, 79, 236.

12 That Heathcliff's legal mind remains intact till the end of his life is suggested when, in answer to Nelly's advice to '[l]et [his] will be, a while', for he will be 'spared to repent of [his] many injustices', he presently says, '[…] as to repenting of my injustices, I've done no injustice, and I repent of nothing—'. See *Wuthering Heights*, p. 296.

13 For Nelly's perfunctorily executed resolutions, see *Wuthering Heights*, pp. 83, 106, 114, 216.

14 See especially *Wuthering Heights*, pp. 134, 217.

15 See *Wuthering Heights*, pp. 226, 286.

16 Heathcliff's use of 'swear' as a sort of substitute for 'promise' is suggested when, in the attempt to persuade Nelly to let him visit Catherine, he says: 'I swear I meditate no harm; […]. I only wish to hear from herself how she is, and why she has been ill; and to ask, if anything that I could do would be of use to her'. See *Wuthering Heights*, p. 134. This tender oath is, however, rendered meaningless both by Heathcliff's aggressive recriminations against Catherine at their tryst and by their fatal effects on her life.

17 See Peter D. Grudin, '*Wuthering Heights*: The Question of Unquiet Slumbers', *Studies in the Novel*, 6 (1974), 396.

The Role of Religion in *Wuthering Heights*

One subject that has exercised a good many Brontë scholars over the years is the role of religion in *Wuthering Heights*. Prominent in this respect has been the aim to establish the theological significance or intention of the novel, whereby the opinion has sometimes been advanced, or, at least, the impression conveyed, that, transcendental or other-worldly as it may be in spirit, Emily Brontë's masterpiece is at heart a more or less anti-Christian book.[1] Of various reasons given for this assumption perhaps the most plausible is the suggestion that Heathcliff's 'mystical' religiosity, because practised in order that he may remain in communication with Catherine after her death, and also ensure their reunion in the afterlife, is 'superior' to the Christian doctrines he implicitly rejects.[2] But if such thinking may have held a certain appeal in this our highly secular era, chiefly among those readers who zealously identify with Heathcliff and his sufferings, it nevertheless fails to do justice to the author's remarkably comprehensive and objective critique of religion.[3] Indeed, in her concern to show us, among other things, the various ways in which the presentation of her characters is bound up with the historicity of the Judaeo-Christian tradition, Emily Brontë is intent on inviting us to consider what relevance Christ's life and teachings may still be thought to have had at the dawn of the nineteenth century, and even to her readers in 1847 and beyond.[4]

This should not, however, obscure the fact that religion in *Wuthering Heights* is, for the most part, depicted in drab colours. We note, first of all, that the action of the novel takes place during a historical period that is marked by conflict and separatism within the Proestant Church, a period in which the steady rise of Nonconformism is paralleled by a perceptible decline in Anglicanism. This is suggested in part by a handful of references to the local clergy, who, despite enjoying an unquestioned standing in society, notably as educators, come across to the reader as lazy, mercenary, given to gossip and lacking in spirituality.[5] Moreover, though traditional Christian practices are generally observed, and deviations from them frowned upon, by the small Yorkshire community here portrayed, it is evident that for those whom Nelly Dean here and there summarily refers to as 'the parish' (*WH*, pp. 33, 37, 40, 87), churchgoing is a perfunctory or social pursuit rather than a pious endeavour. It is, therefore, hardly surprising that the very days when it is obligatory to attend church, namely, Sundays and Christmas Day, also happen to be conspicuous in the novel for a number of blatant acts of uncharitableness or impropriety on the part of some so-called Christians. All the same, religion has a fairly important place in everyday life, and nowhere more so than in Wuthering Heights itself. Indeed, it is one of the ironies of the narrative that the cause of Christianity is upheld principally by two laypersons, Nelly Dean and Joseph, who represent orthodoxy and dissent respectively, and whose disputes or disagreements with one another comically symbolize the schisms obtaining within the Church at the time.

Nevertheless, the question arises: how far can Joseph and Nelly Dean be deemed the Christians they purport to be? As regards Joseph, some readers might be content to assume the answer to lie already in the disparaging generalities made about him by Nelly in Chapter 4, and to be confirmed in that assumption by ironic attitudes towards the Nonconformists suggested elsewhere in the narrative, not least through the somewhat satirical portrait of Zillah. On the other hand, it is reasonable to suppose that a good many Christians in the late eighteenth century, Anglicans no less than Dissenters, would have been quite favourably impressed by Joseph's religious influence over the Earnshaw household. Indeed, his concern for the welfare of the souls of his social superiors, his warnings about the dangers of the devil, his supervision of prayers and devotional offices, his catechizing of the children—all these would have been considered signal examples of religious leadership. And though Joseph's Calvinism sometimes seems pernicious, as when, in moments of crisis, he calls upon God to distinguish between the elect and the non-elect, it is worth remembering that the dogma of Predestination commonly associated with the Nonconformists was not only accepted but even affirmed by many an Anglican clergyman at that time.[6]

Yet, despite the apparent sincerity of Joseph's religious didacticism, as manifest, for example, in his heavy reliance on the Bible, it is not difficult to suppose that his solemn pronouncements, especially with respect to eschatological doctrine, are for the most part theologically presumptuous. Consider, for instance, that moment when he points up the futility of wailing over the sudden death of Mr. Earnshaw by declaring the latter to be already 'a saint in Heaven' (*WH*, p. 42). Consider, too, the contradiction within Joseph's utterance when, in answer to Isabella's asking him, shortly after her arrival at the Heights as Heathcliff's bride, to provide her with 'a place of refuge and means of repose', he mingles his appeals to the Deity with virtually blasphemous interjections as follows: 'Whear the divil, […] The Lord bless us! The Lord forgie us! Whear the *hell* wold ye gang? ye marred, wearisome nowt!' (*WH*, p. 144). The violence of Joseph's language—a violence which is to be sensed in most of his religious interjections and invocations and which is testimony enough to his inveterate misanthropy—is especially ironic here if we recall that, having been entreated by Isabella only a few moments earlier to accompany her into the house, he has replied: 'Mim! mim! mim! Did iver Christian body hear owt like it?' (*WH*, p.138). In similar vein is Joseph's verbal response to Isabella's having flung down the tray holding the porridge she has just made: 'Gooid-fur-nowt madling! yah desarve pining froo this tuh Churstmas, flinging t' precious gifts uh God under fooit i' yer flaysome rages!' (*WH*, p. 144). What is significant for our purposes about Joseph's words in this context is not only his rather untimely reference to himself as a Christian, but the way in which his pronunciation of 'Christmas', with its first syllable sounding like 'cursed', ironically evokes the acerbity he has already exhibited in Chapter 7 towards this traditionally joyous festival.

In the light of what has just been said above, it would, then, seem appropriate that, to Joseph's vociferous complaints in Chapter 32 about her merry singing in the Heights kitchen, Nelly Dean should reply good-humouredly with the following piece of advice: 'But wisht, old man, and read your Bible like a Christian, and never mind me' (*WH*, p. 308). At the same time, the reader may wonder what Nelly herself means here by 'Christian'; indeed, whether her use of that epithet does not beg the question as much it has done when, in conversation with Catherine, she naively summed up Heathcliff's conduct since his return to Gimmerton by declaring: 'He is reformed in every respect apparently—quite a Christian—offering the right hand of fellowship to his enemies all round' (*WH*, p. 98). But if Nelly might have been nearer the truth by saying 'decent person' instead of 'Christian', her somewhat inept description of Heathcliff here is none the less an example of her tendency to judge her fellow creatures by the codes and standards of Christianity. Among other notable examples of this tendency may be mentioned not only her pedantic concern with the observance of solemn rituals or ecclesiastical law, whether it be, say, her insistence on Hindley's funeral 'being respectable' (*WH*, p. 186) or her objection to Cathy's being forced to marry her cousin Linton for being 'felony without benefit of clergy' (*WH*, p. 274), but her readiness to remind her social superiors, Heathcliff and Isabella in particular, of the teachings of the Bible which, in their vengefulness, they appear to have neglected or forgotten. Yet for all that she is thus preoccupied with others, Nelly tells us next to nothing about her own life as a Christian, whether that has to do with such things as going to church or even saying her prayers. Moreover, when, for example, she says to Lockwood, '[w]e don't in general take to foreigners here, [...] unless they take to us first' (*WH*, p. 43), her words seem as little the sign of a practising Christian as do her various acts of deceit and deception, to say nothing of her general vindictiveness.

Nelly's apparent lack of piety, not to say her lack of a sense of sin, as suggested partly by her rationalizations about her sundry betrayals of Edgar, doubtless helps to explain her somewhat 'cosy' notion of the Deity. Thus, not unlike Joseph, though in more optimistic fashion, Nelly is generally confident as to how God will think or act, usually with respect to matters of interest to herself. Among several instances we may refer in particular to the comparison she draws in Chapter 17 between Edgar and Hindley as bereaved widowers, whereby, amid respect for the former's stoicism and disapproval of the latter's unruliness, she recalls that, displaying 'the true courage of a loyal and faithful soul', Edgar 'trusted God; and God comforted him!' (*WH*, p. 183). In this connection, it is noteworthy that, sharing as they do a belief in heaven, and not without good reason in view of what is said here and there in the New Testament about an afterlife for true Christians, Nelly and Edgar seem nevertheless blissfully unaware of the presumptuousness with which they separately take it for granted that the rebellious Catherine has preceded them thither. In Nelly's case, the presumptuousness is doubtless due partly to the unmistakable aestheticism permeating her religiosity—an aestheticism that may be sensed especially when, from the sight of Catherine's elaborately described beauty in death, she infers that the latter is already in heaven and now 'with her Maker' (*WH*, p. 165). Interesting, too, is the way in which Nelly reveals the essence of her religiosity in this reference to the effect exerted on her by the defunct Catherine's facial beauty: 'My mind was never in a holier frame than while I gazed on that untroubled image of Divine rest' (*WH*, p. 164). And though it is understandable that, in that state of mind, Nelly should even go on to corroborate her confident assumption about Catherine's posthumous fate by saying, 'I instinctively echoed the words [Catherine] had uttered, a few hours before. "Incomparably beyond and above us all!"', the reader may be none the less aware not only that, when consulting Nelly about whether or not to marry Edgar, Catherine has repudiated the idea of a Christian heaven, but that Nelly herself has declared her mistress to be by nature 'not fit' (*WH*, p. 80) for heaven. It is this sort of inconsistency which, taken in conjunction with accounts of her moments of irrational fear, inclines the reader to look upon Nelly's religion as being often barely distinguishable from superstition. Indeed, it is her very superstitiousness that raises doubts about the quality of her religious faith.[7]

The fact that superstition seems to have elements in common with religion may suffice to explain its firm hold not only on Nelly Dean but on those characters who, like herself, have been brought up as Christians in an environment steeped in the traditions of local folklore. Yet superstition is clearly much less complex in Nelly than it is in, say, Hindley, Catherine and Heathcliff, perhaps because the last three seem to have been adversely affected by the religious indoctrination to which they were rigorously subjected during their childhood. Consider, for example, Heathcliff's refusal to accept the finality of Catherine's death, together with his conviction that the dead continue to lead some kind of terrestrial existence. Such thinking is, no doubt, connected with the belief in ghosts which he has held in common with Catherine since earliest years and which, for some readers, may be thought validated at the end of the novel by statements about the ghosts of the hero and heroine, even though Heathcliff's experiences of Catherine's ghost may also be understood as symptomatic of his partial insanity.[8] Still, notwithstanding his 'strong faith in ghosts' (*WH*, p. 289), not to mention his apparent rejection of Christianity and his anticlericalism, Heathcliff continues to betray, in much the same way as Catherine and Hindley do, the effects of an austere religious education. Thus Heathcliff's use of 'hell', 'hellish', 'infernal', etc. in meaningless metaphors or interjections, which, like Hindley's use of such terms, are expressive of impatience, fear or despair, seems an unconscious manifestation of the guilt supposedly inculcated into him by Joseph's constant warnings to him and the other children about the dangers of that place of eternal perdition—a guilt which, incidentally, seems to be likewise at the bottom of Heathcliff's (and Hindley's) blasphemous use of 'accursed', 'confound', 'damn', 'damnable', 'damnably' and their cognate forms.

Noteworthy, too, are the references made now and again to heaven, and the way in which concepts of heaven are shown to have been elaborately subjective in childhood. But whereas there is something perfectly 'normal' about, say, Cathy's and Linton Heathcliff's respective descriptions of heaven (in Chapter 24) as ideal places of happiness, it would appear, on the other hand, that Catherine and Heathcliff never quite outgrow their childish notions of heaven, such as the one evoked by Nelly when, describing their plaintive response to Mr. Earnshaw's sudden death, she recalls that 'no parson in the world ever pictured Heaven so beautifully as they did, in their innocent talk; [...]' (*WH*, p. 42). Yet if, as adults, Catherine and Heathcliff will have no truck with the Christian heaven as conceived by, say, Nelly Dean or Edgar Linton, they are evidently persuaded of that transcendentalism of the afterlife which is traditionally associated with heaven. That Catherine, moreover, seems never to have quite abandoned her childish concept of the Christian heaven is unconsciously suggested when she speaks of being 'incomparably above and beyond [everybody]' and also through interjections she utters such as 'please Heaven!' (*WH*, p. 106) and 'Heavens!' (*WH*, p. 115). Again, though Heathcliff's own concept of heaven has by the end of his life come exclusively to mean togetherness with Catherine, just as hell has long meant separation from her, it is interesting to note how, in spite of himself, he seems to acknowledge the existence of a Christian heaven when, speculating somewhat superstitiously about Catherine's fate since her death, he says this to himself in Nelly's presence: 'Where is she? Not *there*— not in heaven—not perished—where?' (*WH*, p. 167).

The impact of a strict religious upbringing can also be felt through the ways in which Heathcliff, Catherine and Hindley conceive of, or refer to, the soul. For example, just as Hindley's overweening certainty about the dreadful fate in store for Heathcliff's soul as well as for his own after death seems to betoken the continuance of Joseph's spiritual influence, so Heathcliff's and Catherine's talk about the soul, though utterly subjective, not to say romantic, seems to bespeak an ineffectual rebellion against that influence. Thus, Heathcliff's use of 'soul' both when he asks Catherine, at their final meeting, whether she would 'like to live with [her] soul in the grave?'

(*WH*, p. 161) and, again, when, in the throes of his monomania, he tells Nelly that '[his] soul's bliss kills [his] body, but does not satisfy itself' (*WH*, p. 333), appears to have much the same erotic implications as Catherine's own use of the term, especially when she gives Nelly Dean the following reason for her doubt about accepting Edgar's proposal of marriage: 'In whichever place the soul lives— in my soul, and in my heart, I'm convinced I'm wrong!' (*WH*, p. 79). That the erotic experience seems for Catherine, no less than for Heathcliff, to be a kind of religion is quite apparent when she goes on to say this to Nelly: 'Whatever our souls are made of, [Heathcliff's] and mine are the same, and Linton's is as different as a moonbeam from lightning, or frost from fire' (*WH*, p. 80). Indeed, the inherent religiosity underlining Catherine's peculiar love for Heathcliff seems to be ultimately confirmed when, puzzled by his momentary remoteness from her at their last tryst, she consoles herself with the image of him that she seems to have all along preferred to the real person by saying, 'he's in my soul' (*WH*, p. 160).[9]

More significant in this context, however, are the references made by all the main characters to God or to the devil. Joseph's persistent talk about the devil as an actual presence in human life may, in part, explain why Catherine and Heathcliff themselves occasionally mention the devil as a real figure; and, no doubt, that concept is at the root of the tendency of various characters to compare Heathcliff to that figure, and even to look upon him as a very personification thereof. It is, however, Hindley who best proves to be Joseph's acolyte on that head, especially when he speaks of the devil, or of some unspecified devil, either as a source of help for, or as a hindrance to, his nefarious intentions. Thus he explains to Isabella his persistent inability to murder Heathcliff: '—it is some devil that urges me to thwart my own schemes by killing him—you fight against that devil, for love, as long as you may; when the time comes, not all the angels in heaven shall save him!' (*WH*, p. 140).

This generally presumptuous, even nonsensical, obsession with the devil is unconsciously manifested in metaphorical interjections of all kinds, which, together with the epithets 'diabolical' and 'devilish', and like the figurative language entailing the use of 'hell', are voiced again and again, usually meaninglessly, down to the youngest generation portrayed in the novel.

Meaningless, too, in similar ways are interjections incorporating mention of the Deity, more especially those which Heathcliff, in anger, despair, impatience or contempt, is given to using more often than any other character, and which, in contradistinction to the interjections referred to above, are, of course, utterly blasphemous for breaking the Third Commandment.[10] These interjections are, however, but one aspect of the theologically questionable relations that Heathcliff continues to entertain with God. We note, for example, that, not unlike Joseph and Nelly Dean, Heathcliff is sometimes presumptuous about God's attitudes. For example, when in answer to Nelly's disapproval of his plan to 'pay Hindley back' for his maltreatment of him and her reminding him that it is 'for God to punish wicked people', he retorts, 'No, God won't have the satisfaction that I shall' (*WH*, p. 60). A like presumptuousness may be noted when, at his final meeting with Catherine, Heathcliff expresses confidence that, had she chosen him instead of Edgar, 'nothing that God or Satan could inflict would have parted [them] […]' (*WH*, p. 161), whereby the conjunction of God or Satan here seems, theologically speaking, to be almost as pretentious as the interjection '[b]y Heaven and Hell' (*WH*, p. 77) uttered by Hindley in an earlier context. It is this sort of indiscriminate language which, moreover, typifies Hindley's own anomalous relations with the Deity, as we gather when, as Nelly tells Lockwood, he 'execrated God and man' (*WH*, p. 65) for the death of Frances, and when, on the morning after his fight with Heathcliff, he says to Isabella: 'Oh, if God would but give me strength to strangle [Heathcliff] in my last agony, I'd go to hell with joy' (*WH*, p. 180). Nor is Catherine herself devoid of an analogously careless subjectivity, as may be seen when, gladdened by Heathcliff's return to Gimmerton after his three-year absence, she says this to Nelly: 'The event of this evening has reconciled me to God and humanity!' (*WH*, p. 99). Yet her readiness in the same context to go further than obeying Christ's injunction to offer the other cheek adds to the intrinsic frivolity of her seemingly contrite utterance, and the more so as she will shortly afterwards contradict it by her unpleasant behaviour towards Isabella. Whether or not Catherine's strangely penitential sentiments here are due in their suddenness to the incompetence of her religious educators or merely to her wrong-headedness is, no doubt, a question related to one that might be similarly raised *mutatis mutandis* as to the language of the other characters we have just discussed above. At any rate, the idea that the blame for all this seems to attach to Christians rather than to Christianity itself, though in some sense already implicit in our findings hitherto, may be thought validated when we have examined Lockwood's presentation in some detail.

★ ★ ★

It is easy to deduce from Lockwood's allusion to Christ's miracle of the Gadarene swine in Chapter 1 that, like the main characters, he has had a religious upbringing.[11] That he seems, moreover, not unlike those characters, to have turned his back on formal religion, is suggested by his occasional use of 'God', 'devil', 'heaven' and 'hell' and their kindred forms in various ironic or meaningless interjections and metaphors. Noteworthy, too, is Lockwood's secular use of words traditionally associated with Christian doctrine, particularly for the connection which he, as frame-narrator, has surely noted between such terms and those which Nelly Dean and other characters employ with secularized meaning. Consider, among numerous examples of the latter, *angel* (*WH*, pp. 99, 106, 199, 213, 243, 299) as 'pet', 'virtuous person' or 'beautiful person'; *blessing* (*WH*, pp. 67, 176, 259, 268) as 'good thing' or 'advantage'; *charity* (*WH*, p. 28) as 'financial support'; *confess* (*WH*, pp. 35, 67) as 'own up'; *redeem* (*WH*, pp. 65, 164) as 'make up for'; *repent* (*WH*, pp. 88, 138, 173, 224, 254, 313) as 'regret'; *soul* (*WH*, pp. 35, 42, 64, 67, 183) as 'individual', and so on. Of particular interest in this connection are various secular uses of 'pray' and 'prayer', the most striking instance being perhaps embodied in Heathcliff's following utterance to the recently defunct Catherine: 'And I pray one prayer—I repeat it till my tongue stiffens—Catherine Earnshaw, may you not rest, as long as I am living!' (*WH*, p. 167).[12] Nor should we overlook Nelly Dean's affected use of such words as 'catechism' (*WH*, p. 77), 'communion' (*WH*, p. 59), 'epistle' (*WH*, pp. 146, 226, 227), 'paradise' (*WH*, p. 100), 'purgatory' (*WH*, p. 58) and 'pilgrimage' (*WH*, p. 197). That Lockwood's own use of religious terms, on the other hand, seems much more affected is suggested through such words as 'miscreants' (*WH*, p. 16), 'hermit' (*WH*, p. 90) and 'charitable' (*WH*, p. 90), and, more especially, when, referring to Hareton's preparations for clearing the snow drifts in the early morning, he facetiously recalls the latter 'performing his orisons, *sotto voce*, in a series of curses directed against every object he touched […]' (*WH*, p. 28). Such a quaint paradox seems typical of Lockwood's outwardly carefree attitude towards religion—an attitude well exemplified when, in his complaint to Heathcliff about the obtrusive ghost child of his second nightmare, he inadvertently combines eschatology with superstition by declaring the girl's twenty years of restless walking on earth to be 'a just punishment for her mortal transgressions' (*WH*, p. 25). Nevertheless, the phrase 'mortal transgressions' may be enough to remind us of Lockwood's religious background, and also to help us to understand why he shows a knowledgeable interest both in the general situation of the local clergy and in the physical state of

Gimmerton Kirk. Indeed, it is owing partly to this interest that the reader may be inclined to wonder whether Lockwood, though cast more or less in the mould of an eighteenth-century Rationalist or Freethinker, was not once a student of theology, and may even be an unfrocked clergyman. Such hypotheses are not as specious as they might appear to be, at least when they are considered in the light of the first of the two dreams that Lockwood describes in Chapter 3.

In view of what has just been said about Lockwood, then, it is not surprising that, having drowsily noted the title of Jabes Branderham's sermon in one of the books he has been leafing through in the oak-panelled room, he should tell of 'worrying [his] brain to guess what [the preacher] would make of his subject' (*WH*, p. 20). And though the full title of the sermon is of itself quite enough to make Lockwood dream of the chapel service in Gimmerden Sough (since he falls asleep immediately after reading it), much of its content is clearly symbolic of the hostility and conflict he has recently experienced in Heathcliff's household, as well as of his aggressive attitudes and reactions to such experiences. For present purposes, however, the interest of the dream derives from its revealing Lockwood's extraordinary knowledge of the Bible. That Lockwood is, first of all, aware that the sermon he is about to read is on Christ's injunction to his disciple Peter to forgive infinitely is presently confirmed when he tells of 'journeying to hear the famous Jabes Branderham preach from the text—"Seventy Times Seven"' (*WH*, p. 21). Significant, too, is the fact that, once his patience with the inordinate length of Branderham's sermon has been exhausted, Lockwood is 'moved to rise and denounce' the preacher 'as the sinner of the sin that no Christian need pardon' (*WH*, p. 22). Although this particular sin has been interpreted by Brontë scholars in various religious, literary or psychoanalytical ways, it will have almost certainly been understood by the earliest readers of the novel, many of whom would have been hardly less conversant with the Bible than Lockwood himself, as blasphemy against the Holy

Ghost, which Christ deems unforgivable, doing so, however, as we note in the gospels of St. Matthew, St. Mark and St. Luke, without either explaining or elaborating on that pronouncement.[13] But what makes probable the idea that Lockwood has this very pronouncement in mind is that it occurs six chapters earlier in St. Matthew's gospel than the one about infinite forgiveness, thereby suggesting, in a manner characteristic of dreams, that the one reference has somehow prompted the other because they both occur in the same biblical book.[14] At any rate, it makes sound theological sense that someone so well-grounded in the Scriptures (as is amply confirmed by the end of this dream) should fall back on this stern dictum of Christ's as a subterfuge by which the more easily to elude the threat of being 'publicly exposed and excommunicated' (*WH*, p. 21). Whether Lockwood acts on this cunning impulse is not stated, though it is interesting to note that, amid the accusations they subsequently aim at one another, both he and Branderham resort to random quotations from the Book of Job, the Second Book of Samuel and the Psalms as means whereby each seeks to justify his exhorting the congregation to attack the other.[15] That Branderham is, to be sure, entirely a creation of Lockwood's unconscious, not to say his 'double', is self-evident when we recall that the latter has only read the title of the sermon. But that Branderham may, accordingly, be seen as a figure symbolic of Lockwood's proclivity to vindictiveness and self-justification, as manifest already in events described in the first two chapters, is buttressed by the fact that Christ's metaphor about forgiving seventy times seven is by both of them taken all too literally. It is, then, little wonder that Lockwood should summarize the conflict in the chapel with words which, occurring here and there in the Old Testament, are utterly antithetical in spirit to Christ's injunction about forgiveness: 'Every man's hand was against his neighbour; [...]'.[16]

Besides the special interest of its biblical references, Lockwood's first dream is significant as a grotesque foreshadowing of events to be later narrated by Nelly Dean. Certainly, the vindictiveness of Lockwood's language, behaviour and attitudes towards Jabes Branderham, as well as towards Heathcliff's household, points forward to the vindictiveness that colours a good many relationships delineated in the novel. This vindictiveness seems to have its roots partly in the authoritarianism of the oldest generation of Earnshaws and Lintons and their servants, being typified most palpably by their proneness to reprove, scold, lecture and punish—a proneness that may also be predicated of some members of the younger generations. Consider, for example, Catherine's readiness in Chapter 11 to blame Heathcliff, Edgar, Isabella, and even Nelly Dean, for troubles of which she has been the prime cause. Another aspect of this 'culture of vindictiveness' is a tendency, especially apparent in Nelly Dean and Joseph, to regard someone's predicament as something they have deserved. Relevant to all this, in turn, is the prominence of such notions as retaliation and repayment, each of which is almost invariably contemplated or realized in a spirit of self-justification. Hareton himself is aware of the advantages of such notions already as a small boy when he gives Nelly Dean the following reasons why he likes Heathcliff: '[...] he pays Dad back what he gies to me—he curses Daddy for cursing me' (*WH*, p. 110). Also important here is the theme of vengeance and the different ways in which it is played out through the malicious intentions or attitudes harboured by some of the main characters. And though extreme forms of vengeance are seldom executed, we are nevertheless aware that Heathcliff, Hindley and Isabella, in particular, remain incurably engrossed with the idea of vengeance as a sort of inalienable right. But whereas of these three characters Isabella is alone in acknowledging the wrongness of vengeance in principle, it may be said that, fraught though it is with inconsistencies and contradictions, her philosophy of vengeance assumes a peculiar interest for us when she utters this somewhat self-contradictory sentiment to Nelly Dean with respect to Heathcliff:

'On only one condition can I hope to forgive him. It is, if I may take an eye for an eye, and a tooth for a tooth' (*WH*, p. 179).[17]

Not unlike the biblical references in the dream of Jabes Branderham, the well-known words from the Old Testament just quoted above serve to justify an obdurate vindictiveness. Yet their significance also derives in part from their exemplifying the idea that for Isabella, as, indeed, for most of the characters in the novel, forgiveness is a goal difficult, if not impossible, to attain without certain conditions. And it is no doubt for this reason that forgiveness tends to be understood in the novel as, say, something that should be asked of God, or that one has to deserve, or that one asks of others, or even something that has degenerated into the meaninglessness of such polite phrases as 'I beg pardon'. In some cases, moreover, forgiveness is quite out of the question. Thus, in Edgar Linton we see someone who is not only unable to forgive others, but is even presumed to be unforgiving by nature. The same may be said of Heathcliff, who, despite his somewhat conditional forgiveness of Catherine at their last meeting, shows himself, rather like Lockwood, obsessed with the idea of neither being in debt to others nor allowing them to be in his debt, as if both seemed quite ignorant of the fact that, as the original form of the Lord's Prayer makes plain, forgiveness meant literally cancelling a debt.[18] For Nelly Dean, on the other hand, forgiveness is, at least formally, part and parcel of human relationships. Thus even though Edgar has told her, among other things, that he has nothing to forgive Isabella concerning her elopement, Nelly does not hesitate to give the latter an utterly garbled version of his actual words when, shortly after arriving at the Heights, she says this to her: '[My master] sends his love, ma'am, and his wishes for your happiness, and his pardon for the grief you have occasioned; [...]' (*WH*, p. 147). At the same time, it is obvious that, being of a rather vindictive disposition, Nelly Dean looks upon forgiveness more as an ideal to be striven after than as something to which she would have ready recourse. This has already been suggested when, having mildly rebuked Heathcliff for his vengefulness against Hindley, she adds: 'It is for God to punish wicked people; we should learn to forgive' (*WH*, p. 60). Again, if, for example, Cathy seems better endowed than almost all the other characters with a capacity to forgive, as we see well enough in her troubled relations with her cousin Linton, it is yet a capacity undermined for us not only by her priggish consciousness of possessing such a capacity, but by her tendency, despite her willingness to forgive those dear to her, to remain obstinately vindictive towards others such as Heathcliff and Joseph and, until their reconciliation, even towards Hareton. But though the spirit of forgiveness is, as Lockwood's first dream ironically foreshadows, for the most part overclouded in the novel by a spirit of vindictiveness, the reader is still bound to wonder about the possible aesthetic or structural function of the text used by Jabes Branderham for his sermon, and especially so in relation to various other biblical passages quoted or alluded to in the narrative.

★ ★ ★

We have already noted in our discussion of Lockwood's first dream how Jabes Branderham and Lockwood himself find support for their vindictiveness in arbitrarily selected passages from the Old Testament. And though there are references to the New Testament that will also be considered here, it is worth mentioning beforehand some of the less obvious ways in which Emily Brontë alludes to the Bible, and not without certain comical implications. Consider, for example, Joseph's apparently unwitting contravention of Christ's dictum, 'No servant can serve two masters' when he says this to Isabella for insisting on making the porridge: 'If they's tuh be fresh ortherings— just when Aw getten used tuh two maisters, if Aw mun hev a *mistress* set o'er my heead, it's loike time tuh be flitting' (*WH*, p. 141); or, again, that moment when, on his return from Gimmerton Fair on Easter Monday, he has overlaid his Bible 'with dirty bank-notes from his pocket-book, the produce of the day's transactions' (*WH*, p. 315), he forcibly reminds us that, as St. Paul says, a bishop should be 'not given to filthy lucre'.[19] Such contradictions, moreover, seem utterly apposite when viewed in the light of Joseph's theologically presumptuous habit of resorting to biblical references of all kinds. Thus we note, first of all, that his tendency to mention certain well-known biblical names is almost always tinged by a vindictiveness quite out of keeping with their particular historical significance. One example occurs when, in his malicious account to Nelly of the riotous goings-on at the Heights, he says this about Hindley: 'He's noan feard uh t' Bench uh judges, norther Paul, nur Peter, nur John, nur Mathew, nor noan on'em, nut he!' (*WH*, p. 103). Certainly it is to be doubted whether Joseph is at that moment conscious of the spiritual significance of those New Testament figures so arbitrarily assorted here any more than he is continuously mindful of the legendary goodness of the Old Testament figure whose name he bears.

More questionable, however, is Joseph's tendency to quote from the Bible without apparent concern for the context of a particular quotation or apparent awareness of the human situation to which it is meant to pertain. Thus when he sums up happenings on the night of Heathcliff's disappearance by saying, 'All warks together for gooid tuh them as is chozzen, and piked aht froo' th' rubbidge!' (*WH*, p. 85), the homage he typically pays to Predestination in the latter part of that assertion is patently incongruous with the biblical passage to which he is alluding: 'And we know that all things work together for good to them that love God, to them who are called according to *his* purpose'.[20] Such careless uses of the Bible are to be also noted, ironically enough, in Joseph's former pupil Catherine, and not only, as we saw earlier, through her frivolous allusion to

Christ's injunction to turn the other cheek, but through her flippant reference to the Tenth Commandment when, afraid lest Heathcliff should take material advantage of Isabella's infatuation with him, she warns him as follows: 'Abstract your mind from the subject, at present—you are too prone to covet your neighbour's goods: remember *this* neighbour's goods are mine' (*WH*, p. 106).[21]

Perhaps the most important thing with respect to our topic, however, is the fact that some of the biblical references and allusions so far considered have had to do with Christ's teachings. Yet occurring as they do at random, such references and allusions are interesting primarily for what they disclose or confirm about those who make them or to whom they apply. Thus it seems characteristic of Joseph that he should take advantage of Christ's more uncompromising statements. For example, when referring to Hindley's growing dependence on Heathcliff's money to pay his gambling debts, he informs Nelly somewhat jocularly that the former 'gallops dahn t' Broad road, while [Heathcliff] flees afore tuh oppen t' pikes' (*WH*, p. 104).[22] Again, when in nervous response to Cathy's teasing him about the Black Art she is clearly pretending to have been using against him, he exclaims: 'Oh, wicked, wicked! [...] may the Lord deliver us from evil!' (*WH*, p. 13), one cannot help inferring from this curious isolation here of part of the Lord's Prayer that Joseph's utterance is indistinguishable from superstition.[23] There is a certain irony also to be felt in one or two allusions to Christ that are made in connection with Joseph's staunchest disciple, Mr. Earnshaw, as, for example, when Nelly Dean, speaking of the latter's delay in returning home from Liverpool, recalls that 'there were no signs of his coming [...]' (*WH*, p. 34), thereby evoking the question that Christ's disciples put to him on the Mount of Olives as follows: '[...] and what *shall* be the sign of thy coming, and of the end of the world?'; and, more particularly, when, having at last arrived home with a child he has rescued from the streets of Liverpool, Mr.

Earnshaw gives well-versed readers the impression of having all too eagerly, not to say misguidedly, realized Christ's parable of the Good Samaritan.[24]

Significant, too, are some of the essentially secular ways in which Christ's Passion and Crucifixion are hinted at in the novel. Thus it might be asked whether Nelly Dean's exclaiming 'Judas!' (*WH*, p. 111) at the sight of Heathcliff making amorous advances to Isabella is, from a theological viewpoint, not as exaggerated as her description of Hindley as 'the Jonah' (*WH*, p. 85) on the night of the severe storm at the Heights is vague. Similarly, when in the oak-panelled room Lockwood notices a highly distraught Heathcliff at one point 'crushing [his] nails into his palms' (*WH*, p. 25), we may wonder whether, by singling out that detail, he is not equating his landlord's sufferings with Christ's sufferings on the Cross as unconsciously as he seems to regard himself as a sort of latter-day Christ, no doubt partly on account of his gentlemanly politeness and partly because of the humiliations he undergoes at the Heights. This is humorously suggested through his use of two words specifically associated with the birth and death of Christ: 'advent' and 'resurrection'. Thus Lockwood records that, having just arrived at the Heights for the first time, he 'charitably conjectured' that Joseph's peevish words 'the Lord help us' had 'no reference to [his] unexpected advent' (*WH*, p. 2); and, again, when referring to the dogs that have knocked him down in his attempt to run off with Joseph's lantern, he relates that, until the arrival of 'their malignant masters', they would 'suffer no resurrection' (*WH*, p. 16).

Yet despite all such telling allusions to Christ's life and teachings, to say nothing of various ironic and even question-begging uses of the terms 'Christian' (*WH*, pp. 22, 36, 98, 138, 308), 'Christmas' (*WH*, pp. 51, 52, 54, 59, 144), 'Christendom' (*WH*, p. 47), 'christened' (*WH*, pp. 36, 182) and 'unchristian' (*WH*, p. 333) in other contexts, it is interesting to note that Christ himself is nowhere actually mentioned by name in the novel, as if perhaps to suggest that Christians in the late eighteenth century have been ignoring an important aspect of his historic significance, namely, his humanity. Yet it is this very aspect that well-versed readers may find themselves indirectly put in mind of through certain references made to Hareton Earnshaw. Consider, for example, Lockwood's noting in his diary that, on his second visit to the Heights, a young man [Hareton] 'hailed me to follow him' (*WH*, p. 8) as a reminder of the way in which Christ would address those strangers whom he sought to turn into his disciples; or, again, Lockwood's evident disapproval of Hareton's 'eating his bread with unwashed hands' (*WH*, p. 11) as an evocation of the burden of complaint which is made by the Scribes and Pharisees about Christ's disciples, but which is presently dismissed by Christ when, by way of contrast with those sins that come 'out of the heart', he asserts that 'to eat with unwashen hands defileth not a man'.[25] Even when Heathcliff, after the evening meal in Chapter 2, orders Hareton to 'drive those dozen sheep into the barn porch' (*WH*, p. 13), we may be prompted to think of Christ's twelve disciples as well as his symbolic function as a shepherd.

Such postulated links might, however, be thought somewhat far-fetched, especially by those readers who would, for example, point out that, as well as being for the most part a boorish fellow given to violence, Hareton is the only character in the novel to be brought up without any religious instruction or influence. And yet of all the characters he is also the readiest not only to feel remorse and to express contrition for his anger or acts of violence, but to bear no grudge against those who have hurt his feelings. This we see most particularly in his relations with Lockwood, Cathy and Linton Heathcliff. Certainly in a novel where, as we have suggested, vindictiveness is all too prevalent, Hareton is practically unique in showing that capacity for compassion, sympathy and forgiveness by which Christ's humanity has ever remained historically exemplary.[26] And though the forgiveness which Hareton agrees to grant Cathy

at her earnest request, and that, significantly enough, on the Easter
Monday of 1802, seems modest by comparison with that embodied
in the text of Lockwood's first dream, it nevertheless marks a turning
point in the action momentous enough for the well-versed reader to
compare it perhaps to the liberation of man by the New Testament
from the dominion of Law as embodied in the Old Testament.[27]

It would, however, be idle to conclude from arguments put
forward above that Hareton Earnshaw's presentation is in some way
intended as an apology for Christianity any more than it is meant to
be an apology for an unreligious upbringing. Nevertheless, it is partly
through Hareton that we may come to realize that, whatever her private
views on religion, Emily Brontë is by no means disposed here to reject
Christianity out of hand but, rather, to indicate in what ways Christians
themselves have failed to live up to some of its basic tenets. That such
a failure should be shown to manifest itself particularly at a time when
the Nonconformists appear to have been working much harder than
the Anglicans to sustain the cause of Christianity, is no doubt one
of the ironies of the novel. At the same time, it is a testimony to its
remarkable unity that we are also made aware of the extent to which the
Judaeo-Christian tradition has influenced the language and mentality,
and even the behaviour, of almost all the characters. Indeed, we have
seen that, recalcitrant as they are to formal religion, neither Catherine
nor Heathcliff ever quite succeeds in sloughing off the effects of their
Christian education. In this connection, much has been made of the
'mystical' relationship between Heathcliff and Catherine, whereby
some scholars have gone so far as to avouch as *de facto* the assumption
that the lovers are reunited in the afterlife. Such an interpretation,
however, has a fancifulness about it that detracts from Emily Brontë's
seriousness as a novelist, and the more so when it is pointed out
that much of Heathcliff's and, indeed, Catherine's 'transcendental'
thinking takes place while they are each separately betraying symptoms
of partial insanity. Still, for many a reader, this outward repudiation of

Christianity on the part of the principal hero and heroine is perhaps understandable, even justifiable, given the fact that they have grown up under the care of those by whom religious conventions and rituals seem to have been observed all too often to the comparative neglect of that love of neighbour which is so central to Christ's teachings and which, as we have seen, is practised best of all by the 'heathen' Hareton.

That religion had become more or less problematic in most Western societies by the end of the eighteenth century, can, of course, be put down in large measure to the growing influence of the Enlightenment and the concomitant spread of secularism. Such factors undoubtedly help to throw some light on the inherent liberalism of Nelly Dean's Christianity.[28] But if there is thus something peculiarly 'modern' about Nelly's religious outlook, it is Lockwood who, with the hotchpotch of religious, superstitious and secular notions coexisting uneasily in his otherwise well-stocked mind, seems to be par excellence the precursor of the type of cultured persons who, though avowedly agnostic or even atheistic, nevertheless have their pseudo-religious moments, even if these constitute little more than paying visits to historical church buildings. This idea is to some extent suggested towards the end of *Wuthering Heights* when we find ourselves wondering whether Lockwood's grumbling to himself about Cathy and Hareton with the words, '*They* are afraid of nothing. [...] Together they would brave Satan and all his legions' (*WH*, p. 337) is not an unconscious seeking of solace in religion for another disappointment in love, just as we may well have been wondering by then, and will again wonder while reading the final paragraph, whether behind the unwonted interest that this apparently unbelieving aesthete has been taking in the decaying Gimmerton Kirk and its churchyard, there does not lie a certain nostalgia for a lost religious faith.

Brontë Studies, 32/1 (2007)

Notes

1 For some religious interpretations of *Wuthering Heights*, see, for example, Charles G. Robertson, 'The Brontës' Experience of Life', *Brontë Society Transactions*, 9 (1936), 43; Derek Traversi, '*Wuthering Heights* after a Hundred Years', *Dublin Review*, 222 (1949), 67; J. Hillis Miller, *The Disappearance of God: Five Nineteenth-Century Writers* (Cambridge, MA: Harvard University Press, 1963), p. 259; John E. Jordan, 'The Ironic Vision of Emily Brontë', *Nineteenth-Century Fiction*, 20 (1966), 8; Wendy A. Craik, *The Brontë Novels* (London: Methuen, 1968), 11; Isobel Mayne, 'Emily Brontë's Mr. Lockwood', *Brontë Society Transactions*, 15 (1968), 212; Francis Fike, 'Bitter Herbs and Wholesome Medicines: Love as Theological Affirmation in *Wuthering Heights*', *Nineteenth-Century Fiction*, 23 (1968), 148; John Hewish, *Emily Brontë. A Critical and Biographical Study* (London: Macmillan, 1969), p. 152; Tom Winnifrith, *The Brontës and their Background: Romance and Reality* (London and Basingstoke: Macmillan, 1973), pp. 28-75; Barbara Munsen Goff, 'Between Natural Theology and Natural Selection: Breeding the Human Animal in *Wuthering Heights*', *Victorian Studies*, 27 (1984), 494; Katherine Sorensen, 'From Religious Ecstasy to Romantic Fulfilment: John Wesley's *Journal* and the Death of Heathcliff in *Wuthering Heights*', *Victorian Notes*, 82 (1992), 4; Emily Brontë, *Wuthering Heights*, ed. Joyce Carol Oates (Oxford and New York: Oxford University Press, 1999), p. xi; Lisa Wang, 'The Holy Spirit in Emily Brontë's *Wuthering Heights* and Poetry', *Literature & Theology*, 14 (2000), 160-173.

2 See, for example, Thomas Reynolds, 'Division and Unity in *Wuthering Heights*', *University Review*, 32 (1965), 31; Larry C. Champion, 'Heathcliff: A Study in Authorial Technique', *Ball*

State University Forum, 9 (1968), 24; Jane O'Neill, *Wuthering Heights: A Worksheet Guide* (Berryville, VA and Braceborough, U.K.: Literary Images Ltd., 1992), p. 52; Claire Bazin, 'Heathcliff ou l'amour de l'argent', *Cahiers Victoriens et Edouardiens*, 35 (1992), 80.

3   It is possible that negative discussions on Christianity in *Wuthering Heights* have been determined in some measure by the supposition that Emily Brontë, though a clergyman's daughter, was somewhat ill-disposed towards conventional religion, and even pagan in outlook. See Winifred Gérin, *Emily Brontë: A Biography* (Oxford, New York and Melbourne: Oxford University Press, 1978), pp. 81, 264. Swinburne, who was a great admirer of *Wuthering Heights*, had even gone so far as to describe Emily Brontë as 'antichristian'. See Lucasta Miller, *The Brontë Myth* (London: Jonathan Cape, 2001), p. 209.

4   For quotations from the novel, see Emily Brontë, *Wuthering Heights*, eds. Ian Jack and Patsy Stoneman (Oxford: Oxford University Press, 1998). For the sake of convenience, the first Catherine will be referred to as 'Catherine', the second as 'Cathy'.

5   See *Wuthering Heights*, pp. 39, 42, 48, 84, 109.

6   See Winnifrith, *The Brontës and their Background*, p. 33.

7   See *Wuthering Heights*, pp. 48, 75. For a discussion on Nelly Dean's superstitions and her assumptions about the afterlife, see Graeme Tytler, 'The Parameters of Reason in *Wuthering Heights*', *Brontë Studies*, 30/3 (2005), 234-235.

8   For a discussion on Heathcliff's partial insanity, see Graeme Tytler, 'Heathcliff's Monomania: An Anachronism in *Wuthering Heights*', *Brontë Society Transactions*, 20/6 (1992), 331-343.

9   The erotic implications of 'soul' also seem to be at the heart of Isabella's reactions to Catherine's warning to her about the dangers of being in love with Heathcliff, when, in defence of the latter, she tells Nelly that he has 'an honourable soul' (*WH*, p. 103).

10 See Exodus 21:7; Deuteronomy 5:11.

11 For the miracle of the Gadarene swine, see Luke 8:33.

12 For other similar uses of 'pray' and 'prayer', see *Wuthering Heights*, pp. 23, 152.

13 See Matthew 12:31-32; Mark 3:28-30; Luke 12:10 in the Authorized (King James) Bible. For scholarly interpretations of the unforgivable sin, see, for example, Becky Levine, '*Wuthering Heights*: Separate Worlds', *Brontë Society Transactions*, 19 (1946), 156; Edgar F. Shannon, Jr., 'Lockwood's Dreams and the Exegesis of *Wuthering Heights*', *Nineteenth-Century Fiction*, 14 (1959), 100; Vereen M. Bell, '*Wuthering Heights* and the Unforgivable Sin', *Nineteenth-Century Fiction*, 17 (1962), 189; William A. Madden, '*Wuthering Heights*: The Binding of Passion', *Nineteenth-Century Fiction*, 27 (1972), 131; Anne Leslie Harris, 'Psychological Time in *Wuthering Heights*', *The International Fiction Review*, 7 (1980), 113; Linda Gill, 'The Unpardonable Sin: Lockwood's Dream in Emily Brontë's *Wuthering Heights*', *Victorian Institutes Journal*, 28 (2000), 97-108.

14 For Christ's injunction about forgiving seventy times seven, see Matthew 18:22.

15 For these biblical quotations, see *Wuthering Heights*, p. 343, n. 22.

16 For biblical references, see *Wuthering Heights*, p. 343, n. 22.

17 See Exodus 21:24; Leviticus 24:20; Deuteronomy 19:21.

18 In his article 'Forgiveness', Haddon Willmer writes: 'The remission of a debt, an early model for forgiveness in the Christian tradition (as in the Lord's Prayer and parables of Christ, e.g. Matthew 18:23-25) shows that forgiving is not purely spiritual, but operates in social and economic practicalities.' *The Oxford Companion to Christian Thought*, eds. Adrian Hastings et al. (Oxford: Oxford University Press, 2000), p. 245.

19 See Matthew 6:24; Luke 16:13; Titus 1:7.

20 See Romans 8:28. For other arbitrary or vague links between Joseph's biblical allusions and statements in the Bible, see *Wuthering Heights*, pp. 85 and 173, in relation respectively to 2 Peter 2:5 and 1 Corinthians 3:15.

21 See Exodus 20:17; Deuteronomy 5:21.

22 See Matthew 7:13.

23 See Matthew 6:13.

24 See Matthew 24:3 and Luke 10:30-37.

25 See Matthew 15:18, 20 and Mark 7:1-9. In his article 'Discipleship', Adrian Hastings writes: 'Jesus called individuals to follow him, sharing his peripatetic and unstable life, and imbibing his teaching. The calls to Simon and Andrew, James and John, Levi and others to "follow me" represent the true start of his ministry, while the discipleship which remitted from their obeying the call provides an enduring model for Christian life.' *The Oxford Companion to Christian Thought*, p. 169.

26 In his article 'Compassion', A. M. Allchin writes: 'In Christianity the thought of an all-embracing compassion, where it prevails, is rooted in a belief in the human ability to suffer with another's suffering. This itself is seen as reflecting God's divine compassion, a compassion already evident in the O[ld] T[estament] prophets; God suffers in the suffering of his people. In the N[ew] T[estament] this vision takes flesh. The human capacity for compassion is understood as flowing from the compassionate love of God and Christ.' *The Oxford Companion to Christian Thought*, p. 128.

27 This idea is succinctly expressed by St. Paul's words, 'For Christ *is* the end of the law for righteousness to every one that believeth.' See Romans 10:4.

28 Nelly's liberalism is especially noticeable when her advice to Heathcliff in the last days of his life includes this detail about the Bible: 'Could it be hurtful to send for some one—some minister of any denomination, it does not matter which, to explain it, and show you how very far you have erred from its precepts, and how unfit you will be for its heaven, unless a change takes place before you die?' (*WH*, p. 333).

Heathcliff's Monomania: An Anachronism in *Wuthering Heights*

When Nelly Dean has recalled how, in bewildered incomprehension, she interrupted Heathcliff's second long confession about Catherine's haunting of him to ask what he meant a few moments earlier by speaking of 'a strange change approaching', she goes on to intimate that he 'might have had a monomania on the subject of his departed idol' (*WH*, p. 324).[1] For the present-day reader, 'monomania' is usually synonymous with 'craze', 'fad', 'obsession', 'hobbyhorse', and the like, as, indeed, it was for a good many people in the mid-nineteenth century, including novelists.[2] Yet 'monomania' originally denoted a type of mental illness, and had often been used in that sense in medical writings by the time *Wuthering Heights* appeared in 1847. That Emily Brontë intends 'monomania' in its clinical sense is suggested by the realistic detail with which she depicts not only

Heathcliff's illness, but also its counterpart, namely, Catherine's 'brain fever', which, like monomania, was a common, not to say fashionable, disease in both life and literature.[3] But unlike 'brain fever', which was already a recognized medical entity at the close of the eighteenth century, 'monomania' can hardly be dated before 1810. Emily Brontë's use of 'monomania' in *Wuthering Heights*, whose action ends in September 1802, is, therefore, strictly speaking, an anachronism.

'Monomania', or, rather, 'monomanie', was first coined around 1810 by the Frenchman Jean-Étienne-Dominique Esquirol (1772-1840), who, though a somewhat forgotten figure nowadays, is regarded as one of the founders of modern psychiatry.[4] Having grown up during a period when insanity was becoming a matter of special interest for the medical world, especially in England and France, even though the treatment of the insane often remained largely primitive, Esquirol was fortunate in becoming the pupil of Philippe Pinel (1745-1826), and later his successor as head of La Salpêtrière in Paris, a hospital renowned in the early nineteenth century for its humane attitudes to mental illness. Committed as he was to observation rather than to theory, however, Esquirol grew increasingly dissatisfied with the term 'melancholy' as used by Pinel and his predecessors to designate a particular type of mental illness, and wanted to replace it with 'lypemanie'.[5] But 'lypemanie' never quite caught on, being soon replaced by 'monomanie', a term Esquirol is said to have brought into medical currency after he had published his article 'La Monomanie' in the *Dictionnaire des sciences médicales* in 1819. Derived from the two Greek words μονος (= one) and μανια (= madness), 'monomania', like 'lypemanie', was to be distinguished from 'mania' as a form of partial insanity, whereby the understanding is diseased in some respects, and healthy and well-ordered in others.[6]

Having achieved a certain clinical respectability by the 1820s, monomania was to become an almost cultish illness in the next two or three decades, and not least through its close association with phrenology and physiognomy, both of which had already been enjoying great popularity throughout Europe.[7] That monomania should have found acceptance as a nosological category across the English Channel is hardly surprising, since some of the most important writings on insanity of the late eighteenth century had appeared in Britain.[8] In this connection, it is noteworthy that Pinel had been profoundly influenced in his quest for the causes of insanity by Alexander Crichton's *Inquiry into the Nature and Origins of Mental Derangement* (1798), a work which he frequently cited and to which he acknowledged a considerable debt.[9] But the debt was in some sense handsomely repaid when the famous British psychiatrist Alexander Morison, having visited Esquirol in Paris in 1818, delivered the first formal lectures on monomania in Britain some five years later.[10] Just as important for the acceptance of monomania in Britain was James Prichard, whose *Treatise on Insanity and Other Disorders affecting the Mind* (1838) Esquirol refers to in his essay on monomania as 'the most complete work we possess on mental diseases'.[11]

With this brief historical background in mind, then, it is interesting to discover that, in the 1840s, one library from which the Brontës are known to have borrowed books, namely, the Keighley Mechanics' Institute, possessed copies not only of *A Manual of Phrenology* and *Walker's Physiognomy*, but, more importantly, of Esquirol's book *On Insanity*, which contained the essay on monomania mentioned above.[12] Whether Emily Brontë actually read these books is, however, less important for us than the fact that, housed as they were in that remote Yorkshire library, they amply confirm for us the topicality at that time of monomania and the sciences with which it was so closely linked. In any case, it is probable that Emily Brontë was aware of monomania from her assiduous reading of national periodicals, or even her knowledge of the York Retreat, which was famous in her day for the humane treatment of insanity, and through her knowledge that George Nussey (the brother of Charlotte's friend Ellen) was, to the family's great distress, being treated for mental illness in a private asylum in York.[13] Postulating that Emily Brontë intends the word 'monomania' in its clinical sense, let us consider how far her presentation of Heathcliff can be deemed an expression of a true knowledge of that illness.

The fact that Esquirol regarded monomania first and foremost as 'the disease of advancing civilization', or, more specifically, the disease of the rising bourgeoisie, with its determined quest for self-fulfilment, already has some relevance to our image of Heathcliff as a man who, through relentless effort, raises himself above his social limitations and achieves conspicuous material success.[14] Relevant, too, is Esquirol's definition of monomania as 'the disease of going to extremes, of singularization, of one-sidedness' when we think of Heathcliff's obsession with power, domination and revenge.[15] Much more significant for our purposes, however, are Esquirol's following remarks on the causes of monomania: 'Monomania is essentially a disease of the sensibility. It reposes altogether upon the affections, and its study is inseparable from a knowledge of the passions. Its seat is in the heart of man, and it is there that we must search for it, in order to possess ourselves of all its peculiarities. How many are the cases of monomania caused by thwarted love, by fear, vanity, wounded self-love, or disappointed ambition.'[16] Such words forcibly remind us of Heathcliff's tragic relationship with Catherine, and it is in their light that we should now examine it in some detail.

Heathcliff's love for Catherine is more or less an obsession, which seems to have begun before he leaves the Heights on the evening of her betrothal to Edgar. That the obsession has continued during Heathcliff's three-year absence is evident when, on the night of his return, he says to Catherine: 'I've fought through a bitter life since I last heard your voice, and you must forgive me, for I struggled only for you!' (*WH*, p. 96). Heathcliff's obsession with Catherine is apparent even after his marriage to Isabella, to the extent that he begins to exhibit abnormal behaviour. Thus Isabella asks in her letter to Nelly: 'Is Heathcliff a man? If so, is he mad? And if not, is he a devil?' (*WH*, p. 136); and, after her escape from the Heights, she describes him as 'a monster' and 'not a human being' (*WH*, p. 172). Nelly herself is disconcerted by Heathcliff's way of disparaging Isabella, which she condemns as 'the talk of a madman' (*WH*, p. 151). Even in his final meeting with Catherine, Heathcliff's vehemence of language and violence of physical contact seem abnormal. Thus he says to Catherine: 'Don't torture me till I'm as mad as yourself', at the same time as Nelly notices him 'grinding his teeth' (*WH*, p. 159). Abnormal, too, is the rage behind Heathcliff's apostrophising the dead Catherine because she has failed to mention him by name on her deathbed, his bidding her to haunt him, his dashing his head 'against the knotted trunk' (*WH*, p. 167), and his crying out 'like a savage beast getting goaded to death with knives and spears' (*WH*, p. 167). Then, Heathcliff's talk of suicide, as connected with Catherine, also has to be taken into account when judging him as a potential monomaniac.[17] Most important of all, however, is his determination to remain in some sort of relationship with Catherine after her death, for it is in that very single-minded determination that lie the roots of his monomania.

If, as the foregoing suggests, Heathcliff seems to show a certain predisposition to insanity up to the time of Catherine's death, and just beyond, it is not until some eighteen years later that he begins to exhibit signs of mental illness. A good deal of Heathcliff's talk and behaviour from Chapter 29 onwards may, for example, be considered essentially symptomatic of monomania—the hallucinations, the sleeplessness, the talking to himself or to Catherine's ghost, the distraction in company, the sighs and groans, even the cruelty to Cathy and to his son Linton, all of which can be matched with monomania nosology and case histories.[18] Whether Heathcliff's rapid breathing, hollow cheeks or bloodshot eyes, as observed and commented on by Nelly in the last few days of his life, are also peculiar to monomaniacs cannot be said for certain, since Esquirol and others say comparatively little about the physical effects of the illness. However, when some five days before Heathcliff's death, Nelly keeps referring to his eyes with phrases such as 'a strange joyful glitter' (*WH*, p. 327), 'the same unnatural […] appearance of joy' (*WH*, p. 328), 'glittering restless eyes' (*WH*, p. 331), and so on, we are reminded of Esquirol's following words: 'The physiognomy of the monomaniac is animated, changeable, pleased: the eyes are lively and brilliant.'[19] It is also interesting to reflect on the extent to which Nelly's detailed account of the five days leading up to Heathcliff's sudden death seems to bear out Esquirol's experience that 'the progress of monomania is rapid and violent' and that 'its termination is often unexpected'.[20]

That Heathcliff's mental illness is, above all, an obsessional disorder characteristic of monomania is strikingly evident in those passages where he confesses to being relentlessly haunted by Catherine's image. This is suggested, for instance, in Chapter 31 when Lockwood, on his third visit to the Heights, overhears Heathcliff muttering to himself about Hareton's resemblance to Catherine: 'How the devil is he so like? I can hardly bear to see him' (*WH*, p. 303). It is also significant that Lockwood immediately afterwards notices 'a restless, anxious expression in his countenance' which he has 'never remarked there before' (*WH*, p. 303), for his words indicate that Heathcliff's illness has now become acute. In other episodes, Emily Brontë underlines the acuteness of Heathcliff's condition by the way in which he is shown to be daunted by Cathy's resemblance to her mother, especially in those moments when she defies his tyrannous domination, and, more particularly, when he detects, probably for the first time, the close resemblance between Cathy and Hareton, as if that resemblance confirmed once and for all the terrible power exercised over him by Catherine, not to say the ultimate triumph of the Earnshaws.[21] Shortly afterwards, in his second long confession to Nelly, Heathcliff makes it abundantly clear that his obsessional disorder has reached a point where Catherine has become an ineluctable physiognomical presence. Thus having dismissed Hareton's 'startling likeness to Catherine' and its fearful connection with her as being 'the least [potent] to arrest [his] imagination' (*WH*, p. 324), Heathcliff continues:

> ... *for what is not connected with her for me? And what does not recall her? I cannot look down to the floor, but her features are shaped in the flags! In every cloud, in every tree—filling the air at night, and caught by glimpses in every object, by day I am surrounded with her image! The entire world is a dreadful collection of memoranda that she did exist, and that I have lost her.*
> *(WH, p. 324)*

In this connection, it is interesting to note that the author seems to be hinting at monomania on the two occasions when Heathcliff speaks to Nelly at length about his sufferings with Catherine. Indeed, just as on the earlier occasion Nelly has observed how, at the end of his long account, Heathcliff's eyebrows imparted 'a peculiar look of trouble and a painful appearance of mental tension towards *one absorbing subject*' (*WH*, p. 291; italics mine), so on this occasion, some seven months later, Heathcliff seems to point up his monomaniacal state when he says to Nelly: '[...] it is by compulsion that I do the slightest act, not prompted by *one thought*, and by compulsion that I notice anything dead or alive, which is not associated with *one universal idea*' (*WH*, p. 325; italics mine). The authenticity of Heathcliff's monomania is also corroborated by the fact that, rather like those mental patients interviewed by Esquirol and his associates, Heathcliff has been driven to make his confessions to someone he can confide in, so as to seek relief from his unbearable sufferings. As he says to Nelly in the middle of his second confession: 'But you'll not talk of what I tell you, and my mind is so eternally secluded in itself, it is tempting to turn it over to another' (*WH*, p. 323).

But despite all the evidence to suggest that Heathcliff does, indeed, end his days as a monomaniac, the question may, nevertheless, arise as to whether the term 'monomania', albeit used tentatively by Nelly, and only in retrospect, can be said properly to describe his illness. The question is not an idle one, all the more as Nelly herself, though often privy to Heathcliff's bizarre talk and behaviour, is never quite convinced that he is really mentally ill. And yet Nelly's unawareness in this respect is, oddly enough, the very thing that happens to justify her use of the word 'monomania', for monomania was, in fact, an illness that tended to remain hidden from all but the most expert eyes, and not least because its victims usually remained in normal physical health.[22] That may explain why a simple country doctor like Mr. Kenneth, though quite cognisant of the dangers of insanity inherent in the delirious fevers he diagnoses in Catherine, but otherwise probably unfamiliar with the latest developments in psychological medicine, should also have been deceived by Heathcliff's good health enough to be, as Nelly recalls, 'perplexed to pronounce of what disorder the master died' (*WH*, p. 336). It may also explain why Nelly, herself deceived by her assumption that Heathcliff is 'quite strong and healthy' (*WH*, p. 324) and by his confidence that that good health will enable him to live to a great old age, should make this comment after reporting his second long confession: 'Though he seldom before had revealed this state of mind, even by looks, it was his habitual mood, I had no doubt: he asserted it himself—but not a soul, from his general bearing, would have conjectured the fact. You did not, when you saw him, Mr. Lockwood: [...]' (*WH*, p. 325).

Nelly's latter utterance, presumptuous as it may seem, is, however, quite valid inasmuch as, notwithstanding Heathcliff's strange behaviour in the oak-panelled room, Lockwood nowhere appears to question his sanity. What is the reason for this? It will be remembered that when Lockwood first visits the Heights, his initial impression of Heathcliff—and probably the reader's—is of a normal, if somewhat morose, country gentleman, whose normality is manifest partly through the more or less light-hearted way in which he reacts to his tenant's fight with the dogs and partly through his efforts to be hospitable to him afterwards. In the eyes of Lockwood, the eighteenth-century man of reason and intellect par excellence, Heathcliff is evidently a godsend in that cultural desert, for he makes a special point of noting in his diary that, having introduced 'a subject of conversation that might be of interest to [his tenant]', namely, 'a discussion on the advantages and disadvantages of [Lockwood's] present place of retirement', Heathcliff proved 'very intelligent on the topics [they] touched'—intelligent enough, it seems, for the tenant to 'volunteer another visit' (*WH*, p. 6) the following day. And if on that volunteered visit Heathcliff at first exhibits the same moroseness as before, his conversation remains, nevertheless, essentially rational, to the extent that he even manages to entrap his talkative guest in a kind of game of logic by keeping him guessing as to how the members of the household are interrelated.

The interest of Lockwood's first two meetings with Heathcliff, however, is that they bear out the experience of practically all those who, whether laymen or experts, found themselves in the company of a monomaniac without realizing it.[23] In this connection, it is noteworthy that Esquirol, Prichard, Linas and others assert the difficulty of recognising monomaniacs precisely because, apart from their specific partial manias, they could reason correctly, logically and coherently, and in some instances, displayed the highest intellectual powers.[24] That is why readers of *Wuthering Heights*, themselves confident of Heathcliff's intelligence and good sense at the outset, are no less astonished than Lockwood at his nervous behaviour on his entry into the oak-panelled room, and at the humourless incomprehension and eccentric manner with which he responds to

Lockwood's complaints about the room being haunted and 'swarming with ghosts and goblins' (*WH*, p. 25). Thus, instead of laughing off Lockwood's explanations of his nightmares as he might have done, say, at the evening meal, Heathcliff reacts in a curiously distracted, even distraught, manner. There is also something utterly abnormal about Heathcliff's 'crushing his nails into his palms, and grinding his teeth to subdue the maxillary convulsions' (*WH*, p. 25) and striking his forehead 'with rage' (*WH*, p. 26). When, in answer to Lockwood's account of spelling the name Catherine in order to help him to sleep, Heathcliff exclaims, 'God, he's mad to speak so' (*WH*, p. 26), we cannot help judging Lockwood's explanation of his nightmares to be perfectly reasonable, but Heathcliff's talk and behaviour, on the other hand, to be close to unreason. What we do not realize at the time, any more than Lockwood does, is that Heathcliff is, presumably, having a severe fit of monomania. Even though Lockwood sees Heathcliff climbing onto the bed and calling out to Catherine's ghost in 'a gush of grief' (*WH*, p. 27), he still seems reluctant to take that curious behaviour any more seriously than he did his own irrational utterances about his nightmares, in that he merely dismisses it as 'a piece of superstition which belied, oddly, his apparent sense' and then declares that '[his] compassion made [him] overlook its folly' (*WH*, p. 27). Moreover, in his determination to classify Heathcliff as a sort of *alter ego* of like rationality and intellect, Lockwood is probably reassured, not only by finding him an hour or two later in the kitchen acting as normally, if as grimly, as on the previous day, but, more particularly, by being able to record that, on a visit to the Grange a month later, Heathcliff was 'charitable enough' to sit at his sick bedside and 'talk on some other subjects than pills, and draughts, blisters and leeches' (*WH*, p. 90). Nor, when visiting Heathcliff for the third and last time at the Heights, does Lockwood seem to attach much importance to the latter's being 'sparer in person' (*WH*, p. 303), or muttering to himself about Hareton's resemblance to Catherine, perhaps because in his bid to retain his image of Heathcliff's rationality, he allows himself to be deceived by the bluff manner with which the latter responds to the news of his imminent departure and then teases him with a warning not to try to get out of paying his rent.

Lockwood's apparent failure to recognize the clinical implications of the contradictions in Heathcliff's personality and behaviour, then, may be adjudged quite typical of a good many ordinary people confronted by a monomaniac in the nineteenth century. The same is also true of Nelly's own failure to understand Heathcliff's illness, except that she is, of course, never witness to anything like the behaviour he exhibits in the oak-panelled room. Like Lockwood, Nelly is especially deceived by Heathcliff's rationality and mental alertness on several occasions. Even when Heathcliff's monomania seems to be at its most acute, Nelly recalls, for instance, that, while conversing with Joseph one morning about some farming business, he 'turned his head continually aside, and had the same exalted expression, even more exaggerated', but, nevertheless, 'gave clear, minute directions concerning the matter discussed' (*WH*, p. 330). The fact that Heathcliff can, moreover, speak quite lucidly and coherently about his mental state, as we see, for example, when having said that his confessions have not relieved him, but that they 'may account for some otherwise unaccountable phases of humour which [he] show[s]' (*WH*, p. 325), is interesting in the light of claims made by Esquirol and others about the rationality with which monomaniacs can talk about themselves and their condition. It is, therefore, little wonder that, despite being 'alarmed at his manner' during his second confession, Nelly should have been certain that Heathcliff was 'neither in danger of losing his senses nor dying' (*WH*, p. 324). Thus we see how, through this constant emphasis on Heathcliff's intelligence and rationality, even during his worst mental crises, Emily Brontë not only justifies her use of 'monomania', but also confirms the authenticity as well as the dramatic skill with which she has delineated the illness in her novel.

What, then, are the implications of our findings? First, there is the inveterate problem of trying to establish a connection between real life and what is essentially a creation of the poetic imagination, and hence, as in this instance, of being in danger of reducing a fictitious character to the mundane level of a case history. That sort of approach has certain obvious snags as far as Heathcliff's complex characterisation is concerned. Nevertheless, we have tried to suggest that his presentation cannot be fully understood without some knowledge of psychological medicine of the first half of the nineteenth century; indeed, that with such knowledge we may find ourselves making a reappraisal of his character that could justifiably cut him somewhat down to size. Moreover, an awareness of this historical background makes it easier for us to understand why, living as they did in that climate of monomania, so many of the earliest readers and critics of *Wuthering Heights* seem to have found the book so horrifying and depressing. Not long after the novel's first publication, however, monomania fell into medical disrepute, and was rarely used as a nosological category after 1870, since when the illness has often been overlooked even in standard histories of psychiatry.[25] Perhaps it is for this reason that, amid the almost exclusive use of 'monomania' in its popular sense down to our time, editors and critics of *Wuthering Heights* have hitherto deemed it unnecessary to comment on the clinical meaning of the term, and that, therefore, the contradictions in Heathcliff's personality tend to be understood as aspects of his heroic stature rather than as signs of his partial insanity.[26] If Emily Brontë may be charged with having committed an anachronism, we should, nevertheless, bear in mind that monomania was, in fact, extant well before 1802, albeit under a different name. As Esquirol himself might have put it with customary French diplomacy, monomania already existed *avant la lettre*.

Brontë Society Transactions, 20/6 (1992)

Notes

1 All quotations from the novel are taken from Emily Brontë, *Wuthering Heights*, ed. Ian Jack (Oxford and New York: Oxford University Press, 1990). For the sake of convenience, the first Catherine will be referred to as 'Catherine', the second as 'Cathy'.

2 For popular uses of 'monomania' and its cognate forms, see, for example, Charles Dickens, *David Copperfield*, Chapter 16 and *Little Dorrit*, Chapter 21; Charlotte Brontë, *Villette*, Chapter 22; Edgar Allan Poe's short story 'Berenice'; Mary Elizabeth Braddon, *The Lady's Mile* (1866), Chapter 33.

3 'Monomanie' is used in its clinical sense, albeit humorously, in Balzac's *La Peau de Chagrin*. See Balzac, *Comédie Humaine*, vol. 10, ed. Pierre Citron (Paris: Bibliothèque de la Pléiade, 1979), p. 260. However, the editor makes no reference to monomania or to Esquirol. For details about brain fever and its influence on *Wuthering Heights* and other nineteenth-century fiction, see Francis Schiller, 'A Case of Brain Fever', *Clio Medica*, 9 (1974), 181-192; and Audrey Peterson, 'Brain Fever in the Nineteenth-Century Literature: Fact & Fiction', *Victorian Studies*, 19 (1976), 445-464. In this connection, it is noteworthy how closely Nelly Dean's description of the facial features and bodily gestures of an enraged Catherine already showing signs of brain fever, as well as her accounts of Catherine's delirious fevers, match standard definitions and descriptions of brain fever and delirium. See especially D. Hack Tuke, *A Dictionary of Psychological Medicine*, 2 vols. (London: J. & A. Churchill, 1892).

4 For details concerning Esquirol's invention of the term 'monomania', see Jan Goldstein, *Console and Classify: The French*

Psychiatric Profession in the Nineteenth Century (Cambridge and New York: Cambridge University Press, 1987), p. 153.

5   Esquirol is said to have subsumed 'lypemanie' under 'monomanie' around 1820. See J. Kageyama, 'Sur l'histoire de la monomanie', *L'Évolution psychiatrique*, 49 (1984), 156-157.

6   For details about Esquirol, his relations with Pinel, and the history of monomania, see Goldstein, pp. 128-196. The French Academy accepted 'monomanie' in 1835. According to the *OED* (1989), the earliest recorded use of 'monomania' in English is 1823; the word is shown to be derived from 'monomanie', and its origin attributed to Esquirol.

7   The idea of partial insanity was, no doubt, an important breakthrough in the treatment of the insane; and though it was questioned in some medical quarters, it found considerable support in phrenology. The fact that Gall and Spurzheim regarded the brain as being made up of several independent organs, any one of which might be adversely affected while leaving the others intact, was one good reason why, in a climate of growing popular interest in phrenology, monomania found widespread acceptance. Moreover, by dwelling on monomania more than on any other form of insanity, Gall and his partisans helped to make monomania as fashionable as phrenology had become. Important, too, both for the understanding of, and the promotion of interest in, monomania was physiognomy, a science that was very closely associated with phrenology throughout the nineteenth century. Esquirol's textbook *Des maladies mentales* (1838) was illustrated with 27 engraved portraits based on original drawings by G.-F.-M. Gabriel; and it was for medical purposes that Géricault's famous series of ten paintings of monomaniacs was commissioned by Esquirol's colleague, Etienne Georget.

8 For details about publications on insanity in the late eighteenth century, see Denis Leigh, *Historical Development of British Psychiatry*, vol. 1 (Oxford, London and New York: Pergamon Press, 1961), pp. 84-93.

9 Concerning the dissemination of monomania in Britain, largely through the agency of Charles Bell and his very influential *Essays on the Anatomy of Expression in Painting* (1806), see Sander L. Gilman, *Seeing the Insane* (New York and Chichester: John Wiley, 1982), p. 91.

10 Morison may well have been influenced by Esquirol when, in 1840, he published *The Physiognomy of Mental Diseases*, whose 108 plates of insane patients Gilman describes as 'the first consistent attempt to create the illusion of transitoriness [of facial expression] discussed by Georget' (p. 100).

11 Prichard's essay on monomania is, for the most part, in line with Esquirol's thinking. Like Esquirol, Prichard found support in phrenology, as we see in the Supplementary Note in the latter's text entitled 'Peculiar Configurations of the Skull connected with Mental Derangement, with Observations on the Evidence of Phrenology, and on Opinions respecting the Functions of the Brain'. See James Prichard, *Treatise on Insanity and Other Disorders affecting the Mind* (London: Sherwood, Gilbert & Piper, 1838), pp. 26-71, 461-483.

12 See Clifford Whone, 'Where the Brontës borrowed Books. The Keighley Mechanics' Institute', *Brontë Society Transactions*, 11 (1950), 353-358.

13 Emily Brontë would also have observed Branwell's behaviour. His mental breakdown as manifest in his sleeplessness, loss of appetite, talk of suicide, and so on, betrays some of the characteristics of monomania. For details, see Winifrid Gérin, *Branwell Brontë* (London and Edinburgh: Thomas Nelson, 1960), pp. 205-206. It is possible that Emily Brontë also heard about monomania in 1842, during her nine-month sojourn in Brussels, a city that was ever quick to pick up the latest fads and fashions going on in Paris. With regard to the York Retreat, see Andrew T. Scull, *Museums of Madness. The Social Organisation of Insanity in Nineteenth-Century England* (London: Allen Lane, 1979), p. 67.

14 E. Esquirol, *Mental Maladies. A Treatise on Insanity*, tr. E. K. Hunt (Philadelphia: Lea & Blanchard, 1845), p. 200.

15 Ibid., p. 219.

16 Ibid., p. 200.

17 Ibid., p. 240.

18 See Esquirol, pp. 93, 108-110, 119, 205, 247, 250, 260, 320, 328, 336; and A. Linas, 'Monomanie', *Dictionnaire encyclopédique des sciences médicales*, 2e série, vol. 5 (Paris: Asselin, 1871), pp. 158, 175-176.

19 Esquirol, p. 320. Emily Brontë's delineation of Heathcliff's mental illness is very much in line with the emphasis Esquirol and his medical contemporaries placed on the study of facial expressions as a means of diagnosing and treating mental patients. See Note 7 above.

20 Ibid., p. 333.

21 The treatment of family resemblances in *Wuthering Heights* is very typical of the influence which physiognomy exerted on literary portraiture in the nineteenth-century novel. See Graeme Tytler, *Physiognomy in the European Novel: Faces & Fortunes* (Princeton: Princeton University Press, 1982), pp. 238-246.

22 Esquirol, passim.

23 Regarding the concealment of monomania, see F. Winston, 'On Monomania', *Journal of Psychological Medicine and Mental Pathology*, New Series, 4 (1856), 501-502.

24 See Esquirol, pp. 321-326, 338, 342; Prichard, pp. 27-31; and Linas, pp. 152-153. Other authorities on the same subject are quoted by Goldstein, p. 170.

25 For the decline of monomania as a nosological category, see Goldstein, pp. 189-196 and G. E. Berrios, 'Obsessional Disorders during the Nineteenth Century: Terminological and Classificatory Issues', *The Anatomy of Madness and the History of Psychiatry*, vol. 1, ed. W. F. Bynum et al. (London and New York: Tavistock Publications, 1984), pp. 170-182n.

26 The only interpretations of Emily Brontë's use of 'monomania' I have found in annotated editions of *Wuthering Heights* published during the past thirty-five years are by A. C. Ward as 'madness about one thing' (London: Longman, Green, 1959), p. 393; by Graham Handley as 'fixed obsession' (London and Basingstoke: Longman, 1982), p. 307; and by Linda Cookson as 'obsession, or madness about one thing' (Harlow: Longman, 1983), p. 334.

However, none of those editors refers to Esquirol. Of recent articles mentioning or alluding to Heathcliff's monomania, but without reference to Esquirol, we may cite: A. Stuart Daley, 'The Date of Heathcliff's Death: April 1802', *Brontë Society Transactions*, 17 (1976), 15; Heather Glen, Introduction to *Wuthering Heights* (London and New York: Routledge, 1988), p. 5; Bette London, *'Wuthering Heights* and the Text between the Lines', *Papers on Language and Literature*, 24 (1988), 51; Cates Baldridge, 'Voyeuristic Rebellion: Lockwood's Dreams and the Reader of *Wuthering Heights'*, *Studies in the Novel* (Denton, Texas), 20 (1988), 284.

The Parameters of Reason in
Wuthering Heights

Doubtless flattered by Lockwood's presumptuous assessment of her as someone who, 'more than the generality of servants', has been 'compelled to cultivate [her] reflective faculties, for want of occasion for frittering [her] life away in silly trifles', Nelly Dean declares that she 'certainly esteem[s] [herself] a steady, reasonable kind of body', elaborating on that sentiment by speaking both of the 'wisdom' she has learnt through 'sharp discipline' and of the books in Thrushcross Grange library she has 'looked into, and got something out of also' (*WH*, p. 61).[1] It is, however, necessary to keep in mind that this dialogue takes place as early as Chapter 7, by which time Nelly's narrative can hardly have failed to give Lockwood—or, for that matter, the reader—a generally favourable impression of her character. We have by then seen a number of episodes that have shown her to be more or less 'steady' and 'reasonable', at least in the popular acceptation of those epithets. Thus as well as having been a willing domestic, not to say a selfless one, especially in her earliest years at the Heights, she has proved an efficient housekeeper and a competent sick-nurse. And even if she has in one way or another been disloyal or disobedient to Mr. Earnshaw and Hindley, usually in connection with Heathcliff, her acts of insubordination seem justified by the somewhat unreasonable behaviour or attitudes of those two masters. Furthermore, by drawing Lockwood's attention to the moral defects or foibles of Mr. Earnshaw, Hindley, Frances, Catherine, and Joseph, Nelly makes herself appear, by contrast, the essence of normality and good sense, and that partly through her apparent determination to maintain peace and order in what would nowadays be styled a dysfunctional family.

There are, to be sure, several contexts after Chapter 7 in which Nelly's view of herself as 'a steady, reasonable kind of body' may be thought to have been likewise substantiated. For example, there is much good sense in the questions and statements she addresses to Catherine when the latter has come to consult her about whether or not to marry Edgar. The same holds in regard both to Nelly's defence of Edgar and Isabella against Catherine's complaint about them in Chapter 10, and to her advice to Catherine to value Edgar's affection for her and not to harass him with her interest in the newly-returned Heathcliff. A good many of Nelly's recommendations are undoubtedly expressions of her peculiarly cautious attitude to life—an attitude apparent not only in her tendency to warn her superiors against the risks or futility of taking certain measures, even when these measures constitute acts of kindness such as those performed by Cathy on Linton Heathcliff's behalf, but, more particularly, in her advocacy of a policy of resignation with respect to what she sees as an irresoluble enmity between Heathcliff and Edgar. At the same time, Nelly is not averse to using the troubles of her superiors as a means of pointing up the intelligence and sobriety of her own mode of existence. One memorable example of this occurs when, having evoked the gloomy atmosphere at the Grange at the beginning of Chapter 12, she tells Lockwood that she 'went about [her] household duties, convinced that the Grange had but one sensible soul in the world, and that lodged in [her] body' (*WH*, p. 120). And, no doubt, it is as a 'sensible soul' that Nelly would expect to have been recognised by Lockwood for conscientiously coping with Heathcliff's vagaries during the last days of his life. Nor should we forget in this connection the degree to which, in her hectic dialogue with a Catherine caught in the throes of brain fever in Chapter 12, Nelly champions the cause of rationality through her earnest attempts to persuade her delirious mistress that what she is mistaking for the black press at the Heights is, in fact, a mirror in her bedroom at the Grange.

What has been said about Nelly Dean in the foregoing assumes an added interest for us when we pause to consider her presentation in a historical light. Indeed, it is useful here to recall that the action of *Wuthering Heights* takes place between the early 1770s and the turn of the nineteenth century, that is to say, during the latter part of the so-called Age of Reason or Enlightenment. Lockwood himself comes across as an intellectual who might not be altogether unacquainted with the writings of Locke, Hume or Kant and, to judge by his gallicisms, with those of the French Rationalists and *philosophes*.[2] This is suggested in some measure by his occasional recourse to the methods of logical argumentation, his aphoristic utterances, his fondness for theorizing on all manner of subjects, his tendency to see people as types and to place them in social categories, his reliance on physiognomy, his politeness, his apparent atheism or agnosticism, and, as we saw in Chapter 7, his concern with the cultivation of the mind. That Lockwood is, moreover, meant to represent, however ironically, the intellectuality of his era is, in any case, plain enough from his very narrative, which is conspicuous for its elegant style and sensitive observations. The same might be said of Nelly Dean herself, whose own narrative, contained as it is within Lockwood's, is remarkable for its many perspicacious comments on the characters depicted therein. And perhaps this in part explains why, amid their favourable assessments of her character and mentality, some Brontë scholars appear to have been content with her view of herself as 'a steady, reasonable kind of body'.[3]

Yet for all that Nelly considers herself an embodiment of reasonableness, there are moments in her narrative when she may be thought, at least *qua* servant, to have fallen short of that self-image. This can be seen even before Chapter 7, when, for example, in her noble concern for Heathcliff's welfare as a boy, she sometimes breaks rank to no good purpose. Thus it is not hard to surmise that one reason why Heathcliff hits Edgar with the tureen of hot apple-sauce is that he has only moments earlier been assured by Nelly, previous to her flattering him with suppositions about his high-born origins and a disparaging reference to Hindley, that, 'being taller [than Edgar] and twice as broad across the shoulders', he 'could knock him down in a twinkling' (*WH*, p. 55). Such words are typical of Nelly's habitual interference in matters outside her proper sphere as a domestic. This can be seen more especially when Heathcliff has returned to the neighbourhood after a three-year absence. Thus we may well wonder, for example, whether Nelly's attempts to discourage Isabella's amorous interest in Heathcliff, or her asking Catherine in the latter's very presence if Edgar would approve of him as a husband for Isabella, have not partly motivated the elopement. At any rate, it would appear that Nelly is not a little to blame for that occurrence insofar as the incident most probably precipitating it, namely, Edgar's showdown with Heathcliff in Chapter 11, may be assumed to have been a direct consequence of her having rather gratuitously informed her master both about Heathcliff's advances to Isabella and about his subsequent quarrel with Catherine. The fact that Nelly's superiors are dependent on her as a confidante may also account for the alacrity with which she gives them advice, sometimes even by butting into their conversations. Such dependency cannot but enhance Nelly's sense of self-importance, as may be seen, for example, when, in response to Isabella's letter of distress, she takes it upon herself to pay her a visit at the Heights, during which, thanks both to her counselling Heathcliff how to treat Isabella and to her dogged attempts to dissuade him from visiting Catherine, she annoys him enough to find herself presently coerced into promising to arrange a meeting for him with Catherine at the Grange. And yet, had Nelly been the 'faithful servant' (*WH*, p. 128) she has only recently made herself out to be in the face of Edgar's stern rebuke of her in Chapter 12, she would surely not have hesitated to break her promise by warning him of Heathcliff's intention, and thus prevented a tryst which, though rationalized by her as something that 'might create a favourable crisis in Catherine's mental illness' (*WH*, p.159), was almost certainly the main cause of the latter's untimely death.

Nelly's inadequacy as a servant is no less noticeable in her handling of Cathy, especially after the latter has been forbidden by her father to associate with Heathcliff's household. Thus, instead of accepting the girl's melancholy mood while they are out on a walk together in Chapter 22, Nelly endeavours to distract her from it, thereby encouraging her to actions that perforce lead to another fateful meeting with Heathcliff. Similarly, rather than letting Cathy cry herself out over Linton's reported sufferings, Nelly decides, instead, to expostulate with her on Heathcliff's 'assertions about his son', only to find herself in the end agreeing to accompany her to the Heights the following morning, partly because she cannot bear to see the girl looking unhappy, but mainly because, in her evident vanity, she hopes that Linton 'might prove, by his reception of [them], how little [Heathcliff's] tale was founded on fact' (*WH*, p. 235). This episode is a signal example of Nelly's persistent failure to keep her young mistress in hand through the authority vested in her by Edgar, and will play no small part in bringing about Cathy's ill-fated marriage to Linton Heathcliff.

The discrepancy that seems to exist between Nelly's self-image as 'a steady, reasonable kind of body' and her sundry follies as discussed above is perhaps easier to understand if we consider it in the light of some of the ways in which her mind works. We note, first of all, not only how prone Nelly is to be slow-witted, uncomprehending, forgetful, and self-contradictory, but, more especially, how presumptuous or fallacious she can be through a good many of her ideas or arguments.[4] Then there are times in her generally perceptive narrative when she frankly confesses to responses or attitudes on her part that are decidedly irrational. Consider, for example, her hallucination of Hindley at the sand-pillar guide post that makes her wonder whether it is 'a sign of death' (*WH*, p. 109), her momentary mistaking Isabella's dog hanging on a wall for 'a creature of the other world' (*WH*, p. 129), her fear of dreams and of the dark, and her dread of being alone at the Heights. But it is chiefly through her religiosity that Nelly is to be seen at her most irrational. Not that being religious necessarily means being irrational, as Locke himself had already made abundantly clear through his tract entitled *The Reasonableness of Christianity as delivered in the Scriptures* (1695).[5] Earlier theologians and ecclesiastics such as St. Augustine and St. Thomas Aquinas had, in any case, already postulated that religious faith was perforce founded on rational argumentation.[6] In *Wuthering Heights*, however, Emily Brontë portrays a society in which (Christian) religious faith, far from being rooted in the cogent theological thinking of the Church Fathers, seems for the most part to be barely distinguishable from superstition. It is true that Nelly Dean shows some familiarity with the Bible, and that she is more or less orthodox in recommending its teachings as a guide to living a Christian life. And though it is just as true that the references she makes, say, to the after-life can be authenticated to some extent by what is said about it in the New Testament, it is not difficult to see that a good many of her religious assumptions are scarcely other than subjective fantasies.[7] The same may, of course, be said of the sentimental, careless, and even blasphemous ways in which some of the other characters, including the fanatical Joseph, speak of the role and function of God or Satan or devils, or disclose their private notions of heaven, hell, angels, the soul and so on, thereby exposing the unsoundness of the religious instruction they have evidently undergone.[8] What differentiates Nelly Dean from the other characters, however, is the optimism with which she occasionally presumes to know how God is thinking or acting. Thus we may refer to the certainty with which, despite having some years earlier deemed her 'not fit to go [to heaven]' (*WH*, p. 80), she takes it for granted that the recently defunct Catherine has already gone there and is now 'with her Maker' (*WH*, p. 165), confirmed as she has already been in this notion by observing the transcendental beauty of the latter's facial appearance in death; or, again, to the complacency with which, in the elaborate comparison she draws between Hindley and Edgar as bereaved husbands, to the obvious disadvantage of the former, she remarks, 'Linton, on the contrary, displayed the true courage of a loyal and faithful soul: he trusted God; and God comforted him' (*WH*, p. 183).

Nelly Dean's religiosity, as glimpsed in the foregoing, may be understood as one of several ways of thinking on her part that seem to be in curious contradiction with one another. We have, for example, already noted moments in her narrative when Nelly reveals a certain superstitious streak in herself, though the instances cited seem moderate in comparison with the demonic image that she continues harbouring about Heathcliff's nature and origin, whether by referring to him with words such as 'goblin', 'ghoul', 'vampire', and the like, or even by describing her squeamish reactions to his dead body in the final chapter. Such language and behaviour might be thought scarcely becoming in someone who purports to be a Christian. Another type of contradiction can be seen between certain assertions that Nelly makes about the fate of those who have died. For example, when, on hearing Heathcliff's account of his removal of Catherine's coffin lid, she reprovingly asks him whether he was 'not ashamed to disturb the dead' (*WH*, p. 310), she appears to have forgotten that, having several years earlier only just announced Catherine's death to him, she went on to ascribe a quite different fate to the latter by saying this to Heathcliff, 'Gone to heaven, I hope, where we may, everyone, join her, if we take due warning, and leave our evil ways to follow good!' (*WH*, p. 166). Yet even when, towards the end of her narrative, Nelly mildly reproaches Lockwood for his facetious talk about ghosts at the Heights by declaring, 'I believe the dead are at peace, but it is not right to speak of them with levity', can we say that her talk is any less superstitious than Lockwood's?

But significant as are Nelly's words just quoted, their interest also derives from their being not unrelated to a practice that both she and Lockwood are given to, namely, that of using words with superstitious or occult connotations, such as 'presentiment', 'omen', 'misfortune', 'ill luck', 'luckless', 'happily', 'fortunately', etc. Such language might, strictly speaking, be deemed anomalous in two people who evidently pride themselves on their rationality—as anomalous as, say, the paradoxicality inherent in some of their other utterances. Thus it might be asked whether Nelly is aware of the glaring contradiction between reason and superstition when, for example, she describes herself as a 'sensible soul' (*WH*, p. 120); or that between religion and superstition when she responds to Heathcliff's 'weird smile' by saying, 'Don't, for God's sake, stare as if you saw an unearthly vision' (*WH*, p. 331).[9] Similarly, one wonders whether Lockwood himself is conscious of the strange juxtaposition of reason and superstition when, for example, he speaks of the girl he encountered at the sea-coast as 'a real goddess in [his] eyes'; or, more particularly, when, having confessed to Heathcliff that it was Zillah who put him in the forbidden oak-panelled room, and in an attempt to propitiate him further, he continues thus: 'I suppose that she wanted to get another proof that the place was haunted, at my expense—well, it is—swarming with ghosts and goblins! You have reason for shutting it up, I assure you!' (*WH*, p. 25).[10]

★ ★ ★

The metaphysical inconsistencies and contradictions instanced above, though perhaps intended, with no little comic irony, to show up the minds of two people seemingly all too confident of their reason or reasonableness, are, to be sure, by no means psychologically out of the ordinary in *Wuthering Heights*. Indeed, it would appear that, notwithstanding their superstitious talk about noumenal beings or phenomena we referred to earlier, to say nothing of their belief in ghosts or their reported encounters with the dead, some of the main characters regard themselves as staunch votaries of reason. But if reason is supposedly equated in their minds with, say, good sense or sanity, and may sometimes be deemed such by the reader, especially when the characters are concerned with the well-being of others, it can also be often seen to be little more than an expression of expediency, not to say egotistical unawareness. This notion of reason may be assumed to have its roots partly in the patriarchal thinking and hidebound conventions which seem to have somewhat determined the mentality and outlook of the oldest generation of Lintons and Earnshaws portrayed and to have, in turn, influenced the middle generation to look upon their own attitudes and actions as being for the most part 'reasonable'. One typical manifestation of this is the assumption that one is in the right or that one has more sense than other people—an assumption implicitly held by Isabella in her rather self-righteous accounts of her life at the Heights in

Chapters 13 and 17. Something analogous may be discerned now and again in Edgar Linton's utterances. For example, just as reason *qua* convention ironically underlies his stubborn refusal at first to believe the news of his sister's elopement, so it ironically underlies his having resigned himself shortly afterwards to the idea of the elopement as an inescapable fact when he makes this reference to Isabella: 'Hereafter she is only my sister in name; not because I disown her, but because she has disowned me' (*WH*, p. 133). Edgar's tendency both to consider 'the other person' as the cause of the failure of his relationship with them and to use that standpoint as an excuse for keeping them at arm's length is later confirmed when, to Cathy's contention that her cousin Linton's whereabouts was kept hidden from her because he 'disliked Mr. Heathcliff', he gives this specious reply: 'No, it was not because I disliked Mr. Heathcliff, but because Mr. Heathcliff dislikes me […]' (*WH*, p. 220). As one may easily surmise, the justifying of attitudes or acts by causes apparently beyond one's control is, in Edgar's eyes, tantamount to being reasonable.

What has just been said of Isabella and Edgar might equally apply to Catherine and Heathcliff, though with the difference that the latter two are conspicuous above all for presuming to be exceptionally rational beings, more particularly when they are having discussions or arguments with some of the other characters. A memorable example of this may be noted when, in an attempt to counter the dialectical skills with which Nelly has been astutely picking holes in the arguments she has put forward for marrying Edgar, Catherine retorts, 'I wish you would speak rationally' (*WH*, p. 78). Such words are already enough to suggest that, for all that she has charmed countless readers down the years with her poetic perorations and her philosophical flights of fancy, Catherine is none the less singularly deficient in reasoning powers. This we are made aware of most particularly after Heathcliff has returned to Gimmerton. Thus we note, for example, that, despite having made use in Chapter 10 of the diversionary tactic of criticizing Isabella's and Edgar's characters and behaviour in order to justify her having upset the latter by her commendations of the lately-returned Heathcliff, Catherine seems quite oblivious of those same commendations when, in an attempt soon afterwards to discourage Isabella from her love for Heathcliff, she draws a most damning portrait of his character. Hardly less contradictory is Catherine's later upbraiding of Heathcliff for having made amorous advances to Isabella, while unmindful of the fact that she it was who tauntingly drew his attention to her sister-in-law's attachment to him in the first place. Nor should we forget the way in which Catherine falsely infers from his dismissal of Heathcliff from the Grange that Edgar had been eavesdropping on her quarrel with the latter, wondering as she mistakenly does, 'what possessed him to turn listener', and just as mistakenly presuming that 'all is dashed wrong by the fool's craving to hear evil of self that haunts some people like a demon' (*WH*, p. 103). Is it any wonder, then, that Catherine should be quick not only to blame Isabella for the clash between Edgar and Heathcliff by saying that 'the uproar is owing to her' (*WH*, p. 116), but to take it for granted that Nelly is 'aware' that she herself is 'in no way blameable in this matter' (*WH*, p. 116)? All such reasoning seems to be of a piece with Catherine's habit of garbling what she or others have said, or of presuming to know what other people are thinking, or ought to be thinking, and suggests that she lives too much in her mind, and not enough in the world of facts and reality.

Like Catherine, Heathcliff, too, comes across to the reader as someone at once confident in, and proud of, his rationality. That this is not without some justification is suggested in Chapters 1 and 10, when Lockwood speaks of Heathcliff's capacity for making intelligent conversation, and, again, when, in Chapter 2, he tells of the latter's humiliating him in a kind of game of logic by keeping him guessing as to how the members of his household are interrelated. Heathcliff is, in any case, remarkable in other contexts for his quickness, his articulateness and his sharp-wittedness, as he is for his preoccupation with reasons, causes, and proofs, especially legal ones, in the planning and shaping of his life as well as the lives of those under his care. Yet the fact that he has managed against all odds to achieve considerable material prosperity may in some measure account for the hubris one senses in his attempts to assert his intellect over others. One striking example can be seen when, in his (successful) quest to persuade Nelly Dean to arrange a meeting for him with Catherine, Heathcliff mingles his threats of violence with a number of plausible arguments propounded in order to prove, among other things, not only that the latter has not forgotten him, but that she loves him better than she ever loved Edgar. What is noticeable about Heathcliff's altercation with Nelly, however, is the degree to which he seems unaware of the fallaciousness of his claims to know precisely what Catherine is thinking or feeling. Fallacies of various kinds can, of course, be predicated of all the characters, including Nelly Dean and Lockwood, as we have already suggested, being somewhat prominent in quarrels, especially where the disputants, as in the case of, say, Cathy and Linton Heathcliff defending their respective parents in Chapter 23, are each clearly bent on demonstrating that they have reason on their side. But whereas Cathy's and Linton's fallacies, whether here or in other contexts, are usually the understandable effects of childish ignorance or presumptuousness, Heathcliff's may be said to be a by-product of his delight in displaying his intellect with extravagant figurative language, and that to a point where he seems to mistake specious rhetoric for sound reasoning. Moreover, disposed as he is both to look upon his fellow creatures as types rather than as unique individuals, and to judge their minds according to his own mentality and experience, he usually fails to reckon with the contingent or the unpredictable. Hence it is that, at Cathy's first reunion with her cousin Linton, Heathcliff is brashly confident that she 'will discover his value, and send him to the devil' (*WH*, p. 217), or that Hareton is 'safe from *her* love' (*WH*, p. 217), just as he will presently assure Nelly not only that Hareton 'will never be able to emerge from his bathos of coarseness and ignorance', but that he 'takes a pride in his brutishness' (*WH*, p. 219). Yet reasonable and cogent as they seem to be at the moment they are being voiced, Heathcliff's predictions and opinions turn out in the end to have been utterly erroneous—as erroneous, indeed, as the way in which, in his indifference to Cathy's anxiety about her father just after she has been trapped in the Heights, he will betray his ignorance of her character by presumptuously telling her that 'it is quite natural that [she] should desire amusement at [her] age; and that [she] should weary of nursing a sick man, and that man *only* [her] father' (*WH*, p. 275).

In view of the fallacies with which Heathcliff so often flaunts his intellect, it is, then, perhaps hardly surprising that he should be swift to doubt the presence of rationality in those with whom he is severely at odds. One example that springs to mind is the occasion when, having by way of prelude to his summary of Isabella's behaviour since their wedding told Nelly Dean that he 'can hardly regard her in the light of a rational creature' (*WH*, p. 150), he is shortly afterwards so far incensed by Isabella's tirades against him as to assure her that she is 'not fit to be [her] own guardian' (*WH*, p. 152). That questioning someone's reason is, indeed, but one step from declaring them insane has by then been amply illustrated in Chapter 10, when, for example, Catherine has not only told her sister-in-law that she is 'surely losing [her] reason' (*WH*, p. 101) for accusing her of being 'harsh' towards her during their walk with Heathcliff the previous day, but presently gone on to repudiate Isabella's confessed love for him as 'idiocy' (*WH*, p. 102) and 'madness' (*WH*, p. 102). Expressing as they do anger, disapproval, or incomprehension, such terms are, to be sure, not uncommon in *Wuthering Heights*, being used most frequently by Nelly Dean, and that, significantly enough, with respect to Heathcliff's and Catherine's language and behaviour.[11] Yet although each vituperative epithet or noun such as 'mad', 'stupid', 'idiot', 'fool', 'simpleton', and the like ironically presupposes that those using it evidently consider themselves rational and sane, it is obvious that all such terms are fundamentally irrational—not unlike, say, the animal comparisons or metaphors with which the characters now and again describe or insult one another.[12] This irrationality is manifest even where such locutions seem somewhat apposite, such as those which Nelly Dean, Joseph, Isabella, and Heathcliff have recourse to, in separate contexts, with respect to Hindley's aberrant talk and conduct, or, more importantly, those which Nelly uses when observing in Catherine the symptoms of what will be subsequently diagnosed as 'a brain fever' (*WH*, p. 134).

The error of calling someone insane is, however, attested principally by the incontrovertible fact that reason somehow continues to prevail in those very characters whose talk or demeanour otherwise gives the impression of being far from wholesome. Important examples of this can be seen in the lucidity with which Hindley confides in Isabella about what might be adjudged essentially irrational, namely, his persistently thwarted attempts to kill Heathcliff, or in that with which Heathcliff conveys his experiences of Catherine's ghost as an utterly empirical phenomenon. Noteworthy, too, in this connection are Catherine's intermittent assertions of her rationality during her incoherent utterances in Chapter 12, as if such assertions were but expressions of that dread of losing her sanity which she has voiced shortly beforehand when telling Nelly how, amid her husband's 'cruelly provoking' her by asking her to choose between him and Heathcliff, she 'couldn't explain to Edgar how certain [she] felt of having a fit, or going raging mad, if he persisted in teasing [her]', but prefaced her account of a revived childhood memory by assuring Nelly that she will inform her 'what [she] thought, and what has kept recurring and recurring till [she] feared for [her] reason—' (*WH*, p. 125). Yet understandable as is Catherine's fear of losing her reason, the question nevertheless arises at this point as to the nature or quality of that reason, and the more so as we have by then come to recognize its apparent limitations. Indeed, one might go further by asking whether Catherine's mental illnesses do not have something to do with improper uses of her reason, as evident, for example, in her proclivity to faulty and malevolent reasoning, and whether there may not be some connection between all this and the apparent disorderliness of her unconscious mind, as suggested in some measure by accounts of her recurrent dreams, some of which, as she tells Nelly, 'appal [her]' (*WH*, p. 124). That the deterioration of Catherine's mental health is, at any rate, most probably a consequence both of living too much in her mind and of being too little aware of the reality and individuality of her fellow human beings is perhaps made palpable for us most of all in that moment when, having just declared, 'Nelly, I *am* Heathcliff', she continues thus: '—he's always, always in my mind—not as a pleasure, any more than I am a pleasure to myself—but, as my own being—' (*WH*, p. 82).

The interest of our foregoing discussion on Catherine lies not a little in the direct bearing it has on the mental illness to which Heathcliff himself gradually succumbs. Whether or not this illness, like Catherine's illnesses, may have been due partly to chronically negative thought processes, it appears to have been touched off by what the latter said to him, and even omitted to say about him, just before her death, and sustained by the many years he has spent thinking obsessively about her—an illness described by Nelly Dean, probably with hindsight, albeit anachronistically, as 'a monomania on the subject of his departed idol' (*WH*, p. 324).[13] That Nelly's use of the term 'monomania' is not simply metaphorical but medical is confirmed by the way in which, with judicious signalling of symptoms, the author demonstrates that Heathcliff is, indeed, suffering from one of various types of partial insanity that had been clinically established by the early nineteenth century. This she does by showing how even at the height of his mental illness, by which time he has, as he confesses, become the mere plaything of his bodily processes, Heathcliff remains none the less capable not only of speaking rationally and coherently about his dire condition, but of continuing to lead an outwardly normal life.[14] Indeed, the notion that one may appear perfectly rational and sane to others in the midst of one's partial insanity is realized for us when Nelly Dean assures Lockwood that, though she was 'alarmed at [Heathcliff's] manner' during his long confession to her in Chapter 33 about his abnormal state of health, he was 'neither in danger of losing his senses, nor dying', and why she adds that, notwithstanding his 'delight from childhood in dwelling on dark things and entertaining odd fancies', as far as 'his reason' was concerned 'on every other point his wits were as sound as [hers]' (*WH*, p. 324).

In view of what was said earlier about Nelly Dean, there is a certain irony about the way in which, through the words just quoted, she looks upon herself as a norm with respect to mental health. At the same time, since rationality is for Nelly the criterion by which to gauge Heathcliff's sanity, it is perhaps inevitable that she should be so readily deceived into thinking, as late as only two days before his death, that he is merely suffering from some minor nervous disorder such as could be cured by sufficient food and sleep, and even by a little religious instruction. Nelly's inability to recognize the enormity of Heathcliff's illness—an inability known to have been common to those confronted at that time by people suffering from partial insanity—may be seen as a consequence of the undue importance she attaches to rationality.[15] Yet it might be asked, of what use is rationality if, however intact it seems to be, as in Heathcliff's case, it exists side by side with a psychiatric disorder over which it can ultimately have little or no control? Indeed, it is partly through Heathcliff's helpless physical state at the end of the novel that we realize that reason or rationality is evidently not enough in itself to determine our humanity or, as we have suggested in our discussions above, to save us from wrong-headed thought or action. And this we see perhaps nowhere more ironically illustrated than through the presentation of Lockwood in that, anxious as he is to pass for a man of reason par excellence, he not only exhibits an inherent stupidity through some of the foolish things he says or does on his four visits to the Heights, but by dint of the accounts of his two nightmares, the second of which is a comically symbolic adumbration of Heathcliff's partial insanity, he gives us a glimpse of his strangely chaotic mind.

It might be tempting to conclude from the evidence hitherto adduced that *Wuthering Heights* is in some sense a critique of the time-honoured concept of man as a rational creature. Certainly, through her concern to suggest that her characters are to be psychologically understood within a polarity between reason and insanity, and against a background of sundry cultural and metaphysical influences obtaining in the late eighteenth century and beyond, Emily Brontë was practically the first English novelist to externalize the idea that the human mind is, in fact, an utterly complex, not to say contradictory, thing. It would, however, be idle to assume that Emily is thereby intent on belittling the faculty of reason; on the contrary, she seems concerned, through her illustrations of its manifold uses (and misuses) in her novel, to invite us, as it were, to put this faculty in perspective, and even to revaluate it as something which, especially in the eighteenth century, was more or less a vague concept and perhaps, therefore, improperly understood. This she does not merely by incorporating some of the advances made in psychiatric medicine, but, more particularly, by showing us that, notwithstanding its scientifically established functions ranging from, say, being a means of apprehending the world in which we live to being a factor in attaining the highest cognitive truths, reason is all too often little more than a manifestation of the prevailing social mores and values. We have seen this ironically illustrated in her presentation of her central characters, all of whom implicitly take pride in their reason, not to say their sanity, but few of whom are much aware of the frailty of some of their opinions, attitudes or assumptions, to say nothing of their superstitions. In this connection, it has sometimes been contended that Emily's novel embodies a kind of conflict between the bold transcendental thinking and outlook of Catherine and Heathcliff and the tame rationality of Nelly Dean and Lockwood, whereby the reader is supposed to award the laurels to the principal hero and heroine for having somehow liberated themselves both from the restraints of human society and from the limits of the human mind. Such an interpretation, however, seems unsatisfactory if it is accepted, partly by virtue of arguments put forward above, that reason is for Emily Brontë the very basis of everybody's humanity without exception, and that it is by the ways in which we use our reason, especially in our relations with others, that we are to be ultimately assessed as human beings. And so it is that, as we reflect once more on Nelly Dean's dialogue with Lockwood at the end of Chapter 7, this time in conjunction with what has since been learnt about her elsewhere in her narrative, we may find ourselves wondering, for example, whether the housekeeper's somewhat complacent image of herself as 'a reasonable, steady kind of body' is not after all more a homage to the ethos of expediency than an expression of moral self-awareness.

Some readers might, nevertheless, view Nelly Dean's triumphant survival at the end as a poetic vindication of that ethos, and the more so as her survival occurs in a novel which, because famous above all for its treatment of illicit love, has sometimes been designated an amoral work.[16] Indeed, it might even be asked how far morality is of relevance to someone who, like Nelly Dean, has no apparent *raison d'être* outside the domestic sphere, nor any personal life to speak of. Certainly, it is understandable that, as 'a poor man's daughter' (*WH*, p. 61), Nelly's primary objective should be to maintain her menial status at all costs, and that she should at the same time strive to lend meaning to her narrow existence through her constant quest for order and orderliness of all kinds. Such a quest is, no doubt, to be expected of 'a steady, reasonable kind of body', as are the different ways in which she affirms the intrinsically conservative values of the hierarchical structure she serves, and that most notably by the primacy she attaches to the family, property, and the law, not to mention physical strength, sound health, beauty, intelligence, literacy, and decorous behaviour. Yet the fact that Nelly's words just re-quoted form part of the very sentence in which she assures Lockwood that she has 'undergone sharp discipline which has taught [her] wisdom' might indicate that her reasonableness was little more than a kind of pseudo-stoicism. Perhaps that is why Nelly, well-intentioned though she is and not without her good points, seems to set limits to her kindness, is inclined to be impatient with the weak and the sickly, and, where it is a question of having sympathy with those in distress, is content to feel pity, especially when she is scarcely in a position to help, rather than to feel compassion such as might have actuated her, as, for example, it now and then actuates Cathy or Hareton, to say or do things that go well beyond the confines of mere 'wisdom'.

Brontë Studies, 30/3 (2005)

Notes

1   For quotations from the novel, see Emily Brontë, *Wuthering Heights*, eds. Ian Jack and Patsy Stoneman (Oxford: Oxford University Press, 1998). For the sake of convenience, the elder Catherine will be referred to as 'Catherine', the younger as 'Cathy'.

2   Lockwood's reference to Cathy's putting 'a few questions to [him] concerning the inmates, rational and irrational, of her former home, […]' (*WH*, p. 300) may be intended as an ironic allusion to Kant's (and Aristotle's and Epictetus') notion of man as a rational creature. See Harold I. Brown, 'Rationality' in *The Oxford Companion to Philosophy*, ed. Ted Honderich (Oxford and New York: Oxford University Press, 1995), p. 744.

3   See, for example, Florence Dry, *The Sources of Wuthering Heights* (Cambridge: Cambridge University Press, 1937), p. 14; B. Ford, '*Wuthering Heights*', *Scrutiny*, 7 (1939), 381; Laura L. Hinkley, *The Brontës: Charlotte and Emily* (London: Methuen, 1947), p. 259; Philippa Moody, 'The Challenge to Maturity in *Wuthering Heights*', *Melbourne Critical Review*, 5 (1962), 30; Barbara Hardy, *Wuthering Heights* (New York: Barnes & Noble, 1963), p. 24; Q. D. Leavis, 'A Fresh Appraisal of *Wuthering Heights*', in F. R. & Q. D. Leavis, *Lectures in America* (London: Chatto & Windus, 1969), p. 97; W. H. Stevenson, '*Wuthering Heights*: The Facts', *Essays in Criticism*, 35 (1985), 161; Graham Holderness, *Wuthering Heights* (Milton Keynes and Philadelphia: Open University Press, 1985), p. 8; N. M. Jacobs, 'Gender and Layered Narrative in *Wuthering Heights* and *The Tenant of Wildfell Hall*', *Journal of Narrative Technique*, 16 (1986), 216; Patrick Murray, *Companion to Wuthering Heights* (Dublin: The Educational Company, 1987), p. 6.

4   For some examples of Nelly Dean's fallacies, presumptuousness and contradictions, see *Wuthering Heights*, pp. 32, 33, 40, 43, 46, 56, 60, 75-77, 82, 83, 89, 93, 94, 103, 120, 121, 127, 128, 129, 130, 163, 166, 172, 183, 192, 197, 198, 203, 204, 205, 206, 223, 224, 227, 230, 231, 233, 243, 250, 256, 275, 278, 283, 286, 313, 316, 335.

5   See Adrian Hastings, 'Reason', in *The Oxford Companion to Christian Thought*, ed. Adrian Hastings (Oxford: Oxford University Press, 2000), p. 597.

6   See Hastings, 'Reason', ibid., p. 596.

7   See Bernhard Lang, 'Heaven', ibid., p. 287.

8   For some examples, see *Wuthering Heights*, pp. 1, 13, 20, 34, 38, 42, 59, 60, 65, 73-75, 79, 80, 85, 93, 99, 106, 111, 128, 140, 141, 160, 167, 173, 175, 180, 181, 183, 217, 233, 248, 257, 274, 284, 308, 328, 333-335, 337.

9   A similar example is suggested in Nelly's following detail about Heathcliff's ghost: 'But the country folk, if you asked them, would swear on the Bible that he *walks*' (*WH*, p. 336).

10 That superstition will have come to prevail over reason in Lockwood's mind by the end of his narrative is suggested not only when he asserts that Cathy and Hareton together 'would brave Satan and all his legions' (*WH*, p. 337) but when, on visiting the graves of Heathcliff, Catherine and Edgar, he wonders 'how any one could ever imagine unquiet slumbers for the sleepers in that quiet earth' (*WH*, p. 338).

11 For similar examples see *Wuthering Heights*, pp. 26, 27, 39, 46, 65, 72-74, 87, 94, 96, 103, 112, 122, 123, 127-130, 136, 141, 144, 150, 151, 152, 159, 160, 162, 169, 177, 180, 220, 270, 272, 279, 308, 319. Noteworthy in this connection is the way in which Lockwood rounds off his complaint to Heathcliff for being attacked by his dogs: 'The herd of possessed swine could have had no worse spirits in them than those animals of yours, sir' (*WH*, p. 5).

12 See Graeme Tytler, 'Animals in *Wuthering Heights*', *Brontë Studies*, 27/2 (2002), 121-130.

13 For a discussion on Heathcliff's 'monomania', see Graeme Tytler, 'Heathcliff's Monomania: An Anachronism in *Wuthering Heights*', *Brontë Society Transactions*, 20/6 (1992), 331-343.

14 See Tytler, ibid., 339.

15 See Tytler, ibid., 340.

16 Among several critics who have suggested that *Wuthering Heights* is an amoral or non-moral work, see especially G. D. Klingopoulos, 'The Novel as Dramatic Poem (II): *Wuthering Heights*', *Scrutiny*, 14 (1947), 271; David Sonstroem, '*Wuthering Heights* and the Limits of Vision', *Publications of the Modern Language Association of America*, 86 (1971), 57; Terence McCarthy, 'The Incompetent Narrator of *Wuthering Heights*', *Modern Language Quarterly*, 42 (1981), 59; Stevie Davies, *Emily Brontë* (Plymouth: Northcote House Publishers Ltd., 1998), p. 55; Marianne Thormählen, *The Brontës and Religion* (Cambridge: Cambridge University Press, 1999), p. 100.

The Power of the Spoken Word in *Wuthering Heights*

A theme that deserves critical attention for being integral to the structure of *Wuthering Heights* is one that might be conveniently designated as the power of the spoken word.[1] Consider, first of all, the uses of the term 'word' or 'words' in the text, often in idiomatic phrases, and sometimes with respect to utterances that elicit emotional responses from those to whom they are addressed or who overhear them.[2] Thus Mr. Earnshaw is 'painfully jealous lest a word should be spoken amiss' (*WH*, p. 35) to Heathcliff; Hindley's 'old hatred' of Heathcliff is roused by '[a] few words from [Frances], evincing a dislike to [him]' (*WH*, p. 40); Hareton defends Heathcliff against Cathy's vituperation of him by saying that he 'wouldn't suffer a word to be uttered to him, in his disparagement' (*WH*, p. 285). Heathcliff is acutely conscious of the spoken word as a means of both aggression and consolation. Thus in a moment of tension between himself and Catherine he says this to her: 'I have a mind to speak a few words, now, while we are at it' (*WH*, p. 99); and, as at their final meeting: 'I have not one word of comfort—you deserve this' (*WH*, p. 142). Ironic by way of contrast is Heathcliff's attempt to persuade Cathy to resume relations with his sickly son by asserting that 'a kind word from [her] would be his best medicine' (*WH*, p. 206). Cathy herself is alive to the way in which one word alone can give comfort when, just before her reconciliation with Hareton, she addresses him thus: 'Say you forgive me, Hareton, do! You can make me so happy, by speaking that little word' (*WH*, p. 279). That the spoken word may even affect one's very physiology is evident when, not long before her brain fever is diagnosed, Catherine asks Nelly: '[W]hy does my blood rush into a hell of tumult at a few words?' (*WH*, p. 111).[3] Also pertinent here are the verbs 'speak', 'talk', 'say' and 'tell' as used of emotional responses to certain utterances. For example, this is how Heathcliff complains to Lockwood for recounting his second nightmare: 'What *can* you mean by talking in this way to *me*!' before saying this to himself: 'God! he's mad to speak so!' (*WH*, p. 23). Isabella's objection to Heathcliff's belittling of Edgar and Catherine's marriage is expressed thus: 'No one has a right to talk in that manner, and I won't hear my brother depreciated in silence!' (*WH*, p. 132). And this is Cathy's reaction to the Heights housekeeper's informing her that Hareton is her cousin: 'Oh, Ellen! don't let them say such things' (*WH*, p. 173).[4]

What has been glimpsed of the power of the spoken word above may be supplemented by another random selection of examples. Take, for instance, the ways in which a word or group of words is repeated, sometimes in slightly varied or modified form, by the person to whom it is directed, the repetition most often denoting a kind of self-assertion through, say, the shock, surprise, anger, contempt or incomprehension evinced by the speaker repeating the word or phrase that has been used immediately beforehand or earlier in a particular dialogue. Thus when on the night shortly before his death, Mr. Earnshaw asks Catherine: 'Why canst thou not always be a good lass, Cathy?', her retort is clearly an attempt to justify her rebelliousness with this insolent modification of his diction: 'Why cannot you always be a good man, father?' (*WH*, p. 37). Heathcliff is much inclined to repeat his interlocutors' words, usually in order to domineer over them. For example, when amid her persistent efforts to dissuade him from visiting Catherine at Thrushcross Grange, Nelly warns Heathcliff that Edgar will 'take measures' against him, Heathcliff instantly replies: 'In that case, I'll take measures to secure you, woman!' (*WH*, p. 135), a threat by which Nelly is, not surprisingly, eventually compelled to yield to his request. Interesting, too, are Lockwood's repetitions of Heathcliff's words and phrases in his somewhat pathetic endeavours to resist the latter's domination of him. Thus when asked by Heathcliff in the wake of his conflict with the dogs: 'What the devil is the matter?', Lockwood instantly tries to save face by answering: 'What the devil, indeed!' (*WH*, p. 5). Again, when, because told by Lockwood that he will be curtailing his residence at the Grange, Heathcliff warns him against 'coming to plead off paying for a place you won't occupy', Lockwood tartly replies: 'I'm coming to plead off nothing about it!' (*WH*, p. 269), thereby inadvertently giving Heathcliff the psychological upper hand. But perhaps even more memorable among such examples of one-upmanship is the way in which Joseph displays both his essential insubordination as a servant and his inveterate misogyny when, for example, shortly after Isabella's arrival at the Heights as Heathcliff's bride, he vociferously repeats with a mixture of outright contempt and feigned incomprehension her words 'parlour' and 'bed-room' (*WH*, pp. 125-126) as places she has asked him to show her to.[5]

Also pertinent here is the repetition of words or phrases as recalled sometime—even a long time—after they have been first uttered. We note, for example, how Nelly and Isabella in particular mention words that they have recalled Joseph using such as 'girned [snarled]' (*WH*, p. 156), 'offalld [dreadful] ways' (*WH*, p. 174) and 'thrang [busy]' (*WH*, p. 259) as if such terms were memorable for being dialectal and possibly even incomprehensible. And yet dialectal words heard recently or in the past may also be repeated affectionately, as happens when Cathy uses one or two of Hareton's such as 'fairishes [fairies]' (*WH*, p. 172) and 'stalled [bored]' (*WH*, p. 266), the latter repetition suggesting that she has by then begun to fall under his spell. There are, moreover, contexts in which something uttered earlier by a particular character has been later recalled in an especially emotional moment. Cathy, for example, is remarkable for remembering important things that have been said to her, whether by her father or Nelly Dean or Linton Heathcliff. Noteworthy, on the other hand, are those parts of Nelly's narrative where she seems to be repeating something she has overheard many years previously. Thus her characterisation of Heathcliff in Chapter 4 with the simile 'hard as whinstone' (*WH*, p. 29) is clearly based on her memory of Catherine's having once warned Isabella against Heathcliff by describing him partly as 'an arid wilderness of furze and whinstone' (*WH*, p. 90). Again, though Nelly overhears Catherine saying, at her tryst with Heathcliff, that after her death she (Catherine) will be 'incomparably beyond and above you all' (*WH*, p. 141), it is not until the latter has died that Nelly seems to take those words with curiously superstitious seriousness. It is also interesting to note how at the same tryst Nelly recollects Catherine's account of her dream of being thrown out of heaven by the angels because 'heaven did not seem to be [her] home' (*WH*, p. 71) when, having momentarily noticed Catherine's ghastly appearance, she remarks: 'Well might Catherine deem that Heaven would be a land of exile to her, unless, with her mortal body, she cast away her mortal character also' (*WH*, p. 140). There are, however, moments of recall on Nelly's part that are not without comical implications. For example, though she has plainly disapproved of Cathy's account of her illicit visits to Linton Heathcliff enough to report them to Edgar, she shows how well she has remembered the details of that account when she makes use of them in order to upbraid Linton Heathcliff for his callous treatment of his new wife: 'Master Heathcliff, [...] have you forgotten all Catherine's kindness to you, last winter, when you affirmed you loved her, and when she brought you books, and sung you songs, and came many a time through wind and snow to see you?' (*WH*, p. 247).

There are, to be sure, a number of other contexts where the spoken word may be seen to have exercised its power over the characters portrayed. Thus it is doubtless natural that children should be much affected by what their parents and elders tell them, one notable instance being the quarrel (in Chapter 23) between Cathy and Linton Heathcliff in that they each base their arguments on what they have been told by their respective fathers.[6] Another such instance is suggested by the shepherd boy's 'phantoms', namely, his vision of the ghosts of Heathcliff and Catherine on the moors one night, which, as Nelly surmises, were 'probably raised [...] from thinking [...] on the nonsense he had heard his parents and companions repeat' (*WH*, p. 299). More important on that head, however, is our realization that Hareton's speech, including not only his 'frightful Yorkshire pronunciation' (*WH*, p. 194), to which Linton Heathcliff mockingly draws Cathy's attention, but even his mastery of bad language has undoubtedly been rendered possible by what he has picked up aurally from Hindley, Nelly Dean, Joseph, Heathcliff, and, later, from Cathy herself. The same is true *mutatis mutandis* of the development of Heathcliff's own speech from the 'gibberish' (*WH*, p. 31) he speaks on his first arrival at the Heights to the brilliant articulateness of his diatribes after his return to Gimmerton; a development surely due in part to the manifold oral influences he has undergone both in Yorkshire and beyond its confines.

Interesting, too, in this connection is Emily Brontë's pointing up the extent to which one's diction and accent are determined by one's social and regional background, one example being Nelly's following comment to Lockwood about Edgar: '—He had a sweet, low manner of speaking, and pronounced his words as you do: that's less gruff than we talk here, and softer' (*WH*, p. 62), a sentiment that helps to explain her occasional marks of deference to her temporary master. Moreover, with our awareness of the elegance of Lockwood's spoken and written language, it is easy to understand why he should set store by good conversation, or what might be regarded as the spoken word at its very highest level. Thus it is because he finds Heathcliff 'very intelligent on the topics [they] touched' at the end of his first visit to the Heights that Lockwood feels 'encouraged', despite his landlord's wish to the contrary, to 'volunteer another visit' (*WH*, p. 5) the next day. Indeed, had it not been for that second, fateful visit, Lockwood's diary might have contained little, if anything at all, of Nelly's 'history of Heathcliff'.[7]

Yet notwithstanding the numerous responses and reactions to the spoken word described in the novel, ranging as they do from cultural emulation to physical violence, and running practically the entire gamut of human emotions in both language and demeanour, the reader might nevertheless wonder how far some of these reactions and responses are necessary, let alone as inevitable as many of them seem to be; indeed, whether the spoken word is not sometimes taken too seriously, even wrong-headedly. Certainly there are contexts where these questions readily spring to mind, one such context entailing the presentation of Mr. Earnshaw. Thus we realize why, depicted as he is as an essentially humourless, superstitious man, Mr. Earnshaw seems stubbornly loath to call in question anything he is told by his servant Joseph. As Nelly recalls: 'By his knack of sermonizing and pious discoursing, [Joseph] contrived to make a great impression on Mr. Earnshaw, and the more feeble the master became, the more influence he gained' (*WH*, pp. 35-36). Furthermore, it is surely Joseph's continual negative talk about Hindley that induces Mr. Earnshaw to agree to the local curate's advice that 'the young man should be sent to college' (*WH*, p. 35). Ironically, Hindley will himself, when master of the Heights, be likewise influenced by Joseph, occasionally to the point of acting punitively on the latter's complaints about Heathcliff and Catherine. The trouble with Hindley, as with his father, is that he is much too prone to credulity. Credulity is no doubt something of a universal foible, as is memorably illustrated by the alacrity with which the local inhabitants, Zillah in particular, believe the story that Heathcliff has had cunningly spread round Gimmerton about his having rescued Nelly and Cathy from 'the Blackhorse marsh' (*WH*, p. 246). And though it is true that credulity now and then betokens innate virtue, as is suggested by Cathy's wholesome, albeit naive, trust in Heathcliff's early utterances to her, it is commonly shown in the novel to be a sign of wishful thinking. This is evident when, for example, we are told that Mr. Earnshaw 'took to Heathcliff strangely, *believing all he said* (*WH*, p. 32; italics mine). The same sort of wishful thinking may be seen on the reverse of the medal, namely, incredulity, some instances of which may strike the reader as faintly risible. Thus we may mention Hindley's repudiation of Mr. Kenneth's prognosis of Frances's fatal illness; a lovesick Isabella's outright rejection of Catherine's damning evaluation of Heathcliff's character; Edgar's denial of his maid's third-hand account of Isabella's elopement; and Cathy's taking exception to the Heights housekeeper's telling her that Hareton Earnshaw is her cousin.

As responses to the spoken word, expressions of credulity and incredulity are typical of those characters who rely all too heavily on what they are told, or rather, wish to be told, by others, especially their servants. Indeed, what we have seen in the case of Mr. Earnshaw and Joseph may be seen in elaborate form in relations between Nelly Dean and her superiors. Thus, for example, we note how dependent

Edgar is on Nelly not only for information of all kinds, but even for her opinions and her advice, particularly advice about Cathy and Linton Heathcliff, and is almost invariably willing to act on it. Thus it is her advice that Heathcliff be banned from the Grange which leads to the showdown between the two men and brings about Edgar's most serious conflict with Catherine. Yet when Edgar presently blames Nelly for that showdown and its consequences, even going so far as to threaten her with dismissal '[t]he next time [she] bring[s] a tale to [him]' (*WH*, p. 113), we may wonder how, wholly reliant as he is on the words of his trusted housekeeper, he could ever know that she was actually bringing him 'a tale'. Again, when Edgar rebukes Nelly for not telling him about Catherine's illness, it does not seem to have occurred to him that he could have visited, or tried to visit, his wife in person instead of safeguarding his pride by waiting for Nelly's messages about her. In this connection, it is noteworthy that, having shortly after the showdown insisted on Catherine's choosing between himself and Heathcliff with a straightforward 'answer' (*WH*, p. 104), Edgar is ironically unaware that her apparent reluctance to give him such an answer, no less than her later refusal to say whether or not she loves Heathcliff, is anything but ominous for their marriage. Indeed, it is because he is all too content with the mere spoken word, as he seems to be here, instead of, say, keeping a watchful eye on his wife, that Edgar will remain utterly ignorant of Catherine's earlier and later complaints about his neglect of her, particularly during her sequestration in her bedroom. That Catherine, in turn, fails to do justice to Edgar by being too dependent on Nelly's utterances about him at this time is ironically instanced when, on seeing him enter her bedroom, she advises him to 'return to [his] books' (*WH*, p. 113), simply because Nelly's earlier statement, namely, that he is 'continually among his books' (*WH*, p. 107) still rankles in her mind.[8] No doubt, Catherine's reliance on Nelly both for her reports on Edgar and for her surmises about him, and even for her influence on him, has its historical roots dating back to the occasion when she asked the housekeeper for her opinion about Edgar's proposal of marriage and reacted with a mixture of wishful thinking and incomprehension to Nelly's unpalatable words of sound common sense.

If, then, Catherine is unduly, even unnecessarily, sensitive to the spoken word because she tends to be too reliant on it, may not the same be said to be just as true of Heathcliff? Certainly no character in the novel is quicker to react not only to things said to him at length, as we have already seen in some measure above, but very often to a particular word uttered by an interlocutor. Thus in her letter to Nelly, Isabella relates that on telling Heathcliff that she was 'staying up so late' at the Heights on the night of their arrival there because he had 'the key of our room in his pocket', she received this reply: 'The adjective *our* gave mortal offence. He swore it was not, nor ever should be mine' (*WH*, p. 128)—a response that, incidentally, reminds us of Catherine's having taken umbrage at Isabella's accusation of her with terms such as 'harsh' (*WH*, p. 89) and 'dog in the manger' (*WH*, p. 93). Heathcliff's sensitivity to the spoken word is already manifest in his boyhood, sometimes with an intensity that leads to unpleasant consequences. For example, his physical violence to Edgar just before the Christmas dinner seems due scarcely any more to the latter's tactless remark about the length of his hair than to Nelly's having only a short while earlier made this flattering comparison between himself and Edgar: 'you are taller and twice as broad across the shoulders—you could knock him down in a twinkling; don't you feel that you could?' (*WH*, pp. 49-50). Much more pathetic, however, is Heathcliff's boyish sensitivity to Catherine's snobbish remarks to him on her return from her five-week sojourn with the Lintons, to say nothing of the talk which he will overhear between her and Nelly about Edgar and himself and which will impel him to take flight. For what proves to have been so mistaken about such sensitivity is that Catherine not only is strangely uncomprehending of the things she has said to upset Heathcliff, but turns out to have completely forgotten what she was saying to Nelly in the Heights kitchen, including her famously poetic comparison between her two men that has fascinated so many Brontë scholars down the years.[9] And yet how different might have been the fate of the principal hero and heroine had Heathcliff taken all those words with a pinch of salt, all the more as Catherine still had plenty of time in which to break off her engagement, given that her marriage does not take place until some three years after Edgar's proposal. Heathcliff's tendency to react to Catherine's talk too earnestly is still apparent after his return to Gimmerton. First of all, it is interesting to note the extent to which he takes the lead from Catherine in maintaining sobriety in their conversations (most of which appear to have turned on his ambition to accumulate wealth) at the Grange and on their walks together, that is, until she carelessly apprises him of Isabella's love for him.[10] Moreover, through her subsequent attempts to minimise the significance of that disclosure, Catherine merely feeds Heathcliff with malevolent intentions he seems to have been far from entertaining since his return to Gimmerton. This she does when, for example, she warns him as follows: '—quarrel with Edgar if you please, Heathcliff, and deceive his sister; you'll hit on exactly the most efficient method of revenging yourself on me' (*WH*, p. 100). Is it any wonder, then, that, nettled as he probably is by Catherine's support of Edgar and perhaps also by her apparent failure to declare her love for himself, Heathcliff should have interpreted Catherine's utterances as a hint for him to resort to a particular course of action that he would otherwise have scarcely taken on his own initiative?

It is, however, in his endeavours (in Chapter 14) to persuade Nelly to enable him to visit Catherine at the Grange that Heathcliff's responses to the spoken word are at their most curiously subjective. And here it is important to consider how far Nelly is herself to blame for these responses. First of all, we note that, instead of immediately returning to the Grange after delivering Edgar's garbled message to Isabella, Nelly takes the opportunity of her visit to the Heights not only to declare Heathcliff a threat to Catherine's recovery from her illness unless, as she says, he moves 'out of this country entirely' (*WH*, p. 130), but even to reproach him quite gratuitously for his neglect of Isabella and to advise him how she should be treated. It is therefore hardly surprising that Heathcliff is riled by Nelly's patronizing utterances enough to retaliate with talk that is almost ridiculous for its blatant subjectivity. This subjectivity seems partly due to his somewhat arrogant, though possibly unfounded, assumption that Catherine loves him in the same way as he loves her. Thus we note how Heathcliff at first takes advantage of Nelly's baseless assessment of Edgar as 'the person who is compelled, of necessity, to be her companion' and as someone who 'will only sustain his affection hereafter by the remembrance of what she once was, by common humanity, and a sense of duty' (*WH*, p. 130). Such a sentiment can nevertheless be shown to have been grossly unfair to Edgar, not only because it seems to be based in part on Nelly's having earlier overheard Mr. Kenneth's warning him that 'his health and strength were being sacrificed to preserve a mere ruin of humanity' (*WH*, p. 118) but because, as Nelly has herself observed, Edgar has lovingly nursed Catherine during her brain fever and her convalescence thereafter. Not unexpected, then, is Heathcliff's treating what is pure speculation as if it were a factual truth when he answers Nelly as follows: 'That is [...] quite possible that your master should have nothing but common humanity and a sense of duty to fall back upon. But do you imagine that I shall leave Catherine to his *duty* and *humanity*?' (*WH*, p. 131).

Nowhere in the text is Heathcliff's sensitivity to individual spoken words more patent than through his angry repetition of the emphasized two words just quoted. Such sensitivity is just as noticeable when, to Nelly's having said that Catherine has 'nearly forgotten' him, Heathcliff presently replies: 'You suppose she has *nearly forgotten* me? […] Oh Nelly! you know she has not!' (*WH*, p. 131; italics mine). Several moments later, when Heathcliff tries once again to get her to grant his request, Nelly answers him with this account of Catherine's mental state: 'The commonest occurrence startles her painfully. […] She's all nerves, and she couldn't bear the surprise' (*WH*, p. 135). That Heathcliff's subjectivity has by now assumed almost maniacal proportions is obvious when, for example, he inaccurately recapitulates some of Nelly's words thus: 'You *say* she is often restless, and anxious looking—is that a proof of tranquillity?' (*WH*, p. 135; italics mine). And though the last word quoted shows how well Heathcliff has remembered Nelly's having just 'urged the cruelty and selfishness of his destroying Mrs. Linton's tranquillity for his satisfaction' (*WH*, p. 135), his summary of Nelly's words here is just as inexact as the one with which he follows it up: 'You *talk* of her mind being unsettled—' (*WH*, p. 135; italics mine). But at the same time as Heathcliff's memory of Nelly's actual statements proves faulty, it is noteworthy how his rabid jealousy of Edgar accounts for his accurate repetition of words that Nelly has used earlier: 'And that insipid, paltry creature attending her from *duty* and *humanity!*' (*WH*, p. 135). In view of the undeniably forceful, albeit specious, rhetoric of that exclamation, it is perhaps hardly astonishing that it has helped to sustain Edgar's unduly negative image among many a Brontë scholar.

Just as the spoken word figures prominently in Heathcliff's relations with Catherine during her lifetime, so it illustrates his intrinsically ambiguous feelings towards her after her death. To begin with, we note Heathcliff's bitter disappointment at Catherine's not having mentioned his name on her deathbed, and perhaps reflect whether the subsequent narrative might not have been altogether different, had Nelly, knowing how easily Heathcliff is contented by the spoken word, told him what he had hoped to hear, even if in the form of a white lie. In this connection, we are put in mind of the significance of names in problematic love relationships, not only the uttering of a name, but also a superstitious dread of doing so, even of hearing it referred to.[11] No doubt, here as elsewhere, Heathcliff is inevitably attaching importance to a would-be spoken word, indeed too much so not to have made it already a primary cause of his later hallucinations of Catherine. This is somehow foreshadowed during his final meeting with her when, to her ironic prediction of his indifference to her after her passing, he gives this resentful reply: 'Do you reflect that all those words will be branded in my memory, and eating deeper eternally, after you have left me?' (*WH*, p. 140). What Heathcliff may have failed to realize here, as he has failed to do in the past, is that Catherine will have almost certainly forgotten all those 'words' as quickly as she has said them. That is why there is something sadly ironic about Heathcliff's loud complaint that Catherine is 'a liar to the end' (*WH*, p. 147) and about his accurately remembering what she has told him at their tryst: 'Oh! you *said* you cared nothing for my sufferings!' (*WH*, p. 147; italics mine). But what is especially conspicuous about this mixture of apostrophe and soliloquy are Heathcliff's incantatory uses of the spoken word by which he seeks to perpetuate Catherine's existence: 'And I pray one prayer—I repeat it till my tongue stiffens—Catherine Earnshaw, may you not rest, as long as I am living!' (*WH*, pp. 147-148). Such words are presently supplemented by these commands addressed to her: 'Be with me always—take any form—drive me mad!' (*WH*, p. 148).[12] What Heathcliff cannot foresee at this stage is that those last three spoken words will have been tragically realized by the time Nelly has tentatively, albeit anachronistically, supposed him to be suffering from a form of mental illness clinically defined as monomania.[13]

It will be evident from the foregoing how much the action in the latter half of the novel has its roots in the words Heathcliff says to

Catherine after her death. But it will also have become evident well before then how much the plot has been shaped by certain utterances of Catherine's heard or overheard by Heathcliff. Indeed, it goes without saying that, having ditched his original plan of revenge owing in part to Catherine's unexpectedly friendly reception of him on his return to Gimmerton, Heathcliff is unlikely to have thought up a second plan of revenge and carried it out if Catherine had desisted from her careless talk about Isabella. It is also interesting to speculate how far Nelly Dean's rank-breaking talk to her superiors helps to motivate some of their subsequent deeds. For example, we might ask in what measure Isabella has been spurred on to elopement by Nelly's attempts to put her off Heathcliff with a piece of advice inspired primarily by Joseph's verbal account of the latter's goings-on at the Heights: 'and, if his account of Heathcliff's conduct be true, you would never think of desiring such a husband, would you?' (*WH*, p. 92). Similarly, it is not improbable that Isabella's flight from the Heights has been undertaken partly because, shocked by Heathcliff's virulent haranguing of his bride as 'the talk of a madman', Nelly has said this to her: '—You are not so bewitched, ma'am, are you, as to remain with him of your own accord?' (*WH*, p. 134).[14] On the other hand, Nelly opens a veritable Pandora's box when, on discovering Cathy at the Heights after a frantic search for her, but then finding her unwilling to return with her to the Grange, she says: 'Well, Miss Cathy, if you were aware whose house this is, you'd be glad enough to get out' (*WH*, p. 172). For it is to those very spoken words that may be partly traced the seeds of the plot involving the second generation of characters portrayed. Furthermore, it is useful here to recall that it is Nelly's indulging in persistent talk in her attempts to dissuade Cathy from renewing her relations with Linton Heathcliff, rather than, say, maintaining a judicious silence or, more importantly, exercising her vested authority over her young mistress, that brings about a fresh complication of the plot—a plot that, strictly speaking, begins from the moment '[o]ne of the maids *mentioning* the Fairy cave, quite turned [Cathy's] head with a desire to fulfil this project' (*WH*, p. 168; italics mine), namely, to go to Penistone Craggs.

The interest of the last quotation derives not a little from its suggesting how easily the imagination can be stirred by the spoken word in the form of a narrative, however brief. The maid's account is, to be sure, but one of several narratives within the main narrative that have a strong emotional effect on those who hear or overhear them. One striking example to cite here is Nelly's being deeply moved by Catherine and Heathcliff's way of comforting each other in the wake of Mr. Earnshaw's sudden death: 'no parson in the world ever pictured Heaven so beautifully as they did, *in their innocent talk*; and, while I sobbed, and listened, I could not help wishing we were all there safe together' (*WH*, p. 38; italics mine). Nelly's reaction here is forcibly linked with her sundry responses to the oral narratives retailed by major and minor characters alike—Heathcliff, Isabella, Joseph, Zillah, Mr. Kenneth, a Heights housekeeper, a Grange labourer, and so on—and with the different ways in which she acts, or fails to act, on those narratives. That a narrative much reiterated, especially a generally affirmative one, may have a marked influence on children, is poignantly illustrated when, on his journey with Nelly to meet the father he has 'not heard of [...] before' (*WH*, p. 180), Linton Heathcliff avows how much his affection for Edgar has been conditioned by what he has heard about him from Isabella: 'She often *talked* of uncle, and I learnt to love him long ago. How am I to love papa? I don't know him' (*WH*, p. 180; italics mine). Linton Heathcliff's words are significant for reminding us that *Wuthering Heights* is itself largely the outcome of hearsay, that is, under the guise of 'Heathcliff's history', which, as Lockwood says to himself at the beginning of Chapter 15, he has 'heard [...] at different sittings' and which he will 'continue [...] in [Nelly's] own words, only a little condensed', adding that she is 'on the whole, a very fair narrator and

I don't think I could improve her style' (*WH*, p. 137). Yet if Linton Heathcliff's implicit trust in his mother's talk about Edgar seems to be founded less on any confidence on his part in the veracity of its content than on the power of the spoken word, may not the same be *a fortiori* true of Lockwood's apparent faith in the narrative told him by a comparative stranger, and that notwithstanding Nelly's admitting every now and then to being by no means an omniscient narrator?[15] Certainly it would appear that Lockwood is not so exercised by the question whether Nelly is a *bona fide* narrator as he ought to be, and that no doubt because he occasionally prefers to be *told* a good story than to read one.[16] It is, incidentally, Nelly's skill as a storyteller that surely helps Lockwood to recover his health much sooner than the village doctor has predicted.

It is, nevertheless, useful to remember at this juncture that Emily Brontë's novel is in part made up of Lockwood's first-hand observations on some of the people that figure in Nelly's narrative from Chapter 4 onwards. That is why it is interesting to compare Lockwood's diary entries about his encounters with, and attitudes towards, say, Heathcliff, Cathy, Hareton, Joseph and Zillah with what Nelly tells him about them and their respective histories. First of all, it is evident that Lockwood's more or less negative impressions of these characters as registered on his first three visits to the Heights are in some cases significantly modified by Nelly's detailed verbal accounts of the lives they have led before his first sojourn at the Grange and between the time of his departure from the North in January (?) 1802 and his return there in September 1802. Consider, for example, the fact that, having inwardly complained of Cathy's 'same disregard to common forms of politeness, as before', on his third visit to the Heights, Lockwood finds her 'not […] so amiable […] as Mrs. Dean would persuade [him] to believe' (*WH*, p. 265). Clearly, the face-to-face encounter with Cathy stands in stark contrast with what Nelly, just after hinting at a possible love match between

Cathy and Lockwood, has gone on to say to the latter: 'You smile; but why do you look so lively and interested, *when I talk about her*—and why have you asked me to hang her picture over your fireplace?' (*WH*, p. 226; italics mine). Indeed, it is through his disappointment with Cathy at their second meeting that we recognize how much it is owing to what Nelly has told him about her that Cathy has been for Lockwood an idealized image rather than a real person. This is somewhat confirmed when, in his efforts to get her to speak to him, he says this: 'Mrs. Heathcliff, [...] you are not aware that I am an acquaintance of yours? so intimate, that I think it strange you won't come and speak to me. My housekeeper *never wearies of talking about and praising you*' (*WH*, p. 266; italics mine). Again, it is surely what he has heard about Hareton from Nelly that will have prompted Lockwood in the same context to defend him against Cathy's derogation of his illiteracy. A more important effect of Nelly's talk, however, is ironically suggested when, discovering to his dismay on his final visit to the Heights that he has lost Cathy to Hareton, Lockwood tries to mask his disappointment by, as it were, paying homage to Nelly's affirmative accounts of the two cousins with this sentimental pronouncement on them: '*They* are afraid of nothing. [...] Together they would brave Satan and all his legions' (*WH*, p. 300).[17] By this time, however, the reader may have come to realize that, but for Lockwood's having heard the word 'Gimmerton' (*WH*, p. 271) voiced by a roadside public-house hostler, *Wuthering Heights* as we know it might never have existed.

Lockwood's response just mentioned above is an ironic evocation of the manifold reactions that practically all the characters of *Wuthering Heights* register in one way or another to the spoken word. That the spoken word is, of course, the main medium of communication between human beings is well illustrated throughout the narrative, corroborated as it is not a little by the author's discreet references to the mechanisms of human speech as well as its psychological and social implications. Yet at the same time as Emily shows us how readily we respond or react to what others say and how in so doing we tend to disclose our strengths or weaknesses of character, she makes us acutely aware that there is something ineluctably magical about the spoken word. This we gather at an important thematic level from the extent to which Lockwood's attitudes to some of the characters are, rightly or wrongly, determined rather by Nelly Dean's verbal statements about them than by his own direct observation of them. The idea that the spoken word can be taken too seriously is, however, nowhere more pathetically pronounced than in Heathcliff's relations with Catherine. It is this aspect of his presentation that deserves to be taken into full account, especially by those for whom his role as the heroine's lover seems to matter more than anything else in a reading of the novel. Moreover, amid such a concern with this world-famous romance it is all too easy to overlook the admirable literary skills with which Emily Brontë has put her text together, exemplified in part, as we hope to have suggested above, by her clever use of the spoken word not only for purposes of characterization and plot, but as a means of ensuring the cohesive structure of her masterpiece.

Brontë Studies, 39/1 (2014)

Notes

1 Although a good many Brontë scholars have touched on or alluded to my topic, it would appear that no one has hitherto published so much as an article on it. Of publications that have some relevance here may be mentioned: Christopher Dean, 'Joseph's Speech in *Wuthering Heights*', *Notes & Queries*, 7 (1960), 73-76; John B. Waddington-Feather, 'Emily Brontë's Use of Dialect in *Wuthering Heights*', *Brontë Society Transactions*, 15/1 (1966), 12-19; K. M. Petyt, *Emily Brontë and the Haworth Dialect: A Study of the Dialect Speech in Wuthering Heights* (Keighley: Yorkshire Dialect Society, 1970); Sandra M. Manley, '"Pale t'Guilp off!"', *Transactions of the Yorkshire Dialect Society*, 13 (1971), 25-28; K. M. Petyt, '"Thou" and "You" in *Wuthering Heights*', *Brontë Society Transactions*, 16/4 (1974), 291-293; J. Copley, 'The Portrayal of Dialect in *Wuthering Heights* and *Shirley*', *Transactions of the Yorkshire Dialect Society*, 14 (1976), 7-16; Luke Spencer, 'The Voices of *Wuthering Heights*', *Brontë Society Transactions*, 24/1 (1999), 82-93.

2 For quotations from the novel, see Emily Brontë, *Wuthering Heights*, eds. Ian Jack and Helen Small (Oxford: Oxford University Press, 2009). For the sake of convenience, the first Catherine will be referred to as 'Catherine', the second as 'Cathy'.

3 For similar references to 'word' and 'words', see *Wuthering Heights*, pp. 9, 11, 32, 36, 45, 52, 82, 84, 98, 118-119, 134, 141, 162, 167, 172, 192, 194, 203, 204, 208, 226, 228, 236, 252, 259, 263, 264. For the spoken 'word' in the sense of 'promise', see *Wuthering Heights*, pp. 115, 122, 144, 214, 218, 220-221, 243. Emily's interest in the spoken word is somewhat confirmed by references made to the function of the word as concept. See *Wuthering Heights*, pp. 120, 131, 134, 200, 204, 272.

4   For other relevant examples of 'say', 'tell', 'speak' and 'talk', see *Wuthering Heights*, pp. 13, 23, 33, 40, 52, 68, 73, 74, 78, 86, 90, 101, 103, 105, 107, 112, 114, 117, 120, 130, 131, 133, 137, 143, 153, 154, 167, 169, 172, 177, 186, 212, 220, 224-225, 235, 264, 278, 297. For synonymous words and phrases for 'speak' and 'say', and at volumes varying from the shriek to the whisper, see *Wuthering Heights*, pp. 26, 33, 34, 40, 43, 45, 50, 78, 79, 81, 86, 92, 103, 109, 116, 123, 124, 126, 128, 130, 135, 143, 148, 153, 162. For references to 'tell' in the sense of 'sneak on', see *Wuthering Heights*, pp. 33, 124, 167, 173, 222, 224. Noteworthy in this connection is how with terms such as 'language', 'tongue', 'voice', 'lips', 'mouth', 'tone', 'pronunciation', 'accent', etc. Emily points up or alludes to the mechanics behind, indeed the physical causes of, utterances that prompt emotional responses, whether it be, for example, through Mrs. Linton's asking her husband thus about Heathcliff: 'Did you notice his language, Linton?' (*WH*, p. 44); through Hareton's quest on two occasions to get Cathy to 'hold [her] tongue' (*WH*, pp. 268, 285); through Heathcliff's 'antipathy to the sound of [his son's] voice' (*WH*, p. 186); through Lockwood's following observation on Cathy at their first meeting: 'She never opened her mouth' (*WH*, p. 7). For similar uses of those terms, see *Wuthering Heights*, pp. 2, 5, 9, 10, 13, 14, 23, 25, 43, 53, 68, 82, 86, 94, 96, 99, 101, 106, 110, 116, 123, 134, 155, 163, 167, 171, 189, 193, 195, 209, 210, 211, 219, 223, 243, 267, 268, 273, 275, 276, 284. For other references to bad language, see *Wuthering Heights*, pp. 24-25, 42, 43, 44, 48, 56, 65, 75, 77, 92, 97, 98, 101, 122, 128, 156, 172, 174, 175, 186, 192, 221, 222, 262, 274, 278.

5   For similar examples of repetition, see *Wuthering Heights*, pp. 1, 7, 8, 9, 10, 13, 21, 23, 28, 44, 47, 51, 52, 57, 61, 62, 67, 70, 71, 72, 74, 76, 85, 87, 90, 94, 99, 100, 104, 107, 109, 112, 115, 118, 125, 126,

129, 132f, 136, 142, 143, 152, 154, 155, 161, 171, 173, 182, 184, 188, 194, 196, 197, 209, 211, 213, 214, 217, 227, 231, 235, 236, 240, 241, 242, 247, 255, 256-257, 260, 265, 272, 278, 279, 280, 284, 291, 292, 294, 296.

6   That Linton Heathcliff is deeply affected by other things said to him by his father is evident elsewhere in the text. See, for example, *Wuthering Heights*, pp. 209, 223, 233, 248.

7   Noteworthy is the fact that, at the beginning of Chapter 10, Lockwood mentions his having refrained from blaming Heathcliff for his illness because the latter was 'charitable enough to sit at [his] bedside a good hour, and talk on some other subject than pills and draughts, blisters and leeches' (*WH*, p. 80). Noteworthy, too, in this connection is the importance of good conversation for Catherine, as is evident not only when one reason she gives for loving Edgar is 'every word he says' (*WH*, p. 69), but even earlier when, shortly before Edgar is expected to arrive at the Heights, she complains to Heathcliff about being bored by his company: 'What good do I get —What do you talk about? You might be dumb or a baby for anything you say to amuse me' (*WH*, p. 61).

8   The irony of Catherine's advice to Edgar is enhanced when we recall that Nelly has earlier remarked that the latter 'shut himself up among books *that he never opened*' (*WH*, p. 106; italics mine).

9   Catherine's incomprehension and forgetfulness as described in these contexts may in some sense be pathologically linked with the signs of mental illness she betrays from Chapter 11 onwards and, more especially, during her tryst with Heathcliff in Chapter 15.

10 As Catherine says to Isabella by one way of warning her against Heathcliff: 'Avarice is growing with him a besetting sin' (*WH*, p. 91).

11 For example, when Edgar asks Catherine: 'Do you love that wretch, Heath—', she cuts him short in mid-sentence with this warning: 'You mention that name and I end the matter, instantly, by a spring from the window!' (*WH*, p. 113). Also noteworthy is that, whereas in the early stages of her infatuation, Isabella, in her complaint to Catherine about being excluded from her conversation with him on their walk together, is too shy to refer to Heathcliff by name, she will begin her account of her life at the Heights before her flight by saying: 'Heathcliff—I shudder to name him!—' (*WH*, p. 153).

12 Heathcliff's apparent awareness of the 'magic' of the spoken word is still noticeable in the last days of his life, when, for example, Nelly overhears him 'muttering terrible things to himself' (*WH*, p. 289), and, later, 'groaning, and murmuring to himself' (*WH*, p. 297), her most important such reference at this time being the following observation: 'He muttered detached words, also; the only one I could catch was the name of Catherine, coupled with some wild term of endearment, or suffering; and spoken as one would speak to a person present—low and earnest, and wrung from the depth of his soul' (*WH*, p. 295). In this connection, see also *Wuthering Heights*, pp. 153, 256, 269.

13 See Graeme Tytler, 'Heathcliff's Monomania: An Anachronism in *Wuthering Heights*', *Brontë Society Transactions*, 20/6 (1992), 331-343.

14 By the same token, it is not inconceivable that, subject as he is to incredulity, Edgar would have ended his relationship with

Catherine after their quarrel in Chapter 8 had Nelly refrained from trying to encourage him to do so by warning him about her young mistress's defects of character. See *Wuthering Heights*, p. 64. In this connection, it is one of the ironies of Nelly's presentation that, while well aware of the dangers of the spoken word through her conspicuous habit of maintaining silence or prevaricating about matters that she could have truthfully disclosed to her superiors, she now and again finds that her strenuous offers of advice to them on how to act are anything but heeded. For references to Nelly's keeping silence or prevaricating, see *Wuthering Heights*, pp. 40, 103, 104, 106, 161, 180, 189, 224, 234, 249, 257.

15 For Nelly's admissions of non-omniscience, see *Wuthering Heights*, pp. 30, 80, 163, 174, 186, 259.

16 At the beginning of Chapter 10, Lockwood writes: 'I am too weak to read, yet feel as if I could enjoy something interesting. Why not have up Mrs. Dean to finish her tale?' (*WH*, p. 80)

17 Nor would it be unreasonable to suppose that the last clause of the final paragraph of the novel had been influenced not a little by the fact that, in response to Lockwood's frivolous suggestion that ghosts will inhabit the shut-up parts of the Heights, Nelly has reproached him as follows: 'No, Mr. Lockwood, [...] I believe the dead are at peace, but it is not right to speak of them with levity' (*WH*, p. 300).

'He's more myself than I am': The Problem of Comparisons in *Wuthering Heights*

One aspect of *Wuthering Heights* that deserves critical attention is the tendency of the characters to draw comparisons.[1] Such a tendency may be deemed a normal part of everyday life, be it in the guise of comparing human beings, or landscapes, or inanimate objects, or experiences with one another in order to point up contrasts or parallels. But although comparisons of these kinds are to be found in Emily Brontë's novel, it is interesting to note the extent to which some of them have a thematic significance. Moreover, the fact that these comparisons are for the most part evaluative rather than objective, especially where they have to do with the differences or similarities between particular individuals, would suggest that their import for the reader derives not so much from what they tell us about the people compared as from what they disclose about those making the comparisons. At the same time, conscious as we become of the unusual number of comparisons present in the text, we may therefore be induced to wonder whether Emily Brontë is perhaps indirectly expressing a certain disenchantment with comparisons in general, chiefly because a good many of them somehow vitiate what would appear to be a fundamental principle underlying her vision of man, namely, the primacy of human individuality.

Let us, first of all, consider at random some of the ways in which Emily Brontë's characters draw comparisons between themselves and others, or between two people apart from themselves. These practices may be noted, for example, in characters vested with a certain authority, such as Mr. Earnshaw, Joseph and Nelly Dean, and that partly through the epithets 'better', 'best', 'worse', etc., which they use with respect to the conduct of youngsters.[2] Thus when Mr. Earnshaw, put out by Catherine's general unruliness, says this to her: 'I cannot love thee; thou'rt *worse than thy brother*' (*WH*, p. 37; italics mine), it is clear that the comparison with Hindley is meant to justify the father's inability to love his daughter, as if he thought that love were something that had to be deserved rather than a gift bestowed even on the undeserving. Again, consider Joseph's reaction to Linton Heathcliff's rejection of the porridge he has brought him shortly after the latter's arrival at the Heights. Thus, since, as Joseph assures the boy: 'Maister Hareton nivir ate nowt else, when he wer a little un', it follows for the old servant that 'what wer gooid eneugh fur him's gooid eneugh fur yah, Aw's rayther think!' (*WH*, p. 184). Joseph's implicit denial of Linton's individuality here is much of a muchness with the practice of presuming that others are thinking the same as oneself. For example, when informing Isabella of his intention to kill Heathcliff, Hindley says: 'I'm sure *you would have as much pleasure* as I, in witnessing the conclusion of the fiend's existence' (*WH*, p. 155; italics mine), he does so on the erroneous assumption that, desirous of Heathcliff's death as she also happens to be, she is therefore willing to be an accomplice in his murder.[3] Of like interest here is Isabella's telling Nelly that during a late stage of her sojourn at the Heights as Heathcliff's hapless bride she would 'rather sit with Hindley, and hear his awful talk than with "t' little maister" [Hareton] and his staunch supporter, that odious old man [Joseph]!' (*WH*, p. 154), having by then apparently clean forgotten that, in her letter to Nelly she had spoken of Hindley as being 'on the verge of madness', wherefore she 'shuddered to be near him, and thought on [Joseph's] ill-bred moroseness as *comparatively agreeable*' (*WH*, p. 124; italics mine).

Somewhat similar in fallaciousness to the examples just given above is the tendency of some of the characters to say what they would do if they were in someone else's shoes, or even to covet someone else's identity. A touching example of this type of comparison may be seen when the servant-girl announcing Hareton's birth to Nelly says this about the newborn baby's fatally ill mother: 'If I were her, I'm certain I should not die. I should get better at the bare sight of it, in spite of Kenneth' (*WH*, p. 56). Yet in thus comparing herself with Frances, the girl fails to realize that, were she Frances in such circumstances, she might still be none the less thinking and acting *qua* Frances. Certainly, comparisons entailing such phrases as 'were I in your place', 'if I were you', 'if he had been in my place', and so on, used as they are chiefly by Nelly Dean, Joseph and Heathcliff, are clearly fallacious. This is evident through the perception that, quite apart from the impossibility of exchanging identities (as Heathcliff, for example, is prone to imagine doing with Edgar, usually to his own advantage with respect to his relationship with Catherine), someone making such a comparison might be unaware that taking on another person's identity, as we have just seen in the case of the servant-girl, would not mean one's being able to act according to one's current wishes.[4] Significant in this connection is the dissatisfaction evinced by some of the characters with their own identities through comparisons with other people. This may be seen at a most pathetic level in Heathcliff's boyish desire to possess specific aspects of Edgar's handsomeness, and that notwithstanding his having earlier assured Nelly that he would 'not exchange, for a thousand lives, [his] condition [at Wuthering Heights], for Edgar Linton's at Thrushcross Grange' (*WH*, p. 42). Hardly less pathetic is Linton Heathcliff's quest to be like Cathy, partly no doubt because, as he admits, he has been taught by his father to be ashamed of his own character. As he says to Cathy: '[…] believe that if I might be as sweet, and as kind, and as good as you are, I would be, as willingly, and more so, than as happy and as healthy' (*WH*, p. 224). The pathos of these comparisons, prompted as they are by way of contrition for his recent callous behaviour towards Cathy, lies partly in our awareness that, not unlike his father in the wake of his very first encounter with Edgar at the Grange, Linton is unable to accept, let alone affirm, the uniqueness of his own identity.

Like the characters discussed hitherto, the two principal narrators, Lockwood and Nelly Dean, are much given to drawing comparisons between people. We see an example of this early in Chapter 1 when Lockwood records his first impression of Heathcliff as follows: 'I felt interested in a man who seemed *more exaggeratedly reserved than myself*' (*WH*, p. 1; italics mine). Nevertheless, in spite of having implied that, thanks to 'a sympathetic chord' within himself, he can interpret Heathcliff's reserve better than anyone else, Lockwood is perceptive enough to acknowledge his own presumptuousness in regarding the latter as a kind of replica of himself: 'No, I'm running on too fast—I bestow my own attributes over-liberally on him' (*WH*, p. 3). Indeed, it is no doubt to his embarrassment that Lockwood will find himself presently obliged to admit that there are, after all, differences between himself and his landlord. Thus at the end of the chapter, and fully resolved, in the face of Heathcliff's wish to the contrary, to visit him a second time, Lockwood writes this in his diary: 'It is astonishing how sociable I feel myself *compared with him*' (*WH*, p. 5; italics mine). Moreover, Chapters 2 and 3 will show Lockwood further disappointed in someone whom he at first declared '[a] capital fellow' (*WH*, p. 1). Certainly, it will be owing to Heathcliff's boorish talk and behaviour that Lockwood will find his identification with him to have been humiliatingly misplaced. Noteworthy, too, is how through his sociological portrait of Heathcliff in the same context Lockwood betrays the naive optimism of the amateur anthropologist who finds himself confronted by an unfamiliar culture. Such optimism, which is patent enough again in Chapter 7 when Lockwood expresses certainty that Nelly Dean has 'thought a great deal *more than the generality of servants think*' (*WH*, p. 55; italics mine), is, of course, as fallacious as his earlier assessment of 'people in these regions' as against those living in towns: 'They *do* live more in earnest, more in themselves, and less in surface change, and frivolous external things' (*WH*, p. 54). And yet even Nelly's seemingly sensible retort: 'Oh! here we are *the same as anywhere else*, when you get to know us' (*WH*, p. 55; italics mine) is no less fallacious in so far as she is unlikely to have come to know people living 'anywhere else' in the first place.

The complacency behind the words just quoted puts us in mind of perhaps the most extraordinary example of Nelly's comparative thinking, namely, her elaborate exposition in Chapter 17 of the differences and similarities between Edgar Linton and Hindley Earnshaw as widowers. Worth noting to begin with is the sentence with which Nelly introduces her topic: '*I used to draw a comparison* between [Edgar Linton] and Hindley Earnshaw, and perplex myself to explain satisfactorily why their conduct was so opposite in similar circumstances' (*WH*, p. 162; italics mine). The fact that Nelly at first speaks of thus perplexing herself may, however, strike the reader as odd, since it would appear from the very concrete portraits she has already given of both men that no two people could be less alike in character. Nelly's perplexity may be due in part to her phrase 'similar circumstances', which makes bereavement seem like a run-of-the-mill experience rather than the peculiarly individual form of suffering it usually is. Significant, too, are Nelly's words 'conduct' and 'opposite' for being redolent of her propensity to attach undue importance to behaviour and to gauge it antithetically as good or bad, right or wrong, and so on.

Nelly then goes on to align Edgar and Hindley generically as follows: 'They had both been fond husbands, and were both attached to their children; and I could not see how they shouldn't both have taken the same road, for good or evil' (*WH*, pp. 162-163). The phrase 'fond husbands' is patently too general to allow for the manifold ways in which husbands may be fond of their wives. Hindley's fondness for Frances, to judge by Catherine's diary in Chapter 3 and by Nelly's comments in Chapter 6, seems to have been a kind of childish dependency, and is hardly to be likened to the self-abnegatory thoughtfulness underlying Edgar's love for Catherine. As for Nelly's assertion that both men were 'attached to their children', it is obvious that, whereas Edgar's attachment to Cathy is in most respects exemplary, Hindley's attachment to Hareton is that of a father who, as well as being 'contented' (*WH*, p. 57) to have his child brought up entirely by its nurse and kept out of hearing, expects to be unconditionally loved by that child, even while frightening it with his drunken antics in Chapter 9. In view of Nelly's apparent obliviousness here of all such particulars and her utterly conventional notion of human life as something to be lived according to pattern and precedent, it is therefore unsurprising that she should have expected Hindley to take 'the same road' in bereavement as Edgar did.

The pleonastic phrase, 'But, I thought in my mind' (*WH*, p. 163) with which Nelly begins her next sentence seems to suggest ironically that she is inclined to think too much or, rather, to think about something without sufficient awareness of its possible bearing on what she has or has not already observed or noted. Thus one looks in vain for evidence to confirm that Hindley had 'apparently the stronger head' (*WH*, p. 163) than did Edgar. Similarly, by positing that Hindley has 'shown himself sadly the worse and the weaker man' (*WH*, p. 163), Nelly seems to turn bereavement into a sort of contest by which to judge manly qualities. This is borne out to some extent by the metaphor with which she shows manliness failing one of the sternest tests: the metaphor of a captain and crew that go to pieces after their ship has 'struck' (*WH*, p. 163). But, apart from being a dubious analogy in so far as the courage needed in a shipwreck is obviously different from that needed in bereavement, Nelly's metaphor enables her to avoid dealing with the actuality of a specific human situation. Nelly's evasiveness is further manifested when she appears to deviate from the concreteness of her nautical image by going on to say this of Edgar: 'Linton, on the contrary, displayed the true courage of a loyal and faithful soul: he trusted God; and God comforted him' (*WH*, p. 163). At the same time, Nelly seems here to have been reluctant to say what she will subsequently relate to Lockwood, namely, that Edgar withdrew altogether from everyday life after Catherine's passing and spent the rest of his days as a virtual recluse. That is why her sentence just quoted may strike the reader, albeit retrospectively, as something of a euphemism, and one unctuous enough to indicate how much her comparison has been weighted in favour of Edgar. Such a sentence is, moreover, a characteristic instance of the quasi-theological language that Nelly is liable to use now and then in her narrative. It is, then, little wonder that the last sentence of the paragraph should have an almost biblical resonance in both diction and rhythm: 'One hoped, and the other despaired: they chose their own lots, and were righteously doomed to endure them' (*WH*, p. 163). Yet for all that Nelly rounds off her comparison with an impressively rhetorical flourish involving judicious use of 'lots' and 'righteously doomed', one cannot but sense a certain pharisaic tone in the solemnity with which she thus sums up the fate of the two men in bereavement.

Nelly's bold comparison between Edgar and Hindley as widowers is not unrelated to her proclivity in other contexts to interpret the minds of some of the other main characters with a like presumptuousness. Take, for example, the episode in Chapter 21 in which, having immediately assumed that Cathy is weeping by her bedside because she has been forbidden by her father to visit Linton again at the Heights, Nelly not only pooh-poohs the girl's grief, but goes on to make this implicit comparison: 'You never had one shadow of substantial sorrow, Miss Catherine' (*WH*, p. 197), evidently unmindful of the very real sorrow that Cathy felt on learning of Linton's unexpected departure from the Grange on the morning after his arrival there. Then, as if to belittle further the supposed reason for the girl's tears, Nelly cunningly falls back on this diversionary tactic: 'Suppose, for a minute, that master and I were dead, and you were by yourself in the world—how would you feel, then? *Compare the present occasion with such an affliction as that*, and be thankful for the friends you have, instead of coveting more' (*WH*, p. 197; italics mine). This comparison is, however, clearly fallacious, and the more so as Nelly still remains ignorant of the true reason for Cathy's tears, that is, both her distress at being unable to keep her promise to see Linton the following day and her painful anticipation of his consequent disappointment.

Nelly's comments to Cathy here are typical of the overweening confidence with which she likes to give advice to the youngsters in her care, doing so perhaps nowhere more blatantly than when she is holding forth on the subject of love. This may be especially noted when, on her journey with Linton Heathcliff to the Heights in Chapter 20, she seeks to distract the boy from his apprehensiveness about meeting his father for the first time. First of all, to Linton's expressing reluctance to leave an uncle to whom he has grown attached and to be taken to a father whose existence he has hitherto been unaware of, Nelly replies that he should be glad to see him, adding: 'You must try to love him, *as you did your mother*, and then he will love you' (*WH*, p. 180; italics mine). Secondly, to Linton's wondering how he is to love a father he does not know, Nelly replies: 'Oh, all children love their parents' (*WH*, p. 180). Thirdly, having described Heathcliff's appearance and somewhat forbidding manner, she gives Linton this piece of advice: '—still, mind you be frank and cordial with him; and *naturally he'll be fonder of you than any uncle*, for you are his own' (*WH*, p. 181; italics mine). But although Nelly's essentially specious comparisons about love here are clearly a well-intentioned means of mitigating Linton's anxiety, they are to be none the less condemned not least for insulting the intelligence of a not unintelligent child.

Involving as they do various comparisons, Nelly's remarks about love between parents and children are, of course, fallacious, indeed as fallacious as some of her ideas about erotic love, particularly as experienced by minors. Thus, on hearing of Cathy's 'loving' her cousin Linton through their correspondence with each other, Nelly exclaims: '*Loving!* Did anybody ever hear the like! I might just as well talk of loving the miller who comes once a year to buy our corn. Pretty loving, indeed, and both times together you have seen Linton hardly four hours in your life!' (*WH*, p. 200). The fallacy of Nelly's comparative reasoning is evident not only from her implication that erotic love is validated only after a considerable lapse of time, but from the presumptuous way in which, in the wake of some quite unfounded interpretations she has recently made of Linton Heathcliff's state of mind, she practically dismisses Cathy's affection for him as mere calf-love through her qualitatively inappropriate reference to the miller. Nevertheless, one wonders whether Nelly's dismissive attitude towards Cathy's relationship with Linton is not after all quite justified when she soon afterwards overhears their dialogue in Chapter 23, involving as it does its questionable uses of comparisons with respect to love. For example, when to Cathy's wishing that '[p]retty Linton', as she addresses him, were her brother, Linton has answered: 'And then you would like me *as well as your father*? […] But papa says you would love me *better than him, and all the world*, if you were my wife—so I'd rather you were that!' (*WH*, p. 210; italics mine), Cathy replies that she would 'never love anybody *better than papa*' (*WH*, p. 210; italics mine). That Cathy's notion of love here seems coloured by her almost incestuous fondness for her father is amply borne out by the four naive comparisons she has used in the previous chapter in order to assure Nelly that it is not concern for her cousin Linton but anxiety about her father's illness that is making her fret: 'I care for nothing in comparison with papa. And I'll never—never—oh, never, while I have my senses, do an act or say a word to vex him. I love him better than myself, Ellen; and I know it by this—I pray every night that I may live after him; because I would rather be miserable than that he should be—that proves I love him better than myself' (*WH*, p. 204).

If the passage just quoted above, with its sundry comparisons, is understandable, even pardonable, as the expression of an adolescent who, having been brought up by her widowed father, has so far barely known erotic love, it is quite another matter when comparisons about this sort of love are pretentiously made by an adult such as Heathcliff. In this connection, it is useful to consider beforehand how far Heathcliff's comments on love have to do with his proneness to speculate comparatively on the mentalities or states of mind of some of the characters portrayed in the novel. For example, in the context of his metaphoric comparison between his son Linton and Hareton as tin and gold respectively, Heathcliff tells Nelly of knowing from his own childhood experiences the very sufferings that Hareton is at present undergoing, at the same time as he expresses confidence that the latter will 'never be able to emerge from his bathos of coarseness and ignorance', partly because, as he adds, he has got him *'faster than his scoundrel of a father secured me, and lower'* (*WH*, p. 193; italics mine). Such words are characteristic of Heathcliff's intensely competitive use of comparisons as manifestations of his inveterate quest to outdo others and, more particularly, to be proved right in his interpretations of other minds.[5] That is why there is something arrogant about the way in which, while perceptive enough to recognize Hareton's 'first-rate qualities', Heathcliff takes it for granted that those qualities are 'lost—*rendered worse than unavailing'* (*WH*, p. 193; italics mine). For, notwithstanding this further comparison, which seems plausible enough to the reader at the time it is made, subsequent events will prove how much Heathcliff has underestimated the scope of those 'first-rate qualities', and how wide of the mark he has been in gauging the mentality of their possessor.

Heathcliff's competitive use of comparisons has, to be sure, already been blatant enough in the assertions he has made in Chapter 14 both as to his love for Catherine and as to hers for him. Take, for instance, the words he says to Nelly about Catherine as follows: 'You know as well as I do, that for every thought she spends on Linton, she spends a thousand on me!' (*WH*, p. 131). The absurdity of this statement, based as it is on pure speculation and made up entirely of comparisons, leaps to the eye. First, there is not only the absurdity of Heathcliff's taking it for granted that Nelly already agrees with what he is about to say, but that of his claiming to know exactly what is going on in Catherine's mind; a sentiment which, amid his dogged determination to visit her at the Heights, he will continue to asseverate until the end of the chapter. Noteworthy, too, is the way in which, as well as implying that Catherine loves him more than she loves Edgar, Heathcliff repeatedly avers, sometimes with extravagant hyperboles, his superiority to Edgar in the capacity to love Catherine, the competitiveness of his attitude being especially noticeable when, having fallaciously dismissed Edgar's love for Catherine as bestowed on her merely out of a sense of '*duty* and *humanity*', he puts this rhetorical question to Nelly: '[...] and *can you compare my feelings respecting Catherine, to his?*' (*WH*, p. 131; italics mine).

The irony of all the words just quoted stems in part from the reader's scarcely knowing at this stage whether Catherine looks upon Heathcliff as a lover rather than as a friend. This uncertainty is later added to by evidence in the text suggesting that, notwithstanding the showdown between the two men in the Grange kitchen, during which she seems to have been more in sympathy with Heathcliff than with Edgar, Catherine nevertheless continues to show a quite heavy dependence on the latter, especially in Chapter 12. The same uncertainty prevails even during her tryst with Heathcliff in Chapter 15 in so far as, despite expressing her love for the latter, she continues to show signs of the mental ill-health she has recently been afflicted with. That Catherine, in any case, generally evinces an immature attitude to love is evident enough even after her marriage when, for example, she makes fun of Isabella in Chapter 10 for being infatuated with Heathcliff. What is significant, moreover, is that, not unlike Heathcliff, Catherine considers love as something that can be measured and compared, as may be noted when, in the same chapter, she taunts Heathcliff as follows: 'Heathcliff, I'm proud to show you, at last, somebody that *dotes on you more than myself*' (*WH*, p. 92; italics mine); and, shortly afterwards, with this garbled version of Isabella's earlier avowal: 'Isabella swears that the love Edgar has for me is *nothing to that she entertains for you*' (*WH*, p. 93; italics mine).[6]

Such frivolous talk on Catherine's part reminds us somewhat of her dialogue with Nelly in Chapter 9 about Edgar's proposal of marriage, in which she betrays her inability to love one man exclusively for his own sake. This she does principally by resorting to nature references such as 'the foliage in the woods' and 'the eternal rocks beneath' (*WH*, p. 73) by which to compare the quality of her love for Heathcliff with that of her love for Edgar, thereby managing to avoid having to make clear that she is, in fact, rather vague about her feelings for either of the two men as flesh-and-blood human beings. In this connection, Catherine's curious unawareness of Heathcliff's love for her—a feeling which he has patently disclosed to her in Chapter 8—is ironically manifested when, having been informed by Nelly that he may have overheard their dialogue, she goes so far as to hope that he 'has no notion of these things'; in other words, that he 'does not know what being in love is' (*WH*, p. 72). That partly explains why the comparisons she has earlier made about her love for Heathcliff may be regarded as but a convenient means of assuaging her bad conscience about her reluctance to marry him. Certainly, there is something puzzling not only about her giving a reason for loving Heathcliff—as if love needed a specific reason for its existence!—but about the reason itself, to wit, 'because he's *more myself than I am*' (*WH*, p. 71; italics mine). For fascinating, even admirable, as readers have found this comparison, to say nothing of her equally famous words, 'Nelly, I *am* Heathcliff' (*WH*, p. 73), such paradoxical assertions of identification indicate as much as anything else how loath Catherine is to view Heathcliff as the unique and separate individual he must needs be in any authentic love relationship. The folly of Catherine's comparative thinking is, in any case, presently made quite apparent for the reader when, afraid that Heathcliff's disappearance is due to his having overheard what she has been saying about love, Catherine exclaims: 'What did I say, Nelly? I've forgotten' (*WH*, p. 74). What Emily Brontë herself made of Catherine's comparisons, or, indeed, of any of the others discussed above, must perforce remain a matter of conjecture. Yet it is possible that, through Lockwood's comparisons between himself and Heathcliff in the opening chapters, the author is indirectly warning her readers of the perils of comparing identities, more especially in that moment when, as we saw earlier, Lockwood queries that tendency in himself.[7]

Brontë Studies, 42/2 (2017)

Notes

1 To my knowledge, no studies have yet been published on my chosen topic, even though comparisons as rhetorical devices will have been subsumed under discussions on the figurative language of the novel. For references to the text, see Emily Brontë, *Wuthering Heights*, eds. Ian Jack and Patsy Stoneman (Oxford: Oxford University Press, 1998). For the sake of convenience, the first Catherine will be referred to as 'Catherine', the second as 'Cathy'.

2 See *Wuthering Heights*, pp. 59, 64, 66, 74, 87, 88, 91, 100, 110, 114-115, 125, 143, 174, 193, 198.

3 See *Wuthering Heights*, p. 134.

4 For examples of such comparisons, see *Wuthering Heights*, pp. 50, 57, 77, 131, 186, 206, 209. For a discussion on Emily's treatment of this and other aspects of identification, see Graeme Tytler, '"Nelly, I *am* Heathcliff": The Problem of "Identification" in *Wuthering Heights*', *The Midwest Quarterly*, 47/2 (2006), 167-181.

5 See *Wuthering Heights*, pp. 8, 10, 36, 44, 46, 49-50, 53, 58, 75, 158, 193.

6 Isabella has in fact said this to Catherine about Heathcliff: 'I love him more than ever you loved Edgar; and he might love me if you would let him!' (*WH*, p. 90). Yet it is interesting to note Isabella later somewhat contradicting these words when, by way of a rejoinder to Heathcliff's deprecation of the nature of Catherine's love for Edgar, she says: 'Catherine and Edgar are *as fond of each other as any two people can be!*' (*WH*, p. 132; italics mine). As may be seen here, Isabella's comparative attitude to love is scarcely different from Catherine's.

7   The idea that problematic comparisons form an integral part of a prominent theme in Emily Brontë's novel may be thought somewhat substantiated by the equally problematic omnipresence of metaphorical comparisons in the text. Consider, for instance, the simile, a time-honoured type of comparison used numerous times in the narrative, and sometimes with no little poetic skill: one thinks in particular of Lockwood's and Nelly Dean's handling of this trope. Yet lacking as it does the capacity to substitute or replace the person or thing whose essence it is intended to convey, the simile may be utterly unsatisfactory, not to say meaningless. This is also true of many a comparison used as a rhetorical device, as is well illustrated by Lockwood's following complaint to Heathcliff about the aggressiveness of his dogs: 'The herd of possessed swine could have had no worse spirits in them than those animals of yours, sir. You might as well leave a stranger with a brood of tigers!' (*WH*, p. 5). Lockwood's two comparisons are clearly grotesque examples of fallacious reasoning. Such reasoning is also often at the root of that extreme form of the comparison, namely, the superlative, especially when it is an expression of strong emotion. Thus it would be as impossible to verify the servant-girl's reference to the newborn Hareton as '[t]he finest lad that ever breathed!' (*WH*, p. 56), as it would be to vindicate Nelly Dean's opinion of Linton Heathcliff as '[t]he worst-tempered bit of a sickly slip that ever struggled into its teens!' (*WH*, p. 214). For other problematic superlatives, see *Wuthering Heights*, pp. 3, 4, 7, 33, 35, 36, 69, 72, 79, 88, 135, 138, 143, 168, 181, 215. For problematic similes, especially animal similes, see *Wuthering Heights*, pp. 4, 27, 30, 33, 37, 65, 76, 91, 93, 122-123, 141, 147, 148, 155, 161, 172, 188, 239, 267, 276, 277, 283, 291. 14

Physiognomy in
Wuthering Heights

The study of physiognomy in the novel has in recent years become a fairly well established domain of literary criticism.[1] Some of this scholarship has been concerned with the novels of the Brontë sisters; and though physiognomy is hardly as conspicuous in *Wuthering Heights* as it is in Charlotte Brontë's novels, which abound in physiognomical (and phrenological) references and descriptions, it is, nevertheless, important enough to deserve critical discussion.[2] Broadly speaking, physiognomy in fiction has to do not only with the moral significance of facial and bodily features, gestures, gait, handwriting, laughter, clothes, national, regional or family characteristics, resemblances between human beings and animals, the effects of inner and external influences on the appearance, and so on, but also with the presentation of narrators and characters as more or less skilled observers of the human appearance; that is to say, elements in fiction which have usually been examined in the light of the physiognomic theories

of Johann Caspar Lavater (1741-1801) and against the background
of their diffusion in Europe from the late eighteenth century
onwards. There is, however, no evidence that Emily read Lavater
or any other physiognomists, or took any particular interest in
physiognomic theory; but it would be hard to imagine her not
having become as familiar with popular physiognomy as Charlotte
appears to have been, especially during the nine months of 1843
when they were both teaching at M. Heger's school in Brussels,
that city which, incidentally, had brought out at least five French
editions of Lavater's physiognomic essays in the 1820s and 1830s.[3]
In any case, by the time Emily began to write *Wuthering Heights*,
Lavater's historic work had already appeared in several English
translations and editions, and been the main impetus behind a
number of British publications on physiognomy, including
Alexander Walker's *Physiognomy founded on Physiology* (1834),
a copy of which is known to have been housed in the Keighley
Mechanics' Institute in 1841, being one of several books to which
the Brontë family had access at that time.[4]

Whatever Emily Brontë's knowledge of physiognomy, her
treatment of personal appearances in *Wuthering Heights* is very much
in line with that of her immediate predecessors, Ann Radcliffe and
Walter Scott in particular, whose detailed descriptions of fictional
characters sometimes include references to physiognomy and
physiognomists, and even to Lavater himself.[5] In this conncection, it
is noteworthy that Emily's two main narrators, Lockwood and Nelly
Dean, are presented as acute observers, with a sensitivity to faces one
might have readily attributed to the numerous disciples of Lavater
who flourished in late eighteenth-century Europe and beyond.[6]
Certainly it would be surprising if, with his dilettante disposition,
Lockwood had not heard of, or even dipped into, at least one of the
English editions of Lavater's essays that had appeared in Britain by
1801, the year heading his first diary entry.[7] Lockwood's familiarity

with physiognomy is suggested, for example, when, seeing Heathcliff give Cathy 'a look of hatred', he qualifies this judgment by adding, 'unless he has a set of facial muscles that will not, like those of other people, interpret the language of the soul' (*WH*, p. 16) and, earlier, when referring to his encounter with a young lady at the seaside, he remarks that 'if looks have language, the merest idiot might have guessed I was over head and ears' (*WH*, p. 7), as it is also hinted at through his physiognomical judgments of Heathcliff's voice (*WH*, p. 15), Cathy's face (*WH*, p. 19) and Edgar's portrait (*WH*, p. 82), as well as his use of the word 'physiognomy' in two contexts (*WH*, pp. 8, 112).[8] Yet for all that Lockwood purports to be a physiognomist in his propensity for reading and analysing faces, it would appear that physiognomy itself has at best encouraged in him a tendency not only to categorize people into types rather than to see them as individuals, but also to keep them at arm's length; indeed, far from teaching him to come to know and love his fellow men, as Lavater would have it, physiognomy may have even enhanced Lockwood's aestheticism and, hence, fostered his preference to remain a detached spectator of life.[9]

A similar predilection for observation may be noted in Nelly— no doubt as the effect of a life lived mainly through those she has served as nursemaid or housekeeper—and, like Lockwood, she seems to be quite familiar with physiognomic theory. For example, Lavater's sundry comments about the influence of virtue or vice on the development of beauty or ugliness, as well as other factors determining the facial appearance, have a certain bearing on the occasion when, having wished that, like Edgar, he had 'light hair and a fair skin' as a means of becoming 'decent' and 'good', Heathcliff is taken by Nelly to a looking-glass, shown his morose facial features in all their grim detail, and then, rather than wish for his rival's physiognomy, is advised, instead, to 'wish and learn away the surly wrinkles, to raise [his] lids frankly and change the fiends to confident, innocent angels [...]' (*WH*, p. 72). Realizing presently, however, that Heathcliff has drawn a false conclusion from her physiognomic premise in assuming she meant him to wish for Edgar's 'great blue eyes and even forehead' (*WH*, p. 72), Nelly retorts: 'A good heart will help you to a bonny face, my lad, [...] if you were a regular black, and a bad one will turn the bonniest into something worse than ugly' (*WH*, p. 72).[10] Characteristic as that aphoristic utterance is of Nelly's tendency to live her life according to fixed principles, it is, nevertheless, borne out to some extent by her observations of Hareton Earnshaw. Thus, despite being aware of a certain loutishness in his general appearance at the age of sixteen, Nelly describes him as 'a well-made athletic youth, good-looking in features', in whose 'physiognomy', as she puts it, she can detect 'a mind owning better qualities than his father ever possessed' (*WH*, pp. 240-241)—a judgment which, apart from bespeaking Hareton's intelligence and good nature, foreshadows that moment when Nelly will describe how Cathy's educative influence has affected his outward appearance: 'His brightening mind brightened his features and added spirit and nobility to their aspect—I could hardly fancy it the same individual I had beheld on the day I discovered my little lady at Wuthering Heights, after her expedition to the Crags' (*WH*, p. 391).[11]

Another aspect of physiognomy used by Nelly, and one to which Lavater was practically the first physiognomist to draw attention, is the human appearance in death or in a moribund state. For example, when he speaks of a certain refinement in one's appearance shortly before death, and even for several hours afterwards, whereby the facial features become 'visibly ennobled', we are forcibly reminded of Nelly's final descriptions of Catherine. Thus, having described the physical effects of the heroine's 'brain fever' with phrases such as 'ghastly countenance', 'strange exaggerated manner' and 'wasted face', and underlined the physiognomic interest of her illness by mentioning the alarm and horror with which she and Edgar have reacted to her haggard looks and changing facial expressions, Nelly inevitably becomes aware of a significant alteration in her appearance on the eve of her death, whereby, conscious of 'unearthly beauty in the change', she recalls that 'the flash of her eyes had been succeeded by a dreamy and melancholy softness' so that they 'appeared always to gaze beyond, and far beyond—you would have said out of this world—' (*WH*, p. 192).[12] No less 'Lavaterian', it might be said, is Nelly's following description of Catherine shortly after her death:

> *Her brow smooth, her lids closed, her lips wearing the expression of a smile, no angel in heaven could be more beautiful than she appeared, and I partook of the infinite calm in which she lay. My mind was never in a holier frame than while I gazed on that untroubled image of Divine rest. (WH, pp. 201-202)*[13]

Furthermore, since Lavater's observations on the dying and the dead are an expression of the Christian theology underlying his physiognomic thinking, they have a particular relevance to the way in which, despite having just remarked on the heroine's 'wayward and impatient existence' (*WH*, p. 202), Nelly is, ironically enough, so heartened by the sight of the latter's corpse 'asserting its own tranquillity' (*WH*, p. 202) as to reaffirm her simple-hearted, not to say naive, belief in a heavenly after-life.

But perhaps the most important aspect of physiognomy in *Wuthering Heights* is the family physiognomy, not least because Emily Brontë's treatment of it entails a remarkably dramatic use of the observational skills of some of her main characters. It is interesting, first of all, to note the way in which the differences between the Earnshaws and the Lintons in character and temperament are already suggested by specific references to personal appearance. The fact that, for example, the Earnshaws have dark eyes and brown hair—Catherine's 'brown ringlets' (*WH*, p. 65) are mentioned, as are Hareton's 'thick brown curls' (*WH*, p. 14) and 'brown locks' (*WH*, p. 372)—and the Lintons blue eyes and fair hair, seems to make physiognomic sense if we accept Lavater's view that '*blue* eyes announce more weakness, a character softer and more effeminate than *hazel* or *black* eyes'; and, again, his statement, made amid vague and, sometimes, unfavourable assessments of dark hair, that 'flaxen hair', to which he assigns the epithet '*noble*', generally announces 'a delicate and sanguino-phlegmatic temperament'.[14] Furthermore, since references to family features are rare in physical character description before 1790, and then usually perfunctory, our comparison here between *Wuthering Heights* and the *Essays on Physiognomy* may be deemed justifiable, all the more because, apart from making simple comments on heredity that were by no means commonplace in the late eighteenth century, Lavater found that none of the great physiognomists before him had said much on the subject of the family physiognomy.[15] And though by 1847 Emily Brontë might have come to know of the sophisticated scientific theories of heredity propounded by Comte, Lamarck and others, there can be little doubt that her elaborate treatment of family resemblances and differences, which is virtually unprecedented in the English novel, is a sort of homage to Lavater's categorical claim that 'family physiognomy is as undeniable as national [physiognomy]'.[16]

Family physiognomy plays an important part in relations between the Earnshaws and the Lintons on the one hand, and in the conflict between the Lintons and Heathcliff on the other. Let us first consider the Linton physiognomy, which is treated in two ways: first, the 'light hair' and 'fair skin' of Edgar Linton are associated, it seems, with social privilege and cultural refinement; secondly, they imply a certain decadence, which becomes evident in the child of Heathcliff and Isabella Linton. By marrying Isabella, Heathcliff has sought to avenge himself both on Catherine and on the Lintons. But fate answers this quest for vengeance with an act of counter-vengeance, for Heathcliff's son proves not only to bear no physical resemblance to himself, but to possess a sickly version of that Linton physiognomy which his father had once so coveted as a boy, and which, to judge by the latter's condemnation of Isabella in front of Catherine for 'that mawkish, waxen face' and for her blue eyes inasmuch as they 'detestably resemble Linton's' (*WH*, p. 131), he has by now come to hate and despise. The irony of this is made plain when Nelly Dean notes Linton Heathcliff's resemblance to his uncle: 'A pale, delicate, effeminate boy, who might have been taken for my master's younger brother, so strong was the resemblance, but there was a sickly peevishness in his aspect that Edgar Linton never had' (*WH*, p. 245). Pathos is then added to irony in Nelly Dean's dialogue with Linton Heathcliff, who learns to his dismay that he is physically quite different from his father with the 'black hair and eyes' (*WH*, p. 252), and then again in the boy's own awareness of this difference as expressed in a letter to his uncle Edgar: 'I believe an interview would convince you that my father's character is not mine, he affirms I am more your nephew than his son, [...]' (*WH*, pp. 314-315). Disappointed for obvious reasons by the physical appearance of his son, Heathcliff resolves, nevertheless, to have him well looked after in order to use him later for purposes of revenge; though, as time passes, his dislike of the boy becomes more and more apparent, being typified, for instance, by his 'antipathy to the sound of his voice' (*WH*, p. 258). However, his plan to win a vicarious triumph over the Lintons by having his descendant 'lord of [the Lintons'] estates' and 'hiring their children, to till their fathers' land for wages—' (*WH*, p. 255) is thwarted; for, though Heathcliff forces Cathy to marry his son, the latter dies an invalid's death shortly afterwards.

The fair hair and blue eyes of the Lintons are also contrasted with the Earnshaws' brown hair and dark eyes, which, in the person of Catherine Earnshaw, represent that boisterous vitality which is lacking in the Lintons. Moreover, the fundamental incompatibility between Catherine and Edgar is suggested to some extent by their being physically quite unalike—an incompatibility which is made symbolically manifest in the mixture of sensitivity and discontent we so often see in the child of their tragic union. Nevertheless, as Nelly Dean implies in her first detailed description of Cathy, the child has clearly inherited the best of both parents:

> *She was the most winning thing that ever brought sunshine into a desolate house—a real beauty in face—with the Earnshaws' handsome dark eyes, but the Lintons' fair skin, and small features, and yellow curling hair. Her spirit was high, though not rough, and qualified by a heart sensitive and lively to excess in its affections. That capacity for intense attachments reminded me of her mother; still she did not resemble her; for she could be soft and mild as a dove, and she had a gentle voice, and pensive expression: [...]. (WH, p. 232)[17]*

Cathy's heredity becomes the basis for her role in the novel. Thus with her Earnshaw vitality and Linton sensitivity, she not only offers resistance, however ineffective, to Heathcliff's tyranny, but manages after a long period of conflict with Hareton Earnshaw (for which her inherited snobbishness is largely to blame) to draw the latter out and, as we saw earlier, to educate him. Not the least interesting thing about this relationship is the cousins' growing resemblance to each other through mutual spiritual and emotional influences, all the more as Lavater observes:

> *I have found the progress of resemblance most remarkable when two persons, the one richly communicative, the other apt to receive, have lived a considerable time together, without foreign interventions; when he who gave had given all, or he who received could receive no more, physiognomical resemblance, if I so dare say, had attained its punctum saturationis. It was incapable of further increase.[18]*

But however 'Lavaterian' Cathy's resemblance to Hareton may be, it serves an unmistakable structural function, for, as we shall see presently, its effect on Heathcliff is such as to mark the final turning point of the action.

The idea that Heathcliff should be profoundly affected by this family resemblance need not surprise us here if we remember the account of his visit to the Lintons in Chapter 6, where, despite his naive assumptions about physiognomy in Chapter 7 mentioned above, his reference to the 'vacant blue eyes of the Lintons' gazing 'full of stupid admiration' at Catherine's 'own enchanting face' (*WH*, p. 63), already bespeaks that gift for observation which Lavater found so often in children.[19] In any case, it may be supposed that Heathcliff's physiognomic sensitivity has already taken root in that moment when, in order to reassure his wife in her terror of the boy, Mr. Linton falls back on the following age-old physiognomic half-truth: 'Don't be afraid, it is but a boy—yet the villain scowls so plainly in his face, would it not be a kindness to the country to hang him at once, before he shows his nature in acts, as well as features?' (*WH*, p. 61). Indeed, it needs only the reference to Mrs. Linton's raising her hands 'in horror' and Isabella's suggesting that he be put down in the cellar because he looks 'exactly like the son of the fortune-teller, that stole [her] tame pheasant' (*WH*, p. 61) for the reader to imagine the essence of Heathcliff's self-consciousness about his personal appearance. All such details, together with several (mainly) derogatory references to Heathcliff as a gipsy and Nelly's constant, and sometimes nervous, awareness of his 'black eyes' and 'black hair' are, no doubt, satirical comments on physiognomic prejudice, not to say outright Anglo-Saxon racism, as manifest most patently in Mr. Linton's contemptuous designation of Heathcliff as 'a little Lascar, or an American or Spanish castaway' (*WH*, p. 62). And though it is true that later in the novel Heathcliff's physicality has, as a consequence of his three-year absence, become strong and refined enough to impress Nelly, Catherine and Edgar, and even to cause the fastidious Isabella to become infatuated with him, it is one of the remarkable ironies of the novel that a man of such impressive physical characteristics should have failed to pass them on to his offspring.

Furthermore, it would be hard to find anywhere in fiction a more admirable treatment of physiognomy than that which Emily Brontë provides us through her presentation of Heathcliff. For just as Heathcliff enters the world of Gimmerton a physiognomic outsider, so he departs it, as it were, a physiognomic wreck, defeated at first by the Linton physiognomy, as we have already seen, and, then, as we shall see presently, overcome in the end by the Earnshaw physiognomy.

The earliest significant reference to the Earnshaw physiognomy from Heathcliff's standpoint occurs in Isabella's letter to Nelly Dean, in which Hareton is described as having 'a look of Catherine in his eyes and about his mouth' (*WH*, p. 167), and Hindley's eyes are likened to 'a ghostly Catherine's, with all their beauty annihilated' (*WH*, p. 168). Such references are, of course, to be expected of the very observant Isabella, though their function here is to adumbrate the moment when, in her brave attempt to intervene on Hindley's behalf against Heathcliff, she will address the latter as follows: 'Now that [Catherine's] dead, I see her in Hindley; Hindley has exactly her eyes, if you had not tried to gouge them out, and make them black and red, [...]' (*WH*, p. 223). That these words should have an ironically painful effect on Heathcliff is only later made apparent; but through them the reader comes to suppose that Heathcliff's inveterate brutality to Hindley may have been much more than a matter of settling a childhood score. Heathcliff's ill-treatment of Cathy can also be similarly explained: some psychologists might even describe it as an expression of inverted love. For example, in one of her many acts of defiance towards Heathcliff, she is described with her 'black eyes flashing with passion and resolution' (*WH*, p. 328). This description prefigures a moment in their conflict when, just after Catherine has demanded the key of the door, Heathcliff is described by Nelly Dean thus: 'He looked up, seized with a sort of surprise at her boldness, or, possibly, reminded by her voice and glance, of the person from whom she inherited it' (*WH*, p. 328).

With each reminder of Catherine's physiognomy, Heathcliff undergoes a kind of psychological jolt, every one of which marks a stage in his gradual spiritual decline. This is first suggested when, just after Hareton has burnt his books out of spite, Lockwood overhears Heathcliff talking to himself about how, in his attempt to discover Hareton's resemblance to his father, he can only detect his uncanny likeness to Catherine—a likeness so painful for him that he 'can hardly bear to see him' (*WH*, p. 367). Another tormenting reminder of Catherine occurs when Hareton and Cathy are behaving frivolously at the breakfast table. On this occasion Nelly Dean describes how, after having 'rapidly surveyed [their] faces', and then been 'abhorred' by Cathy's 'accustomed look of nervousness and yet defiance' (*WH*, p. 386), Heathcliff addresses the latter as follows: 'What fiend possesses you to stare back at me, continually, with those infernal eyes? Down with them! and don't remind me of your existence again' (*WH*, pp. 386-387). Such, indeed, is the impact of this physiognomic resemblance on him that, a few minutes later, when Heathcliff has seized hold of Cathy for refusing to leave the kitchen and, as Nelly Dean observes, seems 'ready to tear [her] to pieces' (*WH*, p. 389), he suddenly relaxes his grip on her while gazing 'intently in her face' (*WH*, p. 390). And as he draws his hand 'over his eyes' (*WH*, p. 390), and then threatens to kill her should she provoke him again, the hero's spiritual decline is further confirmed.

It is, then, little wonder that, with his essentially superstitious nature, Heathcliff should show signs of 'monomania' (*WH*, p. 394) by the time he has become vividly aware of the cousins' mutual resemblance, especially since Catherine's haunting of him is now at its most intense.[20] Thus Nelly Dean relates how, on returning

home unexpectedly from one of his daily rambles, Heathcliff finds
Hareton and Cathy reading together by the fire, their faces 'animated
with the eager interest of children' (*WH*, p. 392). The narrative then
continues as follows:

> *They lifted their eyes together, to encounter Mr. Heathcliff—perhaps you
> have never remarked that their eyes are precisely similar, and they are
> those of Catherine Earnshaw. The present Catherine has no other likeness
> to her, except a breadth of forehead, and a certain arch of the nostril that
> makes her appear rather haughty, whether she will or not. With Hareton
> the resemblance is carried farther: it is significant at all times—then, it was
> particularly striking: because his senses were alert, and his mental faculties
> wakened to unwonted activity.*
>
> *I suppose the resemblance disarmed Mr. Heathcliff: he walked to the
> hearth in evident agitation, but it quickly subsided, as he looked at the young
> man; or I should say, altered its character, for it was there yet. (*WH*, p. 392)*

Nelly Dean's physiognomic interpretation of Heathcliff's agitation
proves to be correct, for, once the cousins have left the room, he feels
impelled to confide in her about his sufferings. That his 'monomania'
is now at its very worst is also evident when he refers to Hareton and
Cathy as 'the only objects which retain a distinct material appearance
to [him]' (*WH*, p. 393). This 'appearance', moreover, causes him,
as he confesses, 'pain, amounting to agony' (*WH*, p. 393): through
Cathy, he is reminded of her mother, while, through Hareton, he
undergoes a kind of *déjà vu* boyhood experience. And having, as he
has just said, now 'lost the faculty of enjoying their destruction' and
feeling the need to 'turn [his mind] over to another' (*WH*, p. 393),
Heathcliff regains much of the sympathy which we felt for him in
his physiognomic dialogue with Nelly Dean in Chapter 7, and which
we feel perhaps more strongly through his following confession to
her:

Five minutes ago, Hareton seemed a personification of my youth, not a human being—I felt to him in such a variety of ways, that it would have been impossible to have accosted him rationally.

In the first place, his startling likeness to Catherine connected him fearfully with her—That, however, which you may suppose the most potent to arrest my imagination, is actually the least—for what is not connected with her to me? and what does not recall her? I cannot look down to this floor, but her features are shaped on the flags! In every cloud, in every tree—filling the air at night, and caught by glimpses in every object by day, I am surrounded with her image! The most ordinary faces of men and women—my own features— mock me with a resemblance. The entire world is a dreadful collection of memoranda that she did exist, and that I have lost her! (WH, pp. 393-394)

With these words, the mystery of Heathcliff's earlier reactions to the Earnshaw physiognomy is at last unravelled; that is to say, they suggest that every single reference to a resemblance to Catherine has constituted part of the ironic leitmotif of her haunting of him. Thus we discover that the heroine's constant presence in the novel, far from being that of some vague apparition, has throughout been an utterly physiognomic phenomenon. It is, moreover, in this penultimate chapter that Emily Brontë shows how skilfully she has used physiognomy in the treatment of her central themes. For just as Heathcliff's downfall, as manifest in the mental deterioration he betrays in this long confession, may be said to be in part the consequence of his physiognomic sensitivity, not to mention his failure to survive physiognomically in his 'descendant', so the resolution of the conflict between the Earnshaws and the Lintons, and hence the establishing of peace and harmony at the end of the novel, which was already foreshadowed in the description of Cathy's physiognomic make-up, may be said to have been symbolically sealed by the growing mutual resemblance of the two cousins as brought about by their love for each other.

Brontë Society Transactions, 21/4 (1994)

Notes

1   For a recent bibliography of such studies, see Graeme Tytler, 'Lavater and the Nineteenth-Century English Novel', in *The Faces of Physiognomy: Interdisciplinary Approaches to Johann Caspar Lavater*, ed. Ellis Shookman (Columbia, SC: Camden House, 1993), pp. 161-162, note 2.

2   For physiognomy in Charlotte Brontë's fiction, see Wilfred M. Senseman, 'Charlotte Brontë's Use of Physiognomy and Phrenology', *Papers of the Michigan Academy of Sciences, Arts and Letters*, 38 (1953), 475-483; Ian Jack, 'Physiognomy, Phrenology and Characterisation in the Novels of Charlotte Brontë', *Brontë Society Transactions*, 15 (1970), 377-391; Graeme Tytler, 'Character Description and Physiognomy in the European Novel (1800-1860) in Relation to J. C. Lavater's *Physiognomische Fragmente*' (Diss., University of Illinois, Urbana, 1970), pp. 143-144, 229n, 242-244, 254-255, 321-322; Graeme Tytler, *Physiognomy in the European Novel: Faces and Fortunes* (Princeton, NJ: Princeton University Press, 1982), pp. 190-192, 236-238, 275-277. For physiognomy in *Wuthering Heights*, see Tytler, 'Character Description and Physiognomy', pp. 234, 250-251, 258-261; Tytler, *Physiognomy in the European Novel*, pp. 227-229, 242-253, 256-259, 278-279.

3   For details, see John Graham, *Lavater's Essays on Physiognomy. A Study in the History of Ideas* (Bern: Peter Lang, 1979), pp. 92-93.

4   For a bibliography of nineteenth-century British publications on physiognomy, see Tytler, *Physiognomy in the European Novel*, pp. 348-349. For the reference to Walker, see Clifford Whone, 'Where the Brontës Borrowed Books', *Brontë Society Transactions*,

60 (1950), 358. Walker devotes a few paragraphs to Lavater's physiognomic essays; and though he dismisses them as scientifically inadequate, he acknowledges them to be 'the most valuable work which has appeared on physiognomical science'. See Alexander Walker, *Physiognomy founded on Physiology* (London: A. K. Newman, 1834), pp. 216-217.

5   For details, see Tytler, 'Lavater and the English Novel', pp. 225-226.

6   For an account of the Lavaterian physiognomic culture in Europe, see Graham, *Lavater's Essays on Physiognomy*, passim; and Tytler, *Physiognomy in the European Novel*, pp. 82-119.

7   Two of the best-known English translations are John Caspar Lavater, *Essays on Physiognomy for the Promotion of the Knowledge and the Love of Mankind*, tr. Thomas Holcroft, 3 vols. (London: G. G. J. & J. Robinson, 1789), and John Caspar Lavater, *Essays on Physiognomy calculated to extend the Knowledge and the Love of Mankind*, tr. C. Moore, 3rd ed., 3 vols. (London: H. D. Symonds, 1797). Since Holcroft's translation of the original *Physiognomische Fragmente* (Leipzig & Winterthur, 1775-1778) contains details that are not to be found in Moore's translation of Lavater's original French edition, *Essai sur la physionomie* (Paris, 1781-1803), and vice versa, reference will be made to both texts in our discussion here. For a list of English editions and versions of Lavater, see Graham, *Lavater's Essays on Physiognomy*, pp. 87-90.

8   For the increasing use of the term 'physiognomy', and the widening of its meaning, in European literature after the 1790s, see Tytler, *Physiognomy in the European Novel*, pp. 117-118, 364. All quotations from the novel are taken from Emily Brontë, *Wuthering*

Heights, eds. Ian Jack and Hilda Marsden (Oxford: Clarendon Press, 1976). For the sake of convenience, the first Catherine will be referred to as 'Catherine', the second as 'Cathy'.

9   For Lavater's concept of physiognomy as an act of neighbourly love, see *Essays on Physiognomy*, tr. Moore, vol. 2, pp. 41-45.

10 Lavater's numerous comments on the relationship between virtue and vice, and beauty and ugliness, are central to his physiognomic outlook. See especially the section 'Of the Harmony of Moral and Corporeal Beauty' in Lavater, *Essays on Physiognomy*, tr. Holcroft, vol. 1, pp. 175-208.

11 For the influence of education and other factors on the human appearance, see especially, Lavater, *Essays on Physiognomy*, tr. Holcroft, vol. 1, p. 184.

12 For Lavater's experience of the physiognomy of the dying, see *Essays on Physiognomy*, tr. Moore, vol. 3, p. 150.

13 Lavater, *Essays on Physiognomy*, tr. Moore, writes: 'As often as I have seen dead persons, so often have I made an observation which has never deceived me: that after a short interval of sixteen or twenty-four hours, sometimes even sooner, according to the malady which preceded death, the design of the physiognomy comes out more, and the features become infinitely more beautiful than they had been during life: they acquire more precision and proportion, you may perceive in them more harmony and homogeneity, they appear more noble and sublime' (vol. 3, p. 149).

14 Lavater, *Essays on Physiognomy*, tr. Moore, vol. 3, pp. 323-324.

15 Lavater, *Essays on Physiognomy*, tr. Holcroft, writes: 'Striking and frequent as the resemblance between parents and children is, yet have the relations between the character and countenances of families never been enquired into. No one has, to my knowledge, made any regular observations on this subject' (vol. 3, pp. 128-129). For Lavater's comments on the family physiognomy and heredity, see *Essays on Physiognomy*, tr. Holcroft, vol. 1, pp. 196-197, and vol. 3, pp. 128-147.

16 Lavater, *Essays on Physiognomy*, tr. Holcroft, vol. 3, p. 128.

17 Of particular interest for Emily Brontë's treatment of the Earnshaw eyes is Lavater's following comment: 'If the eyes of the mother have any extraordinary vivacity, there is almost a certainty that these eyes will become hereditary' (*Essays on Physiognomy*, tr. Holcroft, vol. 3, p. 132).

18 Lavater, *Essays on Physiognomy*, tr. Holcroft, vol. 3, p. 148.

19 See Tytler, *Physiognomy in the European Novel*, p. 64.

20 See Graeme Tytler, 'Heathcliff's Monomania: an Anachronism in *Wuthering Heights*', *Brontë Society Transactions*, 20/6 (1992), 331-343.

The Presentation of the Second Catherine in *Wuthering Heights*

Bronté scholars concerned with the second Catherine in *Wuthering Heights* (or Cathy, as she will be henceforth designated) have for the most part dealt with her somewhat cursorily, their comments about her being generally confined to summary judgements of her character. Several such judgements have been scarcely to her credit, largely because she has tended to be compared unfavourably with her mother, or because she has been frowned upon for clipping Hareton Earnshaw's wings through her educational influence on him. It is true that recent decades have seen an increase in the number of affirmative attitudes towards Cathy, some of which suggest that her role and function in the novel have been examined more objectively than appears to have sometimes been the case before.[1] An objective assessment of a fictional character is no doubt easier to make if that character's presentation is studied step by step and in some detail. Accordingly, rather than settling for an evaluation of Cathy on the basis of, say, key moments in the narrative, my aim here will be to consider her development over a period of some five years, during which she is portrayed not as the grown-up she may give some readers the impression of being but, chiefly, as an adolescent from the age of thirteen onwards. Moreover, contrary to the view expressed by some scholars that the story of the youngest generation in the novel is a kind of let-down for the reader, I would argue that the presentation of Cathy is one of the signal aspects of Emily Brontë's art as a novelist.[2]

Cathy's importance in the novel is suggested as early as in Chapters 2 and 3, where we are given glimpses not only of essential facets of her character through the mixture of childishness and maturity she displays in her talk and behaviour, but also a general idea of the conflicts she is having, and is subsequently to have, with some of the principal male characters.[3] At the same time, Cathy appears to be at a very low point in her life as a young widow, and one with seemingly little prospect of escaping from her very straitened circumstances; a state of affairs that is, incidentally, now and again underlined right up to the last but three chapters by references made to her having practically no future to look forward to either materially or maritally.[4] Nevertheless, the fact that Lockwood learns that Cathy is married neither to Heathcliff nor to Hareton prompts the reader to surmise a possible romance between her and Heathcliff's genteel tenant as a means by which she might find a way out of her dire situation. Such speculation is somewhat encouraged both by Lockwood's admiration for Cathy's beauty and by his intention to reside for several months within walking distance of the Heights, and is further encouraged at the beginning of his conversation with Nelly Dean in Chapter 4.

Although in Chapter 2 there is a hint of rivalry between Lockwood and Hareton, mainly through the latter's apparent jealousy of her concern that his 'rival' should be safely accompanied back to Thrushcross Grange, Lockwood's originally mistaken assumption about Hareton and Cathy being man and wife may be understood as an ironic foreshadowing both of the eventual marriage of the two cousins and of his own failure to win her hand. It is, then, through such details that Cathy, in spite of, or perhaps even because of, her grim existence as Heathcliff's prisoner, to say nothing of her being at no time addressed by name in the first three chapters, seems already to show signs of the worthy heroine she will have become by the end of the novel. Although Cathy is briefly mentioned again in Chapters 16 and 17 as a newborn baby, it is not until just over halfway through the book, namely, in Chapter 18, that we are given an account of her early years. Born prematurely and somewhat neglected by her father at first, Cathy nevertheless shows a remarkably quick physical and mental development as a toddler, which is doubtless a portent for the exceptional energy both bodily and cultural that she will be conspicuous for during her adolescence. There is, to be sure, much that is quite normal about Cathy's childhood, as we gather from, say, Nelly's reference to the usual illnesses the girl has to live through along with all other children, or to the fact that, though obliged to wear a black frock as a token of mourning for her aunt Isabella, the latter's recent death, we are told, impressed Cathy 'with no definite sorrow' (*WH*, p. 176). In most other respects, however, Cathy's childhood is abnormal, for, unlike her mother, she is brought up in a very protected, not to say severely sequestered, environment, her associates consisting, it would appear, entirely of adults—her father, her nursemaid, and servants. Noteworthy here is the particular attention she receives from her father, who, as well as seeing to her formal education alone, is the only person at the Grange to take her out for walks, for, as Nelly recalls, he 'trusted her to no one else' (*WH*, p. 167). That Cathy perforce turns into a 'spoilt brat' is suggested by her tendency to threaten to report servants for the slightest offence and by the very affectionate terms with which she is invariably addressed by everyone in Edgar's household.[5]

With Cathy's early history in mind, then, the reader should hardly wonder at the naivety and narrow-mindedness she often evinces in her relations with people she encounters beyond the circle of those in whose midst she has spent the first twelve years of her life. The first person Cathy meets outside her home is Hareton Earnshaw; and though they both get on well enough at the beginning, it is on discovering that he is not the son of the owner of the Heights that she shows such crass stupidity in her talk and behaviour towards him as to suggest that she has been taught next to nothing about how to deal with those she looks upon as her social inferiors. Certainly, the reader is astonished both at the presumptuousness with which Cathy concludes that Hareton is a servant and, later, at the thoughtlessness with which she insults him for his illiteracy or makes light of his endeavours to teach himself to read. Such episodes plainly go hand in hand with those in which Cathy's stupidity takes on paranoid dimensions. This we see when, for example, in the wake of being turned out of 'the house' together with Linton by Hareton, she not only claims that the latter 'had killed Linton', but also when, completely misunderstanding Hareton's evident attempt to apologize to her for his violent behaviour, she 'gave him a cut with [her] whip, thinking perhaps he would murder [her]', having already assured him that her father would have him 'put in prison and hanged' (*WH*, p. 222). Nor is surprising the extent to which Cathy's sheltered upbringing is reflected in her tendency to fallacious reasoning. Consider, for instance, her way of countering Nelly's malicious support of Heathcliff's conjecture that his sickly son Linton will 'not win twenty' (*WH*, p. 214): 'He's younger than I […] and he ought to live the longest: he will—he must live as long as I do. He's as strong now as when he first came into the North, I'm positive of that! It's only a cold that ails him, the same as papa has—You say papa will get better, and why shouldn't he?' (*WH*, p. 214). As is only too obvious, there is a good deal of wishful thinking inherent in this string of fallacies. Much the same sort of naive optimism colours Cathy's reading of Linton's mind at their second 'official' meeting on the heath, when, having asked him to tell her 'the meaning of [his] strange talk' and to confess 'all that weighs on [his] heart', she goes on to say: 'You wouldn't injure me, Linton, would you? You wouldn't let any enemy hurt me, if you could prevent it? I'll believe you are a coward, for yourself, but not a cowardly betrayer of your best friend' (*WH*, p. 236). No words seem to be further from the truth about someone who, ironically enough, is in fact cleverly playing the invalid in order to lure his cousin into the Heights for their fateful marriage.

If Cathy's notion of Linton's character reflects a bookish knowledge of life rather than a knowledge based on a real familiarity with the world, it is likely that her optimistic assessment of him has much to do with the clannishness she now and again betrays with respect to those related to her by blood or by marriage. That Cathy's clannishness is essentially childish is nowhere better illustrated than when, having blatantly denied that Hareton is her cousin, she resorts to a non sequitur by asserting that her father 'is gone to fetch my cousin from London', adding, 'my cousin is a gentleman's son' (*WH*, p. 173). Founded as it is at this stage mainly on images of Linton, not to mention the fetishism of her attachment to a lock of his hair sent to her father by Isabella, Cathy's clannishness in this respect is further confirmed when, eagerly awaiting Edgar's return from the South, she 'indulged most sanguine anticipations of the innumerable excellencies of her "real" cousin' (*WH*, p. 176). Scarcely less childish is the fact that on learning that Heathcliff, shortly after meeting him for the first time on the moors, is her uncle, Cathy says: 'I thought I liked you' (*WH*, p. 191), and that despite having been gruffly addressed by him for supposedly poaching on his land. No doubt, it is because Heathcliff is her uncle that Cathy at first not only willingly believes his account of his relations with Edgar, but will even take sides with Heathcliff against both her father and Nelly, saying as she does this to the latter on their way home: 'he's *my* uncle, remember, and I'll scold papa for quarrelling with him' (*WH*, p. 195). It is, of course, clannishness of a quite different kind that will induce Cathy to accept Edgar's own account of Heathcliff's marriage to Isabella. Noteworthy, too, is how, during her ordeals at the Heights, Cathy continues to assert her clannishness when, increasingly beset there by a sense of claustrophobia, she tries to get a very uncommunicative Hareton to speak to her and even to be reconciled with her after a long period of enmity between them. But since Cathy's strategy of reading aloud from a book and then leaving it lying around fails to have the intended effect on Hareton, she takes the unusually bold step of joining him at the hearthstone, saying this: 'I've found out, Hareton, that I want—that I'm glad—that I should like you to be my cousin, now, if you had not grown so cross to me, and so rough' (*WH*, pp. 277-278). It is little wonder that such tactless words should incense Hareton quite as much as those with which she will shortly afterwards address him as follows: 'Come; you shall take notice of me, Hareton—you are my cousin, and you shall own me' (*WH*, p. 278). It is only by abandoning such silly talk that Cathy succeeds in her quest, and especially so when she 'stooped, and impressed on his cheek a gentle kiss' (*WH*, p. 279).

Cathy's clannishness is doubtless somewhat bound up with the peculiar nature of her love for those close to her in her early adolescence. The extraordinary selflessness of her devotion to Linton, for example, is probably due very largely to her awareness of their consanguinity as first cousins. In this connection, it is remarkable how brilliantly Emily Brontë renders Cathy's psychology as that of someone who, having been brought up without siblings and had practically no acquaintance with boys of her own age, at one point addresses her male cousin as follows: 'Pretty Linton! I wish you were my brother!' (*WH*, p. 210). Linton's physical appeal for Cathy may be in part explained by the fact that, as Nelly has already remarked, he 'might have been taken for [Edgar's] younger brother, so strong was the resemblance [between them]' (*WH*, p. 177). It is also important to note that when, during their dialogue that will end in an outright quarrel, Linton has told Cathy that, were she his wife, she would, according to what his father has said, 'love [him] better than [her father]', she instantly retorts: 'No! I should never love anybody better than papa' (*WH*, p. 210).[6] Through this sentiment that betokens Cathy's almost incestuous attachment to her father, the author astutely suggests that Cathy is still too young to know the primacy of adult love between the sexes. That Cathy, even just after her second reunion with Linton, cherishes all sorts of childish attitudes to love is comically evident when, for example, in an effort to persuade Nelly to accept her involvement with Linton, she says this to her: 'He's a pretty little darling when he's good. I'd make such a pet of him, if he were mine—We should never quarrel, should we, after we were used to each other?' (*WH*, pp. 213-214). The irony of those words lies in Cathy's having seemingly forgotten that only a short while earlier she has sought to comfort him in the wake of a tantrum he has thrown at the Heights. And though Cathy will later appear to have learnt about erotic love from Linton's letters, edited as they probably have been by his father, it is nevertheless curious to witness the arrogance with which, amid her futile attempts to ingratiate herself with him, she twice lectures Heathcliff quite fallaciously on the subject of love, as if her relationship with Linton entitled her to do so.[7] Further, the priggishness with which she speaks of the noble part she plays in Linton's life is patently exemplified when, having agreed with Heathcliff that his son has 'a bad nature', she goes on to say this: 'But I'm glad I've a better, to forgive it; and I know he loves me and for that reason I love him' (*WH*, p. 254). Few words could better illustrate the idea that Cathy at this stage still has a rather naive concept of erotic love.

To judge by the select examples discussed above, it would not be difficult to assume that Cathy's wrong-headed talk and demeanour, as manifest more particularly in her relations with people she comes across outside the Grange, are forcibly linked with her very privileged and very narrow upbringing. And yet it is a testimony to Emily Brontë's skill as a novelist that she should also show us a Cathy occasionally disclosing a certain strength of character whose existence we might otherwise have scarcely surmised in the contexts referred to hitherto. At this juncture, it is therefore useful to remember that Cathy's adolescence, like her early childhood, is lived out very largely under the dominance of Nelly Dean. We note, for example, that when speaking of Cathy's first twelve years as 'the happiest of my life' (*WH*, p. 167), Nelly seems to imply that that was a period when her charge was comparatively easy to manage. Yet even beyond those twelve years Nelly exercises considerable control over Cathy, especially where she has Edgar's full backing, as we see well enough when she successfully puts an end to the girl's correspondence with Linton Heathcliff. Nevertheless, even before that happens, Nelly sometimes makes unreasonable use of her power over Cathy, and not without dire consequences for herself. Thus Nelly's outright refusal to foster Cathy's initial interest in Penistone Craggs inadvertently encourages the girl to make that place the goal of her very first illicit excursion one July morning. Nelly's authority is again undermined later that day when, on discovering Cathy at the Heights and then angrily rebuking her, she finds herself confronted by her young mistress's frivolous resistance to her ordering her to return home with her at once. It is also noteworthy that soon afterwards, in spite of having been instructed by Edgar that she and Cathy should return to the Grange 'within the hour', Nelly nevertheless fails to get the latter to shorten her ramble across the moors in her search for birds' nests, to the extent that, finding herself a very long way behind her, she symbolically underlines the diminution of her authority with the following words: 'I shouted to her, as she had outstripped me, a long way; she either did not hear or did not regard, for she still sprang on, and *I was compelled to follow*' (*WH*, p. 188; italics mine).

From the moment of Cathy's chance meeting with Heathcliff for the first time shortly afterwards that day, Nelly's authority over her mistress seems to diminish further, and that despite the threatening objections she is later to raise to the girl's affirmative attitude towards Linton Heathcliff. This is suggested not only when Cathy overrides Nelly's refusal to allow Heathcliff to invite them both into the Heights, but, more importantly, when, realizing that she has been deceived by Nelly as well as by her father as to Linton's whereabouts, she resorts to her second major act of deceit against Nelly, that is to say, by secretly disobeying her injunction not to send her cousin a note saying that she cannot keep her promise to visit him at the Heights the following day. What is perhaps more curious, however, is that, owing to Heathcliff's plausible account of his son's near fatal sufferings, Cathy succeeds, largely by means of the tears she silently sheds amid her sincere concern for Linton, in making Nelly accompany her to the Heights the next morning, even though Nelly could easily have prevented such an undertaking by reporting the matter to Edgar. Here, indeed, it can be said that it is through moral strength that Cathy is able to overcome the very real power that Nelly could, if she chose, fully wield over her charge at any time. And though in their conversation on their way back home Nelly is determined not to allow her mistress to become involved with Linton again, Cathy's tart reply, 'We'll see!' marks further resistance on her part, a resistance symbolically reinforced by Nelly's adding: 'and she set off at a gallop, *leaving me to toil in the rear*' (*WH*, p. 214; italics mine). Nelly's authority is again flouted when, at the second 'official' meeting with Linton on the heath, she is quite unable to prevent Cathy from thoughtfully accompanying her seemingly sick cousin into the Heights in preparation for a matrimony at which Nelly will helplessly demur, but which Cathy herself, through her avowed love for Linton, is willing to enter into. No doubt in all these episodes where she rides roughshod over Nelly, Cathy still to some extent comes across as the headstrong child we have noted above, and will pay a heavy price for so being through what will after all turn out to be a very unhappy marriage. Yet although Nelly is bested by Cathy on several occasions, and is in many ways to blame for her failure to keep her mistress under control, the struggles between them seem to have little effect on their friendship and love for each other in the long run, and may even be thought to have been a kind of training for Cathy such as to stand her in good stead in her confrontations with Heathcliff.

Motivated as it has been by Edgar's very negative account of his and Isabella's relations with Heathcliff, Cathy's first hostile reaction to her uncle occurs when, meeting him for a second time by chance, she addresses him thus: 'I shan't speak to you, Mr. Heathcliff! [...] Papa says you are a wicked man, and you hate both him and me; and Ellen says the same' (*WH*, p. 205). While ironically reminding us of Cathy's childish talk discussed above, such words suggest not only that in her immaturity she is easily influenced by what she is told by her elders at the Grange, but also how much she has been thereby encouraged to develop an overweening sense of self-importance. This may in part explain her tendency to be unduly bold, not to say foolhardy, in her outspoken defiance of Heathcliff.[8] It is only when she finds Hareton, after her reconciliation with him, flatly refusing to condone her verbal attacks on Heathcliff that Cathy practically renounces her defiance of the latter once and for all (except briefly in Chapter 33), and that evidently out of love and respect for the young man she is eventually to marry.

In Hareton, Cathy may be said to have at last found a man (other than her father) to look up to, even though she has yet to teach him to read and write. At the same time, it is important to remember that it is Cathy, not Hareton, who takes the initiative for them to be reconciled, thereby reminding us of the many initiatives she has already taken in her relationship with Linton Heathcliff from the moment of his arrival at Thrushcross Grange. As Nelly recalls, Cathy not only shows Linton empathy by putting on 'as sad a countenance as himself' (*WH*, p. 177), but, during tea, has resolved to 'make a pet of her little cousin' (*WH*, p. 178), her strong sense of initiative further confirmed next morning when she is described as rising 'in high glee, eager to join her cousin' (*WH*, p. 186). We also note that, as well as kissing Linton 'fervently' at their first reunion, at their second reunion she 'flew to him', and, though somewhat rebuffed in her attempt to kiss him, asks him: 'Are you glad to see me? Can I do you any good?' (*WH*, p. 209). All such talk and behaviour are, to be sure, by no means out of the ordinary in a thirteen-year-old girl of a markedly clannish outlook. Yet it is also perfectly apparent from the foregoing that Cathy has a quite extraordinary capacity for love and, above all, for the kind of love through which she will come to know suffering as never before in her life. That even the intensely egotistical Linton himself seems to recognize Cathy's gift for selfless love is evident enough when, despite having blamed her for Hareton's evicting them both from 'the house' and spoken of his own terrible sense of worthlessness to the point of even suggesting that she walk out of their relationship, he goes on to eulogize her as follows: 'Only, Catherine, do me this justice; believe that if I might be as sweet, and as kind, and as good as you are, I would be, as willingly, and more so, than as happy and as healthy' (*WH*, p. 224). Linton's glowing testimony here is in some sense an ironic foreshadowing of the unwonted problems she will be subjected to on his behalf during their marriage—a marriage in which she not only puts up with his sundry acts of selfishness with remarkable patience, but with exceptional devotion looks after him during his fatal illness without any help from her fellow residents at the Heights. And if Cathy's love relationship with Linton can hardly be declared a truly adult one, what is significant about it is the fact that it becomes a means whereby she comes to learn about love in ways that even her mother seems hardly to have known or experienced.

Although Cathy's troubled marriage to Linton may be understood to have helped her to grow up in some measure, we nevertheless see the extent to which, at this time and even later, she continues to exhibit much the same childishness in her talk and behaviour as we have witnessed in her early adolescence.[9] All the same, it is necessary to remember that, even amid periods of her silliest and most vicious behaviour, Cathy now and then gives us glimpses of her inherently moral disposition. We note, for example, how in her various dealings with other people, Cathy is ever concerned to keep her word and abide by the truth. Consider, for instance, her constant quest to observe her promises. Thus it is because she has promised Linton that she will visit him at the Heights on the day after their first reunion there that she finds it necessary to send him a note saying that she will be unable to keep her appointment as promised. Linton himself is fully conscious of Cathy's practice of honouring her promises when, in Chapter 24, he says this to her on one of her illicit visits to him: 'I was sure you wouldn't break your word, and I'll make you promise again, before you go' (*WH*, pp. 220-221). For Cathy a promise is indeed absolutely binding unless one is absolved from it for good reason and in good time. There are also contexts in which Cathy keeps her promises to other characters, whether it be promising Nelly to cease corresponding with Linton or respecting Hareton's request that she renounce her vituperations of Heathcliff in his presence. And though Cathy is sometimes compelled, albeit reluctantly, to resort to deceit in order to keep some of her promises, it is noteworthy how much she is concerned with truthfulness. Thus, for example, rather than obliging Nelly by telling her father that she will be happy as Linton's wife, Cathy avoids a blatant lie by simply saying that she 'would not complain' (*WH*, p. 251). Cathy's moral integrity is noticeable even in comparatively small matters, as, for example, when instead of lending the groom Michael books from her father's library (as he has asked her to do) for helping her to make her illicit excursions, she 'preferred giving him [her] own' (*WH*, p. 218). What is especially significant about all such references is that they make the reader realize why it is that Cathy is eventually able to put her childishness behind her and show us, most notably through her education of Hareton, certain unmistakable signs of a pleasing maturity.

The fact that Cathy appears to have grown out of her tiresome forms of infantilism and to have become a sensible young adult by the end of the narrative might, however, seem a rather implausible outcome for some readers. Such demurring, though perfectly understandable from what has been said about her character above, may be countered once we recognize the degree in which Cathy's presentation entails references to her physicality. It is useful here to remember that *Wuthering Heights* is in many ways an expression of the influence exerted by physiognomic theory on British life and culture, particularly during the last decade of the eighteenth century and throughout the nineteenth century.[10] This may be seen plainly enough in the very observant Lockwood's tendency to interpret the meaning of the outward person, as, for example, when before asking Cathy to help him find his way back to the Grange, he apologizes to her for 'troubling' her before adding: 'I presume, because, with that face, I'm sure you cannot help being good-hearted' (*WH*, p. 12).[11] Flattering as it seems intended to be, Lockwood's physiognomic judgement is nevertheless significant for foreshadowing the notion that Cathy, for all her erroneous ways as a youngster, is indeed 'good-hearted'. Just as important, too, are Lockwood's references to Cathy's beauty, reminding us as they do that for physiognomists such as Lavater no less than for those of classical antiquity, beauty is a sign of moral virtue.[12] Also worth mentioning here is that, much more than even her mother, Cathy is specifically remarked on now and again for her beauty, especially by Lockwood.[13] Nelly herself also refers to Cathy's beauty when in her earliest description of her she speaks of her being 'a real beauty in face' (*WH*, p. 167), later alluding to it most poetically on the afternoon she accompanies Cathy in her search for birds' nests, as she tells of 'watching her, my pet, and my delight, with her golden ringlets flying loose behind, and her bright cheek, as soft and pure in its bloom as a wild rose, and her eyes radiant with cloudless pleasure' (*WH*, p. 188).

Hardly less pertinent here are Nelly's references to Cathy's physical energy, as amply suggested by the latter's tendency to move her legs nimbly for various purposes.[14] It is, moreover, Cathy's admirable physicality that is the main reason why Nelly balks at the thought of the girl's marrying her weakling cousin Linton.[15] Also of interest here as expressions of Cathy's moral wholesomeness are references to those postures and gestures of hers that betoken her concern for others, as well as a certain humility. Thus we are told of her bending or stooping or kneeling down in moments of her extreme anxiety about Linton Heathcliff, and even in a moment of tension with Heathcliff.[16] A like tendency on her part is evident when Nelly tells Lockwood of Cathy's grudging 'each moment that did not find her *bending over* [Edgar's] pillow' (*WH*, p. 234; italics mine). And though the same sort of thoughtfulness is still there when, as Lockwood observes, Cathy '*bent* to superintend [Hareton's] studies' (*WH*, p. 273; italics mine), an earlier reference to her 'leaning her hand' (*WH*, p. 280) on Hareton's shoulder in the Heights kitchen symbolically indicates how reliant she already is on the young man to whom she is by now betrothed.

There are, however, other aspects of Cathy's physicality that deserve consideration here for a full understanding of her presentation. We note, for instance, how much her early encounters with people outside the Grange are marked by references to her fits of crying. Such a habit is, of course, hardly to be wondered at in a girl who has enjoyed an unusually protected, not to say pampered, childhood.[17] Yet there are examples of her crying that could be described as somewhat selfless, particularly when her tears are caused by her distress over her father's illness or by her concern for his anxiety over her prolonged absence from the Grange, or by her worries about Linton's physical sufferings both before their marriage and during the time she is single-handedly tending him in his fatal illness.[18] Such references seem clearly linked with those where Cathy seems, at least in manner, to be no longer the crybaby she used to be. This is evident enough from, say, her 'silent weeping' (*WH*, p. 207) at the Grange as brought on apparently by Heathcliff's account of his son's dying as a consequence of her having ceased to correspond with him; or when, as Lockwood observes, she 'drew out her pocket-handkerchief and applied it to her eyes' (*WH*, p. 266) because Hareton has at first forbidden her to read the note sent to her by Nelly; or, again, when rejected outright by Hareton for her attempts to engage him in conversation, she is described by Nelly as 'chewing her lip, and endeavouring, by humming an eccentric tune, to conceal a growing tendency to sob' (*WH*, p. 278). All such details are interesting for suggesting how far Cathy seems to have put her childishness behind her and begun to show signs of a certain maturity. This may be seen most poetically borne out when Nelly observes Cathy still sitting at her father's bedside on the morning after his death: 'Whether Catherine had spent her tears, or whether the grief were too weighty to let them flow, she sat there dry-eyed till the sun rose' (*WH*, p. 251).

The hint of a budding maturity in Cathy, as conveyed by the words just quoted, may be said to mark a significant stage in her development towards adulthood; a development which, as we have already seen, is by no means a steady process, but, rather, an essentially halting one, realistically illustrated as it is by her occasional reversions to childishness in both speech and behaviour. At the same time, it is worth mentioning here that, well before her father's death, Cathy has already in her early adolescence not only looked forward to becoming a woman (so as to be allowed to visit Penistone Craggs), but in her late teens has even considered herself a woman on the occasion she assures Nelly of her ability to take care of her sickly cousin: 'And besides, I'm almost seventeen. I'm a woman—and I'm certain Linton would recover quickly if he had me to look after him—I'm older than he is, you know, and wiser, less childish, am I not?' (*WH*, p. 213). Yet naive as is Cathy's estimate of herself here, it can nevertheless be linked with her somewhat maternal interest in birds, each reference to which, whether symbolic or otherwise, seems to foreshadow her unconscious aspiration to become the mother she has never known in her own life, to say nothing of the grown-up she longs to turn into.[19]

Nevertheless, Cathy's arrival at adulthood would surely have been considerably, not to say indefinitely, delayed had she not had to undergo what may be aptly described as an education in the hard knocks of life as Heathcliff's prisoner, the most important part of which education being undoubtedly the fact that, because inescapably thrown together with Hareton at this time, she is compelled to recognize as seldom before his true worth as a human being. At the same time we should not forget that, trapped though she is in a singularly patriarchal environment during this period, Cathy comes across to the reader as someone quite remarkable for her courage and her personality. For example, it is through sheer moral force that, notwithstanding her very lowly status under Heathcliff's jurisdiction, Cathy succeeds not only in obliging Linton to enable her to escape from their room so that she may return to her dying father, but in rousing the entire Heights household in order that her strongly voiced concern for Linton's fatal illness may be immediately acted on. Indeed, such is Cathy's strength of character in her very confined situation that, quite independently of one another, Lockwood, Joseph and Heathcliff each refer to her more or less nervously as a witch.[20] In Heathcliff's case, Cathy's witch-like nature seems physiognomically corroborated for him by his continual awareness of the dark eyes which she has inherited from her mother and which, by aggravating his mental illness and thereby probably hastening his untimely death, may be understood to have played a crucial part in the eventual liberation of Wuthering Heights.[21] It is, moreover, at this late stage of her adolescence that we come to realize that Cathy's presentation has all along been that of a fundamentally fearless person. And if Cathy's fearlessness is manifested but negatively through the childish talk and behaviour she demonstrates during her early adolescence, it is for all that a fearlessness informing those commendable aspects of her character that have been noted above, among them being more especially her intrinsically moral disposition and her extraordinary capacity for love. Perhaps that is why Lockwood, who by the end of the novel has practically transformed Cathy into a fictional heroine, seems, albeit grudgingly as a disappointed lover, to hint at her heroic stature when, having seen her return to the Heights with Hareton after a nocturnal ramble, he 'grumbled' these words to himself: '*They* are afraid of nothing [...]. Together they would brave Satan and all his legions' (*WH*, p. 300).

Notes

1   See especially Q. D. Leavis, 'A Fresh Approach to *Wuthering Heights*', in F. R. and Q. D. Leavis, *Lectures in America* (London: Chatto & Windus, 1969), pp. 85-130; William A. Madden, '*Wuthering Heights*: The Binding of Passion', *Nineteenth-Century Fiction*, 27/2 (1972), 143ff; Douglas Jefferson, 'Irresistible Narrative: The Art of *Wuthering Heights*', *Brontë Society Transactions*, 17/5 (1980), 345; Joyce Carol Oates, 'The Magnanimity of *Wuthering Heights*', *Critical Inquiry*, 9 (1982), 447; Mary Burgan, 'Some Fit Parentage: Identity and the Cycle of Generations in *Wuthering Heights*', *Philological Quarterly*, 61 (1982), 407; Annette R. Federico, 'The Waif at the Window: Emily Brontë's Feminine *Bildungsroman*', *Victorian Newsletter*, 68 (1985), 27ff.

2   For negative comments on the youngest generation, see especially Pelham Edgar, 'Judgments on Appeal: II, The Brontës', *Queens Quarterly*, 39 (1932), 422; Vincent Buckley, 'Passion and Control in *Wuthering Heights*', *Southern Review* (University of Adelaide), 1 (1964), 23; Wendy A. Craik, *The Brontë Novels* (London: Methuen, 1968), p. 34; Alan Gardiner, 'Does the Novel Deteriorate with the Death of Catherine?' in *Critical Essays on Wuthering* Heights, eds. Linda Cookson and Brian Loughrey (London: Longman, 1988), p. 90.

3   For quotations from the novel, see Emily Brontë, *Wuthering Heights*, eds. Ian Jack and Patsy Stoneman (Oxford: Oxford University Press, 1998).

4   See *Wuthering Heights*, pp. 190, 226, 262, 264.

5   See *Wuthering Heights*, pp. 167, 175.

6   Noteworthy in this connection is that, having earlier denied that she is fretting for Linton Heathcliff, Cathy goes on to correct Nelly thus: 'I fret about nothing on earth except papa's illness, [...] I care for nothing in comparison with papa. [...] I love him better than myself, Ellen; and I know it by this—I pray every night that I may live after him; because I would rather be miserable than that he should be—that proves I love him better than myself' (*WH*, p. 204).

7   See *Wuthering Heights*, pp. 243, 254.

8   See especially *Wuthering Heights*, pp. 25, 232, 233, 238, 254.

9   We see this especially in her impoliteness to Zillah and Hareton, and even to Lockwood. See *Wuthering Heights*, pp. 7-8, 215, 259, 263.

10 For studies on the influence of physiognomy on the English novel, see especially John Graham, 'Character Description and Meaning in the Romantic Novel', *Studies in Romanticism*, 5 (1966), 208-218; John Graham, *Lavater's Essays on Physiognomy: A Study in the History of Ideas* (Bern: Peter Lang, 1979); Graeme Tytler, *Physiognomy in the European Novel: Faces and Fortunes* (Princeton, NJ: Princeton University Press, 1982).

11 See Graeme Tytler, 'Physiognomy in *Wuthering Heights*', *Brontë Society Transactions*, 21/4 (1994), 138.

12 See Tytler, *Physiognomy in the European Novel*, pp. 68-69.

13 See *Wuthering Heights*, pp. 7, 28, 136, 265, 273.

14 See *Wuthering Heights*, pp. 176, 188, 189, 193, 205.

15 See *Wuthering Heights*, p. 240.

16 See *Wuthering Heights*, pp. 197, 199, 212, 236, 243.

17 See especially *Wuthering Heights*, pp. 171, 173, 186, 211, 217, 222, 225, 239.

18 See *Wuthering Heights*, pp. 197, 203, 207, 211, 212, 225, 242, 247, 248, 249, 260.

19 For references to birds thematically associated with Cathy's maternal instinct, see *Wuthering Heights*, pp. 187-188, 199, 203. For Cathy's earliest reference to herself as the woman she longs to become, see *Wuthering Heights*, p. 168.

20 See *Wuthering Heights*, pp. 12, 255, 284, 285.

21 See *Wuthering Heights*, pp. 25, 239, 275, 285, 287. In this connection, see Tytler, 'Physiognomy in *Wuthering Heights*', pp. 143-146.

The Presentation of Hareton Earnshaw in *Wuthering Heights*

I n a good many books and articles published on *Wuthering Heights* since the early twentieth century we may find judgements of one kind or another on Hareton Earnshaw.[1] Some of these judgements are conspicuous for including comparisons between him and Heathcliff. For example, Hareton is commonly declared a pale version of Heathcliff and, accordingly, deemed a scarcely memorable figure in the novel.[2] Again, whereas some Brontë scholars have approved of Hareton's relationship with Cathy, others have dismissed it as a sentimental nonsense, and even deplored it as a let-down in the wake of the love story between Catherine and Heathcliff.[3] There are, to be sure, several comments about Cathy's educational influence on Hareton; and though this influence has, on the one hand, been thought a commendable thing, it has, on the other hand, been frowned upon for clipping the young man's wings.[4] Yet whatever worth may be attached to these critical standpoints, there is no question that much still needs to be said about Hareton's presentation, not only because his comparatively frequent presence in the text, from his birth to his impending marriage at the end, usually serves specific structural functions, but because he is a kind of touchstone by which we may assess some of the other characters portrayed in the novel, and as such someone through whom we are given important glimpses of the author's vision of human society and human nature.

Hareton's introduction to the reader in Chapter 2, striking as it is for references to his ill-kempt appearance and his uncouth behaviour at the Heights, and, therefore, perhaps hardly prepossessing us in his favour, is nevertheless of interest chiefly for indirectly adding to the more or less negative impression we have already gained of Lockwood in Chapter 1.[5] First of all, it is easy to see that Lockwood's general attitude to Hareton is not a little determined by his keen awareness of the presence of Cathy, whose beauty he is clearly much taken with. Indeed, this may well account for Lockwood's belittling comments on Hareton's conduct during the evening meal, and that not without certain comical implications. What is perhaps the most comical of all such comments, however, is the one whereby, having hastily concluded that Hareton is married to Cathy, Lockwood not only assumes that as a cultured gentleman he has reason to make the young woman 'regret her choice', but inadvertently betrays his jealousy of Hareton with this arrogant comparison: 'My neighbour struck me as bordering on repulsive. I knew, through experience, that I was tolerably attractive' (*WH*, p. 10). At the same time, through this comparison as well as through those implying the antipodal social differences between himself and Hareton, Lockwood is clearly intent on recovering and restoring his pride, which has been wounded both by Cathy's earlier coolness towards him and by Heathcliff's teasing of him at the tea table.[6]

Lockwood's superciliousness towards Hareton is still manifest on his third visit to the Heights when, having mentioned Hareton's handsomeness for the first time, perhaps because he has been induced to notice it by what he has heard about him from Nelly, he nevertheless adds that Hareton 'does his best, apparently, to make the least of his advantages' (*WH*, p. 265), as if he still had in mind their rivalry for Cathy's hand. Lockwood's essentially patronising attitude to Hareton is further suggested in the same context when, doubtless remembering what Nelly has already said about the latter's efforts to become literate, he comes to his defence in response to Cathy's sardonic remarks about his bumbling attempts to teach himself to read. What Lockwood may fail to realize, however, is that, by dint of his well-meaning talk with Cathy in Hareton's presence, he is perforce bound to aggravate the latter's sense of inferiority. It is even possible that but for that talk on his behalf, Hareton would not have gone so far as to burn Cathy's books. Finally, it is not a little ironic to note Lockwood's peculiar vanity still prevailing on his fourth and last visit to the Heights when, despite seeing with his own eyes that he has lost Cathy to Hareton, he, nevertheless, still seems to fancy his chances of ending up the successful suitor. Thus, aware that he would have been noticed by the couple on their way out of 'the house' for 'a walk on the moors', Lockwood goes on to record this detail in his diary: 'I supposed I should be condemned in Hareton Earnshaw's heart, if not by his mouth, to the lowest pit in the infernal regions if I showed my unfortunate person in his neighbourhood then, and feeling very mean and malignant, I skulked round to seek refuge in the kitchen' (*WH*, p. 273).

Lockwood's negative references to Hareton in Chapter 2 may be said to foreshadow those that Nelly makes about the latter as an adolescent and as a young adult. Given Nelly's deep devotion to Hareton in his early childhood, such references may seem strange unless they are understood in part as expressions of the somewhat haughty attitude she has evinced towards Wuthering Heights and its residents since becoming housekeeper at Thrushcross Grange. We see this haughtiness especially in Chapter 18 when she discovers Cathy at the Heights after a frantic search for her. For example, in her reaction to the bad language Hareton uses when declining to act the servant to Cathy, Nelly practically gives the impression of disowning any acquaintance with him, just as in answer to Cathy's outright refusal to accept him as her cousin, she tries to mitigate the idea of this consanguinity by suggesting that there are cousins whose company one 'needn't keep' if they are 'disagreeable and bad' (*WH*, p. 173).[7] Nelly's haughtiness is further evidenced when, encountering him with Heathcliff while rambling on the moors with Cathy many months later, she describes Hareton as having 'gained nothing but increased bulk and strength by the addition of two years to his age', whereby he 'seemed as awkward and rough as ever' (*WH*, p. 189).[8] A similar attitude has been manifested only a short while earlier when, anticipating that the newly arrived Linton Heathcliff will, despite Edgar's hopes to the contrary, be unable to stay on at the Grange, she wonders: 'however will that weakling live at Wuthering Heights, between his father and Hareton? What playmates and instructors they'll be' (*WH*, p. 178). Even when Hareton has reacted with understandable aggressiveness to Linton Heathcliff's insults about his illiteracy and his Yorkshire accent, Nelly still shows a certain bias against him by designating him as 'the angry *boor*' (*WH*, p. 194; italics mine). That Nelly's snootiness is still prominent at the time Cathy is endeavouring to win back his friendship is plain to see through her support of the girl with this piece of advice: 'You should be friends with your cousin, Mr. Hareton [...]. It would do you a great deal of good—it would make you another man, to have her for a companion' (*WH*, p. 278). Again, not long after the cousins have become reconciled, one can still sense something of Nelly's old snobbishness as she refers to them both sitting together as 'pupil and teacher' by the fire: 'You know, they both appeared, in a measure, my children: I had long been proud of one, and now, I was sure, the other would be a source of equal satisfaction' (*WH*, p. 286).

As a preface to Nelly's account of the extraordinary improvement in Hareton's facial appearance as wrought by the educational influence he has recently been undergoing, the above-quoted sentence is notable for the phrase 'my children', mainly because, whether consciously or not, Nelly alludes thereby to the fact that Hareton was virtually her child while she was nursing him during the first five years of his life.[9] It is, moreover, this experience that surely helps to explain why Nelly sometimes takes pity on Hareton or rises to his defence, and that, ironically enough, even when she is otherwise showing a generally contemptuous attitude to him. Thus she tells of rebuking Cathy for her cruel response to a second instance of Hareton's illiteracy and of even going so far as to remind the girl that he is as good as her social equal:

> *If you had remembered that Hareton was your cousin, as much as Master Heathcliff, you would have felt how improper it was to behave in that way. […] To sneer at his imperfect attempt was very bad breeding—had you been brought up in his circumstances, would you be less rude? He was as quick and as intelligent a child as ever you were, and I'm hurt that he should be despised now, because that base Heathcliff has treated him so unjustly.* (*WH*, p. 220)

Evoking as they do Nelly's earlier disapproval of Cathy and Linton Heathcliff's teasing of Hareton for his illiteracy in Chapter 21, and linked as they may also be with her later objection to Zillah's jocular treatment of him in Chapter 30, such words show how easily Hareton can be transformed in Nelly's mind from an object of disrespect to an object of pity. (This inconsistency, incidentally, reminds us how, despite the hatred or contempt he expresses for Hareton, Linton Heathcliff occasionally speaks well of him, and that usually when he is annoyed with Cathy.)[10]

Nelly's inconsistency is further illustrated when she now and then alludes to Hareton's good nature, as on the occasion when, imprisoned by Heathcliff in the Heights with Cathy, she says this to the latter: 'I wish [Hareton] would arrive! Who knows but he might take our part?' (*WH*, p. 244). And yet it is as if here, as in other contexts, Hareton were being affirmed, not as an end in himself, but as someone who, so to speak, has his uses. Consider in this connection how Nelly tries to alleviate Linton Heathcliff's apprehensiveness about his new life at the Heights with this cosily worded prediction: 'Hareton Earnshaw—that is Miss Cathy's other cousin, and so yours in a manner—will show you all the sweetest spots' (*WH*, p. 181); or, again, how, after forbidding Cathy to communicate with Linton, she seeks to allay the girl's anxiety about his life at the Heights with, among other things, this presumptuous rhetorical question: 'Hasn't he Hareton for a companion?' (*WH*, p. 197). But although there is no little hypocrisy underlying these two timely affirmations of Hareton, they may nevertheless stem to some extent from Nelly's unspoken awareness of his goodness. At the same time, any affirmative attitude she shows towards Hareton may have partly to do with the fact that he is the latest scion of what she describes as a 'very old' (*WH*, p. 29) family. Such knowledge is almost certainly at the root of the emotionality with which, while alluding to Heathcliff's mastership of the Heights, she says this to Lockwood: 'And Hareton has been cast out like an unfledged dunnock—The unfortunate lad is the only one, in all this parish, that does not guess how he has been cheated!' (*WH*, p. 30).[11]

If, in the same dialogue with Lockwood, Nelly seems, through her remarks on Hareton, to be rather more loyal to the Lintons than to the Earnshaws, there can be no question of any such divided loyalties on the part of Joseph. His devotion to the Earnshaws is unquestionably absolute, being confirmed especially when, on the death of Heathcliff, Nelly relates that he 'fell on his knees, and raised his hands, and returned thanks that the lawful master and the ancient stock were restored to their rights' (*WH*, p. 298). Significant here is the reference 'the lawful master' for signalling Joseph's assiduous championship of Hareton throughout the narrative.[12] One example of this may be noted when, amid his glee at the sight of Hareton evicting Cathy and Linton Heathcliff from 'the house', he remarks: '*He* knaws—Aye, he knaws, as weel as Aw do, who sud be t'maister yonder' (*WH*, p. 221). That Joseph's support of Hareton is, however, anything but disinterested is obvious enough from Nelly's own observations on their relationship. Thus whereas, as she says, Joseph has instilled into Hareton 'a pride of name, and of his lineage', she has earlier in the same context implicitly blamed Joseph for the latter's moral deterioration 'by a narrow-minded partiality which prompted him to flatter and pet him, as a boy, because he was the head of the old family' (*WH*, p. 174). It is because in Joseph's eyes Hareton is, as it were, family rather than an individual in his own right that the old servant indulges his bad language and his bad behaviour, confident as he is in any case that Heathcliff will have to pay the ultimate price for Hareton's being 'ruined' and 'his soul [being] abandoned to perdition' (*WH*, p. 174). By thus washing his hands of Hareton, Joseph indirectly confirms the essential possessiveness of his love for him—a possessiveness that will be especially noticeable in his jealousy of Hareton's relationship with Cathy.[13]

It is interesting to compare Joseph's curious fondness for Hareton, conditioned as it is by many years of service to the Earnshaw family, with the more or less disdainful attitude held towards the young man by two temporary servants. Thus, even in their awareness of Hareton's kinship with the Lintons, it is clear that both Zillah and the unnamed Heights housekeeper regard Hareton as little more than a lout. We see this most particularly in Chapter 30 when, in her comical respectability, Zillah is teasingly helping Hareton to make himself presentable in preparation for Cathy's descent to 'the house' one Sunday morning.[14] Moreover, in her readiness on that occasion to laugh at Hareton for his gaucheness, Zillah makes a point of mentioning in her verbal account to Nelly that she dare not laugh in Heathcliff's presence, thereby enabling us to understand in retrospect why, without realizing that Lockwood has been knocked down by the dogs (in Chapter 2), she is quick to blame Hareton for this mishap simply through 'not daring to attack her master' (*WH*, p. 14). Being an inveterate coward at heart, Zillah would not, of course, be so free and easy with Hareton were she not aware that Heathcliff himself scarcely treats the latter any better than he does the household servants. Certainly Heathcliff's lack of respect for Hareton is quite overt in episodes where, for example, he mockingly denies being his father, bluffly orders him to get off to his work, or patronizingly advises him how to behave while showing Cathy round the Heights grounds; and it is especially overt when he informs Nelly that he has ordered Hareton to obey his son Linton.[15] All this is certainly of a piece with Heathcliff's general attitude towards Hareton, particularly since his return to Gimmerton. Thus as well as indulging his bad behaviour as a youngster, Heathcliff manages, after Hindley's death, to shape Hareton's life in such ways that, as he confidently assures Nelly, he will 'never be able to emerge from his bathos of coarseness and ignorance' (*WH*, p. 193). What Heathcliff fails to foresee, of course, is that nature will eventually undermine his heinous methods of nurture.

Especially pertinent here is Heathcliff's claim to read Hareton's mind, partly by attributing to him the same sort of sufferings he underwent in his own childhood and partly by presuming that he 'takes a pride in his brutishness' (*WH*, p. 193). Such egotistical identification continues even when, caught in the throes of his mental illness, Heathcliff tells Nelly that Hareton for a moment seemed, among other things, 'a personification of my youth, not a human being' (*WH*, p. 288)—words which, however poetic they may be for the reader, plainly confirm that, for Heathcliff, Hareton does not truly possess a separate identity as a human being.[16] But what is tragic about his image of Hareton is that, while admiring his character and recognizing his superiority to his own son, Heathcliff continues to see him as but a painful reminder of his unhappy past. As he says to Nelly: 'I'd have loved the lad had he been some one else' (*WH*, p. 192). And even though Heathcliff is fully cognizant of Hareton's love for him, he seems to make light of it when, in facetious vein, he goes on to inform Nelly as follows: 'And the best of it is, Hareton is damnably fond of me!' (*WH*, p. 193). By contrast, the shallowness of Heathcliff's own feelings for Hareton is amply suggested when, in the same context, he says this to Nelly: 'I've a *pleasure* in him! [...] He has *satisfied* my expectations' (*WH*, p. 193; italics mine). That Heathcliff seems to remain utterly unaware of the depth of Hareton's love for him is never more ironically confirmed than at the time of his death and funeral.[17] Thus it is through his persistently selfish attitude to Hareton that Emily Brontë succeeds both in exposing some of the glaring limitations of Heathcliff's character and mentality, and, more importantly, in suggesting that, notwithstanding his enduring attachment to Catherine, there are severe limits to his capacity to love.

It is noteworthy that at the beginning of the elaborate comparison he draws between his son and Hareton, Heathcliff tells Nelly that Cathy 'will discover [Linton's] value, and send him to the devil' (*WH*, p. 191), aware as he is at the same time that Hareton himself, in spite of being to his mind by far the worthier suitor of Cathy, is, nevertheless, 'safe from *her* love' (*WH*, p. 192). Although both predictions prove to be as mistaken as others made by Heathcliff in this context, they yet seem at the time cogent enough to the reader and, no doubt, to Nelly herself. Thus quite apart from our already knowing that Cathy's first meeting with Hareton has ended badly, it is not hard to imagine her inimical disposition towards him being reinforced when, for example, having heard Linton Heathcliff, at her first reunion with the latter, ridiculing Hareton for his illiteracy, she goes on to ask: 'Is he all as he should be? […] or is he simple—not right?' (*WH*, p. 194). There are, to be sure, other aspects of Hareton's person and behaviour that might have been thought disturbing enough to put Cathy off him for good, most notably when, by way of reaction to her teasing him for his bumbling attempts to teach himself to read, he not only hits her on the mouth but throws her books into the fire. Nor should we forget the revulsion she feels for him when, despite his having offered her a seat by the fire on her arrival in 'the house' from upstairs and then handed down books to her from the dresser, she says this in response to his touching her hair: 'Get away, this moment! How dare you touch me? […] I can't endure you! I'll go upstairs again, if you come near me' (*WH*, p. 263). Even when he has told her how often he has pleaded with Heathcliff on her behalf, Cathy confirms her revulsion for Hareton by saying: 'Be silent! I'll go out of doors, or anywhere, rather than have your disagreeable voice in my ear!' (*WH*, p. 263). It is through such words, to say nothing of the similarly churlish ones with which she has addressed Hareton or which she has uttered in his presence since their first meeting at the Heights, that Cathy for a time comes across as one of the most cruelly snobbish of all female fictional characters.

With the foregoing in mind, then, how are we to explain not only the reconciliation between Hareton and Cathy but their betrothal at the end of the novel? No doubt, such would not have been the outcome unless the cousins had found themselves practically thrown together in the confined space of the Heights kitchen for several days on end or, more importantly, had Heathcliff died while they were still at odds with each other. Again, though Cathy's quest to be friends with Hareton once more is, ironically, prompted by her avowed willingness to accept him as her cousin, her interest in him as a man is surely founded on the fact that, notwithstanding her dislike of the sound of his voice referred to above, she seems to have by then had a quite favourable impression of his physical appearance. This is already evident from the inaudible words she whispers to Heathcliff in answer to his following question about Hareton: 'Is he not a handsome lad?' (*WH*, p. 192).

A more likely reason for Cathy's reconciliation with Hareton, however, is her having been witness to, or heard about, certain worthy acts or utterances on his part, some of which we have noted above. For whereas her early responses to Hareton, both verbal and physical, betoken the spoilt child of a privileged upbringing, it is obvious, even without our being made privy to her actual thoughts, that Cathy is intelligent and sensitive enough to recognize his inherent goodness already through the remorse and kindness he usually shows in the wake of the violent language or behaviour he has exhibited towards her.[18] Even so minor an incident as Hareton's offer to accompany Lockwood on part of his walk back to the Grange in Chapter 2 will undoubtedly have impressed Cathy in his favour as much as did his earlier offer to see her home after her first visit to the Heights. No less impressive for Cathy will have been the moment when, having blamed her for pushing his chair and thereby causing his 'suffocating cough', Linton Heathcliff tries to shame her with the following comparison: 'Hareton never touches me, he never struck me in his life' (*WH*, p. 211). It is true that, in his anger at being insulted once again by Cathy for his illiteracy, Hareton will quite brutally turn her and Linton out of 'the house' but a few days later. And yet the sight of a gravely infirm Linton being carried upstairs by Hareton only a short while afterwards will have doubtless been for Cathy a sign of the latter's essential magnanimity, just as his telling her to go home in the face of her insistence on attending to her sick cousin will have been for her a sign of his strength of character. Such strength of character may be the reason why, even after her reconciliation with Hareton, she keeps her promise to him never again to vilify Heathcliff in his presence. Cathy's obedience in this respect seems, in fact, testimony enough to her apparent readiness at this time to defer to Hareton for guidance. And though much has been made over the years of the importance of Cathy's educational influence on Hareton, it needs to be none the less stressed that Cathy's own moral development would have remained incomplete without the respect that she has gradually come to feel for the young man that she eventually chooses to marry.[19]

If Cathy's relationship with Hareton seems, then, intended in no small measure as a means of delineating her gradual, albeit arduous, growth to maturity, we are nevertheless still left with a number of things to say about Hareton's presentation. It is, first of all, useful to be reminded here that Hareton is seen, not through the eyes of some omniscient third-person narrator, but through the eyes of several first-person narrators as well as through those of characters whose spoken or written words have been recorded by those self-same narrators. And since there are divergences of opinion about Hareton, and even contradictions between attitudes held towards him by particular individuals, it is perforce left to us readers to make up our minds about his character. That Hareton emerges as a more or less sympathetic human being can hardly be denied; it would be odd were it otherwise, if only on account of the heroic stature he acquires by the end of the narrative. Yet no fictional hero ever seemed a more 'unlikely' one to start with, or his subsequent development more unexpected. For whereas it is easy enough to attribute his physical violence and his bad language to his rough upbringing, it is much less easy to account for his readiness to show remorse and contrition, his sundry acts of kindness, or his efforts to become literate in a household that discourages such efforts. And even if these contradictions would seem quite improbable in a mature adult, they are surely credible in someone on his way to becoming a full-fledged human being. At the same time, it is interesting to note the extent to which the author portrays Hareton as someone who, in spite of the disadvantages of his environment and circumstances, is conspicuous above all for his normality.[20] Let us consider this idea in some detail.

We have already seen how much light is thrown on the moral shortcomings of Lockwood, Heathcliff, Nelly Dean, Joseph, Zillah and Cathy through their relations with Hareton; and it is partly by analysing such relations that we come to recognize one of Hareton's principal functions in the novel. In this connection, it is noteworthy how often Hareton appears to be a kind of constant amid the vagaries and eccentricities displayed by the other characters. Take, for instance, that moment when, angered by Heathcliff's refusal to let him sleep on a chair in 'the house', Lockwood relates: 'I uttered an expression of disgust, and pushed past him into the yard, running against Earnshaw in my haste' (*WH*, p. 13). This reference to Hareton, casual as it may look, prepares us for the offer he will presently make to accompany Lockwood part of the way back to the Grange, at the same time as it somehow enhances the folly of the latter's behaviour. But already as a baby, Hareton's normality seems to be a standard by which, say, Catherine's talk and behaviour are now and then gauged to her disadvantage. Thus among episodes connected with her early dilemma between Heathcliff and Edgar may be mentioned one where, to her desire to recount her dream, Nelly, in her dread of 'conjuring up ghosts and visions', responds with these words concerning the child in her lap: 'Look at little Hareton—*he*'s dreaming nothing dreary. How sweetly he smiles in his sleep!' (*WH*, p. 70). Again, the abnormality of Catherine's 'crying outright' (*WH*, p. 75) as she waits in the rain for Heathcliff to return home is underlined by Nelly's following comparison: 'She beat Hareton, or any child, at a good, passionate fit of crying' (*WH*, p. 75). Later that night, while Catherine is lying on the settle in drenched clothes and being maliciously preached at by Joseph, Nelly recalls that she 'betook [herself] to bed with little Hareton, who slept as fast as if every one had been sleeping round him' (*WH*, p. 76). There are also contexts in which Hareton's normality at various other stages of his life stands out against the oddness of language or behaviour in Catherine, Hindley, Isabella, Linton Heathcliff, Zillah and even Heathcliff himself.[21] Nor without interest here are the ways in which as a diligent farmhand Hareton is sometimes shown in ironic contrast with those characters who are leisurely engaged in trivial or malevolent talk and activity, especially where reference is made to his going off to work, being away at work, or returning home from work.[22]

For most of the novel, then, Hareton bears the stamp of an essentially minor character whose chief purpose, as we have suggested above, is to add to our knowledge and understanding of some of the central figures, but whose fate otherwise seems for the most part to be as unpromising as that of the imaginary beggar he is sometimes directly or indirectly likened to.[23] And yet by carefully collating all the references made to him in the text, we come to see how with seemingly random brushstrokes here and there on the canvas of her narrative, Emily Brontë builds up a picture of Hareton as a fundamentally strong character, and one therefore eminently fitted to end up as a kind of hero. This is in part indicated by details about his physicality that occur more often than those usually predicated of a minor character. Consider, for example, how his heroic destiny seems prefigured by the enthusiasm with which a servant girl announces his birth as follows: 'Oh, such a grand bairn! [...] The finest lad that ever breathed!' (*WH*, p. 56), and continues to harp on about his beauty. The idea that Hareton is something of a traditional epic hero by dint of his good looks is corroborated by comments made by Lockwood, Heathcliff and Nelly Dean about his handsomeness, his physical strength and the spiritual depth of his 'physiognomy' (*WH*, p. 173) in his later years.[24] (Important, too, in this respect are references to his brown eyes, which, because remarkably similar to Catherine's, clearly play their part in aggravating Heathcliff's visual hallucinations of her.[25]) Hareton's heroism is no doubt also hinted at by the boldness of his amatory approaches to Cathy—a boldness that enables him against all apparent odds to outrival a somewhat timid Lockwood in the quest to win her love. For some readers, however, Hareton's success with Cathy, let alone his sudden luck in becoming a man of property and wealth in the end, is but the stuff of cheap romantic fiction.[26] Moreover, in spite of this 'happy ending', Hareton is for many such readers an unsatisfactory figure primarily because, compared as he tends to be with Heathcliff, especially with respect to personality and the use of language, he is scarcely someone to write home about.

Such a comparison may nevertheless be shown to be as misplaced as the one drawn between apples and oranges. For if in the eyes of countless readers Heathcliff is, and will continue to be, the true hero of *Wuthering Heights*, then Hareton may be said to be not so much its secondary hero as its anti-hero. Indeed, far from being merely a dull copy of Heathcliff, Hareton, with his ordinary way of life, would appear to represent a kind of critique of the latter for embodying the overbearing qualities of the Gothic, not to say Satanic, type of fictional protagonist. Much more important, however, is the fact that Hareton from earliest years displays virtues that are seldom, if ever, observed in Heathcliff, namely, thoughtfulness, kindness and compassion as well as a considerable capacity for self-control.[27] And though Hareton is portrayed as someone both strong and fearless, it is noteworthy that, in spite of his acts of physical violence, his rages and his bad language, which, in any case, are never gratuitous or unprovoked, he evinces none of that machismo which is all too often shown by Heathcliff towards the main characters in general and towards Isabella in particular. Again, Hareton's boorishness, which is commonly singled out by literary critics in their negative assessments of his character, but which should be understood as going hand in hand with his sincerity, may be interpreted as a symbolic repudiation of that culture of politeness which Lockwood seems to represent in the name of eighteenth-century Gallic civilization.[28] Perhaps that is why Lockwood's stance in that respect seems somewhat satirized when he shows disappointment at Hareton's not 'exchanging civilities' (*WH*, p. 25) with him in the early morning at the Heights, or, again, when, on his third visit there, he complains to himself about Cathy's showing him 'the same disregard to common forms of politeness, as before' (*WH*, p. 265).[29] Certainly it is through Hareton—and through Cathy—that we come to recognize why good manners matter far less than, say, a good heart. How Emily Brontë meant us to interpret her presentation of Hareton cannot, of course, be straightforwardly ascertained, partly because he has been a rather controversial figure for Brontë scholars over the years. Nevertheless, one possible clue to her intention on that head seems to lie at the beginning of the novel, when Lockwood has noticed 'the date "1500" and the name "Hareton Earnshaw"' (*WH*, p. 2) inscribed above the principal door of Wuthering Heights. Now, since 1500 has by some scholars been considered the year roughly marking the end of the Middle Ages and the beginning of the Renaissance, might not this inscription, however fortuitous it may have seemed to most readers of the novel, be understood as foreshadowing the idea that Hareton will symbolically come to epitomize a kind of rebirth of humanism in a Yorkshire setting at the dawn of the nineteenth century?[30]

Brontë Studies, 39/2 (2014)

Notes

1   For favourable or unfavourable judgements on Hareton's character, see, among numerous examples, Laura L. Hinkley, *The Brontës: Charlotte and Emily* (London: Hammond, Hammond & Co. Ltd., 1947), p. 257; Barbara Hardy, *Wuthering Heights* (New York: Barnes & Noble, 1963), p. 56; Wendy A. Craik, *The Brontë Novels* (London: Methuen, 1968), p. 32; David Sonstroem, '*Wuthering Heights* and the Limits of Vision', *Publications of the Modern Language Association of America*, 86 (1971), 59; Anne Williams, 'Natural Supernaturalism in *Wuthering Heights*', *Studies in Philology*, 82 (1985), 123; Patrick Murray, *A Companion to Wuthering Heights* (Dublin: The Educational Company, 1987), pp. 55-56; U. C. Knoepflmacher, *Emily Brontë's Wuthering Heights* (Cambridge and New York: Cambridge University Press, 1989), p. 22; Q. D. Leavis, 'A Fresh Approach to *Wuthering Heights*', in *Emily Brontë's Wuthering Heights, A Reader's Guide to Essential Criticism*, ed. Patsy Stoneman (Cambridge: Icon Books Ltd., 2000), p. 14.

2   For such comparisons between Hareton and Heathcliff, see, for example, B. Ford, '*Wuthering Heights*', *Scrutiny*, 7 (1939), 388; G. D. Klingopoulos, 'The Novel as Dramatic Poem (II): *Wuthering Heights*', *Scrutiny*, 14 (1947), 277; Keith Sagar, 'The Originality of *Wuthering Heights*', in *The Art of Emily Brontë*, ed. Anne Smith (London: Vision Press, 1976), p. 154; Sandra M. Gilbert and Susan Gubar, *The Madwoman in the Attic* (New Haven and London: Yale University Press, 1979), p. 301; Mary Burgan, '"Some Fit Parentage": Identity and the Cycle of Generations in *Wuthering Heights*', *Philological Quarterly*, 61 (1982), 403; Elizabeth R. Napier, 'The Problem of Boundaries in *Wuthering Heights*', *Philological Quarterly*, 63 (1984), 101; Claire Bazin, 'Is Mr

Heathcliff a Man?', *Cahiers Victoriens et Édouardiens*, 34 (1991), 75; Terry Eagleton, 'Myths of Power: A Marxist Study on *Wuthering Heights*', in *Emily Brontë's Wuthering Heights*, ed. Linda H. Peterson (Boston, MA: Bedford Books, 1992), pp. 411-413.

3   For affirmations of Hareton and Cathy's love relationship, see, among several examples, F. A. Bullock, 'The Genius of Emily Brontë', *Brontë Society Transactions*, 9/47 (1937), 126; Emily Brontë, *Wuthering Heights*, introd. Bonamy Dobrée (London: Collins, 1964), p. 15; Gordon Williams, 'The Problem of Passion in *Wuthering Heights*', *Trivium*, 7 (1972), 52-53; Margaret Drabble, 'The Writer as Reader: The Theme of Solitude in the Works of the Brontës', *Brontë Society Transactions*, 16/4 (1974), 268-269. For negative comments on the relationship, see, among several examples, Edgar Pelham, 'Judgments on Appeal: II. The Brontës', *Queen's Quarterly*, 29 (1932), 422; Albert J. Guerard, 'Preface to *Wuthering Heights*', in Emily Brontë, *Wuthering Heights*, ed. Thomas Moser (New York: Harcourt, Brace and World, 1962), p. 215; Vincent Buckley, 'Passion and Control in *Wuthering Heights*', *Southern Review* (University of Adelaide), 1 (1964), 23; Edward Chitham and Tom Winnifrith, *Brontë Facts and Brontë Problems* (London and Basingstoke: Macmillan, 1983), p. 90; Graham Holderness, *Wuthering Heights* (Milton Keynes and Philadelphia: Open University Press, 1985), p. 63; Alan Gardiner, 'Does the Novel Deteriorate After the Death of Catherine?', in *Critical Essays on Wuthering Heights*, eds. Linda Cookson and Brian Loughrey (London: Longman, 1988), p. 90; Rod Mengham, *Wuthering Heights* (Harmondsworth: Penguin Books, 1989), p. 93; Susan Meyer, *Imperialism at Home. Race and Victorian Women's Fiction* (Ithaca and London: Cornell University Press, 1996), p. 122.

4   For affirmations of Cathy's educational influence on Hareton, see, among several examples, Edgar F. Shannon, Jr., 'Lockwood's Dream and the Exegesis of *Wuthering Heights*', *Nineteenth-Century Fiction*, 14 (1959), 105; William H. Marshall, 'Hareton Earnshaw: Natural Theology on the Moors', *Victorian Newsletter*, 21 (1962), 14; Elliot B. Gose, Jr., '*Wuthering Heights*: The Heath and the Hearth', *Nineteenth-Century Fiction*, 21 (1966), 15; Harvey P. Sucksmith, 'The Theme of *Wuthering Heights* Reconsidered', *Dalhousie Review*, 54 (1974), 423; Barbara Munson Goff, 'Between Natural Theology and Natural Selection: Breeding the Human Animal in *Wuthering Heights*', *Victorian Studies*, 27 (1984), 508; Annette R. Federico, 'The Waif at the Window: Emily Brontë's Feminine *Bildungsroman*', *Victorian Newsletter*, 68 (1985), 26; Inge-Stina Ewbank, 'Emily Brontë and Immortality', *Brontë Society Transactions*, 24 (1999), 49. For negative comments on this influence, see Terence Dawson, '"An Oppression Past Explaining": The Structure of *Wuthering Heights*', *Orbis Litterarum*, 44 (1989), 64; Beth Newman, '"The Situation of the Looker-On": Gender, Narrative and Gaze in *Wuthering Heights*', *Publications of the Modern Language Association of America*, 105 (1990), 1036; Claire Jones, *Wuthering Heights. Emily Brontë* (London: York Press, 1998), p. 59.

5   For quotations from the novel, see Emily Brontë, *Wuthering Heights*, eds. Ian Jack and Helen Small (Oxford: Oxford University Press, 2009). For the sake of convenience, the first Catherine will be referred to as 'Catherine', the second as 'Cathy'.

6   See *Wuthering Heights*, pp. 8-10.

7   Nelly's snobbery towards Hareton in the same context is patent enough through such references as 'pretty company', 'rude-bred kindred' and 'such a clown'. See *Wuthering Heights*, pp. 172, 173.

8   Nelly has referred to Hareton at his first meeting with Cathy as 'too awkward to speak'. See *Wuthering Heights*, p. 171.

9   Nelly's devotion to Hareton as a young child continues well after she has left him behind at the Heights. See *Wuthering Heights*, pp. 56, 57, 63, 67, 68, 79, 165.

10 See especially *Wuthering Heights*, pp. 211, 223, 252.

11 For other references made by Nelly to Heathcliff's injustices to Hareton, see *Wuthering Heights*, pp. 166, 298.

12 For other notable examples of Joseph's championship of Hareton, see *Wuthering Heights*, pp. 125, 154, 184.

13 For details, see *Wuthering Heights*, pp. 274, 280, 284.

14 For details, see *Wuthering Heights*, pp. 262-263.

15 See *Wuthering Heights*, pp. 10, 184, 192, 206.

16 Heathcliff's denial of Hareton's individuality is confirmed when he presently says this to Nelly: 'Well, Hareton's aspect was the ghost of my immortal love, of my wild endeavours to hold my right, my degradation, my pride, my happiness, and my anguish—' (*WH*, p. 288).

17 For references to Hareton's loving loyalty to Heathcliff, see *Wuthering Heights*, pp. 97-98, 244-245, 266, 285-286, 297.

18 For an especially memorable example, see *Wuthering Heights*, p. 266. Cathy's recognition of Hareton's goodness is poetically

suggested when she compares him to a dog. See *Wuthering Heights*, p. 276. In this connection, see Graeme Tytler, 'Animals in *Wuthering Heights*', *Brontë Studies*, 27/2 (2002), 122-124. That the good-natured Hareton is, however, anything but a goody-goody in Cathy's eyes is amply suggested when, for example, she informs Nelly about his 'robbing our woods of pheasants' (*WH*, p. 214), or, later, when in response to Cathy's complaint about his having stolen her books, he dishonestly 'stammered an indignant denial of her accusations' (*WH*, p. 267).

19 See the second part of Note 4.

20 Hareton's normality is underlined at various stages of his life from infancy onwards through references to his laughter, tears and blushes as well as to his healthy eating and sleeping habits. See *Wuthering Heights*, pp. 10, 13, 63, 65-66, 79, 125, 172, 192, 194, 209, 220, 222, 262, 267, 282-283, 298-299. The significance of Hareton's presentation is implicit in the remarkable frequency of references to him in the narrative. By way of supplement, then, here is a list of pages on which Hareton's name is mentioned, but which are not referred to elsewhere in this paper: pp. 121, 173, 174, 175, 182, 188, 205, 221, 222, 249, 254, 260, 261, 264, 277, 279, 281, 282, 283, 284, 285, 286.

21 See *Wuthering Heights*, pp. 63, 73, 125, 152, 154-155, 161, 186, 246, 252, 254, 257, 276, 277, 297.

22 See *Wuthering Heights*, pp. 7, 11, 13, 24-25, 181, 184, 208, 213, 238, 265, 297.

23 See *Wuthering Heights*, pp. 124, 164, 285.

24 See *Wuthering Heights*, pp. 171, 173, 189, 265, 273.

25 Towards the end of Chapter 31 Lockwood overhears Heathcliff saying this to himself about Hareton's resemblance to Catherine: 'But, when I look for his father in his face, I find *her* every day more! How the devil is he so like? I can hardly bear to see him' (*WH*, p. 269). This detail is foreshadowed in Isabella's description of Hareton shortly after her arrival at the Heights as Heathcliff's bride: 'By the fire stood a ruffianly child [...] with a look of Catherine in his eyes and about his mouth' (*WH*, p. 121). For other references to the Earnshaw physiognomy, see *Wuthering Heights*, pp. 121, 172, 286, 287, 288. See also Graeme Tytler, 'Physiognomy in *Wuthering Heights*', *Brontë Society Transactions*, 21/4 (1994), 137-148.

26 See especially Peter D. Grudin, '*Wuthering Heights*: The Question of Unquiet Slumbers', *Studies in the Novel*, 6 (1971), 396.

27 For examples of Hareton's self-control, see *Wuthering Heights*, pp. 10, 194, 276, 279. Interesting, too, are the apparent links drawn between Hareton and Christ in Chapter 2. In this connection, see Graeme Tytler, 'The Role of Religion in *Wuthering Heights*', *Brontë Studies*, 32/1 (2007), 52.

28 That Lockwood's politeness is only skin-deep is amply suggested not only by the acts of violence he commits in Chapters 1 and 2, but also by those he perpetrates in his nightmares in Chapter 3. In this connection, it may not be inappropriate to mention that the years heading the two main entries of Lockwood's diary, 1801 and 1802, marking as they do respectively the (Napoleonic) war between England and France and the temporary truce between the two nations, seem to have some symbolic bearing on this particular conflict of values between Lockwood and Hareton.

29 There are much the same satirical implications in Zillah's complaints to Nelly about Cathy's lack of good manners on a couple of occasions as well as her reference to Hareton not being 'a model of nice behaviour'. See *Wuthering Heights*, pp. 259, 262-264.

30 This idea is in some sense prefigured by sundry references to Hareton as a 'young man' and to Joseph with the epithet 'old' and its synonyms. See *Wuthering Heights*, pp. 2, 7, 8, 10, 11, 12, 13, 14, 92, 120, 125, 127, 154, 192, 287. Certainly the contrast between the new and the old eras is underlined by the fact that Hareton will (with Cathy) move to Thrushcross Grange, whereas Joseph, with 'a lad to keep him company' (*WH*, p. 300), will continue to live in a largely shut-up Wuthering Heights.

The Presentation of Isabella in *Wuthering Heights*

Comments made about Isabella in literary criticism since the mid-nineteenth century have for the most part consisted of brief, negative references to her character and conduct. An anonymous writer in *Eclectic Review* (1851), for instance, describes Isabella as 'one of the silliest and most credulous girls that fancy ever painted', a judgement that has been echoed continually down to the present day.[1] Only a handful of critics, it would appear, have spoken favourably of Isabella, including, most recently, Judith Pike, who, as well as deploring the comparative lack of critical attention Isabella has been given over the years, points up the failure of Brontë scholars to consider her function as a narrator. As Pike maintains, it is through her letter to Nelly Dean that Isabella reveals 'the psychological depth of her character', which is 'too often knocked by critics'.[2] It is, then, partly in the spirit of Pike's essay that I intend to say more about Isabella than has been hitherto said, not only because her presentation throws much useful light on some of the other figures portrayed in the novel, but because it constitutes one of several testimonies to Emily Brontë's remarkable understanding of human nature and human society.[3]

What strikes the reader about Isabella at the outset is the degree to which she comes across as a somewhat unsympathetic figure. This is due in no small measure to Heathcliff's boyishly disparaging account of her behaviour in Thrushcross Grange during his illicit visit there with Catherine one Sunday evening.[4] Certainly from this account we gain a strong impression of the eleven-year-old Isabella as merely the spoilt daughter of a well-to-do household. At the same time, in his scorn for Isabella (and for Edgar) on that occasion, Heathcliff seems to betray that class-conscious envy and jealousy which will be at the root of his determination to exercise total power over her during their marriage. Isabella is, to be sure, an easy target for domination even before her elopement, as is evident from the somewhat minor status she enjoys as a young adult at the Grange. The fact that Isabella quickly falls in love with Heathcliff may, then, have something to do with this state of affairs as much as with Catherine's enthusiastic reception of him on his return to Gimmerton. Moreover, foolhardy as it is usually declared, Isabella's elopement with Heathcliff seems to have been for her practically the only means of escaping from her restrictive way of life. But irrespective of what might be said to Isabella's discredit on that head, one of the main reasons for examining her relationship with Heathcliff is that, like his relationship with, say, Hareton or Linton Heathcliff, it gives us insights into his moral shortcomings. For though, as he cunningly informs Nelly, Heathcliff has been careful not to break the law with respect to Isabella, there can be few acts of a husband's physical and mental cruelty to his bride to match those perpetrated by Heathcliff. All such evidence, however, seems to be overshadowed by the force of Heathcliff's diatribes against

Isabella as an utterly stupid, and even brutal, woman in both word and deed.[5] No doubt, his masterly rhetoric is bound to sustain in the minds of some readers the image of Isabella as 'a real little fool' (*WH*, p. 115)—a description made of her by Mr. Kenneth, ironically enough, by the time she has eloped—and hence to suggest why his arrant mistreatment of her seems to be conveniently downplayed or overlooked by those same readers for whom, thanks to his undying devotion to Catherine, he remains none the less a heroic figure.

The aforesaid remarks on Heathcliff's admirers could also be applied *mutatis mutandis* to those readers who, fully persuaded of Catherine's heroic status, may be inclined to connive at her own peculiar domination of Isabella. Such domination can be sensed already in Catherine's childhood when, for example, on their arrival at the Heights from church on a cold Christmas morning, she is noticed taking Isabella and Edgar each by the hand and bringing them into the house in order to 'set them before the fire' (*WH*, p. 51). Even to Isabella's weeping over Heathcliff's violence to Edgar with the tureen of hot apple sauce, Catherine delivers this rather callous response: 'Give over, Isabella! Has any body hurt *you*?' (*WH*, p. 52). That Catherine's domination of Isabella is just as pronounced during the first year of her marriage to Edgar is amply suggested by a number of Nelly's observations, not the least important of which is her remark that Isabella and Edgar were 'both very attentive to [Catherine's] comfort' (*WH*, p. 81). Similarly, when Catherine has complained to Nelly about Edgar's tearful objections to her praise of Heathcliff on the night of his unexpected visit to the Grange, and then gone on to refer to Edgar and Isabella as 'spoiled children' (*WH*, p. 87), it is interesting to note her claim to being disposed to 'humour [them] both' (*WH*, p. 87) tellingly countered by Nelly's retort that Catherine is the one being humoured by the Lintons. And though Isabella also suffers Catherine's domination of her painfully enough during their early meetings with the newly returned Heathcliff, such domination is nowhere more signal than when Catherine is striving with no little ridicule to put her sister-in-law off her love for him. What is ironic about this endeavour, however, is its being seemingly founded on a certain jealousy of Isabella's capacity to love Heathcliff with an intensity that she herself appears to have been unable to do. This may in turn explain why, instead of trying to help Isabella by, for example, forbidding Heathcliff to visit the Grange, Catherine prefers to continue showing her characteristic disrespect for Isabella, particularly by divulging the girl's love for Heathcliff not only in his very presence but also in the presence of a servant (Nelly Dean), and even by going so far, a few days later, as to tell Heathcliff, despite having moments earlier objected to his open courtship of Isabella, that, provided he likes her, he 'shall marry her' (*WH*, p. 99).[6] What Isabella herself desires is, clearly, of no account whatever to Catherine at that moment, or, indeed, at any other time. Such disrespect is, however, at perhaps its most overt when Catherine has earlier taken advantage of the first signs of Isabella's lovesickness by bossing her about in such ways as to induce the latter to complain that 'the mistress would allow her to be nothing in the house' (*WH*, p. 89).

Is it, then, surprising that the servants at the Grange, knowing as servants tend to do where true power lies in their particular household, should exploit Isabella's troubles with Catherine by ignoring her needs or requests for their services? As Nelly recalls, she and her fellow domestics 'let the parlour fire go out on purpose to vex her' (*WH*, p. 89). Such behaviour is manifestly unfair to Isabella, who, apart from having been brought up to depend on domestic help, and supposedly encouraged to practise such dependence, appears at no time to have been overbearing towards the Grange servants. It is, accordingly, understandable that, on arriving at the Heights as Heathcliff's bride, she should expect to be immediately attended to in ways she has been accustomed to being from her earliest years. The only servant she finds, however, is the elderly Joseph, and one whose blatantly insolent manner to her is in part made possible by his having nothing to fear either from a feckless Hindley or from a temporarily absent Heathcliff. What is striking about Joseph's demeanour towards Isabella is that it shows him at his most unpleasant both as a servant and as a human being. And though Isabella may be faulted for, say, taking over and bungling the cooking of the porridge, her particular requests to Joseph for help are neither arrogant nor unreasonable, whereas Joseph's feigned incomprehension of her utterances and his savage mockery of her upper-class accent are unconscionably gratuitous. One unfortunate consequence of Joseph's treatment of Isabella, not unlike that meted out to her by the Grange servants, is that it has probably reinforced the image of Isabella as an essentially silly woman, albeit unjustly when we consider how much the disrespect she has been shown in one or other of the two households has been undeserved.

Our concern with Isabella here is not a little warranted by our awareness that, though an essentially minor character, she fulfils an important function as a narrator both through her letter to Nelly Dean (in Chapter 13) and through her oral account to the latter of life at the Heights (in Chapter 17). What is of some interest about these two 'narratives', however, is the extent to which they have already been foreshadowed by Lockwood's diary entries as recorded in the opening three chapters of the novel, thereby serving as an ironic illustration of a central theme in the text, namely, the phenomenon of repetition or recurrence in human life. Thus we note, for example, that both characters face much the same hostile reception from Joseph on arriving at the Heights; both have a similarly keen eye for the objects and furnishings inside the house; both have to grope their way along the stairways because deprived of candlelight; and both suffer Joseph's same sort of lame excuse for his unwillingness to oblige them with his help.[7] There are also parallels between Isabella and Lockwood as to the insubordination they each have to put up with from servants at the Grange.[8]

Similar, too, are one or two of their descriptions of nature. Thus on her way to the Heights with Heathcliff, Isabella observes that '[t]he sun set behind the Grange' (*WH*, p. 120), a detail symbolically connected, it would seem, with that used by Lockwood on his final visit to Gimmerton: 'I reached the Grange before sunset' (*WH*, p. 271). Again, consider their choice of diction: both mention 'infernal regions' (*WH*, pp. 161 and 273), 'orisons' (*WH*, pp. 24 and 153), 'essay'(*WH*, pp. 6 and 121) and 'hermit' (*WH*, pp. 80 and 122), with Isabella's 'misanthropical' (*WH*, p. 122) forcibly evoking Lockwood's view of Gimmerton as '[a] perfect misanthropist's Heaven' (*WH*, p. 1). Noteworthy, too, is the similarity between their uses of figurative language, especially the hyperbole. Thus Lockwood's complaint to Heathcliff about his dogs is partly voiced with this sentiment: 'You might as well leave a stranger with a brood of tigers!' (*WH*, p. 5), while Isabella tells Nelly that, in her attempt to reason with a murderous-minded Hindley, she 'might as well have struggled with a bear' (*WH*, p. 155). Finally, mention should be made not only of the toilsome snowbound journeys they each have to make to the Grange on foot, but to the fact that, as with Lockwood, Isabella's ultimate destination in the narrative will be somewhere in or near London.

There are, to be sure, other parallels between Isabella and Lockwood worth noting here. For example, both characters are well-bred, well-mannered and cultured, and both are highly articulate, even literary, in their use of written and spoken English, and not without a certain propensity for irony or even a knowledge of grammatical terms.[9] As a narrator, Isabella is surely Lockwood's equal through her observations on the characters, behaviour and physicality of Heathcliff, Joseph, Hindley and Hareton, providing us with information about them that usefully, even startlingly, supplements what we are told about them elsewhere in the text.

Isabella and Lockwood are also memorable for the blunders they each commit at the Heights, though Isabella's clumsy cooking of the porridge is hardly as reprehensible as the carelessness with which Lockwood causes the dogs to turn on him or the rashness that impels him to steal Joseph's lantern.

More important, on the other hand, are the differences between the two narrators in the matter of love. Thus whereas Lockwood remains throughout both timid and cautious as a lover, particularly with respect to Cathy, Isabella is his very antithesis through the whole-hearted risks she takes for the sake of her love for Heathcliff. Seldom, if ever, in fiction could we find a more instructive account of a naive young woman's experience of first love, made aware as we are how realistically each stage of it is delineated, from the moment it is initially betrayed by Isabella's moodiness at the Grange, through the incredulity with which she reacts to Catherine and Nelly's attempts to put her off Heathcliff, to her rantings about the latter before her final departure from the neighbourhood. For wrong-headed though it proves to be, Isabella's love is nevertheless admirable both for indirectly reminding us of Lockwood's fear of love and for seeming far more erotic than the love that Catherine appears to have cherished for Heathcliff. What should be emphasized here, too, is the brilliance with which Emily Brontë renders the effects of disappointed love. Certainly much of what Isabella utters in her dialogue with Nelly in Chapter 17, and indeed of what Heathcliff himself has already said about the nature of Isabella's love for him is, psychologically speaking, remarkably modern, not only through her readiness to subject herself time and again to his cruelty or through the sadistic and masochistic feelings underlying her talk about killing or being killed by Heathcliff, but also by the way in which, notwithstanding her rage against him, she keeps hinting at, and even hoping for, a reconciliation between them.[10]

The extreme emotion with which Isabella expresses her contradictory feelings of love and hate for Heathcliff is clearly of a piece with the profound sense of loneliness she at first suffers at the Heights as his hapless bride. Yet however much she may be at fault for bringing all this on herself, there can be little doubt that Isabella's account of her spiritual isolation shows her to possess a sensitivity deep enough for us to explode the prevalent notion of her as a light-headed young woman. What is noteworthy about this account is the extent to which it betokens her proclivity to nostalgia—a proclivity manifested already by her uncomfortable awareness of the glaring contrast between her present and her former mode of life. This we see poignantly conveyed in the following detail from her letter to Nelly: 'You'll not be surprised, Ellen, at my feeling particularly cheerless, seated in worse than solitude on that inhospitable hearth, and remembering that four miles distant lay my delightful home, containing the only people I loved on earth' (*WH*, p. 122). Of like interest here is how, while sitting in 'the house' reading a book on the night before her flight from the Heights, she suggests the nature of her loneliness by referring to certain aural effects: 'There was no sound through the house but the moaning wind which shook the windows every now and then, the faint crackling of the coals, and the click of my snuffers as I removed at intervals the long wick of the candle. [...] It was very, very sad, and while I read, I sighed, for it seemed as if all joy had vanished from the world, never to be restored' (*WH*, p. 154). Here we see one of several examples of Isabella's obsession with happiness, which is first noticeable when, to Nelly's bid to put her off Heathcliff, she retorts: 'What malevolence you must have to wish to convince me that there is no happiness in the world!' (*WH*, p. 92). For Isabella, romantic as she is by temperament, happiness is, unsurprisingly, something existing in the past, if not in the future. This is ironically instanced when, while cooking the porridge in the Heights kitchen, she speaks of 'sighing to remember a period when it would have been all merry fun', but finds herself 'compelled speedily to drive off the remembrance' because '[i]t racked [her] to recall past happiness' (*WH*, p. 124-125). That Isabella's sentiment here is perforce illusory is somewhat confirmed when, in Hindley's presence, she taunts Heathcliff with these words about her life at the Grange: 'When I recollect how happy we were— how happy Catherine was before he came—I'm fit to curse the day' (*WH*, p. 160). What Isabella seems to have forgotten, however, is, as Nelly will later tell Lockwood, that Catherine was anything but an easy person to live with in the first year of her marriage.

The foregoing might, then, be enough in itself for some readers, especially admirers of Heathcliff and Catherine, to justify their view of Isabella as a fundamentally foolish creature. Certainly it is astonishing, even to more understanding readers, to find that, given her once comfortable life at the Grange, to say nothing of her apparent weaknesses of character, Isabella does not succumb to utter despair during her residence at the Heights. That she does not do so bespeaks her capacity to fall back on resources which, notwithstanding her hitherto heavy reliance on others for all kinds of help, she manages to discover within herself. We note, for example, how, as well as setting up a daily routine for herself in 'the house' and avoiding Heathcliff as much as possible, Isabella gradually learns to overcome her general timidity at the Heights, including that deep fear which, in common with many a well-born lady, she feels in the presence of a long-standing retainer. As she says to Nelly after her flight from the Heights: 'I recovered spirits sufficient to hear Joseph's eternal lectures without weeping; and to move up and down the house, less with the foot of a frightened thief than formerly. You wouldn't think that I should cry at anything Joseph could say, but he and Hareton are detestable companions. I'd rather sit with Hindley, and hear his awful talk, than with "t' little maister", and his staunch supporter, that odious old man!' (*WH*, pp. 153-154). Nevertheless, it is thanks to her more or less unavoidable relations with these inmates of the Heights that Isabella steadily acquires a strength of character that could hardly have been foreseen earlier in the novel. This strength is especially prominent in her relations with Hindley, whereby we come to see how in her strenuous efforts both physical and rhetorical to deter him from his murderous intention against Heathcliff she displays a considerable fund of rationality and good sense.

It is noteworthy that, having witnessed Hindley's fight with Heathcliff, Isabella gives the former a graphic account of the brutality with which he was treated by the latter while lying on the floor unconscious: 'He trampled on, and kicked you, and dashed you on the ground [...]. And his mouth watered to tear you with his teeth; because he's only half a man—not so much' (*WH*, p. 159). This denial of Heathcliff's manliness, interpreted though it might be as yet another expression of disappointed love, should surely be taken into account in any assessment of Heathcliff's character, and the more so as Isabella appears to be hardly shy of telling the truth. Indeed, even if Heathcliff's forceful diatribes against Isabella as his bride seem cogent enough to put all her own objections to his abuse of her in the shade, we should still take quite seriously the words which, in repudiation of his claim that she has been free to leave him, she says to Nelly as follows: 'Don't put faith in a single word he speaks. He's a lying fiend, a monster, and not a human being!' (*WH*, p. 134). Isabella's contempt for Heathcliff is again manifest in her account of his behaviour from the time he goes daily to the Grange to keep vigil over Catherine's corpse until his first visit to her grave. Thus, having told Nelly of his absence from all meals during that week, Isabella goes on to add: 'He has just come home at dawn, and gone upstairs to his chamber; locking himself in—as if anybody dreamt of coveting his company! There he has continued, praying like a methodist; only the deity he implored is senseless dust and ashes; and God, when addressed, was curiously confounded with his own black father!' (*WH*, p. 153). That Isabella is intent on reducing Heathcliff to the lowest social level possible may be gathered plainly enough from the last four words of this passage, as it may be more plainly so from her later references to his 'black countenance' (*WH*, p. 156) and his 'sharp cannibal teeth' (*WH*, p. 156). Much more important here, however, is the open defiance with which, sometimes with outright laughter, she provokes such extreme physical violence on Heathcliff's part as to necessitate her eventual flight from the Heights, and that partly because he has overheard her telling Hindley that he caused Catherine's death, but mainly because, with unwonted sarcasm, she has made light of his love for Catherine as follows: '[I]f poor Catherine had trusted you, and assumed the ridiculous, contemptible, degrading title of Mrs. Heathcliff, she would soon have presented a similar picture! *She* wouldn't have borne your abominable behaviour quietly; her detestation and disgust must have found voice' (*WH*, p. 160).

Such language, which brilliantly expresses the righteous indignation of 'a woman scorned', is notable for suggesting how much Isabella has by now changed from the timid young woman who at one time all too often elicited domination or disrespect at the Grange. Thus it will be recalled in this connection that, though she is generally supportive of her against Catherine, Nelly not only slackens off in her duties to the eighteen-year-old Isabella when the latter is betraying the first signs of lovesickness, but even breaks rank by warning her against her love for Heathcliff. That Nelly somewhat lacks respect for Isabella during that time is evident from such references to her as 'infantile in manners' (*WH*, p. 89), 'the infatuated girl' (*WH*, p. 90), 'the confounded girl' (*WH*, p. 93) and '[t]he poor thing' (*WH*, p. 93), not to mention references to her moping, weeping and sobbing. We also note that, on visiting Isabella at the Heights in answer to her letter, Nelly is dismayed both at her neglect of the household and at her bedraggled appearance, to the extent of making this heartless comparison between her and Heathcliff: 'He was the only thing there that seemed decent, and I thought he never looked better. So much had circumstances altered their positions, that he would certainly have struck a stranger as a born and bred gentleman, and his wife as a thorough little slattern!' (*WH*, p. 130). Noteworthy in the same context is that, apart from tactlessly hinting to Heathcliff about his negligence of his bride, Nelly actually advises Isabella to leave her husband. No doubt, Nelly's sense of self-importance has been enhanced by the fact that Isabella has already confided in her about her troubled marriage, and even looked up to her as someone wise enough to 'explain […] what [she has] married' (*WH*, p. 120). Little wonder, then, that Nelly should continue to see herself as Isabella's mentor, even after the latter has escaped from the Heights. Typical of this mindset, for example, is Nelly's determination to attend to the knife wound on Isabella's neck and to get her to change into dry clothes before obeying her particular orders. This time, however, Isabella is stubbornly self-assertive as never before, both by insisting on having her orders about her travel plans obeyed before allowing Nelly to touch her and by flatly rejecting her advice to postpone her journey to Gimmerton. Thus we see how much Isabella has been toughened by her sojourn at the Heights. It is, moreover, not without significance that Isabella's communication with Nelly, whether in person or by letter, appears to have effectively ended that very night, thereby indicating that she had by then sloughed off her deferential reliance on the servant once and for all.

Much more problematic than Isabella's relationship with Nelly, on the other hand, is that which has by then existed between Isabella and Edgar, and still exists even at that stage. Indeed, Isabella's disinclination to prolong her refuge at the Grange seems hardly more due to her dread of Heathcliff's hunting her down there than to her unease as to Edgar's likely attitude to her at the moment. For though their relations as brother and sister during childhood, with its mixture of squabbles and mutual attachment, appears to have been nothing out of the ordinary, it is apparent that by the time Edgar has married Catherine, such relations have become more or less conventional, not to say formal. Further, one has the impression that, notwithstanding his loving her 'tenderly' (*WH*, p. 89), as vouched for by Nelly, Edgar values his sister not so much for embodying a particular individuality as for representing the Lintons *qua* family. That may be one reason why Edgar fails to persuade Isabella to extricate herself from her involvement with Heathcliff. But it may also explain why Edgar, once having accepted Isabella's elopement as a *fait accompli*, finds it easy enough to detach himself from her by adopting an essentially legalistic attitude to her when, for example, he tells Nelly that Isabella 'had a right to go if she pleased' and that she is henceforth 'only [his] sister in name' (*WH*, p. 117).

All this, as we gradually come to realize, stands in stark contrast with the love and loyalty that Isabella shows Edgar continuously both before and after he has first severed all ties with her. That it is Isabella rather than Edgar who is the truly loving sibling is already confirmed when, early in her letter to Nelly, Isabella writes: 'Inform Edgar that I'd give the world to see his face again—that my heart returned to Thrushcross Grange in twenty-four hours after I left it, and is there at this moment, full of warm feelings for him, and Catherine!' (*WH*, p. 120). Noteworthy, too, is the strength of her respect for him at this time, whether through her concern to keep her marital troubles sedulously hidden from him or through her readiness to jump to his defence in response to Heathcliff's insulting or threatening talk about him—and all that despite her admitting to Nelly, shortly before her final departure from the Grange, that Edgar 'has not been kind, has he?' (*WH*, p. 151). At the same time, Isabella's resolution, as indicated in her very next sentence, not to 'come suing for his assistance' or to 'bring him into more trouble' (*WH*, p. 151), sadly prefigures the separateness of their lives in the next dozen years or so. For though

Isabella will carry on 'a regular correspondence' (*WH*, p. 161) with Edgar soon after she has settled in the South, and will constantly speak affectionately about him to her son Linton, there is none the less something pathetic, even tragic, about the fact that it is only when Isabella has informed him about her fatal illness that Edgar takes the trouble to visit her for the first time since her elopement.

However much Isabella may be to blame for her vexed relationship with her brother, there can be little doubt as to the depth of her love for her family; a love that seems much warmer than Edgar's own strong sense of family. Thus quite apart from instances of her devotion to the latter noted above, we may consider not only her anxiety about Catherine's illness or her grief at her death, but her inability to forgive herself because, as she says to Nelly, they had both 'parted unreconciled' (*WH*, p. 151)—a remorse all the more commendable since she had had to put up with Catherine's humiliations of her not long beforehand. The intensity of Isabella's affection for Catherine is somehow affirmed by the alacrity with which she detects a physical resemblance between her and her nephew Hareton when describing him, shortly after her arrival at the Heights, as having 'a look of Catherine in his eyes and about his mouth' (*WH*, p. 121); and, again, when, on the morning after his fight with Hindley, she responds to Heathcliff's anger at her for accusing him of causing Catherine's death with the following utterance: 'I beg your pardon [...]. But I loved Catherine too; and her brother requires attendance which, for her sake, I shall supply. Now that she's dead, I see her in Hindley; Hindley has exactly her eyes, if you had not tried to gouge them out, and made them black and red' (*WH*, p. 160).[11] This physiognomic sensitivity, which is a significant aspect of the observational skills that Isabella brings to bear on her fellow residents at the Heights during her time there, is especially evident in the last but one of her descriptions of Heathcliff's face as expressive of his own grief at Catherine's passing:

*His forehead, that I once thought so manly, and that I now think so diabolical,
was shaded with a heavy cloud; his basilisk eyes were nearly quenched by
sleeplessness—and weeping, perhaps, for the lashes were wet then: his lips
devoid of their ferocious sneer, and sealed in an expression of unspeakable
sadness. Had it been another, I would have covered my face, in the presence
of such grief. In his case, I was gratified: and ignoble as it seems to insult a
fallen enemy, I couldn't miss this chance of sticking in a dart; his weakness
was the only time when I could taste the delight of paying wrong for wrong.
(WH, pp. 158-159)*

Besides giving us yet another glimpse of Isabella's intelligence and
perception, the above-quoted passage, with its curious mixture of
tough and tender sentiments, seems very much the expression of
the *grande dame*. This image of Isabella, discernible already in her
childhood through the genteel influence she exerts on Catherine
during the latter's five-week stay at the Grange, is to some extent
buttressed by occasional references to her personal beauty, of which
both Nelly and Catherine implicitly admit to being admirers.[12] All
this, taken in conjunction with her ability to overcome the sundry
obstacles confronting her at the Heights, may help to explain why
Isabella succeeds against all apparent odds in keeping her head above
water after settling in the South. The notion that a highly strung
greenhorn of a girl of privileged upbringing, and one prone to
irrational, even nonsensical, utterances as well as to nervous fits of
weeping or laughter and other hypersensitive reactions, can, by dint
of dogged resistance to adverse circumstances, eventually turn into
a seemingly mature and capable woman, though by no means a rare
thing in human history, is exemplified by Isabella nobly enough to
be practically a sermon in itself.

Such resilience may perhaps be due to the fact that, unusually for
an upper-class woman of her period, Isabella at times shows a markedly
amoral disposition. This is not to say that Isabella is devoid of a
moral sense: her resistance to Hindley's criminal intentions suggests

this to be quite otherwise, as does the truthfulness of her account to Joseph of the fight between Hindley and Heathcliff. That Isabella's morality seems nevertheless a manifestation of her respectable fear of the law and of her inveterate family-mindedness rather than an innate quality can scarcely be denied. This in turn makes it easy for us to account not only for her persistent vindictiveness against Heathcliff and her constant longing for his death, but also for her malicious taunting of him amid his grief over Catherine's death.[13] In this connection, it is noteworthy that, while fully cognizant of the dangers of taking revenge, Isabella admits to Hindley that she would be 'glad of a retaliation that wouldn't recoil on [herself]' (*WH*, p. 155). The fact that Heathcliff has himself earlier told Nelly, with respect to his hanging of the dog Fanny, that 'no brutality disgusted' Isabella, and that she has 'an innate admiration of it, if only her precious person were secure from injury' (*WH*, p. 133) would appear to be not unrelated to Isabella's words just quoted, and thus to put us forcibly in mind of the amoral streak in her make-up. Something of this streak is hinted at even in her incidental remarks about her self-sufficiency as, for example, when, aware that Heathcliff and Hindley are both out of sorts on the morning after their fight, she recalls: 'Nothing hindered me from eating heartily; and I experienced a certain sense of satisfaction and superiority, as, at intervals, I cast a look towards my silent companions, and felt the comfort of a quiet conscience within me' (*WH*, p. 158).[14]

It is this rather egotistical spirit of self-sufficiency that doubtless contributes to Isabella's extraordinary survival during the last years of her life, a survival all the more remarkable because she has to make the best of her hereditarily 'delicate constitution' (*WH*, p. 168). Indeed, it is probably owing to this spirit that Isabella also proves to be a competent lone parent, and as such one worthy enough (not unlike, say, the heroine of *The Tenant of Wildfell Hall*) to be deemed a prototype of the modern feminist. Certainly Isabella's personal situation at that time well illustrates the problem of the disadvantaged married woman in a predominantly patriarchal society in late eighteenth-century England, thereby signalling an important aspect of her presentation in *Wuthering Heights*.[15] Still, it must needs be averred that Isabella is the only female character in the novel that deserves special mention as a mother, partly because her son Linton is, physiognomically speaking, '[his] mother's child, entirely' (*WH*, p. 183), as Heathcliff discovers to his great disappointment, and partly because the boy clearly retains pleasant memories of his early childhood with her.[16]

Brontë Studies, 39/3 (2014)

Notes

1   For this quotation as well as for negative comments on Isabella since the mid-nineteenth century, see Judith E. Pike, "'My name *was* Isabella Linton": Coverture, Domestic Violence and Mrs. Heathcliff's Narrative in *Wuthering Heights'*, *Nineteenth-Century Literature*, 64/3 (2009), pp. 347-383.

2   Pike, p. 352. For other favourable comments on Isabella, see, for example, Barbara Hardy, *Wuthering Heights* (New York: Barnes & Noble, 1963), p. 88; James H. Kavanagh, *Emily Brontë's Wuthering Heights* (Oxford: Blackwell, 1985), p. 68; Patrick Murray, *Companion to Wuthering Heights* (Dublin: The Educational Company, 1987), p. 43.

3   It is interesting to note how Isabella's strong presence in the narrative is reinforced by the sympathetic or negative references made to her even after her death. See *Wuthering Heights*, pp. 176, 179, 180, 183, 184, 191, 196, 204, 210.

4   For quotations from the novel, see Emily Brontë, *Wuthering Heights*, eds. Ian Jack and Helen Small (Oxford: Oxford University Press, 2009). For the sake of convenience, the first Catherine will be referred to throughout as 'Catherine'.

5   See *Wuthering Heights*, pp. 132-133.

6   For further details, see *Wuthering Heights*, pp. 99-100.

7   See *Wuthering Heights*, pp. 2, 3, 6, 24, 121, 127.

8   See *Wuthering Heights*, pp. 6, 89.

9 Compare Lockwood's reference to Heathcliff 'chipping off his pronouns and auxiliary verbs' (*WH*, p. 5) with Isabella's comment on Heathcliff's objection to her use of the phrase 'our room': 'The adjective *our* gave mortal offence'(*WH*, p. 128).

10 See *Wuthering Heights*, pp. 133, 134, 151, 152.

11 It is interesting to note that, on arriving at the Heights as Heathcliff's bride, Isabella immediately spots a resemblance between Hindley and Catherine as to their eyes. See *Wuthering Heights*, p. 121.

12 See *Wuthering Heights*, pp. 88, 182.

13 Isabella's amorality is never more patent than when she says this to Nelly: 'But what misery laid on Heathcliff could content me, unless I have a hand in it? I'd rather he suffered *less*, if I might cause his sufferings, and he might *know* that I was the cause' (*WH*, p. 159).

14 Isabella's concern for her conscience seems as amoral as her respect for the law; in which connection, see *Wuthering Heights*, pp. 153, 157. For other references to Isabella's self-sufficiency or her lack of concern for others, see *Wuthering Heights*, pp. 154, 156.

15 Although nothing is said about Isabella's pecuniary resources at this time, we may take it for granted that the money with which she maintains her household comes from the estate she has inherited from her father. See *Wuthering Heights*, pp. 89, 94, 119, 145.

16 See *Wuthering Heights*, pp. 180, 213.

The Presentation of Edgar Linton in *Wuthering Heights*

S ome of the many readers of *Wuthering Heights* who have looked upon Heathcliff and Catherine as among the greatest of all fictional lovers might think it odd that any Brontë scholar should bother to give Edgar Linton's role and function in the novel much more than a passing mention.[1] Such thinking is, to be sure, quite understandable if, as commonly happens, those same readers remember Edgar chiefly as the weakest figure in a famous love triangle, or even as someone now and then derided for his character and demeanour. Nor is this rather limited, not to say caricatural, idea of Edgar much helped by the fact that it has been more or less perpetuated in cinematic and televisual adaptations of Emily Brontë's book. Another possible reason for harbouring a poor image of Edgar may be a certain bias against him for his upper-class background and hence for his being socially superior to the two principal protagonists. Yet notwithstanding these restrictive views of Edgar, we should not forget that he plays an important part in the action, not merely during part of Catherine's lifetime, but for a good seventeen years after her death until his own passing in the very year Lockwood takes up tenancy of Thrushcross Grange. This may be seen especially through the influence he exerts on the movements and conduct of Nelly Dean and of his daughter Cathy and, in some measure, even through the restraining effect he has on some of Heathcliff's deeds or machinations.[2] It is by dint of these and other facets of his presentation to be discussed below that we discover how much more significant a figure Edgar cuts in the narrative than is often assumed, and to what extent he deserves to be rescued from the unsavoury image he seems to have been lumbered with, at least anecdotally, over the years.[3]

Let us first of all consider some of the most noticeably negative aspects of Edgar's presentation. Thus we may recall the contemptuous remarks made about him as a youngster by Heathcliff and by Nelly during his earliest appearances in the narrative. That Nelly generally sees the young Edgar as a feckless creature is evident enough when she refers to him as a 'soft thing' (*WH*, p. 64) for failing to renounce his courtship of Catherine once and for all in view of the bad behaviour she has exhibited in Chapter 8. The notion of Edgar as a sort of weakling is still retained several years later when, for example, Hindley, in an attempt to persuade Isabella to condone his intention to murder Heathcliff, taunts her with the following words: 'Are you as soft as your brother?' (*WH*, p. 155). By that time there have been other references to keep the reader in mind of Edgar's physical limitations, notably the one in which Nelly describes (for the second time) his being inferior in build to Heathcliff on the night of the latter's unexpected appearance at the Grange after a three-year absence.[4] Edgar's image as a weakling is eventually brought to a grim climax during his showdown with Heathcliff in Chapter 11, first, when, just after Catherine has locked the Grange kitchen door and then thrown the key into the fire, Nelly remarks on his being 'taken with a nervous trembling', whereat 'his countenance grew deadly pale', before she adds: 'For his life he could not avert that access of emotion—mingled anguish and humiliation overcame him completely. He leant on the back of a chair, and covered his face' (*WH*, p. 102). The image of Edgar as a weakling, underlined as it is by that detail, is enhanced to an extreme level, not only when, in response to such pathetic reactions on his part and in a bid to assure him that Heathcliff would hardly deign to 'lift a finger' at him, Catherine practically damns Edgar as a human being by addressing him thus: 'Your type is not a lamb, it's a sucking leveret' (*WH*, p. 102), but also when Heathcliff is prompted by those words to criticize Catherine implicitly for marrying 'the slavering, shivering thing you preferred to me' and to refer to Edgar as someone whom he 'would not strike [...] with [his] fist', but whom he 'would kick [...] with [his] foot, and experience considerable satisfaction' (*WH*, p. 102). Nor does the fact that Edgar presently strikes Heathcliff hard on the throat do much to offset the idea of his essential feebleness, and the more so as Catherine has already scorned him for falling back, if need be, on servants to fulfil his aggressive intentions against Heathcliff. And no doubt all such details have left many a reader with a generally adverse opinion of Edgar Linton's character.

Much less unfair to Edgar than what has just been said about him, on the other hand, are references to those contexts where he betrays what might be designated as avoidable shortcomings. Consider, for instance, the fact that, during the three days Catherine is shut up in her bedroom, Edgar 'spent his time in the library, and did not inquire concerning his wife's occupations' (*WH*, p. 105), the implication of those words, as we gradually come to discover, being not so much that Edgar is indifferent to his wife as that he is dependent on Nelly for information as to what is going on in his household, and even elsewhere. Edgar's dependency on Nelly is especially pronounced when, because of Catherine's untimely death, he has chosen to live his life as a virtual recluse, and that to the partial detriment of his relationship with his daughter Cathy. Such a questionable withdrawal from the everyday world perforce adds to his reliance on Nelly, at the same time as Nelly's taking advantage of this reliance casts further unfavourable light on Edgar as her employer.[5] Thus we may recall Nelly's propensity to prevaricate, not to say lie, about what Edgar has or has not asked her to do. This may be noted when, just after Hindley's death, Nelly falsely informs Heathcliff that Edgar 'has ordered [her] to take [Hareton]' (*WH*, p. 165) back with her to the Grange; or when, having found Cathy at the Heights after a frantic search for her, she upbraids her as follows: 'To think how Mr. Linton charged me to keep you in' (*WH*, p. 171), even though he actually instructed her not to allow Cathy to go beyond the Grange grounds. Such blatant fibs cannot but remind us how often Nelly has already exploited Edgar's whole-hearted trust in her as his housekeeper, and nowhere more glaringly so than when arranging Heathcliff's fateful tryst with Catherine while her master is at church. In this connection, it is noteworthy how, perhaps mindful of Edgar's astonishing incredulity at the news of Isabella's elopement, Nelly is all too inclined to shield him from uncomfortable truths of all kinds. This we see most particularly through her tendency to hide her essentially negative opinion of Linton Heathcliff from him in order not to undermine his apparent approval of his nephew as a prospective husband for Cathy. Indeed, it is owing to Nelly's duplicity in this respect that one wonders whether the unfortunate marriage between the two cousins might not have been prevented had Edgar been vigilant enough to take appropriate action on his own initiative.

The fact that Edgar is such an easy master to serve under may explain why Nelly seems not only to turn a blind eye to his failings but to be quite devoted to him. Such devotion may be sensed when, for example, she speaks of him as 'a kind master' (*WH*, p. 81) or refers to 'the mildness of his nature' (*WH*, p. 162); it may also be felt in the lyricism with which she describes his facial features in his fatal illness as well as in the moment she watches him die. It may be even more strongly felt in those contexts where she sides with him against Catherine, as, for example, when asked by the latter to warn him of her uncontrollable bad temper, Nelly shows a determination not to do so because she 'did not wish to "frighten" her husband, as she said, and multiply his annoyances for the purpose of serving her selfishness' (*WH*, p. 104).[6] Interesting, too, is Nelly's following assessment of Edgar's demeanour just after Catherine's death, not least for implicitly showing it to have been in complete contrast to that displayed by Heathcliff in the same circumstances: 'But he was too good to be thoroughly unhappy long. *He* didn't pray for Catherine's soul to haunt him. Time brought resignation, and a melancholy sweeter than common joy' (*WH*, p. 162). Such words may, however, be adjudged rather too sentimental, forming as they do a prelude to her somewhat loaded comparison between Edgar and Hindley as widowers, whereby the latter inevitably comes off worse. Certainly, Nelly's general bias in favour of Edgar raises questions as to those virtues of his she suggests in her narrative. Thus Edgar is shown to be a perfect father, at least to judge not only by his education of Cathy or his recreational walks with her, but also by Cathy's exceptional concern to be loyal and deferential to him as his daughter. Nevertheless, Edgar's ignorance of some of Cathy's movements and actions from her thirteenth year onwards, to say nothing of his handing responsibility for her almost entirely to Nelly, may be felt to detract from the idea of him as a model father.[7] Again, if Edgar may to some extent be commended for his deeds on behalf of Isabella and her son Linton, there can be little doubt as to the unconscionable stubbornness with which, despite corresponding with her, he keeps his sister at arm's length for some twelve years as if, notwithstanding her having bravely run away from her ill-fated marriage to Heathcliff and made a life of her own in the South, he were still ashamed of her for having entered such a marriage in the first place.

Yet whatever might be said—and indeed should be said—for or against Edgar Linton as father, brother, uncle or master, there can be no question that the most important part of his presentation lies in his relations with the two central figures of the novel, Catherine and Heathcliff. Further, by examining such relations, I hope to make a more dispassionate evaluation of Edgar than seems to have been offered by those readers who have looked askance at him as both lover and husband. First of all, it goes without saying that Catherine and Edgar are an ill-assorted couple from the outset, and nowhere more obviously so than when Nelly describes Edgar's bewilderment at Catherine's violent behaviour in Chapter 8. And though they are both reconciled enough later that afternoon for Catherine to accept Edgar's proposal of marriage, we learn that, even after they have got married, Edgar is a nervously timid husband intent on pleasing his wife at all costs to himself and others. As Nelly says of Edgar and his sister Isabella: 'They were both very attentive to [Catherine's] comfort, certainly. It was not the thorn bending to the honeysuckles, but the honeysuckles embracing the thorn. There were no mutual concessions; one stood erect, and the others yielded' (*WH*, p. 81). Such is Edgar's quest to please Catherine that he even expects his servants to pander to her every wish and whim. Nevertheless, it is undoubtedly by dint of her scrupulous observation of Edgar and Catherine's relationship that Nelly succeeds in sounding very persuasive when, alluding to the end of the first six months of their marriage, she says this to Lockwood: 'I believe I may assert that they were really in possession of deep and growing happiness' (*WH*, p. 81), even though Nelly suddenly goes on to imply that such 'happiness' ceased on the day of Heathcliff's return. Yet if Nelly's two-word sentence '[i]t ended' (*WH*, p. 81) may give the reader the impression that Catherine then and there turned her back on Edgar once and for all, such an impression will prove to have been somewhat misleading.

With the return of Heathcliff from abroad, however, Edgar almost instantly changes from the patient, forbearing husband we have hitherto seen him to be through Nelly Dean's eyes to a weirdly domineering one, determined, as if for the first time, to exercise his conjugal authority over Catherine and keep her in her place.[8] What stands out in Edgar's talk and behaviour on the evening of Heathcliff's unexpected appearance is a jealousy he is barely able to conceal, manifest as it is, among other things, in his forcefully stopping Catherine from rushing down to bring the newly arrived Heathcliff upstairs and in his suggesting that the latter be entertained by her in the kitchen instead of the parlour. Edgar's jealousy has probably been already aroused by Nelly's having just beforehand told him that Catherine 'was nearly heartbroken when [Heathcliff] ran off' and then guessed that 'his return will make a jubilee to her' (*WH*, p. 83), just as it will be further aroused when, like Nelly, he notices that the reunited childhood friends are 'too much absorbed in their mutual joy to suffer embarrassment' (*WH*, p. 85). Edgar's jealousy is then clearly stoked by Catherine's praise of Heathcliff later that evening, especially when she asserts that he is 'now worthy of any one's regard, and it would honour the first gentleman in the country to be his friend' (*WH*, p. 87). And though, as she says to Nelly, Catherine thinks that, 'instead of melting into tears', Edgar 'ought to have said it for [her], and been delighted from sympathy' (*WH*, p. 87), she seems quite unaware that her commendations of Heathcliff cannot but have added to Edgar's jealousy of him.[9] Moreover, the irony is that, while Catherine thinks she is being objective in alluding to Heathcliff's recent achievements in the outside world, in Edgar's jealous mind she is simply making it plain that she is in love with Heathcliff. Still, it is thanks to Catherine's reconciliation with him shortly afterwards that night that Edgar's jealousy seems to subside enough for him not only to allow Catherine to take Isabella with her on a walk to the Heights, but to tolerate Heathcliff's occasional visits to the Grange, whereby, it is important to note, Catherine herself 'deemed it judicious to moderate her expressions of pleasure in receiving him' (*WH*, p. 88).

Edgar's benign mood at this time might well have continued indefinitely but for his sudden discovery that Isabella has fallen in love with Heathcliff. From a psychological viewpoint it is then interesting to note how Edgar's jealousy, dormant as it appears to have been for the nonce, is instantly transmuted into a kind of paranoia in so far as he takes it for granted that Isabella's infatuation is the consequence of Heathcliff's 'deliberate designing' (*WH*, p. 89), whereas, it turns out, Heathcliff is himself utterly surprised to learn about Isabella's love for him in the first place. Edgar's paranoia is hardly less glaring when Nelly, rightly or wrongly, claims that he 'had sense to comprehend Heathcliff's disposition—to know that, though his exterior was altered, his mind was unchangeable, and unchanged' (*WH*, p. 89). How far such words betoken Edgar's attitude to Heathcliff rather than Nelly's own observations cannot be known for certain; but there can be little doubt that Edgar's reading of Heathcliff is based on continuous resentment and scarcely on actual evidence. Edgar's paranoia is especially conspicuous in Chapter 11 once he has been informed by Nelly of Catherine's 'being put out by Mr. Heathcliff's behaviour' and, more importantly, about 'the scene in the court' (*WH*, p. 100), namely, Heathcliff's amorous approach to Isabella. Thus, as Nelly recalls, Edgar exclaims: 'It is disgraceful that she should own him for a friend, and force his company on me!' (*WH*, p. 101). In fact, there is nothing to suggest that Catherine is doing any such thing to him. Again, simply on the basis of Nelly's report, Edgar presently asks Catherine why she is still in the kitchen 'after the language which has been held to you by that blackguard?', adding, 'because it is his ordinary talk, you think nothing of it—you are habituated to his baseness, and, perhaps, imagine I can get used to it too!' (*WH*, p. 101). Edgar's accusations are, of course, utterly unfair to Catherine, who has, in fact, only moments earlier been rebuking Heathcliff for his untoward conduct with Isabella. As she will presently apprise Edgar: 'I was defending you, and yours; and I wish Heathcliff may flog you sick, for daring to think an evil thought of me!' (*WH*, p. 102). It is thus obvious that Catherine's resentment towards Edgar turns on his picking up the wrong end of the stick and, as she mistakenly supposes, on his having eavesdropped on her altercation with Heathcliff.

Nevertheless, it is because Catherine all but condemns Edgar as a man on that occasion, first, by taunting him for his cowardly dependence on servants to help him to get rid of Heathcliff, and then by humiliating him with derogatory animal comparisons, that the reader may seriously begin to wonder about her true feelings for him. Furthermore, all this, together with the fact that Catherine has also told Edgar that Heathcliff is far too manly to strike him, cannot but have encouraged the latter to conclude that she is more drawn to himself than to her husband. This, in turn, explains why Heathcliff, having subsequently heard of Catherine's illness, shows a dogged determination to visit her at the Heights, confident as he is by now that she loves him and is even pining for him. Indeed, such is Heathcliff's confidence in this respect that, in answer to Nelly's attempt to discourage him from paying any such visit both by speaking of the radical change in Catherine's character and appearance and by averring that Edgar 'will only sustain his affection hereafter by the remembrance of what she once was, by common humanity, and a sense of duty!' (*WH*, p. 130), he belittles the quality of Edgar's love by saying: 'But do you imagine that I shall leave Catherine to his *duty* and *humanity*? and can you compare my feelings respecting Catherine, to his?' (*WH*, p. 131). Much the same arrogance can be felt in Heathcliff's other utterances in the same context, particularly his claiming that 'for every thought she spends on Linton, she spends a thousand on me' (*WH*, p. 131); or that '[i]f [Edgar] loved with all the powers of his puny being, he couldn't love as much in eighty years, as I could in a day' (*WH*, p. 132); or, again, that it is 'not in [Edgar] to be loved like me, how can she love in him what he has not?' (*WH*, p. 132).[10] Whether or not some such claims are in any way founded on conversations Heathcliff has been having in private with Catherine since his return to Gimmerton cannot, of course, be known or proved. All the same, while the reader may be absolutely convinced of the intensity of Heathcliff's love for Catherine, there is comparatively little evidence to indicate that Catherine herself reciprocates his feelings for her in quite the same degree, let alone in kind.

Although there are passages in the novel that may well be—and have been—regarded as attestations of Catherine's love for Heathcliff, especially those to be found in Chapter 9, it is, nevertheless, necessary to point out that, after her five-week sojourn with the Lintons, such passages almost invariably occur in contexts of her relationship with Edgar. It is true that some of Catherine's statements about Edgar before their marriage as well as Nelly's comments on Catherine's early months as his bride may be deemed evidence enough to indicate that she does not really love him. Indeed, this seems amply confirmed by the vicious language with which, in Chapter 11, she insults him in the Grange kitchen in Heathcliff's presence. Yet despite the fact that Catherine is a difficult and moody wife, there is much to suggest that she is none the less heavily dependent on Edgar for his love and support of her. Thus we note how anxiously disconcerted she is over Edgar's neglect of her during the time she has been sequestered in her bedroom. We gather this easily enough when, having momentarily thought of committing suicide, she says this in Nelly's presence: 'No, I'll not die—he'd be glad—he does not love me at all—he would never miss me!' (*WH*, p. 106); or when she asks Nelly: 'What is that apathetic being doing? [...] Has he fallen into a lethargy, or is he dead?' (*WH*, p. 106); or, again, when, informed by Nelly that Edgar is 'continually among his books' and clearly afraid that he may have thereby lost interest in her, she questions Nelly as follows: 'Are you speaking the truth about him now? Take care. Is he actually so utterly indifferent for my life?' (*WH*, p. 107). Shortly afterwards, it is interesting to read Catherine's account of the blackout she underwent soon after entering her bedroom. For when she tells of 'the abyss where [she] grovelled' through imagining that, at the age of twelve, she had been 'wrenched from the Heights' and from her 'all in all, as Heathcliff was at that time' and 'converted at a stroke' into 'the wife of a stranger' (*WH*, p. 111), namely, Edgar, it is important to remember that she makes only three references to Heathcliff throughout this context, and in each case merely as a childhood friend.[11] The significance of this is quite apparent when, to Edgar's having shortly afterwards asked her: 'Am I nothing to you, any more? Do you love that wretch, Heath—', Catherine abruptly stops him with these words: 'Hush! [...] Hush, this moment! You mention that name and I end the matter, instantly, by a spring from the window!' (*WH*, p. 113). It is perhaps tempting to interpret that utterance as an expression of her love for Heathcliff. But is it? Are those words not rather testimony to her annoyance with Edgar for obstinately refusing to accept that her fondness for Heathcliff is as a friend, and not as the lover he presumes her to look upon? One has already sensed such annoyance more particularly when, to Edgar's having asked her: 'Will you give up Heathcliff hereafter, or will you give up me?', she instantly replies: 'I require to be let alone! [...] I demand it!' (*WH*, pp. 104-105).[12] Considered from a slightly different angle, though, such words might also be a sign that she is annoyed with herself for being quite unable to decide on the true nature of her relationship with Heathcliff, while still intent on maintaining the comfort of being in an ongoing state of indecision with respect to the two men in her life.

At this juncture, it would be useful to go back over Catherine's relationship with Edgar, starting from the time she has returned home after her five-week sojourn with the Lintons. To begin with, it is clear by then that Edgar has gained the edge over Heathcliff as regards birth, personal appearance, intellect and material prospects. We also note that Catherine takes initiatives to encourage Edgar's courtship of her very soon afterwards, at the same time as she makes light of Heathcliff's attempts to get her to revive their formerly affectionate friendship.[13] Still, Catherine's delaying her marriage to Edgar until more than three years later might suggest that she has been hoping for Heathcliff to return sometime during the interim. Catherine's ability to go through with the marriage in the end may, in any case, have had to do with little more than her realization that she had practically no alternative to fall back on as a woman. Further, given her very temperamental nature as well as her severely limited experience of the opposite sex, it is hardly surprising that, in the earliest stage of her marriage, Catherine should be somewhat selfishly eccentric. Thus, if at first, as the observant Nelly recalls, Catherine 'seemed almost over fond of Mr. Linton' (*WH*, p. 81), it soon becomes apparent that she is much more concerned to be loved by Edgar than to show him love.[14] This does not, however, mean that Catherine does not love Edgar; on the contrary, as we have seen above, her seemingly heavy dependence on him is in itself an expression of love. That is why it is a mistake to assume her enthusiastic reception of the newly returned Heathcliff to be evidence that she has stopped loving Edgar. This is to some extent confirmed by our assumption that the second Catherine is conceived on the very night of Heathcliff's return. We may also point to episodes during the time Catherine is convalescing from her brain fever when she demonstrates her affection for Edgar, as, for example, when, in answer to his tender words to her, she says: 'Next spring you'll long again to have me under this roof, and you'll look back and think you were happy to-day' (*WH*, p. 118). And if Catherine at times seems quite irritated with Edgar for trying to distract her from the burdens of convalescence, there is no reason for us to think that such irritation has anything to do with a fretful longing on her part for Heathcliff.[15] That Heathcliff seems, in fact, to be hardly in her thoughts at this time is partly suggested by the comparative slowness with which she mentally registers the authorship of the note he has written to her by way of preparing her for their meeting in Chapter 15. It is, moreover, worth remembering that Catherine's rather rambling demonstrations of love for Heathcliff at their final tryst are none the less made at a time when her mind is evidently still somewhat unbalanced.[16]

But though commonly considered perhaps the strongest evidence of their mutual love, this final tryst still raises questions as to the quality of Heathcliff's attachment to Catherine, and the more so as, amid the sometimes aggressive resentment with which he now and again addresses her, he seems practically unconcerned about the effect that such talk is having on her precarious state of health, and is indeed about to have with fatal consequences.[17] Moreover, the fact that Heathcliff will be presently described by Nelly 'placing the lifeless-looking form in [Edgar's] arms' (*WH*, p. 143) seems almost symbolic of the idea that it is Edgar, not Heathcliff, who is ultimately responsible for Catherine's welfare. It is through this gesture that the reader may be forcibly reminded of the disparaging language with which Heathcliff has earlier dismissed Edgar's capacity to love Catherine, especially in comparison with his own. And whereas there can be no uncertainty as to the intensity and durability of Heathcliff's devotion to Catherine, it is by and large an essentially mental phenomenon, signifying next to nothing of the remarkable selflessness that Edgar exhibits not only in the early stages of his marriage to Catherine, but, more especially, when he is tending her during her brain fever and in its aftermath.[18] In this connection, Heathcliff's dismissal of Edgar as a lover is scarcely different in kind from, say, the presumptuous words he utters to young Cathy in reply to her fearing for her father in his probable anxiety over her prolonged absence from the Grange: 'Not he! He'll think you are tired of waiting on him, and run off, for a little amusement' (*WH*, p. 242). Such statements confirm, as much as similar ones he makes about other characters, how much Heathcliff is prone to attribute to Edgar attitudes quite opposite to those that may be rather more objectively gleaned from Nelly's narrative. But if, like all the other characters in the novel, Edgar has his failings and his shortcomings, we have also seen that, far from lacking the capacity to love Catherine, as Heathcliff would have us believe, he demonstrates that capacity with a maturity that Heathcliff himself seldom gives signs of possessing, whether in word or in action. And though it may be justly said that, unlike Heathcliff, Edgar is scarcely memorable for his personality or for his verbal skills, he remains none the less an interesting figure not merely for the affection variously bestowed on him by Cathy, Isabella, Linton Heathcliff and Nelly Dean, and even by Catherine herself, but, more importantly, for those inconsistencies in his talk and behaviour which, betokening the somewhat uneasy coexistence of a phlegmatic temperament with a strongly emotional disposition in his genteel make-up, admirably exemplify the essential realism of his presentation.[19]

Brontë Studies, 42/4 (2017)

Notes

1 For a striking example of this view of Heathcliff and Catherine (as advocated by the actor Alistair McGowan in the television programme), see '*Wuthering Heights*', in *BBC The Big Read. Book of Books*, eds. Mark Harrison and Hannah Beckerman (London: Dorling Kindersley, 2003), pp. 54-55. For quotations from the novel, see Emily Brontë, *Wuthering Heights*, eds. Ian Jack and Patsy Stoneman (Oxford: Oxford University Press, 1998). For the sake of convenience, the first Catherine will be referred to as 'Catherine', the second as 'Cathy'.

2 One such effect memorably occurs when Joseph threatens to report Heathcliff to Edgar as local magistrate for the near fatal injuries sustained by Hindley in Chapter 17. See *Wuthering Heights*, p. 158.

3 Although Edgar Linton has been discussed in most books and articles about *Wuthering Heights*, with references being commonly made to his strengths and weaknesses of character, especially with regard to his love for Catherine, I have come across only one article devoted entirely to him, namely, Joy Ellis McLemore, 'Edgar Linton: Master of Thrushcross Grange', *RE Artes Liberales*, 8 (1981), 13-26.

4 See *Wuthering Heights*, pp. 49-50, 84.

5 Edgar's reclusiveness may be excused in some measure if we recall that, when informing Lockwood of Isabella's early death, Nelly says that 'she and Edgar both lacked the ruddy health that you will generally meet in these parts' (*WH*, pp. 168-169).

6 See *Wuthering Heights*, p. 87.

7   Edgar's prevarications to Cathy about Linton Heathcliff, though criticized by her after she has discovered the latter at the Heights, may be thought pardonable for being little more than the kind of white lies by which a parent sometimes feels obliged to assuage a child's anxiety.

8   Edgar's domineering streak, though seemingly uncharacteristic, is realistically confirmed by his altercation with Nelly Dean in Chapter 12 and by his heavy-handed treatment of Joseph in Chapter 19. See *Wuthering Heights*, pp. 113, 179.

9   Catherine's praise for Heathcliff in this context is, of course, in markedly ironic contrast to the very negative images of him with which she will try to put Isabella off her infatuation with him. See *Wuthering Heights*, pp. 90-91.

10 For other similar claims on Heathcliff's part, see also *Wuthering Heights*, pp. 131, 132, 135.

11 See also *Wuthering Heights*, pp. 108, 112-113.

12 It is useful here to recall Catherine's having said this to Nelly only moments beforehand: 'Well, if I cannot keep Heathcliff for my friend—if Edgar will be mean and jealous—I'll try to break their hearts by breaking my own' (*WH*, p. 104). See also *Wuthering Heights*, p. 84.

13 For references to Edgar's courtship visits to the Heights, see also *Wuthering Heights*, pp. 30, 77.

14 This is amply suggested when Catherine somewhat flippantly says this to Nelly: 'I have such faith in Linton's love that I

believe I might kill him, and he wouldn't wish to retaliate' (*WH*, p. 87).

15 For other examples of Catherine's impatience with Edgar during her convalescence, see *Wuthering Heights*, pp. 119, 138.

16 In this connection, the fact that Catherine does not mention Heathcliff by name on her deathbed is probably the root cause of his incurable mental illness. See *Wuthering Heights*, p. 147. See also Graeme Tytler, 'Heathcliff's Monomania: An Anachronism in *Wuthering Heights*', *Brontë Society Transactions*, 20/6 (1992), 331-343.

17 Here we may be reminded of Heathcliff's very aggressive utterances to Catherine in Chapter 11. See especially *Wuthering Heights*, p. 100.

18 See especially *Wuthering Heights*, pp. 116-119.

19 For evidence of the affection of all these characters for Edgar, see *Wuthering Heights*, pp. 86-87, 94-95, 120, 122, 150, 152, 161, 171, 180, 181, 202-203, 210, 214-215, 231, 234, 242, 243. Here it is interesting to note how Edgar's handsomeness, coveted as it is by Heathcliff in his boyhood and constituting one of the main reasons why Catherine wishes to marry him, is clearly also admired not only by Linton Heathcliff, who, on his way to the Heights to meet his father for the first time, asks Nelly if he is 'as young and handsome as uncle' (*WH*, p. 181), but also by Lockwood, who, having seen Edgar's portrait painting, reflects as follows: 'I did not marvel how Catherine Earnshaw could forget her first friend for such an individual. I marvelled much how he, with a mind to correspond with his person, could fancy my idea of Catherine Earnshaw' (*WH*, p. 58).

Masters and Servants in *Wuthering Heights*

*W**uthering Heights** is exceptional among great works of fiction for its comprehensive delineation of the relationship between masters and servants.[1] Such relationships constitute a prominent aspect of an essentially hierarchical, class-conscious community in late eighteenth-century England, reflecting in some measure the social differences between the landed gentry and the yeomanry through the two households depicted in rural Yorkshire. Whether or not Emily Brontë's masters and servants reflect the England of, say, the 1830s and 1840s rather better than the England of the late eighteenth century, is perhaps a question that might well be asked, although it is one that appears to have been scarcely raised by any Brontë scholar hitherto. There is, nevertheless, a certain timelessness about the author's treatment of this subject, partly because it shows little of the perfunctoriness that generally colours relations between masters and servants in nineteenth-century fiction.[2] This may be noted, for example, through the ways in which the characters portrayed as masters or mistresses tell us something about themselves by the uses or abuses of the power they exert over others. Although it is plain from the narrative that the servants of both households, so long as they remain, or wish to remain, in service, are ultimately bound to submit to their employers, it is just as plain that no master or mistress can exercise authority effectively without the co-operation of their servants. And it is on the basis of the latter argument that much of the interest of the action turns on the various freedoms that servants enjoy within the contexts of domination to which they are subject. Accordingly, whereas there is a certain predictability about the behaviour of Emily Brontë's masters and mistresses, there is a complexity about her servants that makes their conduct especially worthy of discussion. Indeed, it is by virtue of that very complexity that the author puts the question of masters and servants, as it were, on the operating table, dealing with it not merely as a matter of economics but as a means of adding to our understanding of human nature. In other words, she invites us to consider, and perhaps even to question, a time-honoured system whose workings she astutely takes apart and lays bare for us.

The reader of *Wuthering Heights* is made continually aware of the existence of servants in both households through references to the sundry tasks they perform in the house, in the grounds, on the farm, and in other areas in or near Gimmerton, and even through references to their attendance at church or chapel, presence at a funeral, participation in the leisure pursuits of their superiors, and so on. Conspicuous among such references are those made by Nelly Dean both to the housework she does and to the tasks she delegates to other servants, as if she were eager to impress upon Lockwood the idea of the prestige as well as the seriousness of her role as housekeeper. Nor does Nelly hesitate to suggest that, though generally liked and respected by her staff, she is nevertheless a tough disciplinarian, as may be gathered from her berating her subordinates at the slightest provocation—a practice that forcibly reminds us of her equally important role as nurse or nanny to Hindley, Catherine, Heathcliff, Hareton and Cathy. In this connection, it is noteworthy how much power some servants, Nelly Dean and Joseph in particular, are vested with in the upbringing of the children under their care. Joseph, for example, as well as being chiefly responsible for instructing them in religious doctrine, is now and then described as thrashing Heathcliff or boxing Catherine's ears for their respective misdemeanours. Accordingly, the idea that Joseph should also be said to have 'regularly grumbled out a long string of tales against Heathcliff and Catherine' (*WH*, p. 40) to Mr. Earnshaw and to have 'encouraged [the latter] to regard Hindley as a reprobate' (*WH*, p. 40) is scarcely less surprising than that he should report Catherine and Heathcliff for their bad behaviour to Hindley when he is master of the Heights.[3]

In view of Joseph's delegated authority over the children at the Heights, to say nothing of the supposed authority with which he is understood to 'hector over tenants and labourers' (*WH*, p. 65), it is easy to understand why this elderly servant should be treated by Mr. Earnshaw as a kind of confidant, mainly with respect to religion and education. Not that this is by any means unusual in a novel where almost all the main characters come to confide in Nelly Dean about their private affairs or their troubles. Reliance on servants for help in matters that have little to do with their domestic duties ranges from their being used as messengers for the most trivial purposes to their being resorted to for help in various household crises. One notable example of such reliance is suggested when, in her letter to Nelly Dean, Isabella declares that, being unable to write to Edgar or Catherine about her elopement, she 'must write to somebody, and the only choice left me is you' (*WH*, p. 136). Nor should we forget that the bulk of the narrative is made possible by the fact that Lockwood, in order to offset his loneliness while nursing a bad cold at Thrushcross Grange, obliges Nelly to keep him company and entertain him with 'Heathcliff's history' (*WH*, p. 60). This and other forms of dependency help to explain why some servants are inclined to give their superiors advice of all kinds. It is true that, forced as they are now and again into subservience against their will, both Joseph and Nelly find their advice sometimes ignored or pooh-poohed. Yet when Nelly's advice is acted on, it is almost always done so with unfortunate consequences. Thus we may think of the apple-sauce tureen incident in Chapter 7 as being partly the consequence of the counsel she has only shortly beforehand given to Heathcliff about improving his physical appearance, taken in conjunction with her disparaging comments on Hindley and Edgar. Similarly mistaken are Nelly's attempts to encourage Isabella to renounce her love for Heathcliff, and even her questioning, in Isabella's very presence, whether Edgar would approve of him as a husband, for it is thus that she unwittingly seals Isabella's relationship with Heathcliff. Almost certainly, the main reason for the elopement is the showdown between Heathcliff and Edgar, as induced by Nelly's having both informed and advised Edgar about Heathcliff's amorous advances to Isabella and his subsequent quarrel with Catherine.

What has just been said about Nelly Dean is a reminder of the extent to which servants influence events in the novel, and even shape its plot. To take two early instances: it is partly owing to Joseph's dilatoriness in fetching wine from the cellar that Lockwood gets into a fight with the dogs in Chapter 1, just as it is partly owing to Joseph's setting the dogs on Lockwood at the end of Chapter 2 that Lockwood spends the night in the oak-panelled room. Again, there is little doubt that Lockwood's second visit to the Heights is prompted principally by his finding a maid putting out his study fire at the Grange. But even a remark made casually by a servant can have important consequences for the plot. Thus Cathy's first encounter with Hareton is primarily due to the fact that 'one of the [Grange] maids mentioning the Fairy Cave, quite turned her head with a desire to fulfil this project; [...]' (*WH*, pp. 189-190). Servants are also behind a good many of the reports and rumours that make up parts of Nelly Dean's narrative. Thus Nelly hears of Hareton's birth and the concomitant behaviour of his parents from the girl who brings breakfasts to her and others working in a hayfield; of Hindley's troubled relations with Heathcliff, shortly after the latter's return to Gimmerton, from Joseph; of Linton Heathcliff's conduct at the Heights from his father's (unnamed) housekeeper; of Cathy's way of life there under Heathcliff's guardianship from Zillah, prefacing her account, significantly enough, by saying, 'otherwise I should hardly know who was dead, and who living' (*WH*, p. 292). That servants are much given to gossip both loyal and disloyal is evident when, despite Nelly's refusal to tell him where Isabella lives in the South, Heathcliff nevertheless 'discovered, through some of the other servants, both her place of residence and the existence of the child' (*WH*, p. 182). By the same token, when Cathy inadvertently informs the Heights housekeeper about her cousin Linton, Nelly has 'no doubt of Linton's approaching arrival [...] being reported to Mr. Heathcliff; ...' (*WH*, p. 195); a certainty on Nelly's part that proves to have been well founded when Joseph unexpectedly turns up at the Grange to fetch the newly-arrived Linton Heathcliff for his father. Perhaps that is why, knowing as he does that, in their proclivity for gossip, some servants even go so far as to threaten to report their superiors to the law, Heathcliff makes sure that Joseph and Zillah are out of the way at the time he marries Linton to Cathy.

The propensity of servants to talk to outsiders about the goings-on in their own households may be seen as an expression of the insubordination they are liable to show towards their superiors. There are, for example, occasions when Joseph is surly or defiant, slack or sardonic, in his attitude and demeanour towards those who are not his employers—Lockwood, Catherine, Edgar, Isabella, Cathy and Linton Heathcliff. He is sometimes even outspoken to his own master, as we note when, together with the curate, he 'reprimanded [Hindley's] carelessness when [Catherine and Heathcliff] absented themselves [from church on Sundays]' (*WH*, p. 44). Nelly Dean herself, as well as now and then ignoring their requests or showing a lack of concern for them, can be downright disrespectful towards her superiors. Thus apart from directing outbursts of anger against those belonging to other households, such as Heathcliff and his son Linton for trapping her and Cathy at the Heights, Nelly scolds her master Hindley (in Chapter 9) for his mistreatment of Hareton and is, we are told later, 'many a time' spoken to 'sternly' by Edgar at the Grange for her 'pertness' (*WH*, p. 91) to Catherine. But Edgar, too, no less than Catherine, is subject not only to Nelly's defiance but also to her disobedience, notable instances of which latter occur during the time she is looking after Cathy. Although some acts of disobedience on the part of servants may be adjudged reasonable, as when Nelly ignores Hindley's instruction to keep Catherine and Heathcliff locked out for the night, it is nevertheless interesting to note how ready servants are to disobey their superiors when opportunity permits. There is, for example, the unconscionable disobedience of the servants which Isabella has to put up with at the Grange and which her son Linton is later to suffer at the Heights. Lockwood's own subjection to the vagaries of domestics in both households and, more particularly, to the domination of his housekeeper Nelly Dean (as comically exemplified by her dictating the hours when he may dine) is doubtless intended as a symbolic caricature of the conflicts that so often arise in the novel between masters and servants.

Such conflicts seem due, at least in Nelly's case, partly to her finding herself obliged to be subservient to those to whom she was either once an equal or over whom she had some power at one time, and partly to an awareness shared by other servants, namely, that the masters or mistresses served evince serious limitations of one kind or another. Thus we think of Hindley as a tyrannical, incompetent master; of Heathcliff as someone who, apart from being 'a cruel hard landlord to his tenants; […]' (*WH*, p. 196), is greatly feared as a master by all his servants, including the usually fearless Joseph; and of Catherine as a 'difficult' mistress, whose domination of people at the Grange extends even to allowing Isabella to 'be nothing in the house' (*WH*, p. 101). Moreover, in their strong desire to domineer over other people, each of these three characters seems beset by what might be termed a 'master complex'. Thus in her diary Catherine tells of Hindley's bid to intimidate her and Heathcliff by saying, 'You forget you have a master here' (*WH*, p. 19), and, on account of the fateful Sunday evening visit to the Grange, his swearing that he 'will reduce [Heathcliff] to his right place' (*WH*, p. 20). Heathcliff's 'master complex' has more psychotic dimensions than Hindley's, as we realize when he gloatingly envisages his son's eventual power over the Linton family: 'I want the triumph of seeing *my* descendant fairly lord of their estates; my child hiring their children, to till their fathers' lands for wages—' (*WH*, p. 208). Catherine's 'master complex' is already manifest in childhood inasmuch as she 'liked, exceedingly, to act the little mistress; using her hands freely, and commanding her companions' (*WH*, p. 40). It is also a perceptibly class-conscious one, as we see when, reprimanding Nelly for doing housework in the presence of herself and Edgar, she says: 'When company are in the house, servants don't commence scouring and cleaning in the room where they are!' (*WH*, p. 70). That Catherine's 'master complex' is especially conspicuous after she has returned from her second convalescence at the Grange is evident both from her refusing to speak to Nelly 'save in the relation of a mere servant' and from her also putting Joseph 'under a ban' for lecturing her 'as if she were a little girl' because, as Nelly adds, she 'esteemed herself a woman, and our mistress [...]' (*WH*, p. 88). Noteworthy, too, in this respect is Catherine's angry response to Nelly's having loudly voiced her objections to Heathcliff's amorous advances to Isabella: 'To hear you, people might think *you* were the mistress! [...] You want setting down in your right place!' (*WH*, p. 111). At the other end of the spectrum, however, are Mr. Earnshaw and Edgar Linton, who, though spoken of respectfully and affectionately by Nelly, come across as too weak with, or too trusting of, their subordinates to be deemed exemplary masters.

If the tyrannical or ungracious or unreasonable conduct of a master or mistress may be considered to be a factor underlying a servant's insubordination, it is quite another question whether servants should take advantage of kindly superiors. Although, for example, Nelly Dean's sundry acts of deceit against Edgar Linton are in large part a consequence of his extreme reliance on her, the reader may still wonder why Nelly is not content to be an obedient servant by simply confining herself to her official duties. No doubt, Nelly's reluctance to be obedient has much to do with her character. Consider, for example, several episodes in which she betrays her inherently violent disposition, whether through her general vindictiveness or through her rough treatment of some of the main characters, especially as youngsters. Consider, too, how, for all her skills as an observant and percipient narrator, Nelly betrays her limited intelligence not only through her propensity to be slow-witted, uncomprehending, forgetful and self-contradictory, but through the presumptuousness and fallaciousness of some of her ideas and arguments.[4] Much more important, however, are the various references that Nelly makes throughout her narrative to her lies, prevarications, false promises, secretiveness, evasiveness and other forms of dishonesty, all of which amply underline her lack of moral integrity. This is not to suggest that Nelly has no sense of the difference between right and wrong but, rather, that she regards right and wrong as relative, not absolute, concepts; that is to say, concepts which she considers right or wrong according to the particular circumstances she finds herself in. This may in turn account for her somewhat fuzzy notions about truth. For example, when, on arriving at the Heights in response to Isabella's letter, she assures Heathcliff that she has brought nothing for his wife, we note that, despite supplementing that detail with the words 'thinking it best to speak the truth at once' (*WH*, p. 147), she goes on to give Isabella an utterly garbled, if well-intended, version of Edgar's actual message to her. It may also account for the hypocrisy with which Nelly will give Edgar the impression of being 'a faithful servant' (*WH*, p. 128), even while continuing to betray him. That is why it is especially during the tryst between the two principal lovers that the reader does well to recall that, in reaction to Heathcliff's earlier insistence that she arrange such a meeting for him, Nelly 'protested against playing that treacherous part in [her] employer's house' (*WH*, p. 153). It is, therefore, little wonder that Nelly seems scarcely able to understand the staunch loyalty which, for instance, Hareton consistently shows to Heathcliff, even beyond the latter's death.

At this juncture it might be asked whether Nelly's moral and mental shortcomings do not in some way derive from her role and function as a servant. It is interesting to note that, although she has more or less drifted into service, she seems never to have wished to be anything but a servant, and then only at the Heights or at the Grange. That Nelly might be said (like Joseph) to have a sort of vocation as a domestic is evident not only from her recurrent and respectful use of phrases entailing 'master' or 'mistress' and related terms such as 'my young lady', but from her apparent preference to live vicariously through her employers rather than to lead a life of her own, let alone cherish ambitions of any kind.[5] This is partly implicit in the passivity informing her attitudes to her employers. For example, having told Lockwood that all the servants at the Heights except herself and

Joseph gave notice on account of Hindley's 'tyrannical and evil conduct', she somewhat blandly rationalizes her decision to stay on by declaring that, having been his 'foster sister', she 'excused his behaviour more readily than a stranger would' (*WH*, p. 65). Again, in spite of refusing at first to accompany Catherine to the Grange on her marriage to Edgar, but then finding herself compelled to do so by Hindley, she rationalizes her acceptance as follows: 'And so, I had but one choice left, to do as I was ordered—' (*WH*, p. 89).[6] Such passivity, unmistakable as it is for being expressed here in the guise of a fallacy, may, however, be thought hardly to square with the bold initiatives that Nelly takes in disregard of her employers' expectations. At the same time, Nelly seems to be well aware that the freedoms she permits herself are none the less exercised within, even determined by, the safe and secure confines of her particular employment. This may explain why, in anxious moments with her superiors, Nelly is quick to fall back on her role as servant, and even to take shelter in it. For example, when to her utter dismay she hears Cathy telling her father about her cousin Linton at the Heights, she recalls that, though 'not altogether sorry', she thought 'the burden of directing and warning would be more efficiently borne by [Edgar] than [herself]' (*WH*, pp. 221-222). Similarly, we note how, having failed with her threatening language to make the newly-wed Linton direct her to Cathy's room in the Heights, she tries to win him round by self-pityingly referring to herself as 'an elderly woman, and a servant merely' (*WH*, p. 280).

It may, then, be deduced from the words just quoted that one reason why Nelly gives scope to her character defects is that she (perhaps unconsciously) considers her social status too abject to bother herself unduly with questions of morality. Such an apparent lack of concern on her part seems confirmed by the fact that even her presentation as a Christian who relies heavily on the Bible for advice to pass on to her superiors does little, if anything, to deter her from her malpractices. In this connection, it is well to recollect here that two servants notable for their religiosity and their chapel-going, namely, Joseph and Zillah, come across as figures for whom morality is at best scarcely distinguishable from respectability. Certainly it would appear that Joseph has come to regard his efficiency, reliability and loyalty as a servant over many years as an excuse for him to overlook the basic principles of morality through his inveterate cantankerousness, maliciousness and misanthropy. Yet even for the other servants portrayed in the novel morality seems to have little relevance to their day-to-day existence. This is suggested to some extent in the mercenary nature not only of their attitudes to service in such utterances as 'I was never hired to serve you' (*WH*, p. 195) or '[t]o mind your son is not my business' (*WH*, p. 269), but also of their talk about money and wages. Perhaps nowhere in the narrative, however, is this more pronounced than it is in Zillah, who is presented, appropriately enough, as a shallow, vindictive woman much given to wrong-headed ideas, as we see especially in her conversation with Nelly Dean in Chapter 30. One thinks particularly of the way in which, having predicted a bleak future for Cathy with a characteristic fallacy, she goes on to say this to her interlocutor: 'She's as poor as you or I—poorer, I'll be bound, you're saving—and I'm doing my little all, that road' (*WH*, p. 295). Such words clearly hint at Zillah's inherently self-seeking attitude to her role as Heathcliff's housekeeper—an attitude well illustrated when, in his complaint to Cathy about the slackness of the Heights servants during his father's absence, Linton tells of Zillah's 'constantly gadding off to Gimmerton' (*WH*, p. 237). But practised as they are safely behind her master's back, such acts of disloyalty none the less indirectly bespeak a fear of Heathcliff deep enough to prevent her from defying him with any open act of disobedience, even if that act were morally justifiable. That is why there is something contemptible about the motives she gives for declining to help Cathy with the ailing Linton, to wit, 'for fear of being moved to interfere' and, more especially, as she further explains to Nelly Dean, 'I didn't wish to lose my place, you know!' (*WH*, p. 293).

How far innate character or the hierarchical system is to blame for the unethical demeanour and attitude of the servants discussed above is a question that perhaps can only be answered tentatively. It is tempting, if not altogether justifiable, to conclude from evidence shown hitherto that being a servant brings out the worst in a human being, and that domestic service is likely to appeal most of all to the morally deficient. No doubt, the relationship between servant and employer is, by its very nature, seldom entirely disinterested or honourable. This idea is ironically confirmed by the presentation of a very minor figure in the novel, the groom Michael, through his willingness to betray his master Edgar Linton in order to be rewarded by Cathy with 'books and pictures' (*WH*, p. 247) for enabling her to make her illicit journeys to the Heights. Yet at the same time as servants are liable to be disloyal to their employers, they cannot but play an important part in the maintenance of a household that is governed by a tyrannical head. Zillah, as we have already seen, is a striking case in point in that her outward obedience of Heathcliff, motivated as it is solely by fear, helps to preserve a fundamentally undesirable system of domination. Furthermore, we see how by working in a well-ordered household, some servants may come to emulate the outlook of their masters and—as we may, for example, surmise from the vicious language with which Mr. Linton's servant Robert addresses young Heathcliff in Chapter 6—thereby learn to exert over others the dominance to which they themselves have become habituated.[7]

Another drawback of servants is that they tend to foster laziness and selfishness in their masters and mistresses, and, as we see in Isabella's case, to make them almost helpless.[8] It is, accordingly, not without significance that Lockwood's somewhat unsympathetic presentation derives in some measure from his having apparently long taken it for granted that servants are not only a necessary part of everyday life but an indispensable luxury. This is ironically borne out when, for example, instead of finding out for himself on his return to the North how to get to Gimmerton, he simply 'directed [his] servant to inquire the way to the village' (*WH*, p. 305). Such a trifling use of a servant is perhaps enough of itself to indicate that, rather like Hindley and Heathcliff, Lockwood suffers from a 'master complex', and one which, towards the end of his narrative, may have been enhanced both by memories of the insubordination he has had to endure from servants at the Heights and the Grange, and by his consciousness that he is after all only a tenant.[9] Perhaps for that reason there is nothing quite so comical (among several other comical instances suggestive of his complex) as the occasion when, having quite unexpectedly turned up at the Grange in September 1802, he answers the old woman, who has just introduced herself as the person keeping the house, with this pompous reply: 'Well, I'm Mr. Lockwood, the master' (*WH*, p. 306).

In the light of the foregoing, it seems therefore utterly appropriate that, having been taken into the Heights on his second visit there by 'a young man, without coat, and shouldering a pitchfork' (*WH*, p. 8), and then, shortly afterwards, noticed that the latter has put on 'a decidedly shabby upper garment' and (in Cathy's presence) is staring down hard at him in front of the fire, Lockwood should begin to 'doubt whether he were a servant or not'. Thus having at first inferred from his rough appearance and attire that he is one, he goes on to make this observation: '[…] still his bearing was free, almost haughty, and showed none of a domestic's assiduity in attending on the lady of the house' (*WH*, p. 10). As well as betraying Lockwood's deeply ingrained sense of social hierarchy, this passage is notable for foreshadowing the idea that, notwithstanding Nelly's patronizing image of him as someone living 'in his own house as a servant deprived of the advantage of wages' (*WH*, p. 187), Hareton is clearly reluctant to see himself as a servant in the usual acceptation of that term.[10] Something of this is hinted at in the episode (in Chapter 18) when, already incensed by Cathy's assumption that, since he is not Heathcliff's son, he must therefore be a servant, and then, by dint of that assumption, ordered by her to fetch her horse, Hareton retorts: 'I'll see thee damned, before I be *thy* servant!' (*WH*, p. 194). This is not to imply that Hareton is unwilling to do jobs usually done by servants. Thus, quite apart from the fact that he is a diligent and conscientious farm worker with hands, as Lockwood squeamishly observes, 'embrowned like those of a common labourer' (*WH*, p. 10), we see how, unlike the typical servant in the novel that is inclined to count the cost of services he or she renders, Hareton not only brings Cathy's pony round to her presently, but even offers her a 'terrier whelp' to boot. And what has just been said of Hareton seems to be also true of Cathy, as we may gather from the dialogue that Lockwood overhears in 'the house' between herself and Heathcliff in Chapter 3. Thus to Heathcliff's complaint to her for being 'at [her] idle tricks again', that is, 'reading a book' by the light of the fire; his assertion that '[t]he rest of them do earn their bread' but that she 'live[s] on [his] charity'; and then his ordering her to 'put [her] trash away, and find something to do', Cathy replies: 'I'll put my trash away, because you can make me, if I refuse, [...]. But I'll not do anything, though you should swear your tongue out, except what I please!' (*WH*, pp. 28-29). Yet expressive as those words are of a kind of desperate egotism, Cathy's stubborn refusal to be Heathcliff's servant belies what Nelly is later to reveal, that is, Cathy's capacity (which she has in common with Hareton) to offer all kinds of selfless and disinterested services to others, especially to her father and to Linton Heathcliff.

It is, then, surely no coincidence that Cathy's relationship with Hareton should end happily at a time when, despite the latter's change of status from farmhand to 'the lawful master' (*WH*, p.

335) of Wuthering Heights, as skilfully foreshadowed in Chapter 1 when Lockwood notices 'Hareton Earnshaw' carved above 'the principal door' (*WH*, p. 2) of the building, the old hierarchical system as practised hitherto at the Heights and the Grange seems to be in marked abeyance. This is ironically underlined, first, when asked by Lockwood on his return to the Grange whether she is the housekeeper, the 'dame' (who, significantly enough, is smoking a pipe) replies: 'Eea, Aw keep th' hahse' (*WH*, p. 306), as if puzzled by his particular designation of her; and, soon afterwards, when, on ordering her to get the place ready for him, Lockwood observes her reactions as follows: 'She seemed willing to do her best; though she thrust the hearth-brush into the grates in mistake for the poker, and mal-appropriated several other articles of her craft; […]' (*WH*, p. 306). Certainly, as a sort of ironic dig at the scrupulously house-proud Nelly Dean, that detail seems symbolically to mark the dawn of an era in which, thanks to a youthful master who has known, perhaps better than any of his predecessors, what it is to be a servant in all but name, the relationship between masters and servants promises to become more wholesome than it is generally shown to have been so far in the narrative. Still, there are moments when relations between Nelly Dean and some of the main characters seem to evoke the charm that biographers have conveyed to us as to the friendship that Emily Brontë and her family enjoyed at Haworth Parsonage with their housekeeper Tabitha Aykroyd.[11] Perhaps it is with this knowledge in mind that some readers might be readily disposed to look upon Nelly's triumphant survival as a servant at the end with no little sympathy and admiration.

Brontë Studies, 33/1 (2008)

Notes

1   To my knowledge, no Brontë scholar has so far dealt extensively with the relationship between masters and servants in *Wuthering Heights*. Most of the research pertaining to that subject has centred on Nelly Dean's role and function as a domestic. There is, however, an interesting discussion on servants to be found in Tom Winnifrith, *The Brontës and their Background: Romance and Reality* (London and Basingstoke: Macmillan, 1973), pp. 191-194. For other references related to my topic, see Emily Brontë, *Wuthering Heights*, abr. and introd. R. H. Durham (London: Longman, 1959), pp. xi-xii; Jacqueline Viswanathan, 'Point of View and Unreliability in Brontë's *Wuthering Heights*, Conrad's *Under the Western Eyes* and Mann's *Doktor Faustus*', *Orbis Litterarum*, 29 (1974), 54; Jay Ellis McLemore, 'Edgar Linton: Master of Thrushcross Grange', *R. E. Artes Liberales*, 8 (1981), 13-26; James H. Kavanagh, *Emily Brontë's Wuthering Heights* (Oxford: Blackwell, 1985), pp. 54-55.

2   Certainly relations between masters and servants in Charlotte Brontë's fiction are usually perfunctory, despite the strong individuality of such servants as Bessie and Mrs. Fairfax in *Jane Eyre* and Rosine in *Villette*.

3   For quotations from the novel, see Emily Brontë, *Wuthering Heights*, eds. Ian Jack and Patsy Stoneman (Oxford: Oxford University Press, 1998). The edition quoted from is the original 1998 impression of 372 pages, not the later 1998 impression of 330 pages. For the sake of convenience, the first Catherine will be referred to as 'Catherine', the second as 'Cathy'.

4   For a discussion of Nelly Dean's mental limitations, see Graeme Tytler, 'The Parameters of Reason in *Wuthering Heights*', *Brontë*

Studies, 30/3 (2005), 234 and 241, n. 4. For a striking instance of Nelly's mediocrity, it is enough to recall that Cathy and Linton Heathcliff's illicit marriage would not have taken place had she acted on the words she uttered earlier to Heathcliff: '[…] I'm resolved [Cathy] shall never approach your house with me again […]' (*WH*, p. 215), not to say had she kept constantly in mind Heathcliff's intention to marry the cousins.

5   Joseph's sense of vocation as a servant is suggested when he prefaces his complaint to Heathcliff about the uprooting of his currant bushes as follows: 'Aw mun hev my wage, and Aw mun goa! Aw *hed* aimed tuh dee, wheare Aw'd sarved fur sixty year; […]' (*WH*, p. 318).

6   One notes a similar rationalization when, hearing Zillah's account of Cathy's unhappy life at the Heights, Nelly recalls reacting as follows: 'I determined to leave my situation, take a cottage, and get Catherine to come and live with me; but Mr. Heathcliff would as soon permit that, as he would set up Hareton in an independent house; […]' (*WH*, p. 298).

7   In this connection, it is interesting to note Mr. and Mrs. Linton's domineering behaviour, first, when, on account of Catherine and Heathcliff's intrusion at the Grange, the former comes to the Heights and 'read the young master [Hindley] such a lecture on the road he guided his family, that he was stirred to look about him in earnest' (*WH*, p. 50); secondly, when, referring to Catherine's delirium, Nelly recalls that '[o]ld Mrs. Linton paid us several visits, to be sure, and set things to rights, and scolded and ordered us all; and when Catherine was convalescent, she insisted on conveying her to Thrushcross Grange; […]' (*WH*, p. 88).

8   It should, however, be said to Isabella's credit that, as Heathcliff's neglected bride, she learns to become quite independent of servants at the Heights, and apparently enough so to find the courage to leave Gimmerton for good and start a new life in the South.

9   The idea that Lockwood is never to become a master of a household in the proper sense of the term is suggested when he recalls his mother having predicted that he would 'never have a comfortable home, [...]' (*WH*, p. 4).

10   That Nelly herself may have sensed Hareton's dislike of being taken for a servant is indirectly suggested in her tentative reference to Heathcliff as 'his master or guardian [...]' (*WH*, p. 218).

11   For Tabitha Aykroyd's influence on *Wuthering Heights*, see Winifred Gérin, *Emily Brontë. A Biography* (Oxford, New York and Melbourne: Oxford University Press, 1978), pp. 29, 60, 225.

Animals in *Wuthering Heights*

O ne notable aspect of *Wuthering Heights* is the considerable number of animals of various species referred to therein. Several scholars have already drawn attention to the author's treatment of the animal image, a rhetorical device which, though present in imaginative literature from time immemorial, may in some measure also be historically accounted for.[1] Thus it is probable that, like many of her contemporaries, Emily Brontë was influenced on that head by Sir Walter Scott, who was the first modern novelist to make extensive and elaborate use of this trope, and even by physiognomic theorists concerned with the physical resemblance between human beings and animals.[2] At the same time, some of Emily's animal images are remarkable enough to have induced one influential Brontë scholar to assert that they are 'more than simple metaphors' inasmuch as they 'tell us that man in *Wuthering Heights* [...] is part of nature, and no different from other animals'.[3] Although that assumption is not without a certain grain of truth, it is, nevertheless, something of an overstatement. Our aim here, accordingly, will be to suggest, among other things, not only that Emily Brontë makes fairly traditional symbolic use of animal imagery and, indeed, of some of the animals depicted in her novel, but that, far from negating the fundamental differences between man and beast, she appears intent on alerting us to the follies and dangers of metaphorical language in general.[4]

Prominent among the animals portrayed in *Wuthering Heights* are the dog, the cat, and the horse, and, from an aesthetic viewpoint, undoubtedly the most significant. For example, the horse, which serves here chiefly as a means of communication between the two households or as a means of flight or elopement, may be understood in some sense as an erotic symbol, especially with respect to the tragic or futile love relationships delineated in the novel. More explicit as to symbolic function, on the other hand, are the cat and the dog, the more so when references to them are examined in the light of Emily's essay 'Le Chat', which was written as a French exercise for Monsieur Heger some five years earlier. Thus the cat is seen here as a creature which, while capable of displaying utmost politeness and charm in its quest to obtain what it seeks from us, remains none the less an egotist at heart through its hypocrisy, its misanthropy, its ingratitude, its cruelty—an anthropomorphic interpretation that may be thought to have a definite bearing on the dozen or so references to cats in *Wuthering Heights*. Indeed, it is noteworthy that, as well as appearing most often in contexts of viciousness or killing, cats are referred to figuratively or otherwise mainly by, or of, Lockwood and Heathcliff, and appropriately, it seems, when we consider that both men also betray the moral defects attributed to those animals.[5]

What is most interesting about Emily's essay, however, is that, while alleging certain mental similarities between cats and human beings, she declares that man 'cannot sustain a comparison with the dog, it is infinitely too good'.[6] For though this somewhat idealized image seems occasionally vitiated by the violence of the watchdogs, and even by such references as 'vicious cur' (*WH*, p. 56) and 'mad dog' (*WH*, p. 160), it is yet realized in some descriptions of canine behaviour.[7] Thus as well as being made aware of the dog's loyalty, as when, for example, Isabella sardonically advises Heathcliff to 'go stretch [himself] over Catherine's grave and die like a faithful dog' (*WH*, p. 176), we are also put in mind of the inherent good nature of dogs and their loving disposition, as when told, on Catherine's return to the Heights after her five-week stay with the Lintons, that 'the dogs came bounding up to welcome her' (*WH*, p. 51); or in a later context, that Isabella, on the point of leaving the Grange for the last time, descended to the carriage 'accompanied by Fanny, who yelped wild with joy at recovering her mistress' (*WH*, p. 181). We are also given instances of the spontaneous friendliness of dogs when, in Chapter 3, Lockwood observes that, in her attempt to read by the kitchen fire, Cathy finds herself compelled to 'push away a dog, now and then, that snoozled its nose over-forwardly into her face' (*WH*, p. 28); or when Nelly Dean, having just brought Linton Heathcliff to the Heights, takes the opportunity (albeit in vain) to slip out of the house unnoticed while the latter is 'engaged in timidly rebuffing the advances of a friendly sheep-dog' (*WH*, p. 209). Significant, too, is the way in which Emily Brontë confirms her image of the dog by showing it to be unvindictive towards those people with whom it has only a short while earlier been in conflict. This is well illustrated already in Chapter 2 when Lockwood relates that, on the very day after his fight with the bitch pointer Juno, the latter 'deigned, at this second interview, to move the extreme tip of her tail, in token of owning [his] acquaintance' (*WH*, p. 8).

Although dogs in *Wuthering Heights* are ostensibly utilized partly for purposes of plot and partly as a kind of local colour, there can be little doubt that they have some symbolic relevance to the presentation of Hareton Earnshaw. That this should be so may seem at first blush hardly surprising in view of the sundry references made to his supposed animality. Thus in Chapter 2 Lockwood speaks of Hareton as 'that bear' (*WH*, p. 12), having already noted the latter's whiskers 'encroaching bearishly over his cheeks' (*WH*, p. 10)—details that adumbrate Nelly Dean's account of Hareton, as observed in the aftermath of his first meeting with Cathy, in which she remarks that Heathcliff 'appeared to have bent his malevolence on making him a brute' (*WH*, p. 196) both by keeping him illiterate and by encouraging him, with Joseph's help, to a life of uncouth behaviour and bad language. This image is doubtless reinforced in Nelly's mind when, on a later visit of hers to the Heights, Heathcliff tells her that, having taught Hareton to 'scorn everything extra-animal as silly and weak', he is as confident that the latter will 'never be able to emerge from his bathos of coarseness and ignorance', as he is that he 'takes a pride in his brutishness' (*WH*, p. 219). The irony of these statements is that, confuted as they will be by subsequent events, they are to some extent apposite, though hardly in ways that would be at all obvious to Heathcliff, let alone to Lockwood or to Nelly Dean.

This we realize partly through some of the canine metaphors and similes which are used of Hareton and which, in turn, prompt us to consider what parallels might be drawn between his characterization and the behaviour of the dogs in the novel. For example, when on his third visit to the Heights, while Heathcliff happens to be away, Lockwood remarks that Hareton 'accompanied [him], in the office of watchdog, not as a substitute for the host' (*WH*, p. 299), the aptness of that canine image seems confirmed for us by accounts elsewhere in the novel of Hareton's unswerving loyalty to Heathcliff during the latter's absences and even after his death—a loyalty manifest especially during Nelly Dean's temporary incarceration in the Heights. It is, moreover, by virtue of such accounts that Hareton inevitably reminds us of the trustworthiness of the Heights dogs as shown at various stages of the action. Also of interest here are the canine similes that Cathy resorts to in the Heights kitchen in yet another attempt to make Hareton speak to her. Thus she remarks to Nelly: 'He's just like a dog, is he not, Ellen? […] or a carthorse? He does his work, eats his food, and sleeps, eternally!'; and then, finding him still unresponsive, presently goes on to say: 'He's perhaps dreaming now. He twitched his shoulder as Juno twitches hers' (*WH*, p. 311). Although such words seem merely to typify Cathy's haughtiness towards Hareton, one still wonders whether, because uttered only shortly before the cousins will be reconciled, they do not also argue a certain awareness on her part that Hareton possesses something of that 'suprahuman' goodness which Emily Brontë attributes to the dog in her essay. Certainly, there are episodes in the novel in which Cathy witnesses examples of Hareton's kindness and thoughtfulness. Thus we may recall that, almost alone in his sympathy for Lockwood's discomfiture in Chapter 2, Hareton offers to accompany him on his journey back to the Grange 'as far as the park', even though he has been embarrassed and angered by him earlier at the tea-table; or that, having gruffly refused to be treated like a servant by Cathy, he is presently moved enough by her tears not only to fetch her pony for her as she has requested but also to offer her the gift of a terrier whelp. Again, we note that, despite having forcibly ejected Cathy and Linton Heathcliff from 'the house' in evident rage at being humiliated a second time for his illiteracy, Hareton is, as Cathy later informs Nelly Dean, the very first in the household to bring help to Linton when the latter's continued shrieking at him has ended in 'a dreadful fit of coughing' (*WH*, p. 252). At any rate, what is most apposite about Cathy's canine references is the comparison she draws between Hareton and Juno inasmuch as it perfectly epitomizes for us the idea that, as with Juno in her conflict with Lockwood in Chapter 1, so Hareton's fits of anger and acts of violence are usually the consequence of extreme provocation, and that, quick to feel remorse for such behaviour and even to make up for it, he is, not unlike Juno in Chapter 2, ready, as it were, to forgive and forget.

In their tendency to dismiss Hareton's education at the hands of Cathy as a sort of emasculating process, some critics appear to have ignored the importance of his moral and physical strength for the success of his love relationship with his cousin. And, as with his other qualities of character, this strength is hinted at through certain references to animals. Thus the fact that Hareton's very first encounter with Cathy is marked by a conflict in which her dogs are evidently worsted by his, seems a symbolic foreshadowing of his ability eventually to overcome her, so to speak, and win her hand, just as his light-hearted response to Cathy's warning to him about her pony's kick seems to symbolize the fearlessness with which, despite suffering rebuffs, he will pay his attentions to her. Cathy is doubtless made aware of Hareton's strong character not only when he bravely intercedes on her behalf against Heathcliff, but when, even after their reconciliation, he forbids her to malign the latter or to undermine his loyalty to him. To be sure, Hareton needs Cathy's help in order to learn the literacy skills and social graces such as will befit the landed gentleman he seems destined to become; but in almost all other respects he is already a young man of exemplary character. And though Cathy herself is compelled after the death of her father to undergo a kind of education to unlearn the snobbery acquired through her sheltered upbringing, she is, like Hareton, quite as 'good-hearted' (*WH*, p. 14) as Lockwood estimates her to be from her physical appearance. This we realize principally through her devotion to her father, her extraordinary selflessnness towards Linton Heathcliff, and her capacity to keep her word. That is why it is appropriate that the most 'sympathetic' of the animal images in the novel are those which, involving either dogs or birds, are variously applied to Cathy and Hareton.[8]

★ ★ ★

As has been suggested in the foregoing, animals now and again seem to fulfil an important symbolic function in *Wuthering Heights*. Indeed, it is through references to them that Emily Brontë achieves some of her finest poetic effects. This we note pre-eminently through details about birds, whether it be, say, the silence of the larks at Catherine's death, or the singing of the same on Cathy's sixteenth birthday, or, again, through the account of the indifference of the nest-building ousels to a Heathcliff motionlessly keeping vigil out of doors just after Catherine has died. But if Nelly Dean's designation of Heathcliff's 'history' as 'a cuckoo's' (*WH*, p. 32) and her description of Hareton in the same context as someone 'cast out like an unfledged dunnock' (*WH*, p. 33) seem just as symbolically apt, such expressions are, notwithstanding, rather of a piece with her quite conventional use of animal imagery, which, involving monkeys, mice, foxes, lambs, doves and the like, attests her strong reliance on traditional or proverbial thought. Only seldom does Nelly employ an original animal metaphor or simile, such as the extensive bird image with which she describes Cathy's utter dismay at finding Linton's love letters missing from her drawer, or her choice description of Linton Heathcliff going out at a door held open by his father 'exactly as a spaniel might, that suspected the person who attended on it of designing a spiteful squeeze' (*WH*, p. 274). At the same time we discern in the latter detail that mixture of hatred and scorn with which, in her vexation at his having helped to entrap Cathy into marriage with him, she calls him 'a little perishing monkey' and 'a cockatrice' (*WH*, p. 272). Such words are typical of the vituperative animal imagery commonly resorted to by the main characters, Heathcliff and Catherine in particular, to express anger, irritation or contempt—imagery which entails indigenous and exotic mammals, reptiles, worms, insects, molluscs, and even fabulous creatures, and which goes hand in hand with those contexts where someone is named a 'beast' or a 'brute', or, for that matter, a 'clown', a 'monster', a 'witch', an 'idiot', a 'thing', a 'cipher' and similar derogatory terms.

Inasmuch as it means that those using it have, at least momentarily, lost sight of the humanity or individuality of those at whom it is directed or about whom it is uttered, that kind of language is, of course, the effect of emotionalism or perverted thinking, and as such a signal example of the author's ingeniously varied way of illustrating the limits and limitations of the human mind.[9] That there is, in any case, an obvious presumptuousness about much animal imagery seems to be hinted at throughout the novel. Thus it is evident, for example, that Nelly Dean's memory of Heathcliff as having been 'as uncomplaining as a lamb' (*WH*, p. 37) during a childhood illness is, as a parallel between man and animal, ultimately meaningless, being of interest, rather, as an expression of the housekeeper's admiration for stoical behaviour. Similarly, when Cathy taxes Hareton with taking her books 'as a magpie gathers silver spoons, for the mere love of stealing' (*WH*, p. 301), it is clear that she does so with a wilful disregard for the essentially human motives behind his actions. Even more presumptuous, perhaps, is the use of animals in a type of hyperbole sometimes known as Buridan's trope.[10] Examples of this can be seen when Isabella assures Nelly Dean that 'a tiger or a venomous serpent could not rouse terror in [her] equal to that which [Heathcliff] awakens' (*WH*, p. 145), or when she later tells her that, in her attempts to thwart Hindley's plan to kill Heathcliff, she thought she 'might as well have struggled with a bear, or reasoned with a lunatic' (*WH*, p. 175). Such figurative language is, in its very improbability, not much different from that which Nelly Dean herself employs when she finds herself unable to cope with her almost irrational fear of Heathcliff shortly after his return to Gimmerton. Thus Nelly allows her anxiety for Hindley and others living at the Heights, based as it is almost entirely on hearsay, to reach such a pitch that she 'felt that God had forsaken the stray sheep there to its own wicked wanderings, and an evil beast prowled between it and the fold, waiting his time to spring and destroy' (*WH*, p. 107). In view of these self-righteous sentiments, it is not surprising that Nelly should subsequently come to regard Heathcliff as virtually indistinguishable from an animal. This we see when, having observed him holding a dying Catherine, she recalls that he 'gnashed at [her] and foamed like a mad dog' and that she 'did not feel as if [she] were in the company of a creature of [her] own species' (*WH*, p. 160); and, later, when just after he has apostrophized a dead Catherine, she notes that, 'lifting up his eyes', Heathcliff 'howled, not like a man, but like a savage beast getting goaded to death with knives and spears' (*WH*, p. 167).

These and similar comments about Heathcliff's supposed animal-like behaviour have doubtless done much to determine the view that he is in some sense a sub-human or preternatural being. Such a view, however, seems untenable, once we realize that, in their use of animal images to address or describe one another, Emily Brontë's characters are prone to singular contradictions and inconsistencies, sometimes even within a short time. We see examples of these in, say, Lockwood's description of Hareton as 'bear', 'clown' and 'boor' in Chapter 2, in Hindley's of Heathcliff as 'dog', 'gypsy' and 'imp of Satan' in Chapter 4, and Nelly Dean's of Cathy as 'lamb', 'fox' and 'mouse' in Chapter 18. Heathcliff, too, shows like contradictions when, for instance, having at first called his son a 'puling chicken' (*WH*, p. 207), he will twice afterwards refer to him as 'whelp' (*WH*, pp. 208, 268); or, again, when, having already described Isabella as 'that pitiful, slavish, mean-minded brach' (*WH*, p. 151), he will call her a 'viper' (*WH*, p. 178) for conspiring with Hindley against him. More curious perhaps are the contradictions between Heathcliff's metaphors for Hareton. Thus although, on the death of Hindley, he has at first envisaged Hareton as a tree that will 'grow as crooked as another, with the same wind to twist it' (*WH*, p. 186), later called him an 'infernal calf' (*WH*, p. 208), and shortly after that compared him and Linton Heathcliff to gold and tin respectively, Heathcliff will, nevertheless, in his long confession to Nelly Dean about Catherine's haunting of him, speak of Hareton, as seen sitting at the fireside with Cathy, as 'a personification of my youth, not a human being', and that partly because 'his startling likeness to Catherine connected him fearfully to her' (*WH*, p. 324). Thus Heathcliff's implicit recognition of Hareton's humanity here seems to make nonsense not only of his earlier images of him, but of his original plan to 'animalize' him.

Stranger still are some similar inconsistencies displayed elsewhere in the novel. For instance, during the episode in which she will have designated Isabella, or likened her to, a cat, a tigress, a monkey, a vixen and a dove in quick succession, Catherine makes pointed use of animal imagery in an endeavour to discourage her sister-in-law's interest in Heathcliff by describing him to her as 'an unreclaimed creature, without refinement—without cultivation' and 'a fierce, pitiless wolfish man' (*WH*, p. 102), having apparently forgotten that only shortly beforehand she had told Edgar that Heathcliff was 'now worthy of any one's regard' and that it would 'honour the first gentleman in the country to be his friend' (*WH*, p. 98), not to mention that three years before that, she had said these words: 'Nelly, I *am* Heathcliff—' (*WH*, p. 82). A comparable inconsistency is comically illustrated in Isabella's conflicting attitudes to Heathcliff. Thus amid a context where she refers, for example, to his 'sharp cannibal teeth' (*WH*, p. 176) and his 'basilisk eyes' (*WH*, p. 179), having already angrily denied his very humanity, she makes it plain that she has quite overlooked the fact that not long ago she had repudiated Catherine's aforementioned images of Heathcliff as 'falsehoods' and countered them with the claim that he had 'an honourable soul, and a true one' (*WH*, p. 103). Hardly less comical is Nelly Dean's reaction to Isabella's outright 'dehumanization' of Heathcliff. For in saying, 'Hush, hush! He's a human being!' (*WH*,

p. 172), she seems oblivious of the animal images that she herself has applied to Heathcliff, unaware, moreover, in her affirmation of his humanity at that moment, that, in the last days of his life, she will even ask herself whether he is not 'a ghoul, or a vampire' (*WH*, p. 330).

To the extent that abusive or negative animal metaphors and similes are interchangeable with other images or modes of name-calling, or contradicted by affirmations of someone's human qualities, they are, then, essentially meaningless utterances, and as such likely to tell us a good deal more about the mentality of those who resort to them than about those to whom they have reference. Such language may be supposed an expression or a by-product of societies in which animals are shown living in close relationship with human beings, whether as working creatures or as domestic pets. Sometimes, in fact, the boundary separating man from beast seems quite tenuous in *Wuthering Heights*. We see this, for example, in Lockwood's childish attempts to relate to the Heights dogs as if they were actual human beings, without allowing for their limitations as animals, even as would-be pets. Certainly, his reluctance to see and accept dogs for what they are is amusingly suggested through the metaphors and hyperboles with which, in his resentment at their aggressiveness, he personifies them or likens them to other species. That Lockwood, moreover, seems to betray that unwholesome concern with animals which marks the misanthropist is strikingly evident when, for example, he writes sentimentally about the kitchen cat in Chapter 3, or when, in an effort to persuade Nelly Dean to continue her narrative in Chapter 7, he draws two elaborate animal comparisons, one about a cat washing its kitten, and the other about the value of a spider to someone living in a dungeon as against someone living in a cottage. But whereas Lockwood seems inclined, as it were, to 'humanize' animals, Hindley shows a tendency to treat human beings as if they *were* animals. This is suggested not only when, on catching Nelly Dean trying to hide Hareton in the kitchen cupboard, he pulls her back, significantly, 'by the skin of [her] neck, like a dog' (*WH*, p. 73), but when, having addressed Hareton as 'unnatural cub', he supplements that appellation with an image whereby the latter seems to lose all human identity: 'Now, don't you think the lad would be handsomer cropped? It makes a dog fiercer, and I love something fierce—' (*WH*, pp. 73-74). It is, therefore, little wonder that, ironic as is that momentary confusion between his baby son and a dog with respect to Hareton's presentation, Hindley should go on to vindicate his recommendation with words consistent with that confusion: 'Besides, it's infernal affectation—devilish conceit it is—to cherish our ears—we're asses enough without them' (*WH*, p. 75).

Just as Hindley's and Lockwood's respective ways of blurring the distinction between the species and, indeed, of being now and again harsh or careless in their treatment of dumb creatures help us, then, to understand why they are both more or less failures at human relationships, so Heathcliff's attitudes to animals are crucial for a proper appraisal of his conduct towards his fellow human beings.[11] That these attitudes may be said to have taken root in specific childhood experiences is suggested by those occasions when he was, say, insulted as a 'dog' (*WH*, p. 37) by Hindley, or warned by Nelly Dean not to 'get the expression of a vicious cur that appears to know the kicks it gets are its desert, and yet hates all the world, as well as the kicker, for what it suffers' (*WH*, p. 56). It is, moreover, partly through Nelly's words that we understand why in a society where domestic pets are given personal names, and even eat porridge, Heathcliff should have learnt early in life to conflate the species somewhat. This is already evident when, in his account of Catherine's being savagely bitten by the Grange bull-dog, he refers to the latter as 'he' but to a menial as 'a beast of a servant' (*WH*, p. 47). Such a *quid pro quo* may, in turn, explain why Heathcliff's essential misanthropy should find expression in a persistent cruelty to animals, as may be gathered, for example,

258

from Catherine's mentioning, on her sickbed, his tendency as a boy to shoot birds and set traps for them and, more especially, from Linton Heathcliff's telling Nelly Dean that his father's striking 'a dog or a horse' makes him wink 'for he does it so hard' (*WH*, p. 281).

Heathcliff's apparent disdain of the line separating the two species is, at any rate, already noticeable in the opening chapters in that, not unlike his domestic animals, everybody in his household (with the notable exception of Cathy) is obliged to work for their keep. At the same time, it is through his habit of using people to his own ends that we realize why Heathcliff looks upon animals as designed to perform no more than a utilitarian function. This we sense when, aware that Juno's snarling has been provoked by Lockwood's caress, he advises the latter to 'let the dog alone' as she is 'not accustomed to be spoiled—not kept for a pet', having by then characteristically checked 'fiercer demonstrations with a punch of his foot' (*WH*, pp. 4-5). Certainly, it would appear that, despite their having soon afterwards attacked his tenant, Heathcliff is pleased that his dogs have proved their usefulness, as when he remarks that they 'do right to be vigilant' (*WH*, p. 6). This starkly pragmatic view of dogs is matched by contexts where Heathcliff seems contemptuous of the idea of keeping domestic animals as pets: his reference to the dog quarrelled over by the Linton children as 'a heap of warm hair' (*WH*, p. 46); his assessment of Edgar's significance for Catherine as being that of someone that is 'scarcely a degree dearer to her than her dog, or her horse' (*WH*, p. 149); and above all, his hanging of Isabella's dog—an act which is gratuitous in a way that Hareton's hanging of the puppies is palpably not.[12] Furthermore, in contrast to the other main characters, Heathcliff is nowhere shown being kind or affectionate to an animal; a deficiency which, like his cruelty to animals, would surely have been enough to condemn him out of hand in the eyes of Emily and her sisters, and might even justify calling his long-standing heroic status in question.[13]

No doubt, an attachment to animals can be a kind of affectation, as we have seen plainly enough in Lockwood's case, and may also gather from, say, Isabella's remark about her 'tame pheasant' (*WH*, p. 48), or from allusions to the caged birds kept at the Grange. Yet the author makes it abundantly clear, especially through Cathy's rambles with her dogs, her visits to grouse nests on the moors, and her watching birds feeding their young and teaching them to fly, that animals both wild and domestic can play an important part in the development of one's ability to form loving relationships. But extraordinary as was her own love of animals, and that to a point where she is said to have admitted to preferring the housedog to all the people in a school she was teaching at, Emily Brontë is objective enough in her novel to acknowledge, as it were, that in an imperfect world animals are necessarily subservient to human needs.[14] This idea is borne out for us as much by details about familiar aspects of animal husbandry and the exploitation of local game, as it is through more or less ironic references to 'clusters of legs of beef, mutton and ham' (*WH*, p. 3), 'roasted calf-skin' (*WH*, p. 18), 'feathered beaver' (*WH*, p. 51) and 'furs' (*WH*, p. 56), to say nothing of Catherine's 'cutting up the wing of a goose' (*WH*, p. 58) on Christmas Day. And although the prominence of animals in the novel, whether in symbolic or figurative guise, or as participants in the everyday lives of the characters, might incline us to think otherwise about a work written at a time when evolutionary and physiognomic theories seemed to be minimizing physical and psychological differences within the animal kingdom, it is certain that, in her concern with the primacy of human relationships, man and animals are, for Emily Brontë, not on the same spiritual plane. This is already implicit in a dialogue in Chapter 2 that begins when Heathcliff, having sarcastically revoked Hareton's offer to accompany Lockwood part of the way back to the Grange, goes on to ask: 'And who is to look after the horses, eh?' (*WH* p. 15)—words that ironically prefigure that moment when, asked by Catherine on the night of Heathcliff's disappearance whether he has been looking for the latter 'as [she] ordered', Joseph callously replies: 'Aw sud more likker look for th' horse [...]. It'ud be tuh more sense' (*WH*, p. 84). Yet conscientious yeoman farmer though Heathcliff may sound with his rhetorical question, it is obvious that his concern for his horses here is immoderate and, like Joseph's utterance, little more than an expression of misanthropy. Hence the interest of Cathy's way of countering Heathcliff's standpoint as follows: 'A man's life is of more consequence than one evening's neglect of the horses; somebody must go' (*WH*, p. 15). For though Cathy's comparison somewhat begs the question and perhaps even causes Hareton, in his patent jealousy of Lockwood, to resent her for making metaphysical capital out of what was after all his idea in the first place, it is none the less the mature sentiment of someone who, loving animals as much as she is loved by them, and now standing on the threshold of womanhood, so often represents, as Hareton himself does, the intrinsic humanism of *Wuthering Heights*.

Brontë Studies, 27/2 (2002)

Notes

1   For discussions on animal imagery in *Wuthering Heights*, see, for
    example, Mark Schorer, 'Fiction and the Matrix of Analogy',
    Kenyon Review, 11/4 (1949), 539-560; Ellen Moers, *Literary
    Women* (London: Women's Press, 1978), p. 101; Patrick Murray,
    Companion to Wuthering Heights (Dublin: The Educational
    Company, 1987), p. 61; Linda H. Peterson, *Emily Brontë, Wuthering
    Heights* (Boston, MA: Bedford Books, 1992), p. 298; Sheryl
    Craig, 'Brontë's *Wuthering Heights*', *The Explicator*, 52 (1994),
    157-159; Claire Jones, *Wuthering Heights, Emily Brontë* (London:
    York Press, 1998), p. 60; Helena M. Ardholm, *The Emblem and
    the Emblematic Habit of Mind in Jane Eyre and Wuthering Heights*
    (Gothenburg: Acta Universitatis Gothoburgensis, 1999), p. 135.

2   For a discussion on animal imagery in Scott's fiction, see
    Christabel F. Fiske, *Epic Suggestion in the Imagery of the Waverley
    Novels* (New Haven, CT: Yale University Press, 1940), pp. 10-
    39. For the relationship between animal imagery in fiction and
    physiognomic theory, see Graeme Tytler, *Physiognomy in the
    European Novel: Faces and Fortunes* (Princeton, NJ: Princeton
    University Press, 1982), pp. 249-252. See also Graeme Tytler,
    'Physiognomy in *Wuthering Heights*', *Brontë Society Transactions*,
    21/4 (1994), 137-148.

3   See J. Hillis Miller, *The Disappearance of God. Five Nineteenth-
    Century Writers* (Cambridge, MA: Harvard University Press,
    1963), pp. 166-169.

4   For quotations from the novel, see Emily Brontë, *Wuthering
    Heights*, ed. Ian Jack and introd. Patsy Stoneman (Oxford:
    Oxford University Press, 1998). For the sake of convenience, the

first Catherine will be referred to as 'Catherine', the second as 'Cathy'.

5 See Charlotte and Emily Brontë, *The Belgian Essays*, ed. and trans. Sue Lonoff (New Haven, CT and London: Yale University Press, 1996), pp. 56-58. For references to cats, see *Wuthering Heights*, pp. 8, 27, 28, 29, 30, 60, 72, 275, 327.

6 *The Belgian Essays*, p. 56.

7 The importance of dogs in *Wuthering Heights* has been pointed up in Judith Weissman, '"Like a Mad Dog": The Radical Romanticism of *Wuthering Heights*', *Midwest Quarterly*, 19 (1978), 388-390; Emily Brontë, *Wuthering Heights*, ed. Linda Cookson (London: Longman Group Ltd., 1983), pp. xxix ff; Lisa Surridge, 'Animals and Violence in *Wuthering Heights*', *Brontë Society Transactions*, 24/2 (1999), 161.

8 See, for example, *Wuthering Heights*, pp. 33, 188, 213, 226, 296. Though somewhat dismissed by some critics as inferior versions of Catherine and Heathcliff, Cathy and Hareton have, nevertheless, been affirmed by other critics as individuals in their own right and deserving of our respect and admiration. For the latter viewpoint, see, for example, F. A. Bullock, 'The Genius of Emily Brontë', *Brontë Society Transactions*, 9 (1937), 126; Emily Brontë, *Wuthering Heights*, introd. Bonamy Dobrée (London and Glasgow: Collins, 1960), p. 15; Barbara Hardy, *Wuthering Heights* (New York: Barnes & Noble, 1963), p. 56; William A. Madden, '*Wuthering Heights*: The Binding of Passion', *Nineteenth-Century Fiction*, 27 (1972), 141; Margaret Drabble, 'The Writer as Recluse: The Theme of Solitude in the Works of the Brontës', *Brontë Society Transactions*, 16 (1974), 268ff; Douglas Jefferson,

'Irresistible Narrative: The Art of *Wuthering Heights*', *Brontë Society Transactions*, 90 (1980), 345; Mary Burgan, '"Some Fit Parentage": Identity and the Cycle of Generations in *Wuthering Heights*', *Philological Quarterly*, 61 (1982), 407; Joyce Carol Oates, 'The Magnanimity of *Wuthering Heights*', *Critical Inquiry*, 9 (1982), 447; Annette R. Federico, 'The Waif at the Window: Emily Brontë's Feminine *Bildungsroman*', *Victorian Newsletter*, 68 (1985), 26ff; Victoria Moreland, '"It has devoured my existence": Emotion and Personality in *Wuthering Heights*', *Brontë Society Transactions*, 19 (1988), 269.

9   The fact that Catherine and Heathcliff both eventually succumb to partial insanity may not be altogether unconnected with their being of all the characters the ones most disposed to using opprobrious metaphorical language. In this connection see Graeme Tytler, 'Heathcliff's Monomania: An Anachronism in *Wuthering Heights*', *Brontë Society Transactions*, 20/6 (1992), 331-343.

10 See Robert Brainard Pearsall, 'The Presiding Tropes of Emily Brontë', *College English*, 27 (1966), 27.

11 Noteworthy in this connection are Isabella's allusion to Hindley's brutality to a Heights bull-dog (in her letter to Nelly Dean) and Lockwood's diary entries about the invitation he has received to 'devastate the moors of a friend' (*WH*, p. 305) and about his deciding on 'a sudden impulse', just after arriving in the North for that purpose, to ride to Gimmerton at breakneck speed and hence, as he admits, 'with great fatigue to [their] beasts' (*WH*, p. 305). See also Note 13.

12 The hanging of unwanted puppies was considered normal practice in the eighteenth century. See Miriam Allott, *Emily Brontë* (London: Macmillan, 1970), p. 63.

13 In this connection, Ellen Nussey writes: 'The Brontës' love of dumb creatures [...] made them very sensitive of the treatment bestowed on them. For any one to offend in this respect was with them an infallible bad sign, and a blot on the disposition.' See Winifred Gérin, *Emily Brontë. A Biography* (Oxford, New York and Melbourne: Oxford University Press, 1978), p. 95.

14 For Emily Brontë's love of animals, see Gérin, *Emily Brontë*, pp. 35, 81, 95, 109-110, 115-116.

Eating and Drinking in
Wuthering Heights

When Lockwood visits Wuthering Heights for the first time, he notes that 'the family sitting room', which, as he adds, is called '"the house" pre-eminently', includes 'kitchen and parlour, generally'. But in contradistinction to what he has found in other local dwellings, the kitchen here, he believes, is 'forced to retreat altogether into another quarter', for he distinguishes 'a chatter of tongues, and a clatter of culinary utensils, deep within', and observes 'no signs of roasting, boiling, or baking, about the huge fire-place; nor any glitter of copper saucepans and tin cullenders on the walls' (*WH*, p. 3).[1] No doubt, part of the interest of Lockwood's words just quoted lies in their indirectly foreshadowing the fact that, notwithstanding its most basic function, the kitchen (together with the back-kitchen) serves all manner of purposes throughout the action. For example, it is the servants' living-quarters, a place to which one may be banished for some misdemeanour or in which one may take refuge, and

266

even through which the characters often make their exits or entrances. It is also the setting, whether at the Heights or at the Grange, for some of the most important episodes in the novel. Nevertheless, Lockwood's reference to that hidden room is, perhaps more obviously, also a foreshadowing of the fact that the kitchen is the place in which almost all the meals mentioned in the narrative are prepared out of sight. At the same time it is through Lockwood's very mention of the Heights kitchen as well as his references to 'culinary utensils' and to certain modes of cookery, to the 'immense pewter dishes, interspersed with silver jugs and tankards' in a 'vast oak dresser' and to a 'frame of wood laden with oatcakes, and clusters of legs of beef, mutton and ham' (*WH*, p. 3), that we are put in mind of a prominent aspect of everyday life in a Yorkshire household, and are thus prepared for much that is relevant to our topic of discussion.

The dried meats and oatcakes noticed by Lockwood in 'the house' make up part of a comparatively small number of actual or potential comestibles named in the text; these also include bread (toast), porridge, cheese, cakes (dainties), tarts, gingerbread, sweets, sugar, sugar candy, herring, rabbit, grouse, goose, pheasant, apples (apple sauce), pears, oranges, gooseberries, bilberries, blackberries, black currants, rosehips, turnips, whey and gruel. Some of these comestibles seem to have a specifically symbolic function. Consider, for example, porridge, a staple food at the Heights for human beings and domestic animals alike, as is comically underlined when a dog devours the porridge which Isabella has just made for herself, but which, in her anger at Joseph, she has deliberately flung 'on the ground' (*WH*, p. 144).[2] The social implications of porridge, which are hinted at already in the genteel Isabella's bungled cooking of it, can surely be felt in Linton Heathcliff's outright refusal of the porridge brought to him as breakfast on his first morning at the Heights, as if his mother, chastened perhaps by her one and only experience of porridge, had never prepared him such a dish. The symbolic significance of porridge, on the other hand, is at first suggested in Nelly's account of the morning when, having announced his journey to Liverpool, Mr. Earnshaw 'turned to Hindley, and Cathy, and me—for I sat eating my porridge with them' (*WH*, p. 34) to ask them what presents they would like him to bring back for them. Nelly's words 'eating porridge' rather than, say, 'having breakfast' may be understood, through the very indigenousness of that food, to have been in ironic contrast with the fact that Mr. Earnshaw will later return to the Heights with an 'exotic' foundling. The implicit irony of 'porridge' in this context is presently reinforced when, alluding to her choice of presents, Nelly recalls that Mr. Earnshaw 'promised to bring [her] a pocketful of apples and pears' (*WH*, p. 34), both types of fruit being, significantly enough, equally indigenous. A similar irony may, therefore, be sensed when, just before identifying Heathcliff at the Grange on the evening of his return from abroad, Nelly tells of 'coming from the garden with a heavy basket of apples which [she] had been gathering' and of setting '[her] burden on the house steps by the kitchen door' (*WH*, p. 92).[3] It is, however, interesting to note that oranges, those fruits of patently exotic origin, occur in two contexts in which Nelly practises certain acts of deceit. One is when, in order to get Hareton to answer questions about his life as a small boy at the Heights, she 'bribes' him with the second of two oranges she gives him, and the other when she sends a servant off to buy some oranges so that he shall be out of the way when Heathcliff enters the Grange for his tryst with Catherine.[4] Nor should we forget the symbolic implications of a Linton Heathcliff childishly sucking his no less exotic stick of sugar candy while an indignant and anxious Nelly Dean, having just been released from her forced confinement in Zillah's room, is rebuking him for his callousness and ingratitude to his bride Cathy.[5]

The negative and affirmative symbolism inherent in references to exotic and indigenous viands respectively—a symbolism suggestive of a sort of conflict or dialogue between a Yorkshire country community and the outside world—seems also to be true of various kinds of drink. Thus it is perhaps significant that alcohol, which tends to figure in grim or gloomy contexts, whether as a means of hospitality, or dissipation, or self-forgetfulness, or, not unlike water, as a restorative, is most often an exotic product, or made up of exotic ingredients—wine, brandy, gin, negus. Accordingly, just as, for example, the 'warm wine and gingerbread' (*WH*, p. 247) that Zillah gladly provides for Cathy on her second illicit visit to Linton Heathcliff at the Heights seems, through the exotic connotations of such refreshments, but a portent of a doomed love relationship, so the 'little wine' (*WH*, p. 294) she gives Cathy to comfort her shortly after Linton has died seems symbolically to seal the demise of that relationship.

By contrast, there are clearly no negative associations with ale, an alcohol that may be assumed to be brewed locally. In this connection, it is noteworthy that, having adjudged 'the house' to be the sort of place usually belonging to 'a homely, northern farmer', Lockwood conjures up the latter with the following image: 'Such an individual, seated in his armchair, his mug of ale frothing on the round table before him, is to be seen in any circuit of five or six miles among these hills, if you go at the right time, after dinner' (*WH*, p. 3). Yet since, as Lockwood continues, Heathcliff 'forms a singular contrast to his abode and style of living' (*WH*, p. 3), it is symbolically appropriate not only that the latter should presently entertain his guest with wine rather than with ale, but that Lockwood's image of a northern farmer should be most nearly realized much later by Joseph as described by Nelly in the Heights kitchen, at the beginning of Chapter 23, on the morning when she and Cathy have come to visit Linton Heathcliff: 'Joseph seemed sitting in a sort of elysium alone, beside a roaring fire; a quart of ale on the table near him, bristling with large pieces of toasted oatcake; [...]' (*WH*, p. 236). Hinting as it does at the delight with which Joseph is about to consume the food and drink specified, Nelly's observation seems almost a celebration of indigenous fare, and the more so as Heathcliff happens to be well out of the way at the time she makes it. It is again in the absence of Heathcliff, this time as a result of his death, and consequently amid a generally sunnier atmosphere in the household, that the symbolism of ale is fittingly rounded off when, notwithstanding Joseph's vociferous objections, Nelly provides Lockwood with some on his final visit to the Heights just before she tells him the rest of 'Heathcliff's history'.[6]

Interesting, too, is the part played by non-alcoholic beverages. Milk is now and again mentioned in connection with children, as, for example, when Nelly is instructed to feed the newborn Hareton with 'sugar and milk' (*WH*, p. 63), or advises Heathcliff that, instead of the 'milk-porridge' he has rejected, Linton Heathcliff be given 'boiled milk or tea' (*WH*, p. 209). But milk is also used to reveal the character or psychology of a child. Thus it is clearly a sign of Hareton's sound health as a youngster when, just after Isabella has made the ill-fated porridge, he is seen, to her dismay and disgust, 'drinking and spilling from the expansive lip' of the 'gallon pitcher of new milk' brought in from the dairy, and when, despite her expostulations, and perhaps encouraged by Joseph's moral support, he 'continued sucking; and glowered up at [Isabella] defyingly, as he slavered into the jug' (*WH*, p. 142). On the other hand, Linton Heathcliff's appetite for milk seems almost abnormal, as the unnamed Heights housekeeper suggests when, in her account to Nelly of the boy's finicky attitudes, she complains that he 'must always have sweets and dainties, and always milk, milk for ever—heeding naught how the rest of [them] are pinched in winter—' (*WH*, p. 211).[7] It is this sort of detail that may explain why milk is here and there referred to in contexts of childish conduct. Consider, for instance, the fact that Lockwood snatches the lantern by whose light Joseph is milking a cow at the end of Chapter 2; or, again, the fact that, after she and Linton have been violently turned out of 'the house' by Hareton, Cathy hurriedly seeks Zillah's help at the moment the latter happens to be 'milking the cows in a shed behind the barn' (*WH*, p. 252). Similarly, in view of the somewhat infantile nature of the relationship between Cathy and Linton, it seems symbolically apposite that the letters they write to each other are carried for them by 'a milk-fetcher who came from the village' (*WH*, p. 224), just as it is comically symbolic when, during Nelly's struggle with that milk-fetcher in an attempt to intercept the note he has just received from Cathy, they both 'spilt the milk between [them]' (*WH*, p. 226).

But whereas milk is at once a local and a universal beverage, coffee and tea are beverages of exotic origin for those living in England. Accordingly, we may, for instance, sense a certain symbolic intent behind the idea that coffee, mentioned as it is only twice in the novel, should have been prepared for two 'outsiders', Lockwood and Heathcliff, and in each case in uneasy circumstances.[8] Tea in the sense of 'beverage' or 'afternoon meal' is almost invariably associated with dubious or unpleasant situations. Thus we may think of Isabella in the Grange parlour, shortly after her flight from the Heights, 'seated in an easy chair on the hearth, with a cup of tea before her, [...]' (*WH*, p. 170). It is, no doubt, significant not only that that detail is given just before Isabella effusively expresses her mixed feelings about Heathcliff or that Nelly presently interrupts her invective partly with the words, 'Drink your tea, and take breath, and give over laughing; [...]' (*WH*, p. 171), but that the last sentence of Isabella's graphic account of her terrible life at the Heights should be immediately followed by this statement: 'Isabella ceased speaking, and took a drink of tea; [...]' (*WH*, p. 181).

The negative symbolism of tea is also strikingly manifest during Cathy's relations with Linton Heathcliff, especially after they have become lovers. For example, speaking of the time when she was looked after by Cathy during her three-week illness, Nelly ironically recalls her ignorance of the girl's secret meetings with Linton as follows: 'Poor thing. I never considered what she did with herself after tea' (*WH*, p. 244). That statement forms a direct link with the words Cathy later uses in her long confession to Nelly as to the moderation of her initial sense of guilt about her third illicit visit: '[…] it was beautiful moonlight after tea; and, as I rode on, the gloom cleared' (*WH*, p. 249). Yet the irony of this gradual swell of optimism is that Cathy cannot know that she and Linton are soon afterwards to be violently turned out of 'the house' by Hareton. And there are other apparently casual references to tea with negative implications, such as the one concerning Cathy, who, in the wake of Nelly's burning of Linton's letters, later 're-appeared at tea, pale, and red about the eyes, and marvellously subdued in outward aspect' (*WH*, p. 228); or the one which is made after Cathy's chance meeting with Heathcliff outside Thrushcross park, viz. Nelly's intimation that, on their return to the Grange, she and Cathy 'took [their] tea together' (*WH*, p. 234), and which seems to constitute an ironic link between that fateful encounter with Heathcliff and the visit they will pay Linton at the Heights the following morning.

Much more important than the details quoted above, and certainly more memorable for their unpleasantness, are those episodes in which three or more characters are gathered together for afternoon tea as a meal. It is enough, first of all, to recall the hostility and contempt that Lockwood suffers at the hands of Heathcliff and other members of the Heights household before, during and after the tea he partakes of as a virtually uninvited guest in Chapter 2. Moreover, it is significant that, while Cathy is being watched by Lockwood from the moment she rejects his offer to help her reach one of the tea canisters on 'the chimney-piece' until she 'restored [it] to its place' (*WH*, p. 13) after the meal, her behaviour is at its most childish. This episode may be seen as a foreshadowing of a chronologically earlier one when another unexpected visitor, namely, Heathcliff, who has suddenly turned up at the Grange after a three-year absence from Gimmerton, is asked by Catherine to join her and Edgar (and Isabella) for tea. That the atmosphere on this occasion is scarcely less strained than that experienced by Lockwood at the Heights is evident from Nelly's following words: 'The meal hardly endured ten minutes—Catherine's cup was never filled, she could neither eat nor drink. Edgar had made a slop in his saucer, and scarcely swallowed a mouthful' (*WH*, p. 97).

The two afternoon teas (or high teas) discussed above are symbolically connected with the occasion when Heathcliff, having made Nelly Dean and Cathy his prisoners at the Heights in order to bring about the marriage of the two cousins, somewhat contradicts the spirit of his deed by telling them that they 'shall have tea, before [they] go home' (*WH*, p. 270); and then, after putting down their resistance, 'expeditiously made the tea himself' (*WH*, pp. 271-272). Furthermore, there is no small irony in Nelly's account of Heathcliff's playing the solicitous host with respect to tea both by what he does, 'The cups and saucers were laid ready. He poured it out, and handed me a cup [...]'; and by what he says, 'Wash away your spleen [...]. It is not poisoned, though I prepared it' (*WH*, p. 272). But the negative symbolism of tea is effectively completed when, during Heathcliff's momentary absence from 'the house', Linton delays answering Nelly and Cathy's request for an explanation of his father's strange behaviour, first, by saying, 'Give me some tea, and then I'll tell you', and, shortly afterwards, by complaining thus, 'Now, Catherine, you are letting your tears fall into my cup! I won't drink that. Give me another'. The fact that Cathy 'pushed another to him' and that, 'after sipping some of the liquid' (*WH*, p. 272), Linton then divulges his father's plan to marry them, seems in complete contrast with, and yet a sad evocation of, the equally tense moment when, shortly after his arrival at the Grange from the South, Cathy's loving attentiveness to her cousin in his tearful distress has included 'offering him tea in her saucer, like a baby' (*WH*, p. 201).

Although, like the afternoon teas mentioned in the foregoing, breakfast, dinner and supper are also conspicuous as backgrounds to, or prefigurations of, unpleasant episodes, all four meals nevertheless represent important junctures of the daily routine in both households. That meals are undoubtedly key events in Nelly Dean's life may be gathered when, for example, she relates that, having gone off on one of her excursions on horseback round Thrushcross park, Cathy 'contrived to remain out from breakfast till tea' (*WH*, p. 191); or that, on account of one such excursion, she 'never made her appearance at tea' (*WH*, p. 191); or, again, that after their visit to the Heights to see Linton Heathcliff, she and Cathy 'both reached home before [their] dinner-time: [...]' (*WH*, p. 243).[9] It is in much the same spirit that, conscious of her important role later on as housekeeper to Heathcliff, himself at that time generally a stickler for punctuality at meals and for members of his household to partake of them with him, Nelly proudly recalls, 'I held the mistress's post in making tea and carving; so I was indispensable at table' (*WH*, p. 317). It is, however, through her scrupulous concern with the need to eat properly, whether to sustain or to recover one's health, that Nelly shows her characteristic self, much of that concern being shown on behalf of Heathcliff. Thus we see how she seeks to compensate him for his absence from the Christmas dinner by 'endeavouring to introduce to him a private mess of victuals' (*WH*, p. 58) in the garret where he has been locked up by Hindley and, later, after he has come down to the kitchen, by offering him 'a quantity of good things' (*WH*, p. 59). Nelly's solicitude, as we shall come to see, is especially noticeable in her unsuccessful attempts to get Heathcliff to eat his meals towards the end of his life. Even after Heathcliff's death the old solicitude is still there when, to a Lockwood who has unexpectedly turned up at the Heights kitchen in September 1802 and been told that he will learn 'all about [Heathcliff's] death', Nelly suddenly says: 'Stop, you have had nothing to eat, have you?' (*WH*, p. 309).

Lockwood's self-assured manner of declining Nelly's implicit offer of food by saying, 'I want nothing. I have ordered supper at home' (*WH*, p. 309) stands in ironic contrast with the diffidence underlying the request he has made earlier to the old woman looking after the Grange, that is to say, 'to prepare a corner of a sitting-room for [him] to sup in, […]' (*WH*, p. 306). But the interest of those words here derives chiefly from the assumption that Lockwood will be eating alone, thus reminding us that meals in *Wuthering Heights* are seldom pleasantly convivial occasions. Indeed, Lockwood himself has by then not only recorded that the afternoon tea he took at the Heights in Chapter 2 was a meal with 'no one uttering a word of sociable conversation' (*WH*, p. 12), but also recalled the unpleasantness of the dinner he attended on his third visit there as follows: 'With Mr. Heathcliff, grim and saturnine, on one hand, and Hareton, absolutely dumb, on the other, I made a somewhat cheerless meal, […]' (*WH*, p. 304). Even that most convivial of repasts, the Christmas dinner, turns out to be a little less than such a traditional occasion, partly because of Heathcliff's exclusion from it by Hindley and Catherine's resultant unease at table. Certainly, it is through meals that Hindley and Frances enjoy exercising their tyranny over others in their household and practising their arrant separatism. This is already suggested when the reason Heathcliff gives Nelly for his and Catherine's illicit visit to the Grange is to 'see whether the Lintons passed their Sunday evenings standing shivering in corners, while their father and mother sat eating and drinking […] before the fire' (*WH*, pp. 45-46). Yet it is Hindley and Frances's recognition of Catherine's enhanced social status, thanks to her five-week sojourn at the Grange, that accounts for the fact that, on the evening of her return to the Heights, she 'supped with her brother and sister-in-law' (*WH*, p. 54)—words which, while emphasising the legal relations between the three characters, seem to corroborate what Lockwood has read in Catherine's diary, to wit, that Hindley 'won't let [Heathcliff] [...] eat with us any more, [...]' (*WH*, p. 20). No doubt, the wretchedness of a character's particular circumstances is seldom more pronounced than when that character is deprived of the company of others at a meal, or prefers to eat alone. For example, Hindley's self-imposed isolation as master of the Heights is poignantly evoked by this detail about the supper prepared for him by Nelly: '[Joseph] and I began to quarrel who should carry some to Mr. Hindley; and we didn't settle it till all was nearly cold. Then we came to the agreement that we would let him ask, if he wanted any, for we feared particularly to go into his presence when he had been some time alone' (*WH*, p. 82). Similarly, there is something pathetic about Isabella's narration of the times when, as Heathcliff's neglected bride at the Heights, she describes herself as either having chosen, or being obliged, to eat on her own.

There is pathos, too, when, because of her infatuation with Heathcliff, Isabella is one morning observed by Nelly 'rejecting her breakfast' (*WH*, p. 101) and, more pointedly, when, later that day, Catherine taunts Heathcliff by saying this to him in Isabella's very presence: 'And [Isabella] has fasted ever since the day before yesterday's walk, from sorrow and rage that I despatched her out of your society under the idea of its being unacceptable' (*WH*, p. 105). The significance of such details, however, lies chiefly in our awareness of the extent to which some of the other main characters also abstain from food.[10] Such abstinence, which is comically foreshadowed by Lockwood's being evidently too absorbed in the first part of Nelly's narrative (Chapters 4-9) to bother about the gruel substituted by her for the supper she at first brought him, is one practised in its most woeful ways by the principal hero and heroine. There are, first of all, contexts in which the fervour of Catherine's devotion to Heathcliff is realistically rendered by details about her inability to eat or drink, or about her going without meals. For example, it is her dread of Hindley's flogging Heathcliff for assaulting Edgar with the tureen of hot apple-sauce that induces her to reproach the latter by telling him that she 'can't eat [her] dinner' (*WH*, p. 58). Again, her distraught state of mind on the night of Heathcliff's disappearance is partly illustrated by the fact that, having restlessly watched out for his possible return, she in the end forgoes the supper she had hoped to eat with Nelly. Much more important, however, for Catherine's presentation as an essentially tragic figure is her occasionally wilful refusal to eat or drink. It is, to be sure, one thing for her to be punished by Hindley for her failure to go to church with 'a fast from dinner or supper' (*WH*, p. 44), and quite another when, having locked herself up in her bedroom for three days, she 'fasted pertinaciously, under the idea, probably, that at every meal, Edgar was ready to choke for her absence, and pride alone held him from running to cast himself at her feet; [...]' (*WH*, p. 120). Whether or not Nelly has read Catherine's mind correctly here, this detail bespeaks a childish egotism on the latter's part quite redolent of that informing the intention she will soon afterwards impart in the same bedroom as follows: 'Nelly, if it be not too late, as soon as I learn how [Edgar] feels, I'll choose between these two—either to starve, at once, that would be no punishment unless he had a heart— or to recover and leave the country' (*WH*, p. 121).

Catherine's vow just quoted in some sense ironically affirms the spiritual bond existing between her and Heathcliff, not only because he himself (supposedly) left the country for three years, but because as a child he was seen by Mr. Earnshaw 'starving [...] in the streets of Liverpool' (*WH*, p. 35). Yet casual as the latter detail seems when first read, it may nevertheless be considered a symbolic foreshadowing of the three or four days leading up to Heathcliff's death, marked as they are quite literally by starvation in the form of his total and involuntary abstinence from food. There are also several occasions in between those two extreme stages of Heathcliff's life that are remarkable for his inability or disinclination to take food. To be sure, there is nothing out of the ordinary about the blend of pride and resentment which, doubtless the outcome of his unhappy reunion with Catherine on her return from the Grange, causes him to go without the 'cake and cheese' (*WH*, p. 54) that Nelly has later specially invited him to have in the kitchen. And even though, as Nelly recalls, '[f]asting and reflection seemed to have brought him to a better spirit' (*WH*, p. 55) the following morning in so far as he has asked her to 'make [him] decent' because he is 'going to be good' (*WH*, p. 55), Heathcliff's abstinence from food is nevertheless prolonged soon afterwards by his banishment from the Christmas dinner. Furthermore, notwithstanding Nelly's willingness illicitly to allow him into the kitchen after his escape from the garret, since, as she points out, 'the prisoner had never broken his fast since yesterday's dinner', and despite her offering him, as aforesaid, 'a quantity of good things', Heathcliff's thoughts of vengeance against Hindley help to explain why he 'was sick, and could eat little' (*WH*, p. 59).

Of greater interest, however, is the way in which Heathcliff's grief at the loss of Catherine is conveyed by statements about his absences from meals or his inability to eat. As Isabella says to Nelly after her flight from the Heights: 'Whether the angels have fed him, or his kin beneath, I cannot tell; but he has not eaten a meal with us for nearly a week' (*WH*, p. 173). But once Heathcliff's mourning has transmuted into an incurable obsession with the deceased Catherine, his abstinence from food seems to become more or less pathological. This is already evident when, having told Nelly in his long confession to her in Chapter 33 of the 'strange change approaching' and of his being 'in its shadow at present', he adds, '—I take so little interest in my daily life, that I hardly remember to eat and drink—' (*WH*, p. 323). Such words are attested time and again in the remaining chapters of the novel both by Nelly's elaborate accounts of her vain endeavours to get Heathcliff to eat or drink the sustenance she has prepared for him and by his continually postponing his intake of food from one meal to the next. And though all these references are enough in themselves to arouse or maintain a certain sympathy for Heathcliff, and the more so when, in her account of Mr. Kenneth's perplexity as to the reason for his death, Nelly is 'persuaded' that Heathcliff 'did not abstain on purpose', indeed, that his abstinence from food was 'the consequence of his strange illness, not the cause' (*WH*, p. 336), there may be said to be something none the less futile about a persistent fasting that has been largely the effect of an inherently egotistical abuse of the mind, and that in the name of a dead person. It is, therefore, perhaps significant that nowhere in the narrative is mention ever made of Heathcliff's going without nourishment out of anxiety for someone he is in living relationship with. Certainly, he is not to be compared in that respect to Catherine in her selfless avoidance of food on the night she watches out for his return to the Heights. Nor for that matter do we learn anything about him to match the knowledge that, during the time she was looking after Nelly Dean and her father, Cathy 'neglected her meals' (*WH*, p. 244).

If Heathcliff's involuntary starvation towards the end of his life may nevertheless seem noble enough in the eyes of some readers to be but testimony to his heroic stature, especially as a sign of his enduring love for the memory or ghost of Catherine, it would still not be out of place here to recall our proposition to the effect that Lockwood's description of 'the house' in Chapter 1 in some sense points forward to the 'normality' of eating and drinking at the Heights. It is true that references to food and drink in *Wuthering Heights* are minimal and show none of the variety and abundance of detail, to say nothing of the occasional humour, of similar references to be found in, say, Charlotte Brontë's fiction. Such austerity on Emily's part is integral to the rigorously economical structure of her masterpiece; which is why, as we have tried to show, references to eating and drinking, food and beverages, seem to serve peculiarly symbolic, thematic or psychological functions, but are otherwise seldom given for their own sake. At the same time, through all such references, many of which may be easily overlooked in our preoccupation with the famously romantic plot, Emily Brontë seems to be laying clues to the meaning of her book as well as giving us unwonted insights into her characters.

Be that as it may, it is owing to Nelly Dean's manifold references to meals, and even to abstention from meals, that the reader is made constantly aware of the essential realism of the novel. And though Nelly's fastidiousness as to the necessity of a regular ingestion of food for the sake of physical and psychological health is not without its ironic implications, we may wonder all the same whether the somewhat heroic status of Cathy and Hareton, as suggested at the end of the narrative, does not in part stem from our knowing that at no time does either of them exhibit any abnormality or eccentricity with respect to food. That is why there is a certain charm about their reconciliation being further confirmed by the breakfasts they take together, notably the one at which Cathy's roguish behaviour is specially contrasted with a gloomily silent and distracted Heathcliff at the moment she is 'sticking primroses in [Hareton's] plate of porridge' (*WH*, p. 318) and thereby transcending the symbolism of that indigenous dish.[11] It is, moreover, not without symbolic significance that Hareton's birth is announced by a girl who brings breakfasts to Nelly Dean and her fellow-workers in the hayfields. For breakfast is, of course, the meal that marks the beginning of a new day. Hence it is that, with this earlier detail in mind, we may find something poetically apt in the idea that, at the very time Heathcliff is fast falling further in a steep mental decline amid his chronic abstinence from food, a fresh and happier era seems to be in part symbolically heralded when Cathy and Hareton, having been advised by Nelly to get their breakfast 'ere the master came down', preferred 'taking it out of doors, under the trees, [...]' (*WH*, p. 330).

Brontë Studies, 34/1 (2009)

Notes

1 For quotations from the novel, see Emily Brontë, *Wuthering Heights*, eds. Ian Jack and Patsy Stoneman (Oxford: Oxford University Press, 1998). The edition quoted from is the original 1998 impression of 372 pages, not the later 1998 impression of 330 pages. For the sake of convenience, the first Catherine will be referred to as 'Catherine', the second as 'Cathy'.

2 In Chapter 2, Joseph is described by Lockwood 'bringing in a pail of porridge for the dogs'. See *Wuthering Heights*, p. 13.

3 In this connection, it is perhaps symbolically appropriate that, on his return to the Heights in September 1802, that is, some three months after Heathcliff's death, Lockwood should notice, near the entrance to the building, the 'fragrance of stocks and wall flowers wafted on the air from among the homely fruit-trees' and that Nelly, having noticed Heathcliff's absence from the Heights one fine April morning shortly before his death, should mention 'the two dwarf apple trees near the southern wall, in full bloom'. See *Wuthering Heights*, pp. 307, 326.

4 See *Wuthering Heights*, pp. 109-110, 155-156.

5 See *Wuthering Heights*, pp. 279-280.

6 See *Wuthering Heights*, p. 309.

7 Linton Heathcliff's craving for milk is foreshadowed when Heathcliff sardonically conveys his first impression of the boy's physical appearance: 'Haven't they reared it on snails and sour milk, [...]?' See *Wuthering Heights*, p. 207.

8 See *Wuthering Heights*, pp. 30, 330.

9 For similar references to meals, see *Wuthering Heights*, pp. 119, 201, 206, 230, 321.

10 Isabella's rejection of breakfast is comically foreshadowed when, referring to Heathcliff's household, on the morning after his night in the oak-panelled room, Lockwood remarks that he 'declined joining their breakfast'. See *Wuthering Heights*, p. 29.

11 That porridge is symbolically associated with Hareton Earnshaw is perhaps already suggested when, in an attempt to persuade Linton Heathcliff to eat the porridge he has at first rejected, Joseph says, 'But Maister Hareton nivir ate nowt else, when he wer a little un: und what wer gooid eneugh fur him's gooid eneugh fur yah, Aw's rayther think!' See *Wuthering Heights*, p. 209.

House and Home in
Wuthering Heights

R eaders of *Wuthering Heights* may have wondered from time to
time why a novel so conspicuous for its principal love story
should have been given the name of a house for its title. Such a use
of a fictional building was, of course, by no means unprecedented
in the mid-nineteenth century, as is evident enough from, say,
Horace Walpole's *The Castle of Otranto* (1765), Jane Austen's
Northanger Abbey (1818) and Sir Walter Scott's *The Monastery* (1820).
Yet there can be little doubt that, whatever the aesthetic functions
of these eponymous buildings, whether thematic, symbolic or
satirical, they can each be said to serve primarily as backgrounds
to particular plots, but otherwise to have comparatively little
influence on the human beings involved in those plots. The same
can, on the other hand, scarcely be said of *Wuthering Heights* once
we have come to realize, after careful examination of the text, that,
in contradistinction to the aforementioned dwellings, Wuthering
Heights *qua* house is very closely bound up with the lives of the

characters portrayed; indeed, so much so in some respects as to be regarded, together with Thrushcross Grange, as essential to a central theme of the novel, namely, the concept of home.[1]

It is interesting to note first of all that, constituting as they do the main settings of actions and events in the novel, Wuthering Heights and Thrushcross Grange are remarkable for the very palpable impression they make on the reader. Thus our attention is drawn now and again to exterior parts of a house, to rooms, to parts of rooms, to areas between rooms, to furniture, to furnishings, to implements, to utensils, to outbuildings, to courtyards, to gardens and to fields, all such references amounting to some twelve hundred altogether, including references to objects that are mentioned more than once in the narrative. It is, nevertheless, useful to be reminded that, notwithstanding their having certain domestic features in common, Wuthering Heights, being the domicile of several generations of yeoman farmers, is socially inferior to Thrushcross Grange, a house owned and occupied by apparently the only landed gentry living in the neighbourhood. Even while still residing at the Heights, Nelly Dean shows how well aware she is of this social difference when, in an attempt to allay Catherine's doubts about marrying Edgar, she says: '[Y]ou will escape from a disorderly, comfortless home into a wealthy respectable one' (*WH*, p. 70).[2] Nelly's comparison here in favour of the Grange is no doubt due in part to her having witnessed a deterioration in the Heights as a household since Hindley became its master and, more especially, since Frances's death. As she says to Lockwood: 'I could not half tell what an infernal house we had' (*WH*, p. 58). This in turn helps to explain why Nelly's affirmative attitude towards the Grange becomes more and more entrenched, reaching its extreme point by the time she has served several years as its housekeeper. We see this in some measure particularly when, anxious to discourage Cathy from visiting Penistone Craggs, she tells her, among other things, that 'Thrushcross park is the finest place in

HOUSE AND HOME IN *WUTHERING HEIGHTS*

the world' (*WH*, p. 168), and, again, when, on their journey to the Heights, she assures Linton Heathcliff that, though he will think that building 'old and dark, at first', it is 'a respectable house, *the next best in the neighbourhood*' (*WH*, p. 181; italics mine). Nor should we forget to mention how much the elegance of the Grange has been suggested early in the novel by the enthusiasm with which Heathcliff as a youngster has told Nelly about the drawing room as observed by him and Catherine through a window from outside: '[A]h! it was beautiful—a splendid place carpeted with crimson, and crimson-covered chairs and tables, and a pure white ceiling bordered by gold, a shower of glass-drops hanging in silver chains from the centre, and shimmering with little soft tapers' (*WH*, pp. 41-42). That Linton Heathcliff, too, will respond to the interior of the Grange quite as favourably as his father has done many years before is implicit in his following question to Nelly: 'Is Wuthering Heights as pleasant a place as Thrushcross Grange?' (*WH*, p. 181).

As well as asserting its social superiority to the Heights partly through the merest references to such rooms or facilities as its hall, its drawing-room, its library and its porter's lodge, the Grange clearly enjoys the highest standing in the neighbourhood attributed to it by Nelly. The idea that one's social status is, moreover, practically determined by the type of house one owns and occupies is underlined when, on meeting a somewhat gruff Heathcliff on the moors for the first time, Cathy identifies her 'papa' as 'Mr. Linton of Thrushcross Grange'; and, again, when to Cathy's presently adding, 'I thought you did not know me, or you wouldn't have spoken in that way', Heathcliff sarcastically retorts: 'You suppose papa is highly esteemed and respected then?' (*WH*, p. 188). In keeping with its respectable status, the Grange is, not surprisingly, a well-guarded and well-ordered household. This may be adduced already from the language used by Mr. and Mrs. Linton in reaction to Heathcliff and Catherine's trespassing on their property one Sunday evening. The notion of the Grange as the 'strong-hold' (*WH*, p. 43) Mr. Linton considers it to be still prevails somewhat when, in one of several attempts to deter Heathcliff from visiting Catherine there, Nelly warns him that Edgar will 'take measures to secure his house and its inmates from any such unwarrantable intrusions!' (*WH*, p. 135). Certainly Edgar's jealousy for the 'decent house' (*WH*, p. 44) with which Mrs. Linton alludes to the Grange and which on the fateful Sunday evening she regards young Heathcliff as 'quite unfit for' (*WH*, p. 44) is patent when, uncomfortable with Catherine's enthusiastic reception of Heathcliff on his unexpected visit there after a three-year absence, he says this to her: 'The whole household need not witness the sight of your welcoming a runaway servant as a brother' (*WH*, p. 84). Yet, as Nelly recalls, it is thanks to Heathcliff's advent that Catherine 'rewarded [Edgar] with such a summer of sweetness and affection [...] as made the house a paradise for several days' (*WH*, p. 88), aware as the housekeeper is how much her mistress has disturbed the usually tranquil atmosphere of the Grange through her conflicts with Edgar and Isabella. That Catherine herself is conscious of her disruptive effect on Edgar's orderly household is plain to see when, imagining in her delirious state in Chapter 12 the reactions of those watching her die, she pictures Edgar 'standing solemnly by to see it over; then offering prayers of thanks to God for restoring peace to his house' (*WH*, p. 107).

By contrast with a generally sedate Thrushcross Grange, Wuthering Heights comes across as a rather dysfunctional household for much of the action. It is true that the Heights is the centre of an apparently thriving farm herding sheep and cattle and dealing in agricultural products, and that it continues functioning as such throughout the narrative, at least to judge by intermittent references or allusions to work done on its behalf, chiefly by Joseph and Hareton, in the outbuildings, hayfields and ploughfields as well as in remote parts of the local countryside.[3] That the Heights might have long been a consistently orderly place to live in is suggested by its having existed continuously as the habitation of the Earnshaw family for almost three centuries. Even under Mr. Earnshaw's aegis it appears to have been a stable, happy place, partly through the custom of family and servants sitting together every evening in the large sitting room known as 'the house'. But when Mr. Earnshaw brings Heathcliff home with him from Liverpool the atmosphere of the house starts to change for the worse; and, once Hindley has taken over as master, will deteriorate to its nadir from the time Heathcliff has come back to live there as his lodger. And although, after Hindley's death, as Nelly recalls, 'the house, inside, had regained its ancient aspect of comfort under female management; and the scenes of riot common in Hindley's time were not now enacted within its walls' (*WH*, p. 174), she now and then offsets this indirect tribute to Heathcliff's mastership of the Heights by negative comments about his household. This may be noted, for example, when she tries to undermine Cathy's early interest in the Heights with the following warning: 'Well, Miss Cathy, if you were aware whose house this is, you'd be glad enough to get out' (*WH*, p. 172); or when, dreading the likelihood that Linton Heathcliff, newly arrived at the Grange, will have to go and live with his father, she wonders: '[H]owever will that weakling live at Wuthering Heights, between his father and Hareton? What playmates and instructors they'll be' (*WH*, p. 178). Nelly's negative attitude to Heathcliff's household has doubtless been already aggravated by Isabella's epistolary and oral reports of her life there as his hapless young bride, whose sense of being little more than a prisoner there prefigures Nelly's own account of being incarcerated at the Heights by Heathcliff for several days with Cathy. All this goes hand in hand with the idea that the Heights under Heathcliff's ownership is for the most part a fortress-like place, whose liberation is eventually realized only by his death.

It is, then, curious to reflect that the two houses possessed by Heathcliff in the last few months of his life appear to have been self-sufficiently independent of each other over several generations. Indeed, it is only from the time of Catherine and Heathcliff's illicit visit to the Grange that communication between both houses can be truly said to have begun. And though other buildings are referred to here and there in the novel—cottages, chapels, a clergyman's house, Mr. Kenneth's house, Mr. Green's house, a road-side public house—Wuthering Heights and Thrushcross Grange are the only ones in which the action takes place, and that very often as a consequence of the movements of the characters from one house to the other, whether on foot, on horseback or by carriage. It is, moreover, chiefly owing to some such movements that events and episodes both good and bad are given rise to: the illness and death of Mr. and Mrs. Linton, Edgar's marriage to Catherine, Isabella's elopement with Heathcliff, Catherine's untimely death, Cathy's ill-fated marriage to Linton Heathcliff, Cathy's meeting with Hareton and subsequent betrothal to him. And whereas relations between the two houses seem to cease altogether between the time of Catherine's marriage and Heathcliff's return to Gimmerton and, again, for some twelve years after Isabella's departure from the neighbourhood, they are re-established through Cathy's visit to Penistone Craggs and through her chance meeting with Heathcliff, and subsequently maintained partly through Nelly's failure to exercise the authority over her charge that has been vested in her by Edgar. Also to be taken into account here are the occasional absences of the master of a particular household—Hindley, Edgar and Heathcliff in particular—as means whereby a plot is furthered, and sometimes not without disastrous effects.[4]

Yet however close the connection between the Heights and the Grange may be throughout the narrative, it is still necessary to stress the extent to which the characters are rooted in one or other of the two houses they belong to. Indeed, apart from its being taken for granted that some of these characters, especially the males of the two oldest generations portrayed, have, like their ancestors, been born and died in the houses they have each lived in all their lives, it is obvious that the master of a house, whether he be farmer or landed gentleman, does his work almost entirely in or near that house, even while part of his work entails dealings with tenants renting properties or land from him elsewhere in the neighbourhood. That is why the distinction commonly drawn between the home and the workplace in our own time hardly seems to apply in the novel. In this connection, it is worth noting that the difference between 'house' and 'home' seems virtually non-existent in the text when 'home' is used in sentences about a movement to a particular house. This conflation is obvious enough when, for example, on the night Heathcliff is noticed to have disappeared from the Heights, Nelly believes that 'the approaching rain would be certain to bring him home without further trouble' (*WH*, p. 75).[5] In some sentences, however, 'home' seems more resonant than usual, especially when, as well as indicating a return to the Grange, it refers to a strong intention or an urgent request to do so on the part of Isabella, Nelly and Cathy after the unpleasant experiences they have undergone at the Heights.[6] Sometimes, too, 'home' has a quite ambivalent meaning. Thus, when amid her attempts to get Linton Heathcliff out of bed on the morning she is to take him to the Heights, Nelly tries to mitigate the boy's perplexity by saying, among other things, '[Y]ou should be glad to go home, and to see [your father]' (*WH*, p. 180), she is probably quite unaware that, since he has been living in London for some twelve years already, 'home' is not likely to mean the same thing for him. Again, when soon after his unexpected arrival at the Grange (in Chapter 29), Heathcliff says this to Cathy: 'I'm come to fetch you home' (*WH*, p. 253), 'home', of course, means the Heights. Yet from her dialogue with Nelly shortly beforehand, it is clear that, though by now married to her cousin Linton, Cathy still looks upon the Grange as her real home, where, together with Nelly, she has been hoping to be allowed to continue living.

The importance of a house for one's sense of security, as hinted at in the foregoing reference to Cathy, is nowhere more strongly emphasized than when, amid his continued preoccupation with the latter's well-being after his death, Edgar believes it is only through marriage to her cousin Linton, as much as in accordance with his own 'natural desire', that she 'might retain—or, at least, return in a short time to—the house of her ancestors' (*WH*, p. 229). This is an understandable sentiment in one who has apparently spent all his life at the Grange. At the same time, because Edgar has followed in his father's footsteps as both landed gentleman and magistrate, he seems for the most part to be in some sense a prisoner of the house he has inherited. Certainly, there is little to suggest that, apart from courting Catherine at the Heights, visiting the neighbourhood for professional purposes, or going down south to see Isabella, Edgar has ever been adventurous enough to go much beyond the boundaries of his estate, or even to wish to do so. We note this more especially after Catherine's death, grief over which, as Nelly recalls, 'transformed him into a complete hermit' (*WH*, p. 162). It is, moreover, from that time onwards, and partly owing to chronic ill-health, that, in spite of his concern to maintain an orderly, disciplined household, Edgar remains largely out of touch with that household, particularly where it is a question of Nelly's guardianship of Cathy. Much the same may be said *mutatis mutandis* of Hindley, who, like Edgar, has inherited his house from his father. But, unlike Edgar, Hindley has a fundamentally irresponsible attitude to his household, ranging from outright tyranny over its inmates to complete unawareness of them. That it is sometimes an utterly frivolous attitude is suggested when, in his drunken state in Chapter 9, he says this to Nelly: 'No law in England can hinder a man from keeping his house decent, and mine's abominable!' (*WH*, p. 65); and, again, when, embarrassed and angered by Nelly's scolding of him for dropping Hareton over the bannister, he shows his resentment towards Heathcliff for saving the latter's life, first, by ordering him out of his 'reach and hearing', and then by threatening him as follows: 'I wouldn't murder you to-night, unless, perhaps, I set the house on fire; but that's as my fancy goes—' (*WH*, p. 67). It is through such talk, as well as through Nelly's and Joseph's comments on his incompetence as master of his house, that Hindley betrays the failings of his character, just as Edgar's own limitations as a human being may be gauged in part from his somewhat tenuous relationship with the Grange.

If Edgar and Hindley seem in some sense neurotically dependent on the ancestral homes they own and inhabit, the same can hardly be said of Heathcliff with respect to either of the two houses he has acquired by the end of his life. It is true that Heathcliff's going to lodge at the Heights on his return to Gimmerton after his three-year absence is, at least according to Catherine, due partly to 'an attachment to the house where [they] lived together' (*WH*, p. 88), even though, amid this romantic view, she appears to have forgotten that his original reason for returning there was to kill Hindley and then commit suicide. What encourages Heathcliff to stay on at the Heights is that, as well as wishing to be within easy reach of Catherine, he finds himself, possibly not without malice aforethought, enhancing Hindley's financial reliance on him so far as eventually to end up becoming legal owner of the Heights on the latter's death. That Heathcliff, namely, 'the guest' who, as Nelly says, 'was now the master of Wuthering Heights' (*WH*, p. 165), never seems to be quite at one with that house, is hinted at by Lockwood when, on his first visit to the Heights he describes him as forming 'a singular contrast to his abode and style of living' (*WH*, p. 3)—a detail that is thematically linked with Heathcliff's having as a child been found by Mr. Earnshaw 'starving, and *houseless*, […] in the streets of

Liverpool' (*WH*, p. 31; italics mine) and with Nelly's accounts of his early years at the Heights, especially under Hindley's jurisdiction. Why Heathcliff stays on at the Heights as owner thereof nevertheless puzzles Nelly, considering that, as she informs Lockwood, he is 'rich enough to live in a finer house than this' (*WH*, p. 29). But if the continuance of his residence there has much to do with his concern to supervise the family farm, it would appear later in the narrative that his main reason for staying put, especially from the time his mental health has begun to decline, is that the Heights is the place where he can best experience the visitations of Catherine's ghost.[7] And though Heathcliff is the master of a very orderly, not to say austerely disciplined, household, there is little to suggest that he ever truly feels at home in that household, spending as he does much of his time alone in 'the house', particularly in the last stages of his life. In any case, being or feeling at home in a domicile seems to matter far less to Heathcliff than owning properties and land and making money out of them. This is most pathetically apparent when, undecided how to 'leave [his] property' at his death, he tells Nelly that he wishes he 'could annihilate it from the face of the earth' (*WH*, p. 296).[8]

The fact that Heathcliff seems for the most part ill at ease in the house he owns somehow forcibly evokes the opposite idea as manifest already in the close links we have noted between 'house' and 'home', namely, that being at home, whether actually or metaphorically, is ultimately inseparable from the house one inhabits. At the same time, it is self-evident that being at home in a particular house does not necessarily mean owning the house one resides in. This is eminently true of the servants employed in one or other of the two households featured in the novel. For Nelly Dean, for example, home has been both the Heights, into which she more or less drifted in childhood, and the Grange, whither she accompanied Catherine on the latter's marriage to Edgar and where, after Edgar's death, she hopes, albeit in vain, to be allowed to continue living, because she regards the place as 'my home' (*WH*, p. 253). It is, moreover, interesting to note the way in which Nelly's sense of being at home in either household she is serving is sometimes confirmed by the odd expression of loyalty on her part. We see this especially when, in her anxiety about the newly returned Heathcliff's influence on both households, she tells of wanting 'something to happen which might have the effect of freeing both Wuthering Heights and the Grange of [him]' (*WH*, p. 95). Joseph's own loyalty to the Heights probably has much to do with the fact that he has lived there for a good sixty years, and is likely to end his days there. By contrast, temporary servants such as Zillah and the unnamed Heights housekeeper suggest how little they feel at home in the Heights through the occasional disloyalty of their utterances and behaviour.[9] But since the servants portrayed in Emily Brontë's novel, both temporary and permanent, are perforce obliged to live in houses that do not belong to them, it is perhaps hardly surprising that they seldom, if ever, appear to suffer from the various forms of nostalgia or homesickness that afflict some of their social superiors, Lockwood being a notable case in point.

Characterized as a man somewhat beset by chronic restlessness, Lockwood may, however, give some readers the impression that he is not much inclined to nostalgia for a home. Thus, already in Chapter 1 Lockwood seems, chiefly on account of his failure to marry the girl he saw at the sea-coast, to be quite resigned to the idea that, as '[his] dear mother used to say', he will 'never have a comfortable home' (*WH*, p. 3). Again, when to Nelly's hinting (in Chapter 23) that he should court Cathy, Lockwood has expressed reluctance to 'venture [his] tranquillity by running into temptation', he continues to resist Nelly's hint with this rather lame excuse: '[…] and then my home is not here. I'm of the busy world, and to its arms I must return' (*WH*, p. 226). As is evident from this vague answer, Lockwood avoids specifying whether he even has an actual home to go to. That the phrase 'my home' nevertheless has a certain nostalgic resonance is not improbable when considered in the light of the extraordinary detail with which he describes the sitting room, usually known as 'the house', in Wuthering Heights on his first visit there. Indeed, what is ostensibly a conventional enumeration of furnishings and objects so typical of nineteenth-century fiction since the time of Scott may be interpreted as a strong expression of nostalgia for a house which he describes almost lovingly and which, in Chapter 2, he will consider appropriate as a setting for what, in similarly nostalgic vein, he (mistakenly) assumes to be Heathcliff's happy nuclear family. Lockwood's nostalgia for a home of his own has even been latent in the physical violence with which he has sought to be let into the Heights on his second visit there—a nostalgia whose unconscious nature is confirmed in Chapter 3 by his account of his first dream, in which, having 'set out on [his] way home, with Joseph for a guide', he is astonished to be told by him that he needs a pilgrim's staff to 'gain admittance into [his] own residence' (*WH*, p. 18). Here we have one of several instances of Lockwood's tendency to imagine himself as a homeowner, and that not without comical implications. Consider, for example, the occasion when, arriving in the North in September 1802, Lockwood decides to visit the Grange, having just 'conceived that [he] might as well pass the night *under [his] own roof*, as in an inn' (*WH*, p. 271; italics mine). Especially comical is the moment when, informed by the old woman sitting outside the Grange that she is keeping house there, he introduces himself as follows: 'Well, I'm Mr. Lockwood, the master—' (*WH*, p. 272), before going on to indulge his apparent nostalgia through the detail with which he describes the old woman clumsily setting about her domestic chores on his behalf.[10]

The interest of our foregoing discussion on Lockwood derives in part from its being thematically linked with the presentation of Catherine and Isabella, both of whom are conspicuous for their bouts of nostalgia. But whereas Lockwood seems nostalgic for a house he does not yet appear to own, Catherine and Isabella express their nostalgia in the form of homesickness for the houses they have been born and brought up in. Isabella's homesickness is at first noticeable when in her letter to Nelly she relates that '[her] heart returned to Thrushcross Grange in twenty-four hours after [she] left it, and is there at this moment' (*WH*, p. 120). No doubt, Isabella's nostalgia is partly due to the well-appointedness of the Grange itself, as Nelly herself suggests when, long aware of the superiority of the Grange to the Heights, she taunts Heathcliff by telling him that, but for her 'capacity for strong attachments', his bride 'wouldn't have abandoned the elegances, and comforts [...] of her former home, to fix contentedly, in such a wilderness as this' (*WH*, p. 132). That Isabella as the daughter of well-to-do parents seems to have been more or less neurotically attached to the Grange from earliest years is evident when, in reaction to Heathcliff's violence to Edgar with the tureen of apple-sauce, she is described as 'weeping to go home' (*WH*, p. 51)—a phrase, ironically enough, practically repeated by Heathcliff when he informs Nelly that, 'the very morrow of [their] wedding', Isabella 'was weeping to go home' (*WH*, p. 132). All the same, it is easy to see that Isabella's nostalgia for the Grange is now and again based on her somewhat faulty memory. Thus when in her letter to Nelly she speaks of '*remembering* that four miles distant lay my delightful home' (*WH*, p. 122; italics mine); or, later, when alluding to life at the Grange with Edgar and Catherine before Heathcliff's return to Gimmerton, she says this to Hindley: 'When I *recollect* how happy we were—how happy Catherine was before he came—I'm fit to curse the day'(*WH*, p. 160; italics mine), Isabella appears to have forgotten how often she was unhappy there on account of Catherine's domination of her. It is, of course, understandable that Isabella should make straight for the Grange after her flight and that she should even think of staying on there, since, as she tells Nelly, 'the Grange is my right home' (*WH*, p. 152). But whereas the reason for her not staying on after all has partly to do with her fear of being hunted down there by Heathcliff, it may also have to do with the maturity she has begun to acquire through her ability to cope with the problems she has recently confronted at the Heights as Heathcliff's unhappy bride. In fact, Isabella proves that she is perfectly capable of jettisoning her attachment to the Grange, not only by leaving her childhood home on the very night she has taken refuge there, but by setting up an independent 'abode [...] in the south, near London' (*WH*, p. 161) and living there with her son until her death some twelve years later.

In contrast to Isabella, whose nostalgia for the Grange is invariably felt and expressed consciously, Catherine's nostalgia for the Heights is for the most part buried inside her unconscious mind. This may in part explain why, unlike Isabella, Catherine seems unable, as it were, to put her attachment to her childhood home behind her and thereby achieve something of the maturity that we glimpse the beginnings of in her sister-in-law. Catherine's nostalgia for the Heights is foreshadowed by Lockwood's dream in which, amid her attempts as a waif to get into the house through a window, she says, among other things, 'I'm come home' (*WH*, p. 20), but does not become overt until she is suffering from the delirium which has been sparked off by Edgar's showdown with Heathcliff in Chapter 11 and which is symptomatic of the 'brain fever' (*WH*, p. 118) she is shortly to be afflicted with. Thus amid her rambling talk in her semi-conscious state, Catherine is pulled up by Nelly for mistaking the mirror in her bedroom for a black press, and effectively enough for her to respond to the latter as follows: 'Oh, dear! I thought I was at home [...]. I thought I was lying in my chamber at Wuthering Heights' (*WH*, p. 109). These words in turn give rise to this expression of nostalgia: 'Oh, if I were but in my own bed in the old house! [...] And that wind sounding in the firs by the lattice. Do let me feel it—it comes straight down the moor—do let me have one breath!' (*WH*, pp. 109-110). That Catherine is, as we have just seen, sometimes quite consciously nostalgic for the past is presently manifested when, having given Nelly an account of her black-out, and even suggested that she has been mistaken to marry Edgar, she suddenly exclaims: 'I wish I were out of doors—I wish I were a girl again, half savage and hardy, and free [...]. I'm sure I should be myself were I once among the heather on those hills' (*WH*, p. 111). This forms a prelude to another spell of delirium, whereby memories of her childhood come back to her with remarkable vividness: 'Look! [...] that's my room, with the candle in it, and the trees swaying before it ... and the other candle is in Joseph's garret ... Joseph sits up late, doesn't he? He's waiting till I come home that he may lock the gate ... Well, he'll wait a while yet' (*WH*, p. 111).[11] Few utterances could better illustrate the notion that the sense of being at home is intimately associated with an affectionate awareness of certain mundane aspects of everyday life in a particular household. Yet touching as Catherine's memories here might be deemed, especially as taken in conjunction with her memories of expeditions with Heathcliff at that time, they are none the less far from being healthy or normal recollections of childhood. Indeed, however businesslike Catherine may consider herself as mistress of the Grange, it is probably owing to her quite pathological fixation on her girlhood at the Heights that she seems to lack the maturity to create a genuine home of her own either through marriage or as an independent woman.

What has just been said above might be considered pertinent enough to anyone intent on drawing a comparison between Catherine and her daughter Cathy. To begin with, where house and home are concerned, Cathy seems the more enterprising as well as the luckier of the two characters. The idea that Cathy, by the age of twelve, appears to have found her life at the Grange rather too secure, not to say too happy, is almost certainly one reason why she breaks bounds in order to visit Penistone Craggs. In this respect, she may be said to have been more adventurous in spirit than her mother, and much more so than her father Edgar.[12] It is, moreover, through this illicit excursion that Cathy not only discovers the existence of the Heights, but meets the young man whom she is eventually to marry—an outcome delightfully foreshadowed when Nelly notices, on arriving there after a frantic search for her young mistress, that Cathy's hat 'was hung against the wall' and that she 'seemed perfectly *at home*, laughing and chattering, in the best spirits imaginable, to Hareton' (*WH*, p. 171; italics mine). Nevertheless, Cathy's discovery of the Heights also leads to the sufferings she will have to endure at the hands of both Heathcliff and his son Linton, just as it is inside the Heights that she will spend much of her time in conflict with Hareton. Moreover, from the very day before her marriage to Linton until well after his death, Cathy will be virtually Heathcliff's prisoner at the Heights until the latter's passing. Still, it is within the confines of her temporary home that Cathy will undergo an education the very opposite of what she once received from Edgar at the Grange, namely, an education in the hard knocks of life. Certainly, the severe restrictions imposed on her movements and the grim atmosphere of Heathcliff's household will prove to have been a vital factor not only in Cathy's learning to overcome her snobbery towards Hareton but in her becoming a better person altogether.

In view of the title of Emily Brontë's novel, some readers may have been disappointed that Cathy is not to stay on at the Heights permanently after her betrothal to Hareton, especially those readers mindful both of the latter's patent attachment to what at his very first meeting with the young heroine he has referred to as '"our home" and "our folks"' (*WH*, p. 172) and of his having lived there continuously since the day he was born, conscious as he is, in any case, that his name is inscribed on the front of the building. No doubt, to readers in full sympathy with Catherine and Heathcliff, even as ghosts, the projected move of all the characters but Joseph from the Heights to the Grange at the end of the novel may be something of an ironic let-down. Other readers, however, may be inclined to look upon this device as a kind of poetic justice to Cathy, believing that, for all her failings as an adolescent, she deserves to recover her ancestral home on account of her moral integrity, her strength of character, and her sundry acts of kindness and thoughtfulness to Edgar, Nelly Dean, Linton Heathcliff and Hareton, to say nothing of the courage she displays during her unpleasant sojourn at the Heights. Yet the reason for this particular outcome may have rather more to do with an unusual aspect of Cathy's presentation: her occasionally explicit desire, even in her adolescence, to be accepted as a woman.[13] It is this aspect of her character that makes us aware how different she is from her mother. Thus whereas Catherine, even as a married woman, harbours an unhealthy nostalgia for the Heights, Cathy's momentary longing for the landscape near the Grange is but the natural emotion of one whose freedom of movement has been unfairly curtailed.[14] It is also interesting to note the way in which Cathy's potential development not only into womanhood, but also into a full-fledged homemaker seems foreshadowed through her relationship with birds. Consider, for instance, her quest, on her sixteenth birthday, to 'have a ramble on the edge of the moor' in order to find out whether 'a colony of moor grouse have made their nests yet'; whereby, when caught by Heathcliff 'hunting out the nests of the grouse', she proves with her empty hands that she only 'wished to see the eggs' (*WH*, p. 188). The symbolism of Cathy's possible roles as both mother and homemaker is as obvious here as it is in Nelly's memory of the girl's tendency in summer to lie on the branches of a tree 'watching the birds, joint tenants, feed and entice their young ones to fly' (*WH*, p. 203)—a symbolism at perhaps its most poetic level when Nelly figuratively describes Cathy's dismay at finding Linton Heathcliff's love letters to her missing from her cabinet drawer: 'Never did any bird flying back to a plundered nest which it had left brimful of chirping young ones, express more complete despair in its anguished cries and flutterings, than she by her single "Oh!"' (*WH*, p. 199). And no doubt it is through such references and through others discussed above that Emily Brontë, painfully homesick as she is sometimes known to have been whenever she was away from Haworth parsonage and the moors nearby, has indirectly conveyed some of her own thoughts about house and home.[15]

Brontë Studies, 40/3 (2015)

Notes

1   Although the subject of my essay has been touched on here and there in some academic writings on *Wuthering Heights*, no scholar has, to my knowledge, so far published a monograph of any kind on this subject. But while aware that my approach to house and home in *Wuthering Heights* is for the most part literary, I am conscious that the topic also admits of an essentially historical or documentary slant through discussions on, say, family traditions, inheritance laws, marital rights, property ownership, personal security, the class system, etc. as obtaining more particularly in the England of the eighteenth and nineteenth centuries. Such matters have, nevertheless, been alluded to here and there in my essay.

2   For quotations from the novel, see Emily Brontë, *Wuthering Heights*, eds. Ian Jack and Helen Small (Oxford: Oxford University Press, 2009). For the sake of convenience, the first Catherine will be referred to as 'Catherine', the second as 'Cathy'.

3   Perhaps much less obvious to the reader is that Thrushcross Grange, too, has its own dairy and ploughfields. See *Wuthering Heights*, pp. 199, 200, 202.

4   See *Wuthering Heights*, pp. 59, 60, 92, 136, 137, 206, 208, 261, 265.

5   For similar examples, see *Wuthering Heights*, pp. 31, 34, 45, 61, 171, 180, 189, 199, 222, 228, 237, 240, 243, 256, 257, 277, 280.

6   See *Wuthering Heights*, pp. 12, 22, 25, 170, 186-187, 209.

7   It might be said that Heathcliff's concept of home is inseparable from, indeed an expression of, his love for Catherine. This is especially suggested when, in his anger with her for trying to make up for the past by, among other things, offering him Isabella as a wife, he exclaims: 'Having levelled my palace, don't erect a hovel and complacently admire your own charity in giving me that for a home' (*WH*, p. 100).

8   Especially pertinent here is Nelly's recalling the local villagers speaking of Heathcliff as 'a cruel hard landlord to his tenants' (*WH*, p. 174). Noteworthy, too, is how Heathcliff's possessiveness is underlined by his use of phrases such as 'my house', 'my property', 'my roof', etc. See *Wuthering Heights*, pp. 1, 23, 182, 184, 189, 238, 242, 243, 258. For evidence that Linton Heathcliff has picked up his father's mercenary outlook, see *Wuthering Heights*, p. 247-248.

9   See, for example, *Wuthering Heights*, pp. 22, 25, 170, 186-187, 209.

10 Lockwood's (unconscious) nostalgia for a house may also be sensed in his use of such terms as 'homely', 'retreat', 'sanctum', 'shelter', 'roof' and 'copestone', just as it may be sensed by his references to Cathy as 'the missis' and 'the lady of the house' and by his uses of 'family'. See *Wuthering Heights*, pp. 2, 3, 7, 8, 9, 11, 12, 13, 19, 20, 23, 24, 28, 29, 273, 300.

11 Catherine's delirium is confirmed when, held in Edgar's arms, she contradicts what she has just been saying about the Heights: '[…] but they can't keep me from *my narrow home* out yonder— my resting-place where I'm bound before Spring is over!' (*WH*, p. 113; italics mine).

12 Catherine's rambles on the moors with Heathcliff and her illicit visit with him to the Grange—a visit, incidentally, instigated in the first place by Heathcliff—are clearly much less 'adventurous' than Cathy's lone expedition to Penistone Craggs. This is somewhat corroborated by the following detail that Nelly has earlier given Lockwood about Cathy's childhood: 'Gimmerton was an unsubstantial name in her ears; the chapel, the only building she had approached or entered, except her own home' (*WH*, p. 167).

13 See, for example, *Wuthering Heights*, pp. 168, 178, 213. In this connection, it is interesting to note the comparative childishness of Catherine's own view of herself as a woman when, during her first convalescence (in Chapter 9), she treats Nelly as 'a mere servant' because she has blamed her for Heathcliff's disappearance. As Nelly herself recalls further: 'Joseph fell under a ban also; he *would* speak his mind, and lecture her all the same as if she were a little girl; and she esteemed herself as a woman, and our mistress, and thought that her recent illness gave her a claim to be treated with consideration' (*WH*, p. 78).

14 See *Wuthering Heights*, p. 266.

15 For an account of Emily's tendency to homesickness, see the extract from Charlotte Brontë's Prefatory Note to 'Selection from Poems by Ellis Bell' in *Wuthering Heights*, p. 311-312.

Author's Publications
(in chronological order)

(Books)

Physiognomy in the European Novel: Faces and Fortunes (Princeton, NJ: Princeton University Press, 1982).

Physiognomy in Profile: Lavater's Impact on European Culture, co-edited with Melissa Percival (Newark, NJ: University of Delaware Press, 2005).

(Articles)

'Letters of Recommendation and False Vizors: Physiognomy in the Novels of Henry Fielding', in *Eighteenth-Century Fiction*, 2/2 (1990), 93-111.

'Mansfield's "The Voyage"', in *The Explicator*, 50/1 (1991), 42-45.

'Martha Lacy Hall, Louisiana Short-Story Writer', in *Regional Dimensions*, 10 (1992), 52-80.

'Heathcliff's Monomania: an Anachronism in *Wuthering Heights*', in *Brontë Society Transactions*, 20/6 (1992), 331-343.

'Lavater and the Nineteenth-Century English Novel', in *The Faces of Physiognomy: Interdisciplinary Approaches to Johann Caspar Lavater,* ed. Ellis Shookman (Columbia, SC: Camden House, 1993), 161-181.

'Physiognomy in *Wuthering Heights*', in *Brontë Society Transactions*, 21/4 (1994), 137-148.

'Dickens's "The Signalman"', in *The Explicator*, 53/1 (1994), 26-29.

'Physiognomy in Stendhal's Novels: "La Science de Lavater" or "Croyez après cela aux physionomies"?', in *Studia Romanica et Anglica Zagrabiensia*, 39 (1994), 59-76.

'Lavater and Physiognomy in English Fiction 1790-1832', in *Eighteenth-Century Fiction*, 7/3 (1995), 293-310.

Book review of *La communication non verbale avant la lettre*, by Anne-Marie Drouin-Hans, in *Isis*, 87/2 (1996), 340-341.

'Charles Dickens's "The Signalman": A Case of Partial Insanity?', in *History of Psychiatry*, 8 (1997), 421-432.

'"Know How to Decipher a Countenance": Physiognomy in Thomas Hardy's Fiction', in *The Thomas Hardy Year Book*, 27 (1998), 43-60.

Book review of *Der exzentrische Blick. Gespräch über Physiognomik*, ed. Claudia Schmölders, in *History of Psychiatry*, 9/2 (1998), 257-259.

'"The Lines and Lights of the Human Countenance": Physiognomy in George Eliot's Fiction', in *George Eliot—George Henry Lewes Studies*, 36 & 37 (1999), 29-58.

Book review of *Der exzentrische Blick. Gespräch über Physiognomik*, ed. Claudia Schmölders, in *Isis*, 91/2 (2000), 328-329.

'The Presentation of Herr von S. in *Die Judenbuche*', in *The German Quarterly*, 73/4 (2000), 337-350.

'Some Reflections on Lavater's Physiognomic Analyses of Two Engravings of David von Orelli', in *Gegen Unwissenheit und Finsternis: Johann Caspar von Orelli (1787-1849) und die Kultur seiner Zeit,* ed. Michele C. Ferrari (Zurich: Chronos, 2000), 57-70.

'Animals in *Wuthering Heights*', in *Brontë Studies*, 27/2 (2002), 121-130.

'"Faith in the Hand of Nature": Physiognomy in Sir Walter Scott's Fiction', in *Studies in Scottish Literature*, 33 & 34 (2004), 223-246.

'Lavater's Influence on Sir Walter Scott: A Tacit Assumption?', in *Physiognomy in Profile*, ibid., 109-120.

'The Parameters of Reason in *Wuthering Heights*', in *Brontë Studies*, 30/3 (2005), 231-242.

'"Nelly, I *am* Heathcliff!": The Problem of "Identification" in *Wuthering Heights*', in *The Midwest Quarterly*, 47/2 (2006), 167-181.

'The Role of Religion in *Wuthering Heights*', in *Brontë Studies*, 32/1 (2007), 41-55.

'Masters and Servants in *Wuthering Heights*', in *Brontë Studies*, 33/1 (2008), 44-53.

'Eating and Drinking in *Wuthering Heights*', in *Brontë Studies*, 34/1 (2009), 57-66.

'*Wuthering Heights*: An Amoral Novel?', in *Brontë Studies*, 35/3 (2010), 194-207.

'Physiognomy and the Treatment of Love in *Shirley*', in *Brontë Studies*, 36/3 (2011), 263-276.

'The Workings of Memory in *Wuthering Heights*', in *Brontë Studies*, 37/1 (2012), 10-18.

'Aesthetic Attitudes in *Wuthering Heights*', in *Brontë Studies*, 37/1 (2012), 63-74.

'Physiognomy in Anne Brontë's Fiction', in *Brontë Studies*, 37/3 (2012), 227-237.

'Physiognomy and Identity in *Villette*', in *Brontë Studies*, 38/1 (2013), 42-53.

'Thematic Functions of Fire in *Wuthering Heights*', in *Brontë Studies*, 38/2 (2013), 126-136.

'The Power of the Spoken Word in *Wuthering Heights*', in *Brontë Studies*, 39/1 (2014), 58-70.

'The Presentation of Hareton Earnshaw in *Wuthering Heights*', in *Brontë Studies*, 39/2 (2014), 118-129.

'The Presentation of Isabella in *Wuthering Heights*', in *Brontë Studies*, 39/3 (2014), 191-201.

'Facets of Time Consciousness in *Wuthering Heights*', in *Brontë Studies*, 40/1 (2015), 11-21.

'House and Home in *Wuthering Heights*', in *Brontë Studies*, 40/3 (2015), 229-239.

'Weather in *Wuthering Heights*', in *Brontë Studies*, 41/1 (2016), 39-47.

'Clothes in *Wuthering Heights*', in *Brontë Studies*, 41/3 (2016), 239-248.

'Physiognomy and the Treatment of Beauty in *Jane Eyre*', in *Brontë Studies*, 41/4 (2016), 300-311.

'The Presentation of the Second Catherine in *Wuthering Heights*', in *Brontë Studies*, 42/1 (2017), 26-36.

'"He's more myself than I am": The Problem of Comparisons in *Wuthering Heights*', in *Brontë Studies*, 42/2 (2017), 109-117.

'The Presentation of Edgar Linton in *Wuthering Heights*', in *Brontë Studies*, 42/4 (2017), 312-320.

'The Presentation of Mr. Kenneth in *Wuthering Heights*', in *Brontë Studies*, 43/2 (2018), 147-155.

'The Presentation of Joseph in *Wuthering Heights*', in *Brontë Studies*, 43/3 (2018), 188-197.

(Articles reprinted)

'Heathcliff's Monomania', in *Readings on Wuthering Heights*, ed. Hayley R. Mitchell (San Diego, CA: Greenhaven Press, 1999), 102-110.

'Physiognomical Awareness in the Nineteenth-Century European Novel' (excerpted from *Physiognomy in the European Novel*), in *Nineteenth-Century Literature Criticism*, vol. 212, ed. Kathy D. Darrow (Detroit: Gale, Cengage Learning, 2009), 284-301.

'Physiognomy in *Wuthering Heights*', in *Nineteenth-Century Literature Criticism*, ibid., 329-334.

'Eating and Drinking in *Wuthering Heights*', in Emily Brontë, *Wuthering Heights*, ed. Sunita Mishra (Hyderabad: Orient BlackSwan, 2011), 324-337.

'Masters and Servants in *Wuthering Heights*', in *Brontë Studies* (Special Issue), "Signs of the Times: The Brontës and Contemporary Society, A Retrospective Collection of Essays from *Brontë Society Transactions* and *Brontë Studies*", 38/4 (2013), 320-329.

DIARY
OF A
GYM ADDICT

DIARY
OF A
GYM ADDICT

TOM MOSS

ISBNs
Paperback: 978-1-80541-074-4
eBook: 978-1-80541-075-1

Contents

CHAPTER 1

Introduction

Synopsis

As the great Brian O'Driscoll once said, "Knowledge is knowing that a tomato is a fruit. Wisdom is knowing not to put it in a fruit salad". In fact, as far as we know, this was first coined by humourist writer Miles Kington, although I'm sure it's been said a million times over the years by a million different people. Never has this quote been so applicable as it is to the fitness and bodybuilding industry, where scientists, who may have never lifted a weight, impart their training and diet 'knowledge' on 300lbs bodybuilders, and 300lbs bodybuilders, who have never read a peer-reviewed paper, impart their training and diet 'wisdom' (or experience) on biologists, chemists, toxicologists and doctors! Of course, in terms of practical application, the truth tends to end up somewhere in the middle, but I find this never-ending wrestle of 'science' vs 'bro science' fascinating, and whilst we should all take notice of proven lab results and solid peer-reviewed studies, we must acknowledge that once things get out of the lab environment, wider social, economic, and mental factors are at play. Put simply, 'life happens', and we all know that even the best-laid plans, with a solid evidence base, are completely useless if we don't, or can't, adhere to them.

My name is Tom and I'm a gym addict. It's been 25 years since I first stepped inside a gym, and the passion, obsession, love (and at times hate) for everything that is training, and diet-related has consumed me ever since. This book aims to capture the lessons, musings, successes, and failures of that journey and covers everything from how to set up a diet and training plan, through to my take on some of the big fitness movements and the effect of the online fitness community. I've tried to make this a deeply personal account, detailing my own fitness philosophies, specific prep diets and training plans, and my own experience of being involved in the industry as a natural bodybuilding competitor, ex-personal trainer and general gym obsessive. The book will cover everything from my own apathy and concern with the current state of 'fitness influencers', and the pedalling of questionably useless supplementation, to a personal account of bodybuilding, and an examination of using training and fitness as a tool of focus and strength in overcoming addiction, anxiety, or self-destructive behaviours.

Importantly, I must say that I'm not a doctor, nor am I a psychologist or neuroscientist. I am not an IFBB pro, I don't represent any company and have no affiliation which might lead me to recommend specific products or supplements. At the time of writing this, I'm not even working as a personal trainer, although I am qualified, and did do so for a number of years. In honesty, being a 'qualified' personal trainer isn't an accolade worth celebrating. Not to diminish personal training as a profession, there are some excellent one's out there, but being able to complete a 6-week course and call yourself a 'certified fitness expert' is systemic of the fitness industry on the whole – incredibly unregulated and very misleading! What I can offer you is a very real account of 25 years of consistent training experience, the specifics of my prep for Natural Bodybuilding shows, a unique take on the approach to the mentality of training and a diet plan that has helped me to stay in consistently good shape year-round. I've included some anecdotes from my own training experience, such as 'The Legend of Big Mike' and being on stage with a 'smooth leg', as well as tackling some of the big issues that plague a lot of us, such as substance abuse, mental health, and body dysmorphia. I have a full-time job, working in Sales, and all of my diet and training programmes are planned around a 40 to 50-hour working week. Hopefully, this makes my advice and findings a little more useable and relevant to others who have similar working commitments.

I also want to add that I am not a fitness 'influencer'; I don't seek to be someone you should directly copy or idolise, and whilst I'm going to talk a lot about my approach to training and diet, and hope there are snippets you can learn along the way, I'm also going to be completely transparent about my relationship with alcohol, binge eating and other hedonistic pursuits. I don't advocate or encourage eating fast food, drinking alcohol, or taking drugs, but I don't completely demonise it either, and I refuse to live in a cosy bubble where we pretend these things don't exist. If we're going to tackle issues around a successful mindset and mental and physical wellbeing, we can't ignore these factors. Instead, we should discuss the realities around mental health, anxiety, binge eating, alcohol and substance abuse and examine how you might look to gain some clarity and control of these factors, using physical exercise, proper planning, and goal setting to your advantage.

So, if you love picking up pieces of metal and putting them back down again, you get excited at the thought of mind-blowing, juicy pumps or want to know more about my take on effective exercise, nutrition, and a healthy mindset, you've come to the right place.

Why Do I Train?

For as long as I can remember, I have taken inspiration from sportsmen and women. As a kid, I was awestruck by the skill, power, poise and talent of footballers, athletes, cricketers, golfers, and rugby players. In fact, I could watch just about any sport and find enjoyment and inspiration in watching someone who is truly exceptional in their field. But one thing stood out for me above the skill, strength, and speed............the mindset. The sheer bloody-mindedness to get over the line, to make that last ditch tackle, to put your head in where it hurts, to push through the pain barrier or to keep your cool in the big pressure situations. I became obsessed with a sporting mindset, with the ability to be consistent, to work towards a goal, and to be in control over your time, your training plans, and your emotions in the big moments. I craved to be a professional sportsman, but I wasn't good enough. I was a jack of all trades and master of none. Quick and strong, but not the quickest or strongest. Good at cricket, football, rugby, and athletics, but not great. I was resilient and hard but not compared to some of the lads I saw coming through from tougher, grittier backgrounds.

I couldn't control my ability to become a professional in these mainstream sports. I can say that injuries and being in the wrong schools or junior programmes played their part, but all in all, I wasn't good enough. But what I could control, was the ability to build an impressive, natural physique, develop the knowledge to plan and programme effectively and have the mindset and willpower to push myself to places that 99% of the population simply can't go. And if I could achieve this, would this growing obsession make up for my shortcomings and failures on the sporting field? After all, a life of year-round programming and meticulous dieting to peak for competitive events is basically what a sports person is. It's as close as I could get to living out my dream. But it's given me so much more. So many life lessons! The pain, the injuries, the accountability, the PBs, the failed PB attempts, the discipline of dieting, of cardio and the good that planning and physical activity can do for your mental health! There are so many reasons why I train: perhaps it ultimately has come to define me; maybe I'm scared to stop – what does a weaker, smaller, fatter, less disciplined version of me have to offer to my friends and family? Would people at work have as much time for me? What would I be known for? I think I train for a variety of physical and mental health-related factors, but I know that I also train because it's just become part of me, part of my identity, and without it, maybe I'm scared of who I am, or what is left of me. Am I a control freak who can't let go of planning every part of my life? Or does the planning give me the control, discipline, and fulfilment to be better, happier, and more content? I'm not 100% sure of the underlying motivation… but I do know that there are many reasons why I love to train:

1. **Control**. I've come to realise that in many aspects of my life, I need control. It explains my fear of flying and why I locked horns with so many teachers at school. Bodybuilding is all about accountability. You can control your diet, your programme, and your decision to get up in the morning and go to the gym or stay in bed and sleep. Unfortunately, this trait where you have the need for control is also wrapped up in some pretty complex behaviours that can lead to obsessive tendencies and sometimes manifest in things like eating disorders, over-training, exhaustion and incredibly high expectations that are often unobtainable. I don't think the need to control is always good or healthy, but (in the interest of honesty) I must include it as one of the main reasons why I train.

2. **Mental Health**. I simply feel better in myself when I train. It's a mixture of physical endorphins and the feel-good factor of completing something hard; something that you planned, programmed, and executed. There is something uniquely transformative about the effect that exercise has on the brain. And as Margaret Thatcher once said, **"Look at a day when you are supremely satisfied at the end**. It's not a day when you lounge around doing nothing; it's a day you've had everything to do, and you've done it."** (Love or loathe her, that's a great quote.)

3. **I love the process.** Winning a bodybuilding competition or a sporting league or title lasts for that moment of raising the trophy and perhaps a day or two of celebrations afterwards. But enjoying the process is what it's all about. I absolutely love the science of

putting together training and diet phases and having the mental fortitude to make those plans a reality. It's the daily sessions, tweaking the diet, the form, the tempo, the exercise selection, that really appeals to me. Standing on a stage in my pants isn't all that much fun, but the hard work, dedication, knowledge, and passion to get there is everything!

4. **It drowns out the nonsense, noise, and confusion of the modern world.** There is something simple and sacred about a training session that provides all the escapism that I need from a modern world of virtual meetings, WhatsApp and cancel culture. I'm incredibly old-fashioned at heart and, if truth be told, I shy away from modern technology and social media because I find it depressing! Ricky Gervais had it right when he said that we've lived through the best years… things have gone too far the other way now. The rise of social media, humans as brands and this idea that 'my opinion is as important as your fact', is just ridiculous. People aren't interested in the truth anymore, they're interested in who is making the statement, how they are making it and how the video has been edited and uploaded! But for an hour a day, none of that can touch me. There is something beautifully simple about picking up weights and putting them back down again that satisfies my primal urges and provides a massive contrast to the rest of my day. Being cold or hot or sweaty, tired, hungry or generally uncomfortable, goes against a modern 'cosiness' that may just be making us all soft, docile, and lethargic.

5. **Self-esteem.** I have no shame in admitting that I like to be strong, fit, and lean. I take pride in being in good shape because I know the hard work, knowledge and commitment that goes into achieving the outcome daily. If I don't train, even for a few days, I feel slow, sluggish, and down. It all feeds into the overarching mental health consideration, but ultimately, being in good shape and working hard, hitting goals and PBs is fantastic for self-esteem and self-worth. I have to caveat this statement by stating that if your feelings of self worth are solely focussed on the physical 'aesthetics' of training, such as muscle size and body fat percentage, this can be incredibly damaging in the long run. These things alone should never dominate your self esteem and self worth. It's the effort levels, dedication, resilience to turn up and keep working hard, that should really yield this outcome.

My Training Philosophy – 5 considerations

You will see some recurring themes running through this book that always come back to my own philosophy on training, mindset, and nutrition. Here are 5 of my top considerations that form the backbone of my training philosophy and some of the topics and issues that this book aims to tackle:

1. **Find Your Passion.** You'll be able to tell from the first couple of paragraphs that my passion lies in sports, fitness and bodybuilding. I'm lucky in that a great by product of my hobby, is that it's active. I burn calories,

I move around, I sweat and I get the natural benefit of the endorphins and general feeling of wellness, that exercise can give. What's less spoken about though, is the mental health and self-esteem that throwing yourself into a passion or hobby, can give you. Becoming a student of your passion, striving for better outcomes, more knowledge and applying that knowledge in practical application, executing a plan and seeing the progress, can be transformative. Whilst the book is centred around the gym, different elements of fitness and bodybuilding, it's the premise of finding a passion, being accountable to hard work, and having the discipline to execute your passion day in and day out, that can really transform someone's mindset, mental wellbeing, physical and mental health. It doesn't really matter if that passion happens to be bodybuilding, hiking, yoga or cycling, but I do believe that some form of physical exertion and hard work is necessary for ultimate feelings of wellbeing and contentment.

2. **Do some Weight Bearing Exercise**. Even if you don't want to get strong or big or even care about looking muscular, I would always advocate lifting weights in some guise. As we age, we're generally getting weaker, the production of hormones like testosterone and growth hormone are decreasing and bones become more brittle in the ageing process. The simple act of lifting weights can improve muscular strength, cell function, and hormone production and keep brittle bones and osteoporosis at bay. It's a simple fact of 'use it or lose

it'. Throughout this book, I will often refer to weight lifting protocols in the following way: Bench Press 4 x 10/12. In this example, the 4 refers to the number of sets and the 10/12 refers to the desired rep range. Sometimes I will also follow this up with something like (2 seconds eccentric, 1 second hold, 2 seconds concentric) this refers to the desired tempo of the set.

3. **Apply Progressive Overload**. If you want to make progress, you must create a novel stimulus! For bigger muscles, try to add weight, reps or change up your exercises every few weeks to encourage new muscle growth. If you're trying to lose fat, look to taper calories or add time or intensity to your cardio. Improvement in the gym and kitchen = improvement to your physique, strength and/or body composition. Don't expect progression if you haven't increased weight, volume, frequency or intensity.

4. **Calories in vs Calories out is King/Queen!** When it comes to weight loss or gain, calories in vs calories out is THE most important factor. Of course, we will go on to examine how we achieve this and there are dozens of factors within this statement to consider, but to be very simplistic, diet types, food choices, macronutrients and food timings are all great tools in the bag, but when it comes to moving the scales, they are irrelevant if the calories are not correct. If you are trying to lose weight, you can eat the 'healthiest', vegan-based, organic, superfood-enriched, intermittent fasting, super-duper diet in the world, but if you're in a calorie surplus for

that day, week, month, or year, you WILL gain weight. I will caveat this by saying that once you do have your calories on point, then your macronutrient splits and the prioritisation of quality food (especially protein) will be key to moving you to the next level. To effect the 'calories out' portion further, you should be doing regular cardio, and even in a 'bodybuilding bulk' phase, cardio sessions are vital to protect heart health.

5. **Plan and Track but don't obsess.** Plan what you'll do and track what you've done. One of the worst mistakes that people make is they walk into a gym with no idea of what they're going to do. They'll go through the motions with the same exercises and leave having achieved nothing. I would urge you to build a training and/or diet plan or at least have an idea of some set goals that you want to get out of your sessions and hard work. You should log these in a logbook or on your phone or laptop so you can make it easy to track your progress and make sure you're heading in the right direction. These plans and goals can help to keep you on the right track and once you've started to log your sessions or meals, you can start to use the data to assess what's working and what isn't. On the flip side, whilst I would always have an overarching goal(s), it's important not to obsess over the little things. Being mega-preoccupied with specific form or micronutrients generally leads to 'paralysis by analysis' and this can be as bad as not planning at all. Have an eye on the bigger picture: Plan – do – track – repeat.

Homo Deus – The Narrating Self vs The Experiencing Self

I was relaxing by the pool, with my Partner, in 30 degrees sunshine. She had already finished 2 books and was well into her third of the holiday. I was still scratching around, trying desperately to get halfway through Homo Deus by Noah Yuval Harari. I wasn't struggling because the book is dull, far from it, the book is a masterpiece, and one that had me gripped, but if truth be told, I don't retain 'read' information very well. My reading pace is awful and the reason that I've chosen to write this book in short, sharp, article style chapters, with lots of lists and bullet points, is because it makes you feel like you're making some progress, getting through chapters quickly and having the aid of bullet points and lists, to recap the important info (well it does for me any way!). I knew that if I could re-read and fully understand the chapters, musings and discoveries of this book, it would be time well spent. Reading Homo Deus was the first time that I had been introduced to the notion of the experiencing self vs the narrating self. Whilst I had struggled to fully understand, comprehend, or decipher much of the book, this direct quote from Homo Deus stood out to me immediately:

> '(There are) at least two different selves within us: the experiencing self and the narrating self. The experiencing self is our moment-to-moment consciousness. The narrating self is forever busy spinning yarns about the past and making plans for the future. [...] It doesn't narrate everything, and usually weaves the story using only peak

*moments and end results. [...] Most of us identify with
our narrating self. When we say 'I', we mean the story
in our head not the onrushing stream of experiences we
undergo.'*[1]

The reason this quote was so meaningful to me, is because it instantly took me back to every Personal Training consultation, that I had ever done. Client after client offering differing versions of their narrating self. Many who 'mainly stuck to meat and veg and never ate processed foods,' others 'trained 5 days a week and never missed a session'. And the same would go for future plans; 'Yes, I'm a morning person so I'll definitely be fine with 6am training sessions, 4 days a week.' ' I want to make this my strictest programme ever. Whilst I haven't ever tried calorie counting or intermittent fasting, it's something that I 100% will commit to over the next 6 months.' Hmmmmm but will you really?

Harari even goes on to explain that he could set up a New Year's Resolution to *'start a diet and go to the gym every day. But the following week when it's gym time, the experiencing self takes over. I don't feel like going to the gym, and instead I order pizza, sit on the sofa and turn on the TV.'*

It dawned on me that this area of psychology is crucial for someone's fitness journey. How many people plan a crazy, unsustainable, unrealistic, diet and training plan, only to fail after a matter of weeks, when the 'experiencing self' actually experiences these set of restrictions and emotions. Early mornings, ultra-restricted and low-calorie diets, ridiculous amounts of exercise volume and a sudden absence of fun and freedom. For a training and diet plan to truly work, in the long run, you MUST get a realistic alignment of your experiencing and narrating self. You MUST get to know what training you will enjoy and adhere to, what diets make you feel satiated and satisfied and which times of day you will realistically operate at your best, day after day, week after week and month after month. Anyone who's stuck in this never-ending cycle of fad diet and training protocols, only to fall spectacularly off the wagon time after time, would be wise to really think about this notion. Forget the bullshit you've been conditioned to hear and try to push your narrating selves voice to the back of your head. What has your experiencing self, truly been feeling and why do these plans keep failing? Can you be brutally honest with yourself? Are you really cut out for those 6am sessions? Do you hate the gym environment and trialling other forms of training could be beneficial? Do your 'cheat weekends' derail your whole programme? Is zero carb really the best diet for you?

With new training types, different gym cultures, home workout video's, group circuits, differing meal plans, greater diet info and more access to home and flexible working conditions, there have never been more ways to create a sustainable calorie balance and training programme that works for you. If you can get the narrating and experiencing self-more aligned as a first step and then look to create small and sustainable changes so you can move your reality further towards the reality that your narrating self-craves, it could lead to transformative changes in the long run.

It was after reading this chapter that I finally decided that I would write a book. Of course, my narrating self-had been planning it for about two decades, but this was the inspiration that I needed to immediately open the 'Notes' section of my phone, and start to list chapter ideas, diet, and training philosophies, as well as a whole host of mental health considerations that I had thought about over the years.

A Study into Metabolism (Conducted by John Speakman, The University of Aberdeen, and The Chinese Academy of Sciences)[2]

In 2021, an international team of scientists published one of the most detailed examinations of life's metabolic highs and lows, looking at over 6,500 people, ranging from one week old to 95 years old. Whilst the study concluded that metabolism does change with age, the details around when these changes occur were a revelation. As one would imagine, infants had the highest metabolic rate of all - by the time a child hits their 1st birthday, their bodies are burning calories 50% faster for their body size, than an adult. Equally, as you would have expected, the people who fell into the over-90 category had a comparatively slower metabolism, meaning that they generally needed 20% - 26% fewer calories to sustain their daily activity than a middle-aged person. But one set of results would come as a huge surprise to most and serve as an exciting discovery for the musings of health and fitness enthusiasts the world over. By and large, metabolism peaks in infants and declines at around 3% per year until you reach your 20th birthday, but what happens after your 20th birthday is quite astounding. Namely, not very much at all. The studies reveal that metabolism fixes in your 20s and shows absolutely no change through your 30s, 40s and 50s. Only when an individual enters their 60s does a natural metabolic change occur, and even then, it's minimal.

Post-60, most people can expect a 0.7% decrease, per year, in metabolism, so an average of a 7% decrease per decade. All things being equal, my 69-year-old father can still metabolise around 93% of the daily calories that I can. Whist the study makes fascinating reading in itself, as a fitness and bodybuilding enthusiast, I found it specifically compelling for two reasons:

1. When it comes to metabolism and fat gain, we're far more a master of our own destiny than we once thought. If you're someone who wants to stay lean, fit and healthy into your middle age, your metabolism isn't an area that's going to hold you back. Maintaining good levels of muscle mass, eating a nutrient-rich diet at sensible volumes, and prioritising good sleep and recovery will not be counteracted by your advancing years. Given the evidence, a 20-year-old and a 50-year-old, with the same approach to bodybuilding, health, fitness, diet and recovery, could yield similar results.

2. It helps to confirm that the reasons for middle-age fat gain, poor health and expanding waistlines, are much more a series of environmental, social, economic and educational factors. Yes, we are more exposed to injuries, illness and hormonal decline as we age, but the physical changes that people often attribute to an ageing metabolism are much more likely to be a simple equation of calories in vs calories out, a changing in priorities as we spend much of middle age raising children, working, moving less and eating more. In theory, this positive

revelation around a fixed metabolism through middle age should inspire individuals to take control of their own health and fitness journey. A healthy and able 58-year-old could be just as likely to successfully lose fat as her 25-year-old counterpart.

Before we get too carried away, we do have to acknowledge that hormonal decline, like the ability to produce Testosterone, does take a hit with age. So, building new muscle mass, does get trickier as we get older. But this notion of a 'middle aged spread' being down to a metabolic crash, is just not accurate. Most people are not bodybuilders, and they want to train to stay lean, healthy and functional. And if you've built a good amount of muscle in your earlier years, then maintaining that into your 40's, 50's and 60's is absolutely possible, with the right approach to training and the CICO equation.

The laws of thermodynamics may sound like a mouthful and the small print could confuse even the most learned of professors, but one area that is incredibly simple to understand is the CICO equation. Calories in vs calories out will determine weight gain or loss. Eating will effect calories in and moving will effect calories out. In the midst of this simple equation are a thousand different musings that blur the edges. Body composition, Macronutrients, Micronutrients, NEAT, the thermal effect of food, diet types, exercise selection, programme planning and a plethora of other considerations that are globally confusing the minds of any people who have ever embarked on a fitness journey.

How Are We Soooooo Confused?!

As I was sat on an incline bench press at my local gym in Bristol, generally thinking over a myriad of nonsense between sets, one interesting thought crept into my tiny mind. If you were to take a person from 1970 and place them here in the present day, think of the unimaginable changes that have occurred since that time, and how difficult it would be for them to navigate modern life! For argument's sake, let's assume that the individual is a bodybuilder, armed with the same diet and exercise knowledge as a decent bodybuilder from 1970, and his name is Troy.

Let's take shopping as a great example of an experience that has changed hugely over the years. In 1970, Troy has one option for grocery shopping. He likely goes to a supermarket to get the bulk of his goods, and, whilst credit cards did exist, compared to cash, they were rarely used, so Troy hands over cash to the cashier and then proceeds to go to the butchers, fishmongers and greengrocers for a better version of those products. Fast forward to the modern day and Troy can now place his order over a thing called 'the internet', he can pay online, and someone will bring the shopping to his house. It's a great option for Troy, but he would need some help in how to navigate the internet, online payments, passwords and the setting up of online accounts, not to mention how to use a computer in the first place. I could use this example for so many things: Online dating, virtual meetings, satellite navigation, and the list goes on, but 1970's Troy, armed with the same knowledge, could walk into our present day and use his exact diet and training plan to effectively lose fat and build muscle. It's been fifty-two years of technological advancements, experiments, new training equipment, all the hype from social media and white noise from fitness influencers, but Troy's approach of a calorie-controlled diet, prioritising quality protein and largely whole foods (which generally tend to be more dense and satiating but lower in overall calories) and a sensible approach to training in an 8-15 hypertrophy rep range, applying progressive overload principles to a weekly, body part split, would still yield the same great results in 2022 as it did in 1972! Incredible! So why the fuck is everyone so confused, so frustrated, and so consumed with the wrong information, when the process of building muscle and losing fat has been the same forever?! I think I can offer up a few reasons from what I've witnessed over the last couple of decades: The overload of conflicting information from various online sources, unscrupulous marketing and pushing of supplements by fitness celebrities, new fitness movements being steeped in dogma, and every lift or diet being scrutinised to the nth degree meaning that gym-goers are spending more time getting every millisecond of their lift or intra-workout nutrition 'correct', they forget to actually apply the basic principles of progressive overload, or think about overall caloric intake. It's like everyone's meticulously applying the coolest new add-ons to their car, but they forgot about the engine or the steering wheel.

Don't Be Like Gary

When I was personal training in Bristol, I had a client called Gary. He wasn't called Gary, but we won't use his real name, and Gary seems like a great Bristolian substitute. Gary was (and I'm sure he still is) a lovely guy; I enjoyed my time spent with Gary and we worked together for about 6 months on a variety of aesthetic and strength-based goals. The problem with Gary is that Gary liked to 'research'. He also loved YouTube and would watch, and read about, dozens of different training styles, supplements, and diets, all of them claiming to be the magic bullet for a killer physique. Every single week, Gary would pose a different set of questions, based on a different set of videos or articles that he had read. "Tom," he would say, "I've got a question for you.... What do you think about intermittent fasting, and training fasted, but just taking BCAA as a pre-workout so I don't waste muscle during my session?" "Tom... what are your thoughts on time under tension vs sets and reps for the bench press and a touch and go vs pause at the bottom, for building muscle?" "Tom... I've been thinking, and I think it would make sense for me to do a combo of CrossFit and the hunter-gatherer diet, based on some of the stuff I've read on Matt Fraser."

Now, none of these are outrageous questions, but it's important that we put into perspective the experience and fitness level of Gary. Whilst Gary had been training on and off for a few years, because of his love for the next fitness fad or craze, Gary would rarely string 3 sessions together before he moved onto something new. One week it's bodybuilding, then jiu jitsu, then he was a CrossFitter, and he would constantly start and stop programmes, with gaps in between to 'research'. The other problem with Gary is that he didn't work all that hard. He was so focused on exercise selection, execution and doing the most current fitness trends that he never executed the basics. He was so quick to log a set in his logbook that this was prioritised over actual muscular failure; he changed programmes so quickly that he couldn't apply progressive overload to an exercise; his diets were so focused on the food types and timings that he didn't apply the basic rules around a calorie deficit or surplus, so he never gained or lost weight effectively. Put simply, Gary was trying to run before he could crawl… Don't be like Gary!

When it comes to hitting a specific goal, I find that using a pyramid of hierarchy is a fantastic tool to visualise the importance of the particular components. Take muscle building, for example. Below is a pyramid that shows my opinion of the hierarchy of importance when it comes to building muscle. At the foundations of the pyramid are the most important elements of building muscle, and as we go up the pyramid, the components get less important and more niche. The idea here is to remind us that without a fantastic foundation of the basic components, the smaller elements, further up the pyramid, are useless. For example, for muscle building, there is no point in looking at nutrient timing or supplement use if we aren't eating enough overall calories or lifting weights. We can take all the creatine we like and eat chicken, rice and broccoli at a set time, but if our overall calories are in a deficit and our weight training is suboptimal, and we're not applying basic principles around progressive overload, we simply won't build any muscle. In fact, if we aren't lifting weights effectively, then almost anything we do past that point is completely useless for the act of muscle gain. For the avoidance of doubt, I'm assuming this to be building muscle for a 'natural' individual. If the supplements involved PEDs, this would likely be a different pyramid.

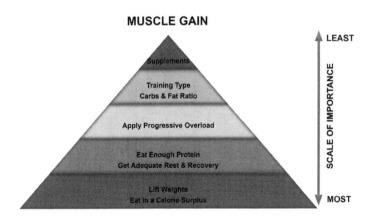

Similarly, we can apply the same thing to losing fat. You could do cardio, eat a wholefood, carb-free diet, apply intermittent fasting protocols and sleep for 10 hours a night, but if you are not in a calorie deficit, you will not lose fat. In so many circumstances I see the wrong things being prioritised. Can I eat bread? Yes, if you're in a deficit, you'll lose weight. Can I eat pasta? Yes, if you're in a deficit, you'll lose weight. Shall I go vegan or carb-free or high-carb? For fat loss, it really doesn't matter. You can choose any of these options and still lose weight if you're in a calorie deficit. The real question you should be asking yourself is, "Which of these diet choices will be best for me to adhere to? Which of these diets will I enjoy and therefore be more likely to continue with? Which of these diets contains the right food choices, so I can eat a reasonable volume, feel full, but still be in a calorie deficit?" Ultimately, we shouldn't be looking at the next block in the pyramid until we're nailing the one underneath. Once we're doing the big, simple things, we can have the confidence that we're ready to move onto the smaller blocks in the pyramid and use these add-ons to advance our progression.

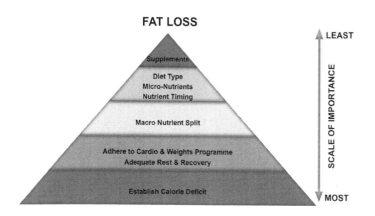

The Mental Fight – I look like an empty tube of toothpaste

Ultimately, I feel for Gary, and I understand why people might change from diet to diet or goal to goal in search of the next magic fix. As I write this paragraph, I've just come out of a 'bulking' phase myself and have just started a slow cut towards a bodybuilding show later in the year. If I reflect on my physique, my feelings, and what I see in the mirror, I can see how people very quickly abandon and back out of diet and training goals. It's so common for people to start a 3-month 'bulk' phase, only to stop 6 weeks in when they feel too full, uncomfortable and their physique doesn't look as ripped in the mirror. Equally, how many people stop short of a full cutting phase, struggling with strength loss, feeling skinny and fed up with counting calories and starving? No one is protected from these feelings. Sometimes they need addressing and examining - should you be that hungry in a cut? Should you gain that much fat in a bulk? But often, they're just varying degrees of body dysmorphia, or the body's natural response to the stimulus that we're putting on it. Unfortunately, things don't often work in the linear fashion that we'd like, and unwanted side effects can accompany our goals. When we go into a 'cutting' phase of any note, it's almost guaranteed that you will lose some strength, especially if you're an experienced lifter, and even more likely if you want to get into single-digit levels of lean. Equally, this weight loss will be accompanied by phases of water retention and muscle glycogen depletion. Glycogen will fill again during different phases and water weight will release, but these things happen during a diet. At various stages of my last prep, I felt and looked horrible. Halfway through my cut, I questioned everything! Was I even losing fat? Had I lost masses of muscle? Why did I look so watery? Would my skin tighten up, or would my lower abs look like I'd just had an emergency C-Section on stage?! I felt like an empty tube of toothpaste. Skinny, but loose, my muscles were flat and I looked watery and blurry. But you have to trust in the process. The body is a complicated beast and you'll never reach a bulking or cutting goal if you back out halfway through. As the cut went on, fat came off those stubborn places, skin tightened around previously bulkier areas, and manipulating muscle glycogen became easier as I cycled carbohydrates. No phase of bodybuilding is ever plain sailing, but applying the basics around calories, macronutrients and exercise selection, and having conviction in your process, is absolutely key. You must accept that this is an adaptive process and that gaining and losing weight will always come with some unwanted effect along the way. If we can accept and expect these fluctuations in water weight, strength and muscle glycogen, it'll make the mental journey that much easier. There are times when we all overanalyse, but this quest for the perfect diet, the perfect plan and the perfect programme, generally has adverse effects on our training goals.

'Good Science' has a lot to answer for – Paralysis by Analysis

Over the years, I've trained several people who loved to analyse every little detail of training, specifically overthinking correct lifting form, tempo, programming, and exercise selection, to a point where the detail seemed to matter more than the output. I remember working with one guy, many years ago, who had faultless form. He was a real purest and his kettlebell, deadlift and squat technique was flawless. The only problem, though, is that in all the years I knew him, he barely got stronger, never put on any meaningful muscle, nor did he lose very much fat. He stayed in reasonable shape and (for the most part) was injury-free, but his massive preoccupation with overanalysing every part of his lifts, and often stopping woefully short of true failure, meant that he seldom improved from a strength, endurance, body composition or aesthetic perspective.

'Paralysis by analysis' is a term that's used a lot in the fitness industry. It means overthinking the science and overanalysing the data to such an extent that we don't apply the fundamentals of training, constantly reimagine our programmes and diets and end up in a state of continual limbo when it comes to making significant improvements to our strength, fitness, and physiques. Often, we see different papers and studies published that conflict with the one from last week. Is low volume and high intensity best, or is high frequency and low volume best?

What about training to failure or using reps in reserve? Should we have a classic 'bro' split of 5 days a week, or is a push/pull/legs split the best way forward? And how about specific tempo? Is it about sets and reps or about time under tension? How intense should sessions really be? Could training to failure actually be hindering my progress to make advancements and gain muscle? Am I overtraining? Am I undertraining? And we've not even started on diets, supplements, and cardio! Fuck me, it's a minefield. So how can we overcome 'paralysis by analysis' and make sure we use important aspects of scientific training knowledge without getting caught in the headlights? Here are some tips:

1. **Work Hard!** Don't overthink this element. Not working hard enough in the gym is still the biggest problem when it comes to making progress. Comparatively, there are very few people who have to genuinely worry about 'overtraining' or working so hard in their sessions that they're unable to recover before the next one. If in doubt, training to failure on each set is still the best way to go. If you are making small, consistent improvements to your training goal, avoiding injury, and getting plenty of quality rest, then it's unlikely you are training too hard.

2. **Get Enough Sleep.** This is one of the most important factors that can contribute to your overall health and wellbeing, both physical and mental. It also ties in well to point number one; it's not overtraining that we should be concerned with, it's much more about poor quality of rest, recovery, and sleep. Sleeping is crucial for

maintaining healthy cell and brain function, supporting growth and development, and fighting harmful health issues. Numerous studies link a lack of sleep with poor body composition, poor cognition and concentration, increased risk of heart disease and a poor immune system[3]. So don't fall for this nonsense of 4 am training being magical or impressive! Unless these people go to bed at 7 pm every night, then they'd probably benefit from moving their sessions back a couple of hours and getting some prolonged, quality, deep sleep!

3. **Keep it Simple.** If in doubt about the best lifts, exercise execution or how many reps and sets to include in your programmes, my advice would be to keep it simple. You will hear conflicting info on these topics all the time, and it's simply because these are mainly anecdotal, personal accounts of what works for each person. It's also because there is more than one way to skin a cat and a variety of approaches work well for different people. I've seen people get great results with very high intensity, training past failure, with heavy weights and high frequency (5 sessions per week), but lower volume (e.g., around 10 working sets). I've also seen people train with higher volume (20 working sets) but at a lower intensity (still going very near to failure but using higher reps, with lighter weights and prioritising tempo, time under tension and mind/muscle connection) at the same frequency and get equally great results. Even people who train less frequently (3 days per week) but with a high intensity and high volume… this can also yield the same outcome.

Use this checklist for a simple but effective programme:

- If in doubt, use a full range of motion at a controlled, smooth tempo to execute exercises.
- Train a muscle to (or very close to) failure. Once you're experienced enough, you can even go beyond failure with spotted reps or partials to help push through plateaus.
- For hypertrophy, work a muscle in a variety of rep ranges, with sets that fail at 5-8 reps, 8-12 reps and 15-20 reps. This means a muscle is more likely to be taken through the lower-end strength and power, mid-range hypertrophy and higher-end muscular endurance phases, thus recruiting more motor units and covering all muscle fibres.
- To apply progressive overload, look to increase weight, reps, frequency of training or exercise difficulty as the programme goes on.

If you want to take it a step further and explore volume, intensity, and frequency as a means of programming, and since using high volume, high intensity **and** high frequency generally has a shelf life, I would urge you to programme your training by prioritising 2 of these 3 components and base your choices on:

- **Which aspects of training do you enjoy?** If you love training heavy to failure and breaking strength PBs, then a higher intensity might be for you.
- **What is your training goal?** If your goal is purely aesthetic, then you can take any of these approaches and make them work. The same goes for general fitness, health,

and wellbeing. If your goal is strength-based, you will need to use some high-intensity, lower-rep work, as strength is really measured using close to maximal loads for reps of 1-5. It's hard to truly build and assess strength using frequency and volume alone. If your goal is to become very fit from an aerobic and anaerobic perspective for specific sports or something like CrossFit, you will be best served in designing a good training programme that prioritises different areas of frequency, volume, and intensity in different micro/mesocycles throughout the year.

• **Are there limiting factors such as injuries that you need to think about?** If you have recurring injuries that generally occur under maximal loads, you might prefer a volume centric approach that uses lighter weights and allows you to hit failure in the 15-20 rep range, than going balls out for heavy sets of 5.

• **What are your weekly time constraints?** If, due to other commitments, you can only train 3 times per week, you should train with high intensity and high volume to offset the lack of frequency.

• **You don't have to stick to 2 out of the 3 forever.** With good programming, you can scale these components up and down during the training year and even change them for different sessions or body parts within the same programme or training cycle. On a personal level, I've learnt that my legs respond best to higher volume and lower intensity, whilst my triceps respond better to higher intensity and frequency. I've also found that I can push weight on lifts like the chest press, lat pull or bicep curl, but using a very heavy weight to failure for a deadlift or high pull gives a high chance of injury. I can programme my sessions to take this into account for different body parts, even within the same training phase or cycle.

Fitness Movements as Dogma – has fitness replaced religion?

From the dawn of humanity, it's been evident that people like to belong to communities. Hunter-gatherers belonged to small tribes that would depend on each other for food, shelter, protection and to reproduce. Forging bonds meant that you were more likely to thrive in the wild landscape and we've evolved to realise that we're stronger together. As social animals, we often crave belonging to a friendship, club, or community. This is evident in the fitness and sporting community, where different clubs, gyms and fitness movements build strong identities that aim to stand out from the rest. When run well, these communities can be incredibly special, uplifting, and inspirational places to train, form friendships and find a sense of belonging. I know that the Bristol gym that I train in (Trojan Fitness) can be a fantastic community of varying disciplines, where bodybuilders, CrossFitters, powerlifters, strength athletes, martial artists, boxers, and everyday fitness enthusiasts train and support each other. The gym is prominent in the local community, doing a lot for people's mental wellbeing and helping individuals who might otherwise find themselves lost without the focus of the gym. But when it comes to specific fitness movements or the latest online crazes, there is certainly a darker side.

Dogma can be described as 'a belief or set of beliefs that is accepted by the members of a group without being questioned or doubted'. In a similar way that religions rely on faith rather than evidence, many of today's training and diet movements seem to do the same. Rather than scientifically backed evidence, much of today's fitness industry seems to rely on funky advertising and sensationalist claims of the next perfect diet or magical supplement. Priests and preachers have been replaced with shirtless and bikini-clad models, pushing a variety of supplements that often have worryingly little evidence of being efficacious when it comes to burning fat or building muscle. Worse still, many of these 'influencers' are attributing their incredible gains to these supplements, which, at best, downplays their effort, adherence, and genetics and, at worst, completely ignores the real supplements they're taking, which are often various forms of performance-enhancing drugs (PEDs). I'll explore the use of PEDs in a later chapter, but forgetting any legal or health-related factors, the simple act of peddling a supplement that you don't use, and then attributing it to gains that were made using PEDs, is incredibly misleading and morally wrong. Thankfully, I've managed to stay away from a lot of this world due to my limited use of social media, but in researching for this book, I'm absolutely blown away by the amount of 'influencers' who are advertising useless, under-dosed supplements and energy drinks and directly attributing them to breaking plateaus in their physiques, completely ignoring the blatant use of PEDs, consistent training and diets. Later in the book, I'll explore some of the popular supplements and examine how effective these really are for our training and dietary needs.

The startling lack of regulation in the fitness and supplement industry makes it ripe for frauds and charlatans to push poor material, but we've also got to be careful about being dogmatic about our own fitness movement or chosen sport. For years now, bodybuilders, powerlifters, CrossFitters, gymnasts, strength athletes, dieticians and endurance athletes have often clashed over a number of fitness-related issues such as correct exercise form, the best way to build muscle, the best diets and how to train for fat loss. The problem with all of these 'groups' or 'communities' is that they often push one ideology and its participants become so wrapped up in being a member of that community that they forget there is often more than one way to do it. So, whilst we must be careful about the bombardment of useless information from every social media outlet, we should also be cautious of doing things just because 'that's the bodybuilding way'. A great example comes from my own training. Over the years, I've found it hard to develop my traps in line with other body parts. By adding in some Olympic Lift variations (that you'd typically find in CrossFit, training for Olympic Lifting, or power training for athletes) and loaded carries (that you might find as part of a Strongman training session), I was able to build my traps more effectively, which related to the stage. It would have been easy to say that 'bodybuilders don't do power cleans or farmer's walks', but these sets were incredibly effective for my goal. Equally, the use of kettlebell swings, whilst using techniques from Pilates, has helped me to train whilst managing worn discs and spinal (Pars) fractures that I suffered as a teenager. I would encourage everyone to look at these different methods of training and see what they can apply to their own programme. Of course, this will always come on a trial-and-error basis, but this can be a fantastic way to overcome plateaus in performance and find renewed enthusiasm in your routine.

Appearance Trumps Knowledge – Beware of false prophets and fad programmes

In the build-up to writing this book, I was having a chat over text with one of my good mates. He sent me the following text: *'Please tell me you're going to use one of your competition photos as a front cover?'* to which I replied *'Ha, ha, No I won't, but the harsh reality of the industry is that I will probably need a pic of that ilk somewhere on the front, back or inside cover... people will take more notice of a decent physique than they will of decent knowledge. So, I may well do that, and then ironically tear it apart on the inside pages.'*

Let's not be naïve. There's a grim truth that an impressive set of abs, biceps, or booty seems to gain more kudos, respect and 'sells' than solid knowledge. The internet, magazines and billboards are littered with shirtless models selling us supplements, diet, and training advice, and purchasing this book is probably no different. There will be many of you who will have bought the book on the strength of some of my bodybuilding pictures, with the hope to follow my training, diet and mindset advice and work towards a similar physique of your own. This is fine, but there are some serious industry pitfalls you need to look out for, and I have a responsibility to tell you some truths about my own programming and how you might respond:

1. **Just because someone looks the part doesn't mean they have an elite knowledge of training, dieting or supplementation**. In fact, it can be horrible to take advice from some of the most genetically gifted unless you have the same genetic makeup. Trying to follow a similar routine to an elite IFBB pro or professional athlete may not work for you. There are people out there who seem to look at a weight and gain muscle or fat falls off them as soon as they start a 'cutting' phase of a programme. Try to look past the physique and critique what they are telling you. If it sounds too good to be true or is littered with nice sounding but conflicting approaches to dieting, reps and sets, it's probably best avoided.

2. **If you do my specific training and diet plan, you won't necessarily look like me**. That's not to say you will look worse; you may respond better and look and feel incredible, but my genetic makeup is specific to me and there will always be differences. I can't directly attribute my abdominals to hard work and dieting. I'm lucky in that I genetically have thick and long abdominals, which are usually visible, even when I'm bulked up. Most people don't. On the other hand, no amount of direct work or calorie surplus seems to help grow my glutes and hamstrings past a particular point and my traps seem destined to stay weak and puny! We all have our genetic strengths and weaknesses, and you won't change muscle insertion sites, bone, or limb length. We can all become better versions of ourselves,

gain muscle, burn fat and feel better in the pursuit of health and fitness, but we're always working within the boundaries of our own DNA and genetic makeup.

3. **Causation and Correlation**. I know this example has been done to death, but it's still the perfect way to explain this notion - You might see a swimmer and be in awe of their long limbs, narrow waist, developed lats and wide shoulders, and because of this, you want to take up swimming. Whilst swimming might help to contribute slightly towards elements of this physique, most of these people aren't this way because they swim; they swim because they're already genetically predetermined to have these traits. Much in the same way that basketball doesn't make you taller, tall people are just better at basketball. You have to be careful of attributing the wrong factors to a set outcome. That magic supplement, incredible new workout or crazy new diet might not be the contributing factor to the impressive physique you see in the adverts. Of course, eating raw cuts of meat, plunging daily into cold water or going 40 days without masturbating might play a part, but if you examine the whole picture, it's generally a mix of good genetics, hard work, consistency in the gym, a sensible diet approach and perhaps a dabble into the saucy cupboard of PEDs that yields the actual results. Because the reality is not nearly as sexy, as easy to market, to cash in on and exploit, we're often fed the magic pill, crazy new diet or special exercise, rather than the truth.

Gym Etiquette and Beyond

Gym etiquette sounds like a dull and dry start to a chapter! We should all know the basics around proper gym use. The gym is a public place and it's important to be polite, friendly and cognizant of others. Lifting too close to the Dumbbell Rack, taking up equipment for hours on end and not returning weights after use, are all annoying habits that should be stamped out. But in this brave new world, rules around social media use, online shaming, and general acceptance, also need to be mentioned. It's become more and more common to see people filming their own sets at the gym. If you are one of these people, then you must acknowledge that you are in a public space; not everyone wants to be captured in your video, and you have no right to huff and puff if an individual walks into your shot by accident. Equally, if people are filming for social media content, to check their form or their physique progress, you shouldn't be deliberately awkward. I've seen people purposely walking into shots, moving someone's phone or even verbally abusing them for filming. Whichever side of the fence you land on, you can be polite, reasonable and kind in the process.

Anyone who follows any form of fitness-related social media, would have also witnessed a growing trend of 'shaming' others, who happen to be caught in the background of training videos. Someone who dares glance over for a split second is labelled a creep, pervert or a weirdo and put on the internet for millions to view. If you are filming content, you have to expect that other people will probably notice you, be intrigued and look over at what you are filming. They might just be inquisitive, they might be genuinely impressed by your physique, form or strength or they might feel uneasy that they're likely caught in the background of your video. Making any kind of content that aims to mock someone, and putting it online without that person's consent, is unacceptable.

In reality, most gyms make their own culture. A lot of gyms will say it's frowned upon to take your shirt off, drop weights or 'grunt' too loudly during a set. For other gyms, where bodybuilders are checking their physique progress and practising their posing, powerlifters are attempting one rep maxes and crossfitters are pushing themselves to the absolute maximum, all of the above things would be expected and accepted. As an individual, the responsibility is on us to understand the gym that we are training in and exercise some emotional intelligence. When I train at my local Pure gym, I don't practice my posing routine in the mirror or apply exactly the same level of intensity and 'noise' to some of my lifts. When I train at 'The Trojan', where competing bodybuilders more commonly train, I absolutely do these things, and no one bats an eyelid.

It all comes down to being kind, accepting and creating a collaborative gym culture. The gym should be a space where everyone feels safe and comfortable, irrespective of their gender, age, race, sexuality, or training level. Everyone is there to improve some aspect of their physical or mental wellbeing, and no one deserves to be made fun of, singled out or harassed.

We're Not Defined by Our Bodies – Finding Self Worth elsewhere

I want to state quite quickly in this book, that having, what the mainstream would call, a fantastic physique, does not make you a good person, nor should people be idolised, put on a pedestal or lorded for simply 'looking the part'. If I'm wiring a book that focusses on fitness, bodybuilding, dieting, and features facts around calorie equations and 'progress pictures' then it would be irresponsible for us to ignore the potential harm, that this industry and these factors can cause. Specifically, I want to focus on the detrimental effect that this can have on the mental and physical health of youngsters, with special focus on young Women. Of course, Men of all ages are also affected by unobtainable body images and body dysmorphia, but I do believe that marketing, social media and attitudes of the general public, leads to many more women, having 'body confidence' issues, than men. If you look at the Statistics from the 'Priory' website, it explains that 75% of people living with an eating disorder in the UK are female[4]. Statistics from the USA show a similar percentage, and if you were to focus on Anorexia Nervosa specifically, this number rises to 90% female. Not only is Anorexia the biggest killer among 'eating disorders' it also reports the highest death rate of any mental illness in the USA, accounting for double the deaths of sufferers of Schizophrenia, triple that of people living with Bi-Polar and triple the death rate of those suffering from depression. For deaths from Anorexia, one in five is from suicide. I won't disrespect the genuine experts in this field by digging too deeply into mental illness or eating disorders, but it's fair to say that anyone operating in the fitness industry has a responsibility to address the role of their own literature or online content, when it comes to marketing, advertising and wider content creation. And as a society, on the whole, we all have a responsibility to ensure that we're doing our part to protect our youngsters who have an interest in this industry. We don't want to discourage a passion for nutrition, fitness and 'gym' related pursuits, but we have to be cognizant that if the self worth from these pursuits is too closely linked with the physical aesthetic alone, we might be walking a very dangerous line. And for our female athletes specifically, we need to be better in how we talk about female bodies, inside the sporting and fitness industries. One of the biggest disappointments is that many of these athletes, bodybuilders and figure competitors are still highly sexualised and outwardly judged on sex appeal rather than performance. The social expectation of what a feminine body 'should' look like needs to change. The amount of times I overhear people in the gym talking about some of our female bodybuilders and figure athletes, and every compliment is followed by a 'but'. "She looks amazing, so ripped, so big, but I don't find that attractive", why the fuck do you need to? She's a bodybuilder, not someone you've matched on Tinder. I doubt you would say that "Ronaldo is a class footballer but I don't really want to shag him." This is also a consideration outside of the aesthetic sports and in the wider, Female sporting world. I recently read an excellent article, written by England Rugby player Sadia Kabeya. In it she explained that she would 'shy away from gym sessions to avoid muscles' and went through a phase of eating salads, in a bid to stay smaller. She would enter the rugby field woefully short of energy and not perform at her best. Like many young women, whilst Sadia wanted to perform well, be strong, quick and powerful, she was doing these things in a bid to look (what society would deem as) 'more feminine'. As she's got older and more accepting of herself, Sadia realised that she can "be aggressive, lift heavy weights, have muscles and still be feminine." And she's realised that the fact she is strong and has muscles, is why she's able to be one of England's top players in the upcoming six nations. If she was avoiding the gym and eating salads, this wouldn't be the case. In this example, Sadia is able to realise that her genetics, hard work and talent means she can do the things that she loves, and the self worth and self esteem derived from performing well and playing for England, can trump any self worth taken from looking stereotypically, more 'feminine'. As I dug into the research surrounding female athletes, I found some alarming stats that were gathered by Barbara Spanjers at the Centre for Discovery (Eating Disorder Treatment). In the USA, it was found that a third of female division 1 NCAA athletes reported behaviours that demonstrate risk for developing anorexia nervosa. 41% of athletes in aesthetic sports like cheerleading, gymnastics, figure skating and dance, reported an eating disorder. And even 60% of women surveyed in the military, met criteria for an eating disorder[5]. So whether you're someone who is sharing content online, selling supplements, workout advice or simply training in a gym, we all need to look at our own attitude towards women in sport and fitness, check the words we use and the things that we choose to comment on. In more positive examples, I've also spoken to dozens of women over the years, who have actually used the gym and developed an excellent knowledge of nutrition, to overcome some of these struggles. Despite the statistics, I still believe, that with a slight shift in attitudes, the fitness and sporting world can be an incredible and fulfilling industry for everyone's physical and mental health journey.

Social Media and the Rise of 'Influencers'

It's hard to write this chapter without starting with the line 'back in my day' which, as a 38-year-old, seems a silly thing to say. When it comes to social media use and anything technical or technology based, I'm absolutely useless. Whilst I've dabbled in some online platforms, as I type this, I don't have an Instagram or Facebook account, I've only been directly on TikTok a handful of times, and whilst I use YouTube daily, I don't make content myself. You might think, therefore, that I'm the most under-qualified person to have an opinion on the fitness community for social media, or to critique influencers, but such is the bombardment of fitness advertising, and the abundance of various YouTube 'fitness lifestyle' videos, that I feel immersed in the whole world. I don't want this to be the ramblings of a grumpy old man, so let's start with the positives, and there definitely are some.

When I first entered a gym in the late 90s, it was a case of learning from fellow gym-goers and reading the odd book. Whilst personal trainers existed, there were certainly none in my local gym and for the first 6 months of training, I remember training bench press and bicep curls daily and becoming obsessed with how many pull-ups I could do. Progressive Overload was an accident of being competitive with my mates, deadlifts, squats (or any effective lower body training for that matter) didn't really happen, and I would perform exercises and not really know what they were meant to be doing. (For example, for the first 6 months of training, I thought an incline dumbbell chest press was solely to work your triceps! I know… clue's in the name!) But fast forward some twenty-five years and the internet is a hive of fitness and bodybuilding information. You can search for exercises and watch a step-by-step tutorial within two minutes. Literature on diet plans and effective training is available at the touch of a button and bodybuilding pros, power lifters, sponsored athletes and qualified nutritionists are all over the internet, imparting tons of great information and musings from their own research and experience. Of course, it's a minefield of conflicting info, false prophets, and scrupulous marketing, but if you can navigate to the right channels, there's plenty of excellent info out there. Such is the ever-changing landscape of the online fitness world that I'm almost nervous to recommend channels or people, as, by the time you read this, they may have been caught up in the latest social media spat, be accused of using fake weights, pedalling poor supplements, or found to be committing the ultimate cardinal sin of being a 'fake natty' (someone who claims to be 'natural' when in reality they are using 'performance enhancing drugs' or PEDs). Anyhow, I'll take the risk and give a few recommendations for people whose content I enjoy, who have my respect and with whose opinions I generally concur with, and from a sports science, education and performance perspective, have a lot more qualifications and knowledge than myself.

1. **Jeff Nippard**. I would recommend Jeff Nippard for natural bodybuilding programming advice, diet information and general fitness information when it comes to effective supplementation, fat loss or muscle gain. Jeff also seems like a pretty humble, down-to-earth

guy who uses peer-reviewed journals to back up claims, comes from a sports science background, but also 'walks the walk' and I believe is a natural bodybuilding pro at the time of typing this.

2. **Tia-Clair Toomey**. Six-time Crossfit games champion and former Olympian, Tia-Clair Toomey is one of the fittest people on earth, and she also has a pretty successful YouTube site that she runs with her partner and Coach, Shane Orr. Their site is a goldmine for anyone interested in Crossfit, and covers lifting technique, diet and training programmes. Perhaps the most useful tool from this channel is to see how Tia and Shane peak for competition, with details of microcycles, mesocycles and an overview of the whole Macrocycle. Even if you don't love Crossfit, you can't help but be inspired with her elite level of strength, agility and fitness.

3. **Ross Edgley** – Ross Edgley comes across as a really positive and inspirational guy. He's done some insane fitness challenges and comes from a sports science background with sound advice around programming and dieting for a mix of performance and aesthetics. I would recommend Ross for fitness motivation, training for endurance challenges (especially any swimming events) and for insights into mindset and what it takes to mentally overcome huge physical undertakings.

4. **Layne Norton**. Layne Norton is incredibly knowledgeable on all things powerlifting, nutrition and natural bodybuilding and has excelled both on the platform and on the stage. His passion and area of expertise seem to lie more on the nutrition side

these days, with lots of great content online, including podcasts, diet plans and information around effective programming, fat loss and micronutrients.

5. '**More Plates, More Dates**' – Derek from 'More Plates, More Dates' has done an incredible job of bringing PED awareness to a mainstream audience. As someone who has used PEDs himself, and who seems to have a genuine love and passion for the bodybuilding and fitness scene, Derek has a non-judgemental approach to steroid awareness. He's not scaremongering or preaching, but he is completely honest about the potential upsides and downsides of using PEDs. He's well-versed in pharmacology and hormonal profiling and talks in an impressive manner about the subjects. Derek has probably done more for a generation of gym addicts to be more clued up on various PED use than anyone else in the modern landscape. If you want to know more about PEDs or the efficacy of certain supplements or micronutrients, 'More Plates, More Dates' is a great place to visit.

6. '**Coach Greg**' – Greg Doucette is a Canadian pro bodybuilder, coach, nutritionist and all-round sports scientist. His presentation style splits opinion, but his actual content and his ability to cut through all the nonsense and present simple and effective diet and training advice, are second to none. I would recommend his content if you wanted to know more about setting up effective diet plans, bodybuilding training, or general health.

7. **Renaissance Periodization** – Dr Mike Israetel holds a PHD in sports Physiology, has been a University Lecturer, Coach and competitive bodybuilder. From

all of the channels and people I recommend, I think Mike Isratel makes my favourite content. His advice on nutrition, training, bodybuilding and athletic performance is second to none and his presentation style is fantastic, conveying simple, common-sense protocols, often delivered in a lighthearted manner. Even when he's disagreeing with another person's training style or point of view, his content is rarely personal or particularly cutting. As well as short YouTube style video's, you can also find longer and more serious lectures and discussions on all things training and nutrition. Some brilliant Mike Isratel lectures have seen me through many a boring cardio session.

There are loads of other channels and people that put out quality content. Ryan Humiston, Jonni Shreve and the late John Meadows all have excellent channels for exercise execution and general bodybuilding info. Jesse James West and LeanBeefPatty both have broader 'bodybuilding lifestyle' channels that are probably aimed at a slightly younger audience, and cover some really important topics around body dysmorphia, relationship with food and mental health, as well as training and diet content. Channels like BashBros and Fouad Abiad Media, have bodybuilding specific podcasts, with excellent guests, Andrew Huberman is an incredible neuroscientist with a lens on wellness, training and dieting, and 'Nick Strength and Power' brings a selection of bodybuilding and fitness related news.

And if you really want to see inspirational and motivational content, slightly outside of the mainstream fitness and gym world, check out Ed Jackson and his charity Millimetres to

Mountains. I've listened to dozens of Podcasts where Ed details his recovery from a serious spinal cord injury. He now runs a charity that raises money and supports people with spinal cord (and other serious) injuries, by undertaking numerous outdoor adventures, like climbing mountains and traversing ice caps. More proof, that whatever your perceived, physical limitations are, the ability to plan and attempt physical challenges, can be transformative for your mental wellbeing and fulfilment. It was listening to the story of Ed's recovery that really made me think which sources of inspiration we seek out. Of course, if you're interested in bodybuilding and the gym, some of these channels, influencers and professionals are brilliant sources of information, but when I really stopped to analyse what inspires me to train, to improve my physical and mental wellbeing, session to session, it's not impressive physiques, or feats of strength. The things that really inspire me are stories of overcoming adversity and extreme, mental fortitude. It's Ed Jackson coming back from the brink of never walking again, to raise masses of money and awareness, to help improve lives across the world. It's my Mum, who had a brain tumour removed, suffered terrible seizures and went on to make a full recovery, it's my Sister who has learned to live with a Spinal Cord Injury, and now has a fantastic personal, family and professional life, it's my Partner, who's has helped (and continues to help) hundreds of kids, from disadvantaged backgrounds, get through some awful, personal circumstances, it's my two mates who have battled with addiction and have got clean and gone on to be incredible Fathers and great people. So taking some inspiration, interest and knowledge from the aesthetics of bodybuilders or the strength and fitness of crossfitters and powerlifters is great, but perhaps you are finding yourself obsessing over a flat stomach, perfect glutes, a massive bench press or a 'crazy v taper'. To look past the aesthetic, and for a chance to take inspiration from other sources, we should also look at some of the great success stories, the adversity, and the mental fortitude of everyday folk, as sources of real inspiration, and to remind ourselves of what's really important, and truly impressive.

Before I get into 'The Bad', I also want to state that I am absolutely not judging the vast majority of fitness enthusiasts and 'influencers' who use social media to document parts of their fitness lifestyle. Sharing progress pictures on social media can be a great way to keep you motivated and bring a sense of pride to your achievements. There is nothing wrong if you take pleasure in sharing your hard graft and knowledge and invite others to take part in that journey. Many of these transformations, progress pictures and general 'fitness posts' can be hugely inspirational and impressive and help others who might be looking to get into health and fitness. If you have great glutes, a rippling 6-pack or huge shoulders and you want to share that journey on a social platform, then go ahead - no one should make you feel bad, shallow, or stupid for doing so. If you've just started out and you want to show your one-month progress as a 'fitness newbie', then go for it. Sharing how you got into the gym and the effect it's having on you might inspire others to go down the same path, and, by the time you read this, I may well be back on socials myself, documenting a bodybuilding prep or marketing my fabulous book. So, to be clear, my specific gripe is not with the majority of these channels, it is when these great physiques are being used to sell magic supplements, mythical new workouts and snazzy diet fads, and the reality of what really went into building these physiques is ignored. If you are sharing a true account of your fitness journey, then more power to you; I can only wish you the best in your endeavours and hope that many people take knowledge and inspiration from your posts and shares.

Sifting out the Nonsense

As I've already stated, I'm not on many of these platforms, and so I've had to do some specific online research to really measure the extent of the problem. In the last 12 months, I've seen a Bollywood star, with millions of followers, state that Whey Protein takes 3 years to digest. I've seen a chap who has sworn blind that he is natural and attributed his incredible physique to eating a variety of raw meats and following a set plan (that he marketed and sold for millions), only to find out that he's been spending over £10k per month on Performance Enhancing Drugs (PEDs). I've seen shirtless fitness influencers be exposed for using their platform to peddle Ponzi schemes and dodgy forex trading, and I've witnessed dozens upon dozens of videos, critiquing foods, exercise selection and supplements, only to completely contradict themselves in a video 2 weeks later. I've seen influencers warn us about the dangers of processed foods (like Whey Protein!), only to be videoed in 10,000-calorie eating challenges in the shape of a Mukbang and I've seen 18-stone men and glamorous women, dancing around on Tik Tok, whilst marketing their latest supplement line, shamelessly targeting a teenage audience with high stimulant products and largely unobtainable (natural) physiques. The whole process has left me saddened and incredibly apathetic about much of the online industry.

There are some fantastic benefits to social media but getting fitness info online is a bit like shopping at TK Maxx; There are some bargains out there, but you have to sift through a lot of shit to find it. Unfortunately, there is a huge amount of poor info, sensationalist claims, and, in the worst cases, downright lies about the efficacy of supplements and the use of PEDs. This unscrupulous marketing seems to be targeted at young, inexperienced and impressionable 'newbies' and has even been coined as the 'newbie trap' by some channels such as 'Shredded Sports Science' who aim to call out these shysters and highlights trendy marketing, cool videos and the promotion of a 'glamorous lifestyle' to sell useless supplements, fitness programmes and diets. There is so much misleading and bad info online that it's hard to know where to start. Fake nattys, poor exercise advice, poor nutrition advice, false positivity or overwhelming negativity - it's become a largely toxic culture, driven by businesses who seemingly have no real interest in fitness, health or bodybuilding, and are out to sell a false dream for big bucks. Everyone seems to have a supplement line; everyone sells their version of a diet or training plan that often promises impossible results within a matter of weeks. What's even more disappointing is that some of the guys and girls who do have fantastic physiques, along with sound exercise and diet knowledge, are still selling lies and crappy supplements to make a quick buck and misleading audiences by selling branded diet pills, energy drinks and quick fix diets, whilst completely ignoring (or deliberately lying about) their use of performance enhancing drugs. It seems a different 'influencer' is caught out monthly, revealed as a 'fake natty', but by then, they're already millionaires! It's been an eye-opener to dip my toe into the murky, interesting and, at times, downright tragic world of the online fitness community. More pictures of peachy butts than I've ever witnessed, a dice roll of decent and awful training advice and growing trends like Mukbangs, dry scooping and something I can only describe as 'TikTok, fitnessy dancing'?! On the face of it, a bunch of teens and 20-somethings having a bit of fun, but is there a darker side to what appears to be the pushing of questionable supplements, the glorification of unobtainable bodies and blatant marketing techniques that seem to be aimed at children? I'm all for kids being into sport, training and learning about sound nutrition, but high stimulant supplements, full of caffeine, the preoccupation with every girl needing a tiny waist and big booty and the bombardment of huge and shredded guys, often being advertised using funky music and childish dances, sometimes by a juiced-up man or woman in their 30s… it all just seems a bit weird.

For me, the overwhelming feeling that researching the online fitness community gave me was one of apathy. It was a disconnect from the physical world of the gym that I know for myself; a world of like-minded training partners, trying hard to achieve a set goal, build a healthy mindset, add to training knowledge and have fun whilst doing it. I had kind of gone full circle with emotions, seeing the great, the good and the horrific. I felt anger and confusion at influencers who were making broad claims like 'this is **THE** best exercise to get a shredded back' or 'this is the **number one** supplement to burn fat', but I also felt some apathy towards the channels that aim to call these people out. It seemed that anyone with any level of muscle mass was automatically a 'fake natty'. Dozens of sports stars, influencers, film stars or musicians were being called out for PED use as if it was fact, without any hard, supporting evidence. People were being torn down for the slightest chink in their bench press or squat form and publicly shamed in front of the masses. At times, these videos could be educational, but there's something uncomfortable about the personal nature of these attacks and some of the videos were just plain wrong! People rarely stopped to consider the training goal and I saw one video which suggested someone should 'slow down the eccentric phase of their power clean', which is such a ridiculous statement, I can't even begin to pull it apart. But in honesty, when it came down to the success of these videos and posts, the content barely seemed to matter; it was all about getting the most views, shares and likes, using 'clickbait' titles, and was far more about the accompanying physique or branding that went along with the content than the content itself. It became apparent that a girl with a round ass could tell you any which way to complete a squat and it would be accepted. A girl with a less obvious 'butt shelf', with less glamour and sex appeal, could tell you a perfect, technical model of a squat, and no one would listen or watch. We are truly in the 'data' age. It seems that likes, shares and comments beat knowledge and hard work. Likes, shares and comments build a brand identity and a strong brand identity can reach and influence millions of people with the touch of a button. All of a sudden, the 'gym world' that I once knew had been turned into a collection of cleverly edited videos, product placement and quick-fix promises, all being run by a collection of people with the highest sex appeal and the most charisma. Much like the dogmatic nature of the big 'fitness movements', we've now got individual people, pushing their own brand of supplementation, workout styles and fitness lingo. Like any of these movements, some information will be poor and some will be great, but the ability of a 13-year-old, who is new to training, to distinguish between the bullshit and the facts, is a definite concern.

Mukbangs, Dry Scooping and TikTok Fitnessy Dancing!

Let me state that I don't specifically judge these three things in their own right, other than the fact that dry scooping a pre-workout is ineffective, compared to taking it with water! If someone wants to dance to music, in a gym, take a pre-workout with no water, or eat huge amounts of food, it doesn't make them a bad person. I'll also state that I have been guilty of binge eating, I sometimes go out and get very drunk, and I can cut some serious shapes, given the right music on a 4 am dance floor. The reason I am calling these three things out is because they have become viral crazes that have somehow infiltrated the fitness industry: Viral crazes, where videos garner millions of views, and off the back of them, thousands of terrible products and ideologies are being peddled to kids. Because, let's get real, very few people over the age of 18 are watching YouTubers dance about, eat loads of calories in one go, or take a dry scoop of their pre-workout. I'm sure there are some, but the vast majority of these videos are directly aimed at teenagers and complete fitness newbies.

The Urban Dictionary, quite brilliantly, describes a Mukbang as 'the unholy but inevitable bastard offspring of pigging out and social media. It involves eating and preparing large quantities of food on camera.' Basically, filming yourself eating shit loads. Somehow, the fitness community has adopted this craze as some sort of way to monetize 'cheat meals' or 'refeeds' and these 'Mukbang' videos have gone to viral levels. I don't want to seem overly stuffy or judgmental, but this nonsense perfectly typifies the state of the current industry where 'influencers', who preach about a sensible approach to diet, fitness and health, seem to indulge in more and more extreme feats of eating – aiming to eat 10,000 calories of junk in one sitting and somehow, get kudos for doing so. I would have no real problem with this if it wasn't being done by the same people who are preaching health and fitness and selling plans and supplements off the back of it. This level of contradiction is taken to new heights by some influencers who seem to preach about healthy living, eating and supplementation, even calling out Protein Shakes for being 'synthetic' and 'bad for you', whilst indulging in huge calorie challenges of junk food, peddling an array of high-stim supplements and, sometimes, using (assumingly huge amounts) of PEDs. And it's this level of hypocrisy and conflicting messaging that is absolutely rife throughout the fitness industry. I have no problem with people eating lots of food, I have no problem with people taking PEDs (as long as they're honest about it and don't seek to compete in sporting events that will give them an unfair advantage), and I have no problem with people selling fitness supplements and products (as long as they're backed by science and they're effective), but when someone makes big anecdotal claims about health and fitness, puts themselves out there as someone to aspire to and follow, and then proceeds to film weekly videos that completely contradict claims that they've made the week before, that's just ridiculous and lacks any kind of credibility. And that hits the nail on the head here – the startling lack of credibility in a lot of these 'influencers' and their videos.

'Dry Scooping' has also become a ridiculous viral craze that seems to make no sense at all. To the uninitiated, this is the practice of pouring a scoop of pre-workout into your mouth, dry and with no water, as some kind of proof that you belong to the fitness community. In itself, who really cares? It probably won't do you any harm and there are plenty more things to be worried about. But again, this is another great example of something that offers no tangible benefit to a training goal. Dry Scooping is reasonably unpleasant and actually less effective than taking your pre-workout with water. If you want your pre-workout to try and facilitate more of a 'pump' as part of your workout, the absence of water is going to likely hinder the ability for the pre-workout to enter the blood and the muscle, as water can act as a 'transporter' for compounds such as citrulline mallate. I would imagine the acidity is also horrendous for your teeth and perhaps your stomach but more troubling is that this craze seems to have directly influenced some kind of game where 'influencers' and everyday folk attempt to ingest as much caffeine through 'dry scooping' as possible. I've seen videos where kids are taking up to 800mg of caffeine – about 4 times the dose of a standard pre-workout, and, in the worst cases, this could be fatal. This is yet another fad craze that seems to garner huge amounts of views, likes, shares, comments and therefore revenue, for fitness influencers.

I could only stomach a few of these 'TikTok dancing fitness videos', which gave me just enough evidence to include in this book, but I'll keep this short and not so sweet. Again, someone comically dancing to music whilst lifting weights is hardly something to be overly concerned with, but the worry here is that these pointless videos get millions of views, likely by 11-17-year-olds, which gives these 'influencers' massive platforms. In turn, these platforms are being used to peddle huge amounts of rubbish supplements, poor training and terrible diet advice to these teenagers who may well become the fitness morons of tomorrow. Many of these videos seem to include a girl doing a squat or deadlift variation whilst facing away from the camera (of course), and are often executed with average form, usually accompanied by an advertisement for some kind of pre- or intra-workout, dry scooped for good measure. They're perpetuating a culture that's miles away from fitness or health, completely dependent on looks and sex appeal and which carries absolutely no value when it comes to exercise selection, correct form or supplementation use. Perhaps I haven't dug far enough in my research, but after watching dozens of these clips, I couldn't stomach much more. I'm sure many of the excellent channels and genuine experts who I watch on YouTube have a TikTok presence that includes fantastic info, but this subsection of some kind of 'fitness dancing comedy' doesn't seem to offer anything in the way of useful diet or programme advice, nor any stimulating discussion or debate that would be of any use to an informed or curious individual.

To Conclude

I think there should be a genuine concern and far more regulation and rigour when it comes to targeting children with advertising and marketing campaigns that sell high stimulant and/or ineffective supplementation and promote physiques that are largely improbable for most individuals to achieve naturally. From a general point of view, like so much of the fitness industry, from personal trainers, to training methods, classes, sporting coaches, gyms and health clubs, the world of social media fitness includes excellent, average, and horrendous people and channels. To say that all is bad would be grossly misleading and completely unfair to many of the quality professionals who operate across a variety of these platforms. It's fair to say that seeking fitness advice on social media comes with a health warning, so you should do your homework and try to navigate to credible sources who are giving you useable, common-sense advice, backed by science, and ideally, personal experience, with evidence that these men and women have talked the talk and can also walk the walk, showing that their fitness philosophies can be translated into useable programmes, diets and outcomes. Having spent the last couple of years looking at a cross-section of the social media fitness landscape, I would be specifically looking out for the following pitfalls and asking yourself some of the following questions:

-   'Have I found the actual information useful and useable, or am I attracted to the content because the individual has a great physique?' If it's the latter, whilst this could still be a source of inspiration, and potentially fun to watch, are you going to be able to apply any of this info to help your overall training/diet plan or exercise selection/execution?

- Be cautious if an individual is marketing a supplement, and if they are specifically claiming that this supplement played a pivotal role in creating their own physique or performance goals. If this is the case, you would be wise to seek wider supplement reviews from peer-reviewed studies or some of the channels that I mentioned at the start of this section.

- Be incredibly sceptical of anyone who claims that a particular exercise is 'the best' exercise for a specific body part as if it's fact. If they're saying that the deadlift is one of the best exercises for overall size and strength, then this is fine, but statements like 'the hanging leg raise is THE best exercise for abdominal development' is just unscientific and plain wrong. It may well be up there for some individuals, but you can never make a sweeping generalisation like this when things like training history, injury history, limb length, mind-muscle connection and a range of other factors have to be considered.

- Pay special attention to conflicting information. I've seen so many influencers back a set of supplements, exercises or training methods, only to directly contradict themselves on videos that are weeks apart. This is a great way to know if a source is credible and if they have a genuine training and diet philosophy, or if they're happy to jump ship in the name of selling a shiny new product or marketable diet.

- Equally, decent fitness professionals should be happy to try new things and be proved wrong. If we're really taking a proper scientific approach to training and diet, we should all be open to new methods that are evolving, and new research that is coming from credible sources. You can still be open to fresh ideas and maintain a healthy scepticism for things that look too good to be true or include sensationalist claims.

- Be careful of taking too much inspiration from, or overwatching channels that predominantly deal in the aesthetics of bodybuilding and fitness. Obsessing over our appearance isn't a good thing and there is no doubt that over indulging on pictures and video's of ultra shredded guys and girls, can give you an unrealistic expectation of what an average human body looks like. Even if bodybuilding is you passion, realising that we are more than our bodies, and finding inspiration from other avenues of fitness performance, human endeavour, overcoming adversity and hard work, would be wise.

- The biggest piece of advice I can offer is to find your own way. Align yourself with some of these credible sources, learn about varying approaches to programming, exercise execution and diets, and see what works for you. See what you enjoy, what fits your body and mindset, and build your own training philosophy and approach to give you the best chance of adherence and results. If you can navigate the online minefield, it can serve as an incredible tool for helping improve knowledge and achieve your goals.

Chapter 2

Training

I've found a gym!

I'm on holiday, I've done my research and I think I've found a gym! According to Google, it's down these stairs, turn left, a 5-minute walk and I should be there. It's 8 am and it's a beautiful morning. Already 28 degrees, people are swimming in the ocean, the sun glistens off the water, fishing boats are leaving for the day and I've left my Partner in bed on day one of the holiday to find somewhere to lift weights… I don't think this is how normal folk start a holiday, but for me, it's crucial. Don't get me wrong, I'll relax and eat and drink and sunbathe, but, for 45 minutes in the morning, I just want to lift weights! I start to get jittery as I keep walking with no sight of a gym and my weird, overactive mind starts to imagine the next 2 weeks without my fix of iron and pain… but wait, what's that I can see…? And there it is, a sign on the street saying, 'Gym 2000 Herceg Novi'. I walk in and can barely believe it! I've hit the jackpot! It's a proper bodybuilding gym! A Hack Squat, fixed benches, fixed inclines, Smith machines, leg press, plenty of dumbbells and more 'plate loaded' machines than I've ever seen.

Dopamine floods my system, giving me the same excitement that most people feel eating an expensive steak or enjoying a beer! A thing of beauty and a whole week for only 20 Euros! It's day one so it's obviously chest and triceps. A quick few warm-up sets on the cables and it's onto the incline bench for a juicy pump. Within 5 minutes, I've been told off for not putting a towel down and sweating all over the equipment. "Sorry," I say, whilst still grinning at the euphoria of finding this little gem. After incline, it's onto some flyes, a chest press machine variation, some triceps overheads, and a nasty dip and press-up finisher before a morning coffee in the sun. Back and biceps tomorrow at the same time… this should be a great holiday!

Pick your Goal before you Pick your Training Method

This seems like the most obvious statement of the year so far, but it's amazing to see how many people are choosing training methods that don't align with their desired goals. There are many subtle changes in exercise selection, tempo and execution, that can make all the difference, depending on whether we're trying to become stronger, leaner or bigger. What's more, I often see people being judged, trolled or 'corrected' at the gym or online, when the individual often has no idea of what the lifter is actually trying to achieve. Examples like telling someone to 'slow down and control' the bar more on a bench press, when in fact, the lifter is doing speed work for powerlifting, is extremely frustrating. Until you understand someone's goal, you can't possibly judge their exercise selection, tempo and ultimate execution. If you want to see the best example of this in action, go and look at a video of Lu Xiaojun's weight-lifting technique review. Lu is one of the greatest Olympic Lifters of all time, but his incredibly rapid weight-lifting tempo has attracted negative attention from armchair experts, who simply don't understand his training goal. Yes, his training tempo is incredibly fast, and wouldn't be optimal for muscle hypertrophy, but this is not the aim of Lu's training. In fact, muscle hypertrophy could actually be an unwanted side effect of weight training, given that Olympic Lifters compete in weight categories and extra muscle mass would equal a heavier category. Of course, Lu's training is all about rapid muscle contraction - the ability to exert speed, force and power onto the bar as quickly as possible. Whereas bodybuilders look to isolate muscles and use a controlled tempo to create muscle tension and minimise momentum (rocking, dipping, swinging weights), Lu would be looking for the exact opposite in his training - looking to maximise efficiency of movement, deploy huge amounts of speed and power onto the bar and lift the maximum weight, utilising as many muscles as needed to make the lift efficient and seamless. If Lu is pressing overhead, it makes little difference to him how much of that lift is activating the front deltoid vs the triceps. On the other hand, a bodybuilder, looking to isolate the front deltoid for his/her shoulder session, wants as much tension on that front delt as possible. Over the next few chapters, we'll examine how your training goal should change your training methods, how to effectively programme for strength, size and speed, how you could set up a training plan for a newbie, and a selection of cardio options for performance, health and fat loss.

Training for Hypertrophy – Rep Ranges and Proximity to Failure

When it comes to training for pure muscle growth, there has been growing evidence that suggests the classic 'hypertrophy rep range', with a sweet spot around 8-12 reps, might not be all that accurate, or, to be more accurate myself, that this rep range may be way broader than we first thought[6]. Newer studies suggest that when it comes to building muscle, it doesn't seem to matter if you fail at 5 or 25 reps; what seems to matter is that you're pushing your lifts to the point of muscular failure, therefore, recruiting more muscle fibres and performing 'effective reps' to stimulate muscle growth. Think about how you feel in a set of 5 compared to a set of 25. If you do 5 reps at a proper '5 rep max' weight, then all 5 reps are hard. The weight is moving at a slower pace because it's near your upper threshold for maximal strength. Now, compare that to a set of 25. The first 12 reps are likely to fly up, with growing fatigue coming in between reps 13 and 20 and the last 5 reps being a slow grind to get over the line. Similar to the 5-rep max, you might say that although you've done 25 reps, it's only the last 5 that were actually 'effective' in taxing the muscle and eliciting the potential for a growth response to the stimulus. So, if the 'effective reps' model is to be believed, then, when it comes to hypertrophy, there is little to no difference between using sets of 5 to sets of 25, as long as the proximity to failure is the same. Now, that's perhaps true in itself, but how should we use this knowledge to programme an effective muscle-building plan and what factors might limit this research?

1. Doing higher rep sets of over 20 reps is all very well, but it doesn't significantly improve high-end strength performance. You may say that you don't care about this for pure aesthetics or bodybuilding, but most people would agree that building some kind of useable strength in the lower-end rep range is useful, enjoyable and just damn right cool.

2. Doing higher rep sets of over 20 reps seems a lot of time wasted if only the last few reps are going to be deemed as 'effective'.

3. Doing lower rep sets of 5 will recruit a lot of fast twitch fibres, increase strength potential and help to build power, but the likelihood of creating enough time under tension is small. A set of 5 will likely take no more than 15-20 seconds (and probably a little lower) with heavier loads much harder to control and manipulate. It's unlikely that this creates enough tension to be optimal for muscle growth potential, if using 5 rep sets, for the whole session.

4. Doing lower rep sets of 5 will likely be incredibly taxing on the central nervous system, meaning that your ability to recover and push through high numbers of sets in this rep range is small.

5. Doing lower rep sets of 5 will likely lead to a greater increase in injury potential, because you are using loads that are much nearer to your 1 rep max.

6. Staying within a very narrow 'rep range' might become boring, and therefore, not optimal for adherence to the overall plan. Including sets that hit failure, in a variety of rep ranges, may be far more optimal.

The Answer – use a variety of rep ranges:

Given the evidence that there are positives and pitfalls in both rep ranges, I would look to programme my sessions to work a muscle through the whole spectrum of rep ranges: Taking advantage of the lower end strength, power and Central Nervous System - building rep range for heavier loads, adding in a mid rep range for medium loads but better control and time under tension, and moving into higher rep 'finishers' utilising drop sets, super sets and giant sets to really fatigue the muscle and provide interesting and taxing sets for a great mental battle.

Hypertrophy – Time Under Tension, ROM, Eccentric Phase

So, we know that hypertrophy can occur in a variety of rep ranges, as long as the individual is taking the set towards muscular failure. I also think that hypertrophy can occur using a range of training methods and lifting tempos. For example, I certainly don't fall out with heavy sets of 5 reps, with the bar being shifted at pace, which might be more aligned with a powerlifting or maximal strength, tempo. The ability to load the bar up and get the body used to moving heavy weights, tax the central nervous system and potentially promote the natural release of things like testosterone and growth hormone, are all great by products. Not to mention that the fun and satisfaction from hitting PB's in that rep range, shouldn't be underestimated from an adherence perspective. However, if your main goal is muscle hypertrophy, then it would also be wise to look at the time under tension and range of movement, of your working sets, specifically addressing the eccentric and concentric phases of each lift, to return maximal muscle gains. Anecdotally, for muscle hypertrophy, I've always favoured a full Range of Motion, with a slow and controlled eccentric phase, and an explosive, or 'athletic', concentric phase. So if the lift was an incline dumbbell Press, I would be coming down in a slow and controlled manner, perhaps 3 to 4 seconds, making sure I fully stretch the chest at the bottom of the movement (full range of motion), pushing up with more force and speed (perhaps a one second concentric phase) and squeezing the lift for a brief second at the top of the movement (full range of motion). If you have never lifted with this sort of deliberate tempo, it won't take you long to imagine, why this would elicit, maximal muscle growth. These reps are painful! Most research seems to support this theory, with multiple studies pointing towards the fact that, will all things being equal (reps, sets, exercise selection) muscle hypertrophy tends to occur most frequently when the muscle is in a lengthened position, during a dynamic movement. This lengthened position occurs during the mid to end point of the eccentric phase. But it's important to acknowledge the 'dynamic' part of this statement. We can't just stand there statically stretching our hamstrings and expect them to grow. Yes, the stretch (or eccentric) portion of a stiff leg deadlift is crucial to hamstring growth, but it's because that muscle is battling the tension of the weight, in a dynamic movement – shortening, lengthening and shifting the weight. An isometric hold can make our hamstrings stronger or lead to greater muscular endurance, but only in that specific, static state, this won't contribute greatly to actual hamstring hypertrophy. We should also be careful of simply focussing on 'time under tension' as if every part of a working set is the same. We could easily spend 60 seconds on a set of squats, but if the vast majority of that set is to pause at the top of the movement, then the quads and glutes are actually under very little 'tension' at all. Equally, if you were to simply fall into the lower portion of a squat, with absolutely no emphasis on the eccentric part of the movement, you're potentially robbing yourself of half the muscle building potential – if gravity is doing half the work, you'll likely get half the gains.

Putting it all together in a session:

I want to prioritise a big, compound-type lift upfront, where I can maximise weight and work on strength and lower-end hypertrophy. I'd then programme a secondary 'big lift', still aiming to load decent weight, but with a bit more emphasis on creating tension for slighter higher and more deliberate reps. Then I would add two 'assistance' exercises, which would be slightly less about hitting big weights and more about hitting different parts of the muscle, maximising strict form and tempo to exhaust the muscle in a higher rep range. And finally, a nasty finisher, really finishing off the target muscle in a high rep range, pushing as much blood as I can into the muscle and chasing 'the pump' to finish. This is also as much about a mental battle and cardiovascular hit as the full fatigue of the muscle. Every set is pushed to the max, failing in my target rep range. If I push past the target rep range, then the weight has to go up. If I fail short, then the weight comes down. Here's what a sample shoulder workout might look like:

Shoulders – a sample session using the 'proximity to failure' model, through a variety of rep ranges:

Military Press: 4 x 5/8 reps (no specific tempo, just look to move as much weight possible in a smooth, safe manner. Longer rest periods here of 2-3 mins between sets)

Seated shoulder press machine: 4 x 8/12 (controlling the eccentric for 2 secs and powering up the concentric phase)

Rear Delt Flyes: 4 x 12/15 reps (looking for each rep to be around 4 seconds of time under tension. Good control of the lift, especially through the eccentric phase and a great mind/muscle connection)

Lateral Raise: 4 x 12/15 (same as above)

The finisher: Front Raise superset Lat Raise finisher. Pick a weight you can perform around 20 reps with and complete the following with as few rests as possible: 20 reps of both, 15 reps of both, 10 reps of both, 5 reps of both. The only rest you get is when you physically or mentally have to stop. If you do stop at all, you should start again ASAP.

The Takeaway:

As long as you are training with adequate intensity, lifting to failure and placing a decent amount of tension on the desired muscle, hypertrophy can occur in a variety of rep ranges, and you'd be best placed to cover all angles if you can. Whilst I believe a variety of rep ranges and exercises would be optimal, you can also use this info to take some comfort in the fact that no set rep range is absolutely necessary for building muscle.

Those with certain injuries and concerns in lifting heavier loads can, in theory, lift lighter weights in the 20-30 rep range, in an acceptable proximity to failure, and still achieve muscle hypertrophy and progress.

Sports-Specific Training - Power and Athleticism

When I was much younger, I was a naturally lean kid, much more on the athletic side and far from being big and bulky. Whilst I didn't have the size or brute, static strength of other kids, I was reasonably explosive and quick. The natural way that I moved around a sports field or chose to lift weights was with pace and power but very little control. I used to look at bodybuilders, who had incredible control and mastery over the weight they were lifting, completing reps with precise tempos, slow eccentrics and squeezing the right muscle at different parts of the lift. As I progressed in my own training, I started to gain better control over the same lifts, executing reps and sets with more deliberate form, supporting muscles strengthened, and I was able to place more deliberate tension on the main agonists to promote muscle growth. One thing I noticed though, is that as my lifts got more deliberate and strict, whilst my muscles grew and my physique changed to better suit bodybuilding, I had started to lose that natural explosiveness from my early days. I had focused too much on perfect form, time under tension, and lording complete control over the weight and lifting tempo, that I had lost that 'snap' of power in my lifts. In turn, the ability to generate raw pace, power and plyometric force through jumping, leaping, bounding and other movements that are key for sports performance, had diminished. So, whilst specific form, tempo, time under tension and deliberately controlling the weight can work for hypertrophy and bodybuilding, going too far in that direction can be terrible for athletic performance. At the time, I was still playing rugby and cricket so I didn't want to lose the ability to exert power and speed on the sports field. Nor did I want to lose the ability to exert the same power on a weights bar and become slower or less athletic in the pursuit of a bodybuilding physique. So, I set out to change my uber-hypertrophy-focused programme to something that would still elicit muscle growth, but also aid sports performance, fitness, speed and power.

Compound and Olympic lift variations – the power of triple extension

From the S&C workshops I had attended, and research I had done into the UK Strength and Conditioning programming for athletes, I knew that mastering the 'triple extension' movement was paramount for effective power and explosive force. The term refers to the simultaneous extension of three lower body joints: the ankles, knees and hips. The explosive extension of these joints generates huge amounts of power that are effectively turned into quicker sprinting, higher jumping, and longer striding and are used to hit tackles harder or throw balls further. Becoming more effective, stronger and quicker in the extension of these three joints would directly correlate with increased pace and power and lead to better sporting outcomes. Of course, some of these lifts would directly make muscles like the glutes, quads and traps stronger, thereby leading to a greater force potential of the muscle. But this training is much more about the learned pattern of exerting force on a weight or object, and the brain's ability to work in tandem with the central nervous system (CNS), sending messages via neurons for muscle fibres to contract with extreme force and precision, helping to shift massive loads at a frightening pace. Just look at the tiny size of some Olympic Lifters compared to the massive weights that they lift. They probably don't have the brute strength of some other athletes, but their nervous system is so trained to fire in perfect sequence, that the weight flies from the floor to overhead at scary speeds. Barely before a specific muscle looks like it's even fired, the snap of the ankles, knees and hips has that bar travelling above their head. But these lifts are hard and can take years to master. The risk to reward for a bodybuilder or amateur footballer to be doing heavy snatches on a regular basis is highly questionable. So, let's consider the best ways that someone can look at adding in these variations that promote efficiency, strength and speed through triple extension:

1. If you do want to add any Olympic lifts into your programme, I would look to add in variations rather than the full lift. For example, a power clean from the hanging position can be just as effective for athletic performance as a full clean and doesn't require as much precision or learning. A kettlebell or dumbbell snatch might be the way to go before you progress to learning the barbell variation.

2. Plyometrics – leaping, jumping, and bounding exercises are excellent for sports performance. Box jumps or squat

jumps can be programmed into certain days without causing too much disruption to a session.

3. When it comes to sets and reps, we can still use a variety of approaches to achieve power, strength, speed and efficiency through these types of movements:

- **Power Training** - Heavy loads for sets of 1-3 reps. Pick a load that you can still exert speed with (not a slow grind; think a quick snap) and perform 1 – 3 reps but stop well short of failure. This isn't about grinding out slow reps to place tension on the muscle, so whilst you'll feel overall CNS fatigue and a cardio hit, it won't feel like muscular failure. Pick lifts like power clean, clean and press and snatch variations.

- **Power / Strength** – Heavy loads of 3-5 reps, getting closer to failure but still keeping a rep or two in reserve. Again, this is about accelerating with the bar, moving with pace and precision and not creating muscular tension or eccentric fatigue. Lifts like the squat or deadlift would be applicable.

- **Explosive Power** – Lighter loads, performing a cluster of 'singles' (1 rep at a time) with maximum effort or force for each rep, varying rest in between reps to recover. You could either use lighter loads or use things like boxes or markers for varying levels of difficulty. Exercises like squat jump, box jumps, vertical jump or medicine ball throws would be good choices.

- **Movement efficiency and posterior chain activation** – Lighter loads for higher reps of 10-20 per set. Focusing on the correct movement patterns, making sure the hips 'snap' and the movement is being created by the flow of the posterior chain rather than specific muscles. Kettlebell swings or variations of 'power cable rotations' are great exercises for this.

- **For Bodybuilding** – If you're someone who competes, but still wants to keep an eye on power and sporting performance, you're better to programme these exercises outside of a bodybuilding prep. Depending on how far you want to go with it, you could dedicate a specific 'power and athleticism' day during your off season, or add lifts like power cleans, power high pulls and rack pulls to various training days. You could also programme some speed work into existing movements, working on executing the concentric phases of presses, pulls, deadlifts or squats, with maximum speed and power. Of course, to achieve the muscle hypertrophy necessary for bodybuilding, these have to be programmed into a training programme that will still be dominated by a deliberate lifting tempo, eliciting time under tension and maximising growth potential.

Carries – the forgotten movement

Though they're a staple of a Strongman's plan, they're often the forgotten movement when we plan a training programme for the everyday gym-goer. Everyone thinks of push, pull, squat and hip hinge, but in my experience, carries can be an incredibly good movement for muscular endurance, strength, postural integrity and even hypertrophy for the traps and rhomboids. Think back to those times in the gym when you've directly hammered your traps with shrugs, high pulls, rows and face pulls and whilst you felt some connection, it wasn't as consistent or specific as you would have liked. Fast forward 4 days and you're carrying your shopping back from Tesco, one bag in each hand, and your traps are on fire! You can barely believe how much they're burning as you adjust your grip and hope your partner hasn't clocked that you're struggling with the weekend essentials! Specifically, I like carries for two main reasons:

1. They carry over very well to daily life. I hate to use the term 'functional' but if any movement is going to carry over well for a variety of functions, it's carries. Literally, any time you have to move an object from A to B, such as in gardening, DIY or housework, it involves a carry. I've been there myself many times, helping my parents in the garden and I've tweaked my back, my posture is failing me, my legs are knackered and I get the old classic line from my old man, "All those muscles and you're struggling to help your old Dad in the garden. Hahaha". Truth is, a lot of the mainstream bodybuilding movements and machines are perfect for hypertrophy and very specific strength, but they don't always carry over that well for everyday tasks and manual labour. Doing carries to bolster your traditional strength and hypertrophy workout may well help you with that.

2. They're fantastic for training postural integrity. Loaded carries train the postural muscles: by focusing on keeping your chest high, shoulders back and down,

you'll feel it in your Rhomboids, traps, rear delts and whole posterior chain and they can be progressively overloaded by adding weight or even making the carries 'uneven' with a weight on one side at a time, forcing the postural muscles to keep you aligned and strong in that movement.

I would absolutely advocate adding some farmer's walks or uneven carries into your programme if you're struggling with posture, grip strength, connecting with your traps or you feel that whilst you look the part, your strength isn't carrying over well for everyday use. You could programme these into a circuit-style session or add them to the end of a more traditional weights session as a taxing finisher. If you've never done carries before, start with a couple of kettlebells and do 4 sets of 30-second carries with a one-minute rest to gauge how that feels (it's impossible to give you a starting weight as 20kg kettlebells will be impossible or easy depending on your starting strength).

Sample Weekly Programme – Strength, Conditioning and Sports Performance

If you're still wanting to achieve some strength and hypertrophy, but also keep an eye on sports performance, speed and power, here is a sample 4-day split that aims to increase the potential for sports performance, power and conditioning:

Below are 'working sets'. Always warm up adequately with 5-10 minutes on your choice of cardio machine and a variety of muscle activation exercises using body weight, bands or cables to activate target muscles, core, glutes and postural muscles.

Session 1 – Push / Pull upper body

Any free weight chest press variation - 3 x 5/8 reps

Any lat pull or pull-up variation - 3 x 8/12 reps

Any overhead shoulder press superset any row variation - 3 x 12/12 reps

Any bicep curl superset any triceps exercise - 3 x 12/12

Barbell Complex Finisher. Complete the following in as quick a time as possible, resting only when absolutely needed. Repeat the following 3 times through with a one-minute rest in between sets:

8 overhead press, 8 bent-over rows, 8 upright rows, 8 bicep curls, 8 triceps overheads.

Session 2 – Lower Body

Any Squat variation 4 x 5/8 reps

Leg Press 4 x 8/15 reps

Walking Lunges or Bulgarian Split Squats 4 x 12/15

Leg Extensions superset Ham Curls 4 x 12/12 (only rest for the time it takes you to walk between the machines – you can do this in a drop set fashion if necessary but you should be hitting failure for each set).

Calf raises – 4 x 25

Session 3 – Conditioning

After an adequate warm-up, complete the following circuit as many times as possible in a 20-minute timescale. You will need to play with the weights in order to find something that suits your starting level. Look to up the weight and complete more rounds as you progress. This should be done as quickly as possible, resting only when necessary.

Rowing machine or assault bike – 12 calories

Single arm KB clean and press – 10 reps each arm

Pull-ups – 5 reps (use a band to assist if needed)

Press-ups – 10 reps

KB Swings – 15 reps

DB farmer's walk – 20 metres

Session 4 - Power for Sports Performance

Barbell Power Clean from Hang - 3 x 3/5 reps

KB Snatch - 3 x 8 reps each arm

Deadlift - 3 x 5/8 reps

Box Jumps - varying heights:

Low jump for 5 reps, no rest. (Choose a height you find easy.)

Medium jump for 3 reps, no rest. (Choose a height you find moderately hard.)

High jump for 5 sets of 1 with adequate rest in between each rep to recover and exert maximum power. (Choose a height that is near your max.)

Finisher: Complete the circuit 3 times with as little rest as possible:

10 kettlebell swings, 10 med ball slams, 5 burpees, 10 hanging leg raises.

Newbie Gainz – setting up a bodybuilding style plan to get in shape

OK, you've decided that this is the year that you get in shape, jacked, swole, absolutely Dame Judy Denched. You might be completely new to the gym or you might have dabbled over the years but never consistently followed a successful programme or plan. Where should you start? What exercises should you do? How do you best achieve your goals? It can be hard to cut through all the noise and not fall into the 'newbie trap' of various quick-fix programmes, diet hacks and magic supplements.

It's important to state that there are dozens of other options for you to get in general shape, get stronger, fitter and work on your mental health. However, if you specifically want a bodybuilding style programme and you've never trained before, here's a 12-week starter programme, step by step, phase by phase, to get started.

Programme length – 12 weeks to get you started

Goals – get into the gym, learn new exercises, build foundational strength, gain some muscle, make this the start of a new 'lifestyle'.

Phase 1 – Whole body sessions! Weeks 1, 2, 3

Main Phase Advancement – Just Turn Up

The worst error you can make is to go from no experience to a 5-day bro split, counting calories, training to failure and getting jacked up on a ton of supplements! Don't be tempted to miss phases here; just start by simply turning up, getting your body used to a range of exercises and movements and getting out within 20 to 30 minutes. Below, I have laid out a sample session for you, but you can swap these exercises for any push, pull, and legs movements. At this stage, you don't need to overthink your diet. Quite simply, if you think you drink too much or eat too much fast food, consider cutting back, even by one day. That's progression compared to the weeks gone by. On the other hand, whilst you're a newbie to the gym, if you are already experienced with setting up calorie-controlled diets, then go ahead and put yourself around maintenance.

Train – 4 to 5 days per week depending on your commitments.

Rest days – come when most convenient to you. If you want to do 5 days on and 2 days' rest, that's fine, there is no right or wrong. From an adherence perspective, I would plan your rest days when it's most convenient, e.g., you know on Wednesday you're working away or you know on Thursday it's your turn to pick the kids up from school.

Diet – No specific diet consideration other than to limit alcohol and 'fast'/'takeaway'-style food.

The sessions – Complete a version of this session 4 to 5 times per week for 3 weeks. You should pick a weight that you can complete 10 reps with and there should always be a couple of reps in reserve. For now, prioritise good form and lifting technique. It should be hard but short of complete exhaustion.

You can swap out any of these exercises for any push, pull, or legs exercises. Ask a friend or gym instructor which options are available in your gym. I've listed some more options below for you.

Warm up with 5 mins of moderate exercise bike, cross trainer or treadmill.

Tri-set 1:

10 press-ups, 10 lat pull-downs, 10 squats with no weight. (Repeat 3 times. You should have minimal rest between each set of 10 and a 1-minute rest between each tri-set).

Tri-set 2:

10 shoulder press, 10 seated rows, 10 quad extensions. (Repeat 3 times. You should have minimal rest between each set of 10 and a 1-minute rest between each tri-set).

Tri-set 3:

10 lateral raises, 10 seated rows, 10 hamstring curls. (Repeat 3 times. You should have minimal rest between each set of 10 and a 1-minute rest between each tri-set).

Here are some variations so you can swap some exercises around:

Push – chest press, dumbbell press, dips, triceps extension, front raises, flyes, pec deck.

Pull – pull-ups, any row variation, bicep curl variations, rear laterals, high pull.

Legs – any squat variation, lunges, walking lunges, split squats, leg presses.

Phase 2 – Upper / lower splits – Weeks 4, 5, 6

Main Phase Advancement – Push Towards Muscular Failure

In Phase 2, we're progressing to a new level by splitting up your upper and lower body days. This will mean your training volume and intensity for a specific body part will be increased. From a diet perspective, I want you to limit alcohol and 'fast food' even further and think about prioritising a protein source with every meal. This may be in the shape of various meats, eggs, fish, a protein shake or the Vegan/veggie equivalent.

Train – 4 weights sessions per week, with 1 day of conditioning and abdominals.

Rest – Whenever is most convenient for you, as long as you hit your sessions.

Diet – Similar to weeks 1-3, I want you to further limit alcohol and fast-food options. For every meal, I want to ensure you include a protein source. This can be any cut of meat, eggs, fish, tofu, soya or protein shake variations.

The sessions – Complete these two sessions twice per week and the conditioning session once. You should pick a weight that you are nearing failure at the desired rep range, but still have a rep or 2 in reserve. Keep that emphasis on form and smooth tempo.

Similar to weeks 1-3, warm up with five minutes on your choice of cardio machine.

Session 1 – Upper Body:

Push/Pull superset 1 – Any chest press variation superset any row variation 3 x 10/10

Push/Pull superset 2 – Any shoulder press variation superset any lat pull variation 3 x 12/12

Push/Pull superset 3 – Press-up superset assisted pull-ups 3 x 12/12

Push/ Pull superset 4 – Any bicep variation superset any triceps variation 3 x 12/12

Session 2 – Lower Body:

Any Squat variation - 4 sets of 10/12 reps
Leg extensions – 3 sets of 12/15 reps
Hamstring curls - 3 sets of 12/15 reps
Walking lunges superset with calf raises 3 x 12/12

Conditioning, abdominals and core training:

Pick a cardio machine of your choice and do the following session:
5 mins of steady state warming up followed by 5 rounds of:
30 seconds of hard work at around 80% of your perceived maximum effort

1 min of easy effort at around 30% of your perceived maximum effort

Finish off with another 5 mins of steady state.

Core/abdominals circuit finisher: complete the following, only resting when needed:

3 sets of the following:

10 full sit-ups, 10 leg raises, 10 seconds of side plank holds each side, 10 seconds of normal plank, 10 crunches.

Phase 3 – Push, Pull, Legs – Weeks 7, 8, 9

Main Phase Advancement – specific session focus on body parts and movements. Push towards muscular failure. Count calories for the first time.

Train – 4 days per week (push, pull, legs, conditioning)

Rest – Whenever is most convenient

Diet – Multiply your weight in pounds by 15 to get your calorie maintenance. So, if you weigh 200lbs, your calorie goal is to hit 3000 calories per day. The only rule here is that you must hit your calories (not over, not under) and you must get **at least** 25% of these calories from protein. So, for the 200lbs person, this is 750 kcals from protein, which translates as 187 grams of protein. Use an app like MyFitnessPal to track what you are eating on a daily basis. Your other calories should be a good mix of fats and carbs. (See diet section for more info.)

The Sessions – Complete these 4 sessions once per week. You should now be training to failure for each set. So, if

I prescribe 3 x 12, you should be failing at, or around, 12 reps for each set.

Upper Push

Any chest press variation 3 x 8/12 (rest for 2 mins between sets; aim to recover and lift heavy to failure)

Any shoulder press variation 3 x 8/12 (rest for 2 mins between sets; aim to recover and lift heavy to failure)

Any flye movement 3 x 12/15 (rest for 1 min between sets)

Lat raise 3 x 12/15 (rest for 45 seconds between sets. Don't let the muscle fully recover and go again)

Any triceps exercise 4 x 12/15 (rest for 1 min between sets)

Finisher – dips, superset press-ups (no rests - 15 reps of both, 10 reps of both, 5 reps of both)

Pull

Pull-ups – 2 sets to failure. Use an assist to hit around 8 reps if you struggle with full pull-ups.

Any Lat Pull Variation - 3 x 10/12

Any Row variation – 3 x 12/15

Rear Delt Flyes any variation - 3 x 12/15

Any Bicep curl variation - 3 x 12/15

Finisher – Any row machine, complete 4 sets in a 'drop set' fashion for 10 reps of each set. No rests should be taken, only the time to drop the weight in between each set of 10.

Legs

Any Squat variation - 4 x 8/12

Leg Press - 3 x 8/12

Leg ext. superset ham curl - 3 x 12/12

Calf Raise - 3 x 20

Finisher – 50 walking lunges with no weight. Complete with as little rest as possible.

Conditioning and abs

Steady-state cardio for 400 calories on either the bike, cross trainer, assault bike, treadmill or rowing machine. You don't have to kill yourself here; this is about burning the calories and helping the body recover from the three intense sessions this week.

Abs Circuit: We're going to do the same from the previous phase but up the reps and add a circuit: Four rounds of:

12 full sit-ups, 12 leg raises, 12 seconds of side plank holds each side, 12 seconds of normal plank, 12 crunches.

Phase 4 – Progress the diet and apply progressive overload – Weeks 10, 11, 12

Main Phase Advancement: The sessions for this phase don't change, but your aim is to progress all your lifts. In the last phase, we introduced 'training to failure' for the first time. Now the emphasis is on progressing those lifts to achieve progressive overload and start to create a new stimulus for muscle growth.

You should keep a logbook to log each session and start to properly record your weights, reps and sets. For each lift, you should be aiming to lift a heavier weight or be able to do more reps for the same weight. Aim to advance, even by 1%, at each and every session for this phase. The diet will also change and become more specific, as stated below.

Diet – This is where I invite you to make your own decisions when it comes to the diet. We're going to start to track calories and introduce accurate macronutrient numbers for the first time. As you are new to training and we're starting to ramp up training to failure and creating a novel stimulus for growth, I would expect you to become stronger and achieve muscular hypertrophy, even in a small calorie deficit. Therefore, depending on how you feel about your own body weight and appearance, the following choices are yours:

1. I'm reasonably happy with my body composition, I just want to get a bit stronger, leaner and more muscular. **If this is you, then you can eat at 'maintenance'.**
2. I feel too small, weak and skinny but carry little fat. I would like to focus on muscle, strength and size. **If this is you, then you can eat in a 200-calorie surplus for this phase.**
3. I am overweight and carry too much fat. Whilst I want to get stronger, I also need to work on reducing fat and becoming leaner in the process. **If this is you, you can eat in a 500-calorie deficit.**

As before, you can work out your maintenance calories by multiplying your body weight in pounds by 15. From there, you can make the necessary adjustments based on your above choice. We're now going to add specific macronutrient goals into our day, which we will set up as 40% carb, 30% protein and 30% fat to begin with. For ease, you should use an app like MyFitnessPal to calculate and record your daily calorie and macro numbers.

To Wrap Up

And that's it. Where you choose to go from here greatly depends on your training goal moving forward. This programme should have given you a solid base of training knowledge, an array of exercise options, programme choices, the beginnings of a diet plan, how to achieve progressive overload and a basis to record progress. Hopefully, you've progressed as the plan intended, moved from body weight exercises to using weights, to using bigger weights, and have gained some strength and hypertrophy along the way. Hopefully, your body has started to change as you've made better food choices and started to understand the importance of calories and macronutrients. And, perhaps most of all, you've felt those endorphins along the way, felt better about yourself, and about your hard work and commitment. Perhaps you have felt a greater mental clarity and satisfaction in your hard work and endeavours. The main thing to take away is that an effective plan has a start point and an end goal. That end goal should present progression, whether that be for strength, fat loss, cardio output, injury rehab or hypertrophy, and an effective plan will always have the ability to record and show how you've gone from A to B. And really, however long you train for, each training phase, programme or cycle has a new goal in mind that moves you from A to B and from B to C. To create a proper fitness lifestyle that works for you, each plan or phase is just another way to move along that progression pathway, until one day, you look back and realise that after years and years of gym work, after more programmes, phases and plans than you care to remember, you've slowly gone from A to X. Slow, steady improvements, one tangible goal at a time, can add up to a lifetime's worth of progress.

The Magic Question... Can I burn fat and build muscle at the same time?

Let's cut straight to the chase with this one. Yes, in theory, it is possible to burn fat and build muscle at the same time, but this Unicorn of a goal relies on some quite specific factors and situations:

1. If the individual is brand new to weight training, that training stimulus is so novel that he or she, could build muscle, even in a calorie deficit.
2. If the individual carries enough body fat, he or she could burn fat in a calorie deficit and have enough energy (surplus body fat) that the body can use to help build muscle, if the weight training stimulus is strong enough.
3. If he or she is taking performance enhancing drugs, it is possible to burn fat and build muscle simultaneously. But even this will have diminishing returns as the individual becomes more experienced and advanced.

Outside of these three groups, whilst you might experience very small levels of body re-composition, it is nearly impossible to make any meaningful strides in either direction at the same time. This is especially true the more advanced you get with your bodybuilding journey. As you get leaner, or more used to shifting big weights, creating a 'novel stimulus' becomes harder and harder. In the 'Diet' portion of the book, we'll look at the benefits of 'maingaining', an approach to body re-composition, where you look to hover at around maintenance calories, making small advances to strength and muscle size. But it's important to say that whilst this approach could be utilised as an alternative to the traditional bulk and cut, it also relies on the individual being very close to their desired goals, and adding a large amount of muscle, or cutting large amounts of fat, just isn't going to happen at the same rate as a dedicated training phase.

Generally speaking, outside of the three groups that I mentioned, you will get better and quicker results if you prioritise one goal at a time. A slow and sustained bulk, followed by a slow and sustain cut, will yield better results in both directions and should lead to a better outcome. Once you are happier with your overall physique, a 'maingaining' approach could be utilised to make small advancements in each direction, without gaining the fat or losing the size that we might experience in a big cut or bulk.

If I was Purely Training for Optimal Health

It would be fair to say, that pure bodybuilding, extreme 'cutting' and 'bulking' and getting down to a stage level of lean, with body fat well into single digit numbers, can easily compromise your health. This is especially true if the individual uses Performance Enhancing Drugs, and if he or she, 'dirty bulks,' overeating large amounts of calories, in a bid to put on as much mass as possible. Not only can this lead to physical issues, but the mental health, of people who are gaining large amounts of weight, dropping to incredibly low body fat percentages and using PEDs may also be compromised.

I have to be totally honest here and state that, from time to time, my training goals, obsessive tendencies and preoccupation with the 'aesthetics' of bodybuilding, has led me to compromise my health. There is no doubt that over the years I've grossly over trained, taken my daily calories to woefully low numbers and used an extreme 'binge eating' and 'binge drinking' approach to 'cheat meals' or diet breaks. So, if we were to ignore aesthetics and specific performance goals altogether, and focus purely on health, longevity, and quality of life, what might we need to consider and how should we build a sustainable training and diet plan?

1. **Stop PEDs**. Most research shows that any use of PEDs past a doctor prescribed dose (TRT/HRT) will not contribute to longevity of life[7]. Not to demonise PEDs completely but if health and longevity is your main goal, you would be wise to think twice. When you hear Celebs and influencers who tell you that 'longevity is their number one consideration' and they use super physiological amounts of PEDs, you should be sceptical.

2. **Do Cardio**. Using a mixture of intense and steady state cardio would be optimal for heart health, mental wellbeing, and weight management.

3. **Body Fat**. Maintaining a healthy body fat percentage of around 10% - 17% for men and 18% - 32% for women. In many ways, too low is as bad (sometimes worse) than too high. I can't seriously look you in the eye and say that health and longevity was my main consideration when I was about 6% body fat on stage. In reality, I felt terrible and performed horribly. My strength was down, I couldn't concentrate, and my energy levels were awful.

4. **Less is More**. I don't want to demonise the cutting and bulking process, but for optimal health you should be cautious when doing both. If you're looking to lose weight, I would limit your calorie deficit to 500 below maintenance. If you're looking to gain weight, I would limit your calorie surplus to 200-300 calories above maintenance. If you are already with in a healthy fat percentage, look to take a 'maingaining' approach, eating at around 'maintenance' calories, whilst looking to make small improvements to fitness and/or strength.

5. **Weights**. Even if you don't care about muscle mass from an aesthetic perspective, you should still be doing weight bearing exercise to maintain strength into later life, keeping brittle bones and osteoporosis at bay and maintaining muscle tissue, which in turns gives you a higher BMR and the ability to eat more calories, without fat gain.

6. **Start your Sessions with 'muscle activation'**. A good warm up is paramount to maximising performance and minimising the likelihood of injury. For optimal health, you should prioritise a good amount of muscle

activation, priming the muscles that will be the main agonists in your session e.g. warm up lats for back day, but also working on key muscles for posture and stability, especially if you spend long hours sitting at the desk or in the car. Some good glute and core activation warm ups may include 'bird dogs', glute bridge, leg raise variations and unloaded variations of squats, lunges and rotational work.

7. **Get Outdoors**. I'm not someone who believes that we should all be moving, eating and living like our Cavemen ancestors, most of these guys and girls died in their 20's and 30' and it would be ridiculous to ignore the modern advancements in food, medicine and technology, that make our lives a whole lot easier, longer and more fulfilled. However, I do agree that the modern landscape seems to pull us further away from physical endeavour and from time spent in nature, and there is something about both things that can be so powerful as fantastic pursuits of dopamine. Perhaps it's a pull back towards our ancestral roots or just how we've evolved, with Human's learning that physical endeavour was necessary for survival and the site of a forest, mountain or lake, could mean food, shelter or water, and would therefore elicit a unique dopamine response in the brain. Perhaps that's why physical exercise and time in the outdoors generally leads to greater feelings of wellness and fulfilment. In turn, these feelings can have a transformative effect in the other areas of your life. Physical endeavour, embracing discomfort and stepping outside of a 'warm and cosy' space may have positive

impacts on a variety of professional, personal, and social situations and relationships.

8. **Balance**. In nearly all aspects of life, a balanced approach is intertwined with health and longevity. From a diet perspective, I would advocate a balanced approach to protein, fats and carbs, and a diet that sees you eat at around your maintenance calories. Using alcohol or fast foods sparingly, should have no significant bearing on long term health and could serve as necessary mental breaks from training and dieting.

9. **Prioritisation**. I spend a lot of this book banging on about priorities, and this chapter is no different. If you look at the hierarchy of importance for health, many of us are still getting it woefully wrong. Whilst you may find health and longevity benefits in various supplements and by considering aspects of gut health and diet types (like Keto, Paleo or IF) these things should take a back seat when compared to the bigger considerations like cardiovascular exercise, strength training and the daily calorie equation. Someone who is supplementing with an Omega 3 fish oil but frequently eats in a large calorie surplus and only trains once per week, would be wise to rethink their priorities. Someone who is claiming to reap cell regeneration and growth hormone increasing effects from Intermittent Fasting, but smokes 20 cigarettes per day, will not find themselves in a better boat for longevity. And if you're taking a plethora of supplements to maximise your gut microbiome health but struggle to run a mile or lift your

own bodyweight, you're probably prioritising the wrong things from a mortality perspective.

10. **Adherence**. Adhering to a plan is still King/Queen, so we must make sure we find exercises, diets and goals that make us fulfilled and excited. So even though maximal strength or running a mile as quickly as you possibly can, isn't completely necessary for optimal health, these training goals and short-term training programmes, can help with enjoyment and adherence. Just because we are looking at health and longevity, it doesn't mean every session should suddenly be tentative, overthinking pushing it too hard, causing injuries and leaving you feeling bored and unfulfilled. You can still work incredibly hard and have these strength, fitness, and endurance goals in mind.

11. **The Extras**. Once you are on point with the more important aspects of fitness, looking at injury prevention, wellness and supplementation is the next step. You may benefit from the regular use of a physio, chiropractor, or osteopath. You may also get some mental and physical benefit in things like cold water therapy, Yoga or Pilates. These things are generally down to the individual and how you mentally and physically respond to the treatment and tasks. Personally, I see a Chiropractor monthly and the 'prevention is better than cure' approach, is certainly working for me to keep my back issues at bay. The final extra is supplementation. Notice I put it last! Not because supplements are always a waste a time, but more that I want to emphasise

the word 'supplement.' If your diet, training, mental wellbeing, injury prevention, plan adherence and body fat percentage is way off, then please don't fall into the trap of thinking a 'supplement' is going to magically fix you. It won't. If you do want to supplement, the ones that have been well researched and proven to be effective for an array of hormonal, muscular, fitness, performance and cell functional benefits, are Creatine, Omega 3's, Whey (or other such as Pea) Protein, Glucosamine and the use of Caffeine at appropriate times, to aid sports performance and focus. I speak in more depth about these supplements later in the book, but if you want to look deeper into micronutrients and supplementation, effective doses and how they work from a physical and mental health capacity, I recommend reading literature or looking at channels like Layne Norton, 'More Plates more Dates' or Andrew Huberman.

Training and diet example week for health and longevity:

-   **Diet** – aim to maintain a healthy body fat range, eating at around maintenance calories, with a good balance of protein fats and carbs. Looking to get around 0.8g of protein per pound of bodyweight and splitting the remaining calories in a 60% carb and 40% fat split. An example for a 200lbs male might be: 3000 calories, 160g protein, 354g carb, 104g fat. If you need to lose some bodyweight, set yourself up in a daily deficit of 500 kcals and use the same approach to the macronutrients.

- **Food Type**. Whilst I don't want to demonise all 'processed' foods as automatically bad, I still like to prioritise a whole food approach, including a variety of lean meats, complex carbs, vegetables and fruits. Using the simple hack of 'have a variety of colours on your plate' certainly works for me. This generally means you've got a number of essential vitamins, minerals and micronutrients, and you've not fallen into the trap of eating exactly the same foods, day in, day out. For me, variety helps with adherence and using a 'whole food' approach means I can eat more food volume. You'll notice that it's much harder to 'overeat' on Beef, Potatoes, peas, carrots, broccoli and spinach, than it is on Burgers and Pizza.
- **Weight Training –** A three day split of Upper Push, Upper Pull and Legs. Prioritising big compound lifts at the start of the sessions like squats, deadlifts, overhead press and pull ups, some hypertrophy sets of 8-15 reps in the middle section and a higher rep finisher. You should be aiming for 12-16 working sets per session.
- **Bodyweight training –** Your weight training sessions should include a good amount of bodyweight training like pullups, dips, and press ups. Being able to use, control and move your own bodyweight is incredibly important for longevity. It's shown that those who struggle to lift their own bodyweight and have a lower muscle mass are at higher risk for injuries, illness and death, especially in later life.
- **Outside Steady State –** Using the outdoors for steady state cardio on most days. Whether this is in the shape

of walking the dog, gardening, hiking, or waking the kids to school.

- **High Intensity Cardio** – Using 1 to 2 days per week of high intensity, interval style cardio. This doesn't need to last any more than about 20 minutes and could be programmed in a 'CrossFit' style, using a mix of weights, bodyweight and cardio machines or by doing interval training on a piece of cardio equipment like a bike, rowing machine or treadmill.

- **Alcohol.** Using a sparing approach to alcohol. Either by drinking infrequently or by restricting the amount of alcohol you drink in a sitting. For example, if you are going to have heavier nights out with friends, you might limit to once per month. If you are going to drink a few times per week, you should limit this to a drink with dinner. Of course, not drinking altogether would be 'optimal' from a physical health perspective, but if drinks with friends is an important part of your life and social happiness, then you'd be wise to put some rules around your drinking.

- **Supplement with.** Omega 3's, Creatine, whey protein, Glucosamine and using Caffeine as a 'pre workout'. Ideally limiting caffeine use to pre midday.

- **Sleep.** For at least 6 hours, ideally 8, per night.

- **Smoke.** Just don't.

It's All About the Arse

Anyone who has worked regularly with a PT, S&C coach, or physio, would have noted that there's a huge emphasis on glute activation, function, and strength. At some point in the early 2000's, the Glutes replaced the 'core' as the main area of obsession and focus, for fitness professionals throughout the globe. Whilst there is no doubt that this can be over obsessed, over trained, and over analysed, there is also very good reason for wanting to create an optimal 'back door'. The Glute Max plays a pivotal role in creating strength, speed, and power, leading to quicker sprinting and the ability to jump higher and further. The Glute Med, one of the main pelvic stabilisers and plays a crucial role in the stability of most things that are happening from the hips down. Any number of back, hip and knee issues, are regularly attributed to poorly functioning, weak, or lazy glutes. Add to this, an early 2000's Kardashian influence, and whether you're looking at maximising athleticism, working on high end strength, want to create an enviable booty, or looking to keep a number of injuries at bay, there are two things that every gym, fitness and sports enthusiast should be doing:

1. Phase 1 - Work on Glute activation, function, and hip stability by using a variety of stabilising exercises like Bird Dogs, Leg raise variations, glute bridges, single leg movements and abductor / adductor exercises.
2. Phase 2 – Apply progressive overload to the glutes by training a variety of hip hinge, single leg, and squat movements.

Looking at Phase 2- Applying progressive overload to the Glutes is simple enough. Look at adding weight to the bar or reps to your sets, in a variety of movements like the Back Squat, Front Squat, Lunge, Split Squat, Deadlift, Glute Bridge and Leg Press. There are many lifting cues that can help to focus your lifts away from other muscles and onto the glutes. Pushing more through the heels, creating a feeling of 'tearing' the carpet outwards with your feet, focus on driving the knees out and placing the bar lower on your shoulders, can all work. But it's actually phase 1, activating the glute max and glute med and creating a strong mind, muscle connection, that can be quite tricky. And if (like me) you're great at getting into the gym, lifting weights, and focussing on the fun stuff, but not so good at paying attention to less glamorous exercises, it can be difficult to juggle strength, aesthetics, bodybuilding, and activation, when you may only have a 45-minute window, in which to train. What I have realised over the years though, is that any back, hip, neck, and knee issues that I've developed, are almost always better, when I complete certain activation exercises, during the week. These can be completed as a whole session or used as a warmup & activation circuit before other gym sessions. Here is what I've done, most weeks for nearly 20 years, in a bid to (try and) stay healthy and functional:

Sample of a very simple, Glute activation, posture, and stability circuit:

Complete 3 rounds of the following:

12 Bird Dogs each side.

20 Glute Bridges (weight optional).

20 Clams each leg.

20 side leg raises each leg.

Complete 3 rounds of the following:

12 Kettlebell Swings.

10 Kettlebell front squats.

12 static lunges with no weight (lifting the opposing arm upwards throughout the movement, to feel a stretch on the hip flexor).

12 abductor & 12 adductor machines.

I find that this 15-minute circuit, can be the perfect warm up for a Strength / Hypertrophy Leg session, or can be done on its own and added to an abs & cardio session, to make sure the glutes are staying healthy and activated. Whilst this is great for activation and you can make some gains using this style of training, if your goal is strength, hypertrophy, or power, then you're best served in progressing these lifts to ones that can bear more load. Applying progressive Overload to variations of Squats, Deadlifts, Glute Bridges, Lunges, Leg Press, and variations of plyometrics and Olympic Lifts, can all be fantastic for Glute strength and athletic performance. So if you have been suffering from back and knee problems or to improve athletic performance, strength and power, make sure the Butt is being given it's fair share of attention.

Getting Jacked Biceps!

If there's one muscle that the mainstream deems to be synonymous with bodybuilding, it's the biceps. If you ask the average man, woman or child off the street to 'show you their muscles', they'll immediately lift their arms, tense for their life and go into a classic 'front double bicep' pose. In a similar way that 'direct training of the abs' has become uncool, unscientific, or unmodern, so too has directly training the biceps. Just this morning, I overheard a group of young lads chatting about bicep training and how 'biceps are actually grown through heavy deadlifts, rows and pulls' and directly training the biceps is 'a complete waste of time'. Well, it is true that you can build significant mass and strength through a variety of compound 'pull' lifts, but just like the abdominals, you're going to get more motor unit recruitment and muscle fibre activation by directly targeting the biceps. By manipulating wrist and elbow angles, you're able to hit different parts of the biceps, namely, the long head, short head and brachialis, and, much more importantly, you're able to apply specific 'progressive overload' to the muscle. After all, how can you actually attribute progressive overload to a muscle when it's not the main agonist in the movement? Yes, deadlifting 5kg more than last week means you are stronger overall, but how much of that lift will directly impact the hypertrophy of the biceps vs the traps, lats, erectors, hamstrings and glutes? There is too much going on to really ensure that biceps growth will occur. So, if biceps hypertrophy is your goal, then you should absolutely train the biceps directly and not just as an afterthought on back or pull day. If your main goal is aesthetics and you want to look jacked in a t-shirt, and, for the record, there's nothing wrong with that, having thick biceps with a defined peak will absolutely contribute to that end. So how should you train your biceps to cover all the bases, get a thick brachialis, impressive long head peak and meaty short head? Well...**here's the problem**...

- If I google 'exercises to hit the short head of the bicep', I seem to get a number of pages that attribute the same lifts to the building of the long head.

- I also get the same exercises that target the brachialis for the targeting of the short head.

- Common sense and most 'gym bros' would assume that externally rotating the shoulder will automatically hit the long head (outer part of the bicep) and the opposite will hit the short head (inner part of the bicep) and lifting with a pronated grip (palms down) or a neutral grip, like a hammer curl, will target the brachialis... but according to recent studies[8], this is unfortunately not always the case. In some cases, hammer curls activate the long head more than the brachialis, and internally rotating the weight activates the long head just as much as the short head.

- What's also become obvious over the years is that different people seem to feel different parts of the bicep by changing different things. For some, it lies in the angle of the wrist, whilst others feel more of a change in differing elbow positions, shoulder placement or even cues like 'pull with the pinky'. I can take this one step further from a personal perspective, where I actually feel my biceps differently from my left to right sides. This is because of specific shoulder, elbow and wrist injuries over the years – a cue that works to feel my long head on the right arm, doesn't work the same for the left.

- As with so many of these lifts, the issue lies in your specific anatomy. Injuries, shoulder mobility, limb length and a dozen other factors can specifically affect which part of the bicep takes over... **so what should we do?**

Don't focus on the 'part of the bicep'; focus on the movement:

For most people, the biceps are too small and fiddly to genuinely target the different heads and areas. By focusing on the movement, angle of the wrist, grip, shoulders and bar path, you can be confident of hitting different parts of the muscle, even if you're not 100% sure which exercises are activating which parts the most. And this is an uncomfortable truth for most lifts and most body parts. Unless you literally go into a gym with a ton of lab equipment to measure muscle activation and muscle excitement, (yes, that's the real name for it,) you don't truly know if your incline bench press hits your upper pecs more than a machine flye. Because of the angle, we assume it does, but in reality, we should just be incorporating these different angles, tempos, bar paths and grips to ensure we have all bases covered. Some of these lifts will lend themselves better to heavy weights, while some will lend themselves better to time under tension and 'mind-muscle connection'. So, if I was programming a decent biceps session, I would look at the following exercises. Of course, this can be moderated and added into back, pull or arm day, but if you have the goal of bigger, stronger arms and the biceps are a weak point, try hitting 8/12 sets of differing angles, grips and exercises in your next bicep session and see how it feels:

1. **Heavy barbell curls with a standard grip for 2 sets of 8/10 reps.**

   Why – you can shift a good amount of weight giving an overall hit to the entire biceps including the brachialis. Using the barbell whilst standing and with shoulders pulled slightly forward should, in theory, hit more short head. You can apply progressive overload by adding weight to the bar but you don't need more than 2 working sets here. This is the 'heavy' part of the workout and we don't want to over-exhaust the biceps up front.

2. **Seated DB curls with weight externally rotated to the side - 3 sets of 10/12 reps.**

   Why – I'm hoping this targets the long head more but my focus is just on the external rotation, keeping the shoulders back, and feeling like I'm gripping the weight with my little fingers. Focus on feeling the bicep and progressively overload by adding weight, reps or time under tension.

3. **Hammer curl with DBs - 2 sets of 12/15 reps**

   Why – Hoping this targets the brachialis more but focusing on squeezing the weight at the top for a split second, coming across my body, and fully extending and stretching the bottom.

4. **Machine or preacher curl - 3 sets of 12/15 reps in a drop set style**

   Why – Really focusing this one on the full eccentric stretch and contracting at the top of the movement, for me, this gives the best 'mind-muscle connection' for the bicep. It'll likely hit both heads but you can pull more with the pinky and pull your shoulders back to try and hit that long head more or lean forward into the bench and pull the hands more in towards each other as you squeeze the top to potentially achieve greater short head activation. Try to really squeeze at the top, with the cue of 'pull through your forehead'.

5. **Close grip underhand or close grip neutral pull ups 2 x failure**

   Why – I feel like this movement seriously finishes off the bicep. My hope is that it hits the short head, contributing to that inner arm line from a front double bicep position. If doing a back or pull day, you can add this grip variation into your pull-up routine. If you are heavier or really struggle with pull-ups, you can do this at the start of a session or use an assist to help you hit 8-12 reps.

Go and Check out:

I've seen tonnes of different Biceps training video's over the years that would concur with (and sometimes contradict some of) my musings above. The video that I would recommend you checking out is an experiment by Ryan Humiston, where he uses an EMG machine to measure the muscle activation for different parts of the biceps. Whilst it wasn't as cut and dry as saying that 'every lift we've been assuming to target a specific bicep head is wrong,' there were certainly some very surprising results. What the video did affirm and recommend, is that if we're unsure exactly what we're working, we're best off hitting the muscle with a variety of exercises, from a variety of angles. Especially if our main goal, is Hypertrophy.

(My take on) Training Abs!!!!!!!!!

I've never seen more debate, conflicting info and absolute nonsense than when it comes to the subject of training the abdominals. So many articles or videos are entitled 'The Truth' about training abs and the vast majority of these seem to be vague, misleading or just incorrect. We see such a variety of new 'truths' when it comes to ab training.

Here are some of the favourite 'truths' that I see time and time again and my thoughts on each point:

1. **Training the abs is pointless if you are above a certain body fat percentage.**
   Whilst there is some truth for aesthetic purposes, it's ridiculous to discount a whole body part based on this notion. Yes, you will struggle to have a visible '6-pack' if you're carrying too much fat around the abdominal area but there is clearly merit in making the abdominals, TVA and obliques strong and functional. This will serve to improve overall strength and mobility and limit injuries. Like any other body part, you can also build the size of your abdominals through hypertrophy, which will become more visible when you do lose body fat. There's also a myth that there is some magical fat percentage where abs do and don't show. This is absolutely not true. Where we store fat is all part of the genetic lottery and I know lots of people who can be pretty lean and not have visible abs, and other people who can carry more fat, but less around the abdominals. I'm a good example of this as I generally have 4 visible

abs even when my body fat is substantially higher than normal. My chest, subscapular and quads, however, are much less forgiving. We all have slightly different areas where we seem to store more fat and we all lose fat in a different order. I know for me, the fat from my glutes, quads and chest is last to shift, whilst the fat from my face and abdominals shifts pretty quickly. If you are only training the abs for a visible 6-pack, then lowering your body fat is going to be a more important factor than direct ab training, but you should do both in conjunction for optimal results.

2. **Direct training of the abs with sit-ups is useless** ✗

   Again, this is nonsense. Whilst it might not be cool or edgy to say it, direct abdominal training with high volumes of sit-ups, crunches or leg raises does work for abdominal hypertrophy. This doesn't mean these are the only exercises you should do and it doesn't mean that you should ignore other ways to hit the abs and surrounding muscles, but it would be a lie to say these are not effective and I personally use these varieties in my training programmes. The things to be aware of here are: how to create progressive overload within these exercises, thinking about your posture and other weaknesses that these positions may create, and making sure that other work around TVA activation, bracing and hollowing is also implemented. As we discussed earlier in the book, hypertrophy is about proximity to failure for a specific muscle. If you are able to feel a strong mind-muscle connection with your abs through sit-ups and can use tempo or weight to get close to muscular failure, they will absolutely work for abdominal hypertrophy. I do sit-ups in nearly all my ab sessions and can use tempo, weight and angle to make sessions harder and keep progressing.

3. **You should only train the (magical) 'core', not the abdominals** ✕

If you want a classic '6-pack' look, then you are best advised to directly train your abdominals (or Rectus Abdominis) for abdominal hypertrophy and shoot for a low enough body fat to make these muscles visible. However, when it comes to strength that will convert to other compound lifts, staying fit and injury-free, it's also important to consider the 'core' muscles and namely the TVA or transverse abdominis. The TVA is the deepest layer of abdominal muscle, spanning from the lower ribs down to the pelvis and wrapping around your midsection like a belt or corset. A strong TVA can serve to protect the spine and keep you strong and solid in everyday life, as well as during weight training, and maintaining good posture and strength during endurance activities like cycling and running. There are a multitude of ways to activate and train the TVA that include exercises such as the vacuum, Superman, cable twists and variations of plank and leg raises. In my opinion, there is no magical 'core' muscle and the 'core' is really defined by the strength and health of all of these muscles. The TVA can play a crucial role here but the strength and health of the rectus abdominis, pelvic floor, obliques, glutes and erector spinae are just as poignant.

4. **You should treat the abs like any other muscle and train them in the same way as the chest or quads** ✓ ✗

I don't fall out with the sentiment here and the statement makes sense, but I don't think I have ever seen this actually put into practice from a programming perspective. I've seen this line used in certain articles and videos, and when I've looked at the training programme of the same 'PT', 'influencer' or bodybuilder who's made the statement, I've never seen an actual 'Ab Day'. I've seen push, pull, legs and I've seen the classic bro split of chest, back, shoulders, legs, and arms. But I'm yet to actually see 'abs' as its own day or training session. Also, where I have seen abs included as part of a day, e.g. pull and abs or chest and abs, it is fair to say that the 'abs' portion of the workout carries far less time, thought or volume than the other part of the workout. There is some good in this statement though and I do believe we should seek to train abs with some similarities to other body parts but need to acknowledge that this rarely gets put into practice. Here are the things that I think we should take from this statement:

- Try to apply progressive overload to your abdominal training. This can be achieved by upping the reps, sets, or weight, or by advancing the difficulty of the exercise.
- Try to do a mixture of higher weight, lower rep sets and lower weight, high volume sets.

- Try to train near to form or muscular failure in the same way you would other body parts.
- In the same way as you hit different heads of the shoulder or different parts of the chest, try to hit different parts of the trunk muscles. Direct ab work like a sit-up, deeper 'core' work for the TVA, bracing the abs through big compounds and rotation for obliques should all be included.

5. **You should target the abs and core by 'bracing' during big compound lifts rather than direct abs or core work**

Yes, you should brace your abdominal wall in big lifts such as the deadlift, squat or overhead press. This will give you more stability, protection and strength during that lift and will clearly work the abdominal area. However, you will not get the same level of targeted, rectus abdominis contraction throughout the whole range of movement as something like weighted sit-ups. It is also incredibly hard to apply progressive overload to something like a deadlift when you're solely thinking of the abs. Yes, a 200kg deadlift is a progression from a 150kg deadlift, but is it definitely a progression for the abdominals specifically? It's incredibly hard to tell. When I 'brace' my trunk muscles for a 200kg deadlift, I brace them just as hard as I do for a 150kg deadlift and because the rectus abdominis are not the prime movers or agonists in a deadlift, it's impossible to tell if they work any harder in lift A or lift B, and therefore, it's impossible to tell if they will react to a new growth stimulus in the same way that they would when I do 100 sit-ups instead of 50. A combination of direct ab work, big compound movements and foundational work on the TVA, glute activation and posture, is the best recommendation for all-round health, strength and aesthetics.

How I actually programme my 'abs' work

During the off-season, I do not train abs on back or legs day, due to abdominal bracing needed for lifts like the squat, leg press, lunges and rowing variations. However, in the run-up to a bodybuilding show, I will train the abs 5 days per week. On the days when I do train the abs, I tend to do this at the start or the end of a weight training or cardio session. A sample programme is detailed below. I would use these sets and reps as the basis for all my abs sessions but change the specific exercise selection.

Option 1 – I do this style Abs workout 2 to 3 times per week. The emphasis here is on progressive overload, improving weight or volume from week to week.

1. Any weighted crunch or sit-up - 3 x 12/15 reps (we have a brilliant plate loaded, sit-up machine). Here, the emphasis is to increase the weight and apply progressive overload.
2. Any leg raise variation - 2 x 15/20 reps (slow tempo, induce muscular failure).
3. Any rotation exercise (cables, sit-ups, twists) - 2 x 12 each side (same as above).

4. Circuit. Pick any 3 abs exercises and perform in a circuit manner for 20 reps, 15 reps, 10 reps and 5 reps, aiming to improve efficiency and decrease rest periods as the programme goes on.

5. Finish with 5 sets of 10-second hollowing/vacuum. I will do this every day as I near a show and aim to increase the sets or time for each set, as the show gets closer. The ability to control the abdominal wall, tense the abs and create a vacuum with the TVA, is paramount to the overall stage look.

Option 2 – I do this Abs style workout 2 to 3 times per week, especially when training with a partner. The emphasis here is on completing the circuit with as little rests as possible. Therefore progressive overload is achieved through muscular endurance, rather than weight or volume.

The 'Abs Surprise' circuit. The Circuit is a continuous set of varying exercises that are generally picked by your gym partner and called out along the way. You only know 2 things; firstly it's going to last for around 100-150 reps, and secondly, it's going to hurt. A sample of that this looks like is below:

12 weighted sit ups, 12 leg raises, 15 side plank pulses, 20 crunches, 10 V ups, 10 beatles, 10 twist sit ups, 12 scissors, 12 single leg raises, 20 crunches.

Even if you aren't making big advancements, from a 'progressive overload' perspective, I would still endorse abdominal training from an 'activation' perspective. On the days that I have worked on my abdominals, TVA and obliques, I just feel a better connection, like the awareness of my trunk muscles mean that my posture is better, I feel more stable and I'm keeping a more hollowed and 'flatter' stomach, because those muscles seem more 'switched on'. Even if you are carrying too much body fat for a visible '6 pack' or you don't overly care about abdominal strength or aesthetics, I would fully endorse training the 'trunk' muscles, a couple of times per week.

Cardio choices – HIIT, Steady State – what are the options?

Whether you are cutting, bulking or maintaining, I would always encourage you to do some form of cardio. Most people think of cardio as a way to burn calories, melt fat and lose weight, but, as the title suggests, cardiovascular training is all about working your heart and lungs and therefore contributing to overall health, longevity and wellbeing. Even in a weight-gaining or bulking phase, I would encourage you to do some form of cardio to protect long-term heart health.

By now, you're probably becoming bored of me banging on about exercise adherence and 'enjoying the process', and you're expecting me to say that cardio type, in itself, doesn't really matter for body composition; it's much more about the overall plan, and being in an overall calorie deficit or surplus. Well, you'd be absolutely correct, but as usual, there are many things to consider that can improve your chances of enjoyment, adherence and success. So, let's look at some of the different cardio types, what we're looking to achieve, and which option(s) might be best for you.

Factors to consider:

- **For general health**, we want to use cardio to help contribute to fat/weight loss (through calorie expenditure) and towards improving heart health and function through taxing the lungs, heart and whole cardiovascular system. To achieve these two things, you can use a variety of high intensity or steady-state cardio, but for heart health, I would look to get the heart rate up to 80% of your heart rate max a couple of times per week. Walking the dog or playing a round of golf is great to burn some extra calories, but something that goes beyond this and taxes the cardiovascular system, like weight training, circuits, sprints or cycling, will push your fitness and heart health to a higher level.

- **For ultimate fitness and cardiovascular performance,** you need to move beyond steady-state cardio and look at ways to up the intensity of your training, improve aerobic capacity, anaerobic capacity and lactate threshold. For this, a variety of exercises or approaches can be utilised. Using shorter, circuit-style weights and body weight sessions can improve anaerobic capacity and lactate threshold, as can sprint intervals using a variety of cardio machines in the gym. Aerobic capacity can also be increased in a variety of ways, utilising longer, steady-state sessions, improving times for middle distances or more intense, shorter intervals. For ultimate performance, I would look at safely programming a 'CrossFit'-style programme, using a variety of weight training, body weight, plyometric and cardiovascular training in a circuit-style approach, ensuring progressive overload by completing circuits quicker than before, adding weight to the bar or progressing specific movements to make them harder.

- **For aesthetics or bodybuilding,** whilst both approaches can also be effective, and I would still encourage you to 'go with the one you enjoy the most', the vast majority of bodybuilders or 'physique competitors' do opt for a slower-state cardio. It's important to consider that, as competitors working towards a show, you will be in a calorie deficit and must work hard to maintain muscle mass and use your energy for weight training sessions. The idea of a bodybuilder doing high intensity sprints, intervals or circuits as they approach a show, and still performing well in the weights room, is probably unrealistic. In this circumstance, I would opt for a steady-state approach, where you could walk, cross-train or cycle with a specific calorie goal in mind. Always look to prioritise the weightlifting portion of your programme, where more intensity and energy will be needed. However, this can be different when 'bulking' or 'maingaining' and when you're in a calorie surplus or at/above maintenance. Adding in some higher-intensity sprints, intervals or circuits can be a great way to promote cardiovascular health and break from the monotony of traditional weightlifting and steady-state cardio. If you do want to do higher intensity cardio and still add strength, weight and muscle mass in a bulk, you just need to be careful that you stay in a calorie surplus and you have enough energy to achieve progressive overload (and therefore get bigger and stronger) in your weight training sessions.

- **For the competitive ones among you…** I have a friend who's never particularly enjoyed any aspect of fitness, training or the gym in itself. The idea of going to a gym, lifting weights or running on a treadmill made sense for training goals, but the process was too dull and unenjoyable. He stayed in good shape by playing a variety of competitive sports, but as we get older, injuries and other commitments can mean that our ability to offset calories with sporting matches alone becomes a lot harder. In the last two years, he's lost a ton of weight and is as fit and healthy as I've ever known him. The reason is that he's found a variety of training that feels like a competition. For him, it's a mixture of intense training on the Peloton, the steady-state cardio workout provided by golf, and counting his weekly steps. The Peloton gives a good mix of high intensity cardio, steady-state cardio and weightlifting, in a circuit style. The thing that has really worked is the competition option that sees you go against other Peloton users and measures things like distance travelled, calories burned or completing various workouts for time. Without even knowing it, he's been applying progressive overload as his competitive edge means he strives for longer distances, quicker times and more calories burned with every session in a bid to beat other Peloton competitors and set his own PBs time and time again. When you love competition and therefore enjoy the process, a workout no longer feels like a workout; it's just a great by-product of an enjoyable competition or session. Instead of focusing on burning calories or lifting weights, your focus is on winning competitions and setting new records. Whilst I'm sure he missed the odd workout and had to talk himself into getting on the bike on occasion, generally speaking, this increase in enjoying the process almost always leads to an increase in adherence, which is the life force of successful training programmes.

Of course, there is nothing magical about Peloton. You could achieve similar outcomes with a variety of sports and fitness options. CrossFit, group circuits, and even things like 5-aside football or 7s rugby could work for you, but the ability to measure output and see progress would be preferable. Knowing your times are getting quicker, you're going further or burning more calories, is what will translate to tangible health, weight and performance improvements. One thing I had never really considered before is how much competitive people love data - something that is measurable, and recordable, where the victory or loss shows up in the stats, numbers, facts and figures. As well as his best times, placings and distances for the Peloton, he'd also note how often he's played rounds of golf and how many steps he's travelled that day. At the end of the year, he's able to note that he's played 140 rounds of golf, 26 games of cricket, completed 70 Peloton workouts, and averaged 14k steps per day, around three times the UK average. No doubt he will want to beat that number next year. No wonder his weight is down and he's lowered his resting heart rate and his blood pressure. If you do have a competitive streak and can use these data metrics to your advantage, you might be surprised how simply keeping a logbook and recording weights, times, distances or scores can contribute to your ability to apply progressive overload, improve performance, and make huge strides in your health and fitness journey.

Exercise execution

Over the last 20 years, I've learned that, by and large, exercise execution is a reasonably personal thing. Things like training goal, injury, exercise history and limb length all decide what 'good exercise form' should actually look like. Someone training for maximal power output will generally move a bar much quicker than someone training for hypertrophy. Someone who's rehabbing from a knee injury will take greater care during the eccentric portion of a squat. But, when it comes to some of the more mainstream, bodybuilding-esque exercises for hypertrophy, I do have some tips on correct execution to maximise mind-muscle connection and muscle growth, and hopefully, minimise injury. I've found that there is a lot of confusion and conflicting information when it comes to these three lifts, often leading to radical changes in form, tempo and angles. These tips have tended to connect with most of the clients that I've used them with over the years, but you'd have to try them yourselves and see if they're appropriate for you. So, if you struggle to connect with any of the following, give these versions a try:

- **The Dumbbell Lateral Raise.** You could look on YouTube for 2 minutes and find 10 different ways to complete this lift. None of them is necessarily wrong, but I find that prioritising absolute simplicity, lighter loads and 'mind-muscle connection' in this lift works best for me. I've trialled this lift with so many form variations, grips, rep ranges and loads over the years, with varying degrees of success, failure and pain. There's the old-school pinkies up/thumbs down approach, that's pretty effective at getting into the side delts, but definitely exposes the rotator cuff and forward rotates the joint, causing potential pain in anyone with shoulder issues. Using heavier weights with a smaller range of motion, rocking from the waist with a high chest, can also be effective for moving bigger loads, but similarly, anyone with elbow issues (like tennis elbow) can really feel this one, and the likelihood of heavier weights activating traps over side delts is reasonably high. I much prefer a seated approach, neutral grip, with a very controlled and smooth concentric and eccentric phase. 2 seconds up, 2 seconds down, soft elbows, taking the weight to just above level with the shoulder, pinning the traps/ rhomboids back and down, and focusing on keeping the backs of my hands facing the ceiling. I use a higher-end hypertrophy rep range of 12-20 reps per set and keep the rest periods to around 1 minute, championing muscular failure over specific weight. You should be failing through muscular pain, lactate build-up and muscular exhaustion rather than pure, mechanical tension based on the weight being too heavy. I find that in these specific lifts, if the form fails too early on due to the heavy weight, you're unlikely to feel the specific connection with the side delts, and the likelihood of using the traps, forearms, biceps and sheer momentum takes over. In itself, this isn't always a bad thing, but for all-out shoulder strength or to train the CNS, much better exercises are available. The DB lateral raise should be used as a specific hypertrophy tool for building the side delts and programmed alongside other lifts, like overhead press variations, rear delt flyes and shrug variations, to hit different deltoid heads, work the traps and develop overall shoulder strength.

- **Bicep Preacher Curl.** This is one of my favourites for building the meat of the bicep. For me, this lift lives and dies by a super strong connection in the eccentric phase (stretching out the muscle) and a strong 'squeeze' at the top of the lift. It doesn't really matter if you use an EZ bar, straight bar or even a preacher curl machine, but I would urge you to try and really connect with the bicep and aim for a super, explosive pump! 2 seconds lowering the weight during the eccentric phase, 1-second pause and active 'stretch' at the bottom, coming up on the Concentric phase slightly quicker at around 1 second but pausing and squeezing at the top, feeling the bicep fully contracting, with a cue of 'imagine you're trying to pull through your forehead'. You'll know this is working when the bicep starts to feel super full of blood, hard and pumped. A combo of muscular pain and fatigue will end the set as you struggle to complete the full rep towards the end. You can add some 'partial reps' to really finish off the bicep on the last set, coming up to halfway but still using the slow, controlled stretch of the eccentric phase. If you want to try and target the long head more, I would retract the shoulders and feel like you're pulling up with your little fingers. If you're looking for more short head activation, lean your shoulders slightly forward into the pad and pull more with the ring finger.

- **Lat Pull-Downs.** There are lots of variations of lat pull-down machines, but we'll assume a standard weight stack, with pin, where you would face the stack, in a seated position and fix your legs under a bar. You can use many different grips to execute this lift and a lot of this is about feel and a personal mind-muscle connection. If you are struggling to connect with this lift, then I would suggest using a long bar and setting your grip just outside of your own shoulders. For me, this is a position where I can actively squeeze and flare my lats. Any wider and I struggle to get any contraction at all. Any narrower and it can push the elbows too far forward and forward rotate the shoulder joint. Next, I want to pin my scapula back, keep the shoulders compressed throughout the movement and keep my chest up and high. (To get this feeling, I may even reset the scapula and shoulders between every rep). In terms of tempo, I get the best feeling here when I'm as deliberate with the concentric phase as I am with the eccentric, opting for a strict 2 up, 2 down motion, with a 'shoulder reset' at the top of the movement. You should feel like you're locked in and that the weight is being moved and controlled solely by the lats. It can help to try and take the grip out of it completely and use straps, almost using your hand as a kind of hook that latches on, instead of manically gripping the weight, which can jump into your forearms and biceps. Although I want to pin the shoulders down and keep the chest high, I am also focussing on pulling the weight directly down (not back and towards my own chest). If you want to see an example of this in practice, check out a fantastic video where Brandon Curry is training with John Meadows. He sets up an amazing lat pull set, where the reps start off super strict, pulling the bar down in a straight line, in front of his chest. As he tires, he progressively makes the movement a little bit easier, rocking and pulling the bar back towards him, to help prolong the set and push past the point of failure.

I'm aware that a book isn't the most ideal resource when it comes to explaining exercise execution, but I thought I'd put my descriptive powers to the test with these three explanations. There are tons of decent channels that discuss exercise execution, angles, hand placings, tempos and body alignment. People like Jonni Shreve, the late John Meadows, or Ryan Humiston, are well worth checking out. I expect all of them would question the above explanations of all three lifts as they'd have their favoured cues, tempos and alignments. But that's fine. If there's a sound biomechanical reason to try a certain exercise style, you should give it a go and see if it works for you. Ryan Humiston has recently released an incredible set of videos (that I refer to earlier) that measure the muscle contraction rate and ability to isolate a specific muscle contraction for dozens of lifts. As well as the videos being brilliantly narrated from a biomechanical point of view, what's even more impressive is that based on a series of surprising results, he happily admits that some of his execution over the years has been suboptimal, finding that certain angles, shoulder placement, wrist placements and ranges of motion have targeted different muscles than he once thought. If someone with his experience and knowledge is open to experimenting, proving himself wrong, and then sharing it with his audience, we should all be open to different training ideas, philosophies and exercise execution. It's long been my belief that anyone who is truly interested in the science bit of 'sports science', is always open to being proven wrong, exploring different viewpoints, evolving their philosophies and sharing their evolving ideas.

Injuries, burn out and exercise selection

I like to think of every exercise selection as an assessment that asks two questions:

1. What is the **risk to reward** for this exercise? (What is the best outcome vs the worst outcome and, therefore, is it worth the risk, based on my training goal and injury history?)
2. What is the **return on investment** for this exercise? (If I carry out this exercise properly, what results will I likely yield and is that worth being included, at the expense of other exercises?)

As an example of how this works, let me take the Deadlift, my favourite lift of all time, a lift I used to complete at the start of every back workout. This is one of the best mass and strength builders, perfect to train the posterior chain, grow and strengthen the whole back, spinal erectors, hamstrings and traps. Given the above statement about deadlifts, you would think that I perform these with regularity, as part of any great strength, hypertrophy or mobility programme. However, sadly, this is not the case, at least not the conventional, barbell deadlift or any variation with any 'high end' weight or intensity. So how did I get to this bitterly disappointing decision?

The Deadlift – Risk to reward musings – specifically for bodybuilding and specifically for me:

Best Outcome – maintain and improve strength of posterior chain and hypertrophy of lat/trap/rhomboid/hamstring muscles.

Worst Outcome – Severely injure my (already) worn discs and make my spinal fractures worse.

Options of how to offset the 'worst' outcome and still do deadlifts – train at a lighter load, using a slightly higher rep range. Change to a trap bar, 'Sumo' style, or train part of the movement using something like a rack pull.

Problems with this – I've tried this before and a combination of poor concentration (e.g. not bracing or concentrating enough due to lighter loads) and a specific mindset to training (e.g. creep the weight up after a few weeks as it 'seems ok') have led me to still get injured, with regularity, whilst completing the deadlift. Equally, I've experienced similar problems with the trap bar, 'Sumo deadlift,' and don't believe the rack pull to have an adequate 'return on investment' specifically for bodybuilding, e.g. the fatigue to the CNS and potential for injury still outweighs its activation of specific muscle fibres compared to a full deadlift.

What's the alternative – Replace with kettlebell swings, Kettlebell deadlifts, carries and single leg variations to keep training the 'hip hinge' movement for posterior chain health and glute activation. Increase reps and sets of exercises such as ham curls, row variations, lat pulls, shrugs and pull-ups to try and minimise strength and size loss in these key areas.

Outcome – Don't do conventional deadlifts. (sad face).

The above may seem like an extreme step to take for such a great and revered movement, but it took me nearly a decade of consistently trying to work around this problem before I cut the deadlift from my bodybuilding plan. I would urge all of you to look at any exercise that seems to injure you and carry out the same risk assessment. Ask yourself if the exercise is paramount for your goal, if there are ways to tweak the movement to make it safer, and what the alternatives would be if you chose to leave it out. In my opinion, there is no one magical exercise that can't be subbed or changed in some way so that you can train safely and effectively with the same progress for aesthetics, fat loss and muscle gain. Of course, when it comes to specific competition like powerlifting, choices are far more limited and if you can't effectively squat, deadlift or bench press without frequent injury, you do have more of a problem. It's likely that serious time and effort will be needed to go back and make improvements to weak body parts and movements. Perhaps a series of micro/mesocycles looking at injury rehab, activation and muscle pattern work (posterior chain sequencing, for example) and a period of forgoing the big lifts for some specific flexibility and strength assistance work on key muscles like the rhomboids, glute med and hamstrings. And whilst it's possible to work on getting back to these big, heavy lifts, you have to be honest about the time and effort it will take to get there. If you chose to go back and start a rehab plan (and in many circumstances, you should), this time and effort will likely be at the expense of training other goals. If your goal is more towards bodybuilding, aesthetics, fat loss and general health, then it's not all that hard to replace some of the classic lifts with variations that will serve your injuries better and keep you fit. Over the years, I've replaced back squats with hack squats, military press with seated DB press and deadlifts with a combination of Kettlebell deadlifts and higher volumes of rows, lunges and shrugs, to offset injuries and keep me in the gym more consistently throughout the year. Even if the exercises themselves are 5% less effective, the fact that I don't take 2 months off injured means that I'm in better physical and mental shape overall.

Return on investment – exercise selection

But it's not just injuries that should shape our exercise selection. We should also question our return on investment for a particular exercise and really examine what we are trying to achieve for every single exercise that we select. The reason that you have selected that exercise should help to determine the tempo, sets, reps and angles that you're trying to achieve. Let's look at setting up a Chest session as an example. To get the most out of each part of the chest, you want to think about which exercises will hit different muscle fibres and what we can use in terms of intensity, sets, reps and tempo to really maximise this. Here is a sample chest day that I've used over the years:

Let's assume a good warm-up of adequate stretching and starting with something like cable flyes - activating the chest using submaximal loads of around 30% of 1rm for 10/15 reps stopping well short of failure for 2-3 sets and some initial warm-up/prep sets on the bench press before the working sets:

Barbell Bench Press - 4 x 5/7 reps hitting full muscular failure (good smooth form but no specific tempo).

Incline DB Press - 4 x 8/15 reps hitting full form failure (3-second eccentric and 1-second concentric. Smooth and controlled).

Machine Flye or Pec Deck – 4 x 12/15 reps to 'pain failure' or leaving 2/3 reps in reserve, with a very specific tempo of 3-second eccentric, 1-second stretch hold, 1 second concentric, 1 second squeeze hold.

Machine Chest Press – FST-7 style finisher. 7 sets of 8/15 reps with only 30 secs rest between.

Now let's examine each exercise, why it was included and why the tempos and intensities might change between each lift, to fully maximise the return on investment:

Bench Press – This is a big compound lift, hitting the meat of the pec, but also has a great overall effect on natural growth hormone and the central nervous system. Excellent for building overall strength and size, this lift should be included at the start of your programme for these reasons but isn't the best exercise for specific 'mind-muscle connection' to really target the chest. I would do this lift in the lower end of hypertrophy and the higher end of 'strength' reps at 5-7 reps. Although these lifts will have some effect on the CNS, the volume isn't high enough to significantly impact the rest of your session. You should be applying progressive overload principles of more load or more reps to this lift.

Incline DB Press – The DBs allow you to bring the elbows further across your body, feeling and squeezing the chest. The incline element gives a slightly increased focus on the muscle fibres of the upper pec, hitting the 'shelf' of the chest. A smooth and controlled tempo and failing at 'form failure' around 2 reps short of full muscular failure allow you to concentrate on isolating and squeezing the chest muscles whilst still dealing with a decent load. You should be applying progressive overload principles of more weight or more reps to this lift.

Machine Flye / Pec Deck – This is a really interesting one because we clearly can't handle as much load with this movement. Therefore, it's incredibly important to maximise the benefits that a flye movement gives us, which is namely that the angle we can create gives us a much easier chance to stretch and squeeze the chest at varying ends of the lift. So, we need to set this up using submaximal loads and placing a huge emphasis on the tempo of the lift. There is no point in loading up a heavy weight and blasting out reps at breakneck speeds. If we're going to do this, we might as well just bench press more; after all, we can handle much bigger loads on the bench press. This is all about making use of the unique angle of the flye movement. We should feel an incredible stretch at the bottom portion of the lift and a strong contraction (or squeeze) at the top portion on completing the set. If done properly, pain, form and muscular failure will probably all come at once!

Machine Press FST-7 sets - This is using Hany Rambod's FST-7 approach, FST standing for fascia stretch training and 7 standing for the number of sets. The idea here is to simply flood the muscle with blood, creating a deep pump that volumizes the muscle, leading to the deep muscle fascia being stretched out and becoming thinner. A thinner fascia will give the muscle a rounder, more ripped and 3D appearance. So, given the goal of bodybuilding, it's obvious why we'd pick this method, and given this is almost a drop set, very high volumes under extreme fatigue, it's much better to choose a machine option that targets the muscle but provides an easy A to B movement, reducing the chance of injury or time wasted in putting free weights down, and picking them back up again.

So, when you next put a training plan together, really examine the risk to reward and return on investment for each exercise and make sure you're programming effective tempo, reps, sets and execution to fit the goals for each one.

Any C*nt Can Do 5! The Magic of Training Partners

Over the years, I've had, and continue to have, a number of fantastic, like-minded training partners, who help to keep gym sessions fun, focused and painful! There's no doubt that a good training partner can eke 5% extra out of a given set or session, and the friendships and bonds that are forged from egging each other on, hitting PBs and grinding under a bar, can be unbreakable! I've trained with one mate (Jimbo) for well over a decade and the gains in strength, hypertrophy, fat loss and fun from keeping each other on the straight and narrow are immeasurable.

I would never recommend doing so, but one day, we turned up at the gym in about a foot of snow! Roads were closed, cars were abandoned, it was the worst snow the UK had seen in 20 years, and there we were, driving across Bristol at 6 am to meet for a shoulders session. I still remember the texts now. *'Are we doing this big man?'* James texted me… *'Well, it is juicy shoulders……we did promise 2 PBs this week… I'm game if you are.'* I replied, *'Yeah Fuck it, I'll see you there.'* I know this is irresponsible and not one to be proud of, but it does serve to illustrate the power of a great training partner. Both of us were itching to get to the gym and try to hit the PBs we had promised ourselves as part of the weekly plan. Neither of us wanted to take the easy option of staying in a warm, cosy bed. There are so many occasions when I might not have turned up if it hadn't been for the thought of letting a training partner down and vice versa. So, training partners can be great for getting to the gym, but the real gains happen during the sessions. There's a different feeling, a different mindset, when someone's shouting at you to get another rep out or to do one last set. There's the competitive edge that a training partner can bring to a session, going against each other for reps, tempo and effort. Whose mentality will crack first; will you finish the set; will you leave a rep in reserve, or push yourself past failure? One absurd saying that has become a kind of mantra for our training is that 'Any C*nt can do 5.' It's a stupid line that we use towards the end of drop sets, giant sets, supersets or nasty finishers that basically calls out that if you just switch off from the pain, you can nearly always do 5 more reps... 5 more reps that I probably wouldn't have done without my mate shouting in my ear. Usually, your brain quits before your body, and that's definitely the case when I look around most gyms and gauge people's general proximity to failure. Now, it's important I add that this doesn't apply to a 5-rep max, or lifting any weight in what would be a classic hypertrophy rep range of 8-15 reps to failure. Sadly, this can't improve high-end strength, but it can absolutely improve mindset, muscular endurance and the ability to handle pain and keep going. This is about the sick finishers, the body weight exercise, the giant sets and the drop sets. This is the set of press-ups to failure to finish a chest day or a massive drop set on the bicep curl machine. With anything that's high rep, using sub-maximal loads, you can generally eke out 5 more reps with sheer bloody-mindedness, grit and will. Whilst I wouldn't recommend or condone shouting the C word out in the middle of a mainstream gym, I would absolutely recommend pushing yourself to this level of failure on your last set of the session. The satisfaction and carryover that going beyond your perceived ceiling can create is incredibly powerful both physically and mentally. If that last set, those last 5 reps, are the hardest, most gruelling thing you do that day, it's amazing how much easier some of your daily tasks can seem. Work meetings, that difficult chat with a colleague or a daunting sales call may just seem a little bit easier compared to those last 5 reps of your session, and if any c*nt can do 5, he or she can surely give that bit of extra grit, determination and effort into a plethora of other professional and personal tasks. Maybe we should get it printed on t-shirts and caps like Donald Trump's 'Make America Great Again'?! All I know is that training partners have helped me to turn up to the gym, to push hard in sessions, and to give me positive and affirming feedback when I'm doubting myself in the lead-up to shows. If you find the right person, I do believe that everyone would benefit from training with a partner.

Chapter 3

Dieting and Food

The Post-Show Binge

It's the summer of 2021 and I've just completed a natural bodybuilding show. This is the strictest I've ever been on prep; I was absolutely dialled into my calories and macronutrients and, for the first time, I'm genuinely proud of how I looked on stage. I get back to my car as I'm about to embark on a 3-hour journey from London back to Bristol, but only one thing is on my mind. Before I left for the competition, my Partner had given me a bag that read 'not to be opened until after the show'. I knew that it would contain a plethora of delicious foods that I'd been abstaining from for what seemed like years! In reality, it was more like 12 weeks, and even then, I had had some planned cheats along the way, but this is the first time I could genuinely get stuck in, guilt-free. Now, going by the textbook, I shouldn't really be doing this. Sure, a nice treat after the show is expected, some cake or doughnuts or a big meal, but this all-out splurge, where you end up gaining weight and fat incredibly quickly after the show, isn't all that healthy and it's counter-productive from a physique perspective. If you have the mental fortitude, then 'reverse dieting' is the way to go – slowly adding back calories and cheat-style foods so that you slowly gain weight and add muscle but keep a certain level of leanness… I can confirm that I did not have the willpower, the inclination, or the interest to do this! I had put myself through hell, and now I was going all out! I opened the bag and there were treats of all kinds - doughnuts, sweets, chocolate, sandwiches, crisps, a pork pie and a scotch egg. I had barely got out of the car park and all of it was gone! But I wanted more… I pulled straight into the nearest garage and bought even more food. A foot-long meatball sub, more crisps, more chocolate, cans of fizzy drink and more sweets that I could pick at on the way home. It wasn't long before I was pulling over thinking I might be sick, feeling absolutely horrendous but hell-bent on finishing the last Peperami! I drove home on autopilot, in a food coma, disgusted with myself but still determined to go out for dinner when I got back… and we did… pasta, pizza and a few beers… Within a week, I had put on 18 pounds of weight. Of course, I was so lean before that I still would have been around 10% body fat, still shredded by normal standards, but the body dysmorphia that can accompany being stage lean, is unbelievable. I felt horrid. I felt bloated and watery and soft. My 'all or nothing' brain had a lot to answer for! I needed a new programme, a new diet plan and a new goal ASAP.

The Bullet Point Bail Out

There is so much confusion and detail to consider when we talk about diet choices, calories, macro and micronutrients, that I want to start by giving you an easily digestible set of bullet points up front. I'll go on to discuss these points in more detail, but I know that my own brain seems to read and digest short bullet points easier than reading paragraphs of detail. So, if like me, your brain hurts at the sight of equations and calories, here is the 'Bullet Point Bail Out', highlighting the main take aways from this whole chapter:

- The CICO equation will dictate weight lost and weight gained. No matter diet type, timing, macronutrient split or micronutrient content, if you are in a calorie surplus, you will gain weight.
- Macronutrient Splits will help contribute towards the calories out portion, can be important for body composition, aesthetics, fuelling workouts and diet adherence.
- Micronutrient content is key for optimal health.
- Protein is an incredibly important macronutrient. It's vital for growth and repair of muscles and has a thermic effect, which means your body has to work harder to use it. In fact, for every gram (4 Kcals) of protein ingested, it costs our bodies around 1 kcal to use it. This means that protein contributes more towards the 'calories out' portion than fats and carbs. Due to this thermic effect, and preference for muscle growth/repair it's much harder to 'overeat' on protein, compared to fat or carbs
- To lose around a pound of fat per week, put yourself in a 500-calorie deficit per day.
- When aiming to build muscle, things may need to be more conservative, unless you don't mind gaining

fat in the process. Most natural lifters are limited to building a maximum of 0.5lbs of muscle per week, and this number will be vastly reduced as you get more experienced. Knowing this, we should start off with a conservative 200-300 calorie surplus per day and look to increase from there.

- You should aim to eat around 0.8g to 1.2g of protein per pound of bodyweight. The rest should be split between fats and carbs.

- When it comes to body composition, once we've applied the 0.8g to 1.2g of protein per pound of bodyweight, it doesn't seem to matter whether you take a carb- or fat-centric approach thereafter.

- The energy in a pound of muscle is around 700 calories, but it takes around 2700 calories to build a new pound of muscle. It's easier to maintain what you have once it's there, but harder to build new tissue.

- Because fat plays a crucial role in normal hormonal and cell function, I would urge you to stay above 15% of your calories coming from fats, even in the most carb-dominated approach.

- If you have a big appetite, you should consider that there are 9 kcals in a gram of fat compared to 4 kcals in protein and carbs. Having a higher fat diet will generally mean less volume. If you are a big eater, you may find that prioritising a protein and carb, whole food approach, is better for adherence. The sheer volume that these lower calorie alternatives can offer you is greater. 0% fat yogurt, rice, potatoes, veg, chicken breast and tuna will yield a bigger food portion than fatty cuts of meat, nuts, oily fish or avocado. This isn't to say these foods are healthier, but if you need to be in a calorie deficit, you should pay attention to the foods that make up the biggest portions of your diet.

- 'Maingaining' or 'body re-composition' could be a healthier alternative to the traditional bulk and cut but rely on the individual being very close to their desired training goal. You will not 'maingain' your way to significant body weight, strength or fat loss improvements.

- Creatine is a well-researched and worthwhile supplement for general health, muscle and strength gains. Whey Protein can be a convenient, safe and inexpensive way to hit your protein numbers. BCAAs and 'Fat Burners' are probably not worth the effort and expense of taking them.

- Those who have suffered with eating disorders or have a complicated relationship with food, should be cautious when counting calories. Health and Fitness goals might be best centred around strength, fitness performance and wellbeing, and any diet-related goals might be better centred around food quality, food type and micronutrient content.

Calorie Set Up

When it comes to losing or gaining weight, the simple equation of calories in vs calories out (or CICO) should be the building block from which MOST diets are formed. Of course, just saying 'consume fewer calories than you use' is about as useful as saying that you 'win a game of football by scoring more goals than the other team'! It ignores vital elements like team selection, formation, strategy, refereeing decisions and home advantage, so it's important that we examine 'how' we get into a calorie deficit/surplus in the first place, and how we keep it sustainable. There are many different routes to take and lots to consider, but it's important to note that most of these considerations, such as diet type, meal timing, workout nutrition and supplementation, are simply tools to get you into that calorie surplus or deficit and not the main thing that will affect fat loss or muscle gain. For example, you can use a vegan diet as part of a weight loss programme, but the fact it's vegan isn't making you lose the weight; you're losing the weight because you're in a calorie deficit.

Now, the vegan diet may be a big contributing factor to adhering to that calorie deficit, especially if you love vegan food and have found loads of food choices that are delicious, low in calories and satiating, but it's the calorie deficit that is the actual factor in losing the weight. Some people will argue that this isn't the case, but this is often because they generally don't understand the 'calories out' part of the CICO equation. For example, it is true that 100 calories of protein is going to interact with the body differently than 100 calories of fat or carbs. More of that protein will go towards a muscle repair and growth function and the body has to use more calories to actually break down protein and make it useable than it does for carbs or fat (for every 4 kcals ingested, it takes 1 kcal to use it). So, whilst we have still ingested the same 100 calories, the 100 calories from protein is actually going to make a bigger impact on the 'calories out' portion. Protein's ability to contribute to muscle growth and repair and its thermic effect makes it a vital macronutrient for optimal performance, aesthetics and health. But whether we lose or gain weight will still depend on how those 100 calories of protein have contributed towards our daily, weekly or monthly CICO equation.

The factor that affects your 'Calories In' is simply the amount of food you eat. The factors that affect calories out are a little more complex. There are four main considerations for the calories out portion. Firstly, the planned exercise that you do will affect how many calories are burned. Think gym work, cardio, running, walking. Secondly, the actual food that you eat will affect the calories out portion. The body uses energy to break down foods and make them 'useable' for energy, growth and repair. A higher protein diet will have a bigger impact on your 'calories out' as it takes more energy to break down protein vs fat/carbs. Thirdly, your NEAT (non-exercise activity thermogenesis) will affect how many calories you are using for tasks that you are not cognizant of doing. Things like blinking, fidgeting, and small body movements when you're at your desk, all make a small dent in your calorie equation. Anyone who has been in a big calorie deficit would have noticed that their NEAT goes to drastically low levels after a while, as the body adapts to try and save as many calories as it can. And finally, your resting energy expenditure. This is simply the energy that your body uses to 'keep the lights on'; things like keeping your heart beating and organs functioning.

The other thing to mention is that whilst CICO is the most important factor for weight loss, it isn't the most important factor for health. You could eat an incredibly unvaried diet and lose weight but be starved of vital nutrients, vitamins, minerals and energy. It's important to also think about macro and micronutrients, gut health, food quality, inflammation and allergies, but you have to consider that simply being overweight in itself can be harmful to blood pressure, organ health, joints, connective tissue and normal cell function, and before we get overly carried away with all of those factors, the simple act of losing body fat may make more of a dent in our health woes than taking the right supplements or using organic produce. Of course, we must also consider the same fact for being in a constant calorie deficit. Eating woefully under your maintenance calories day in, day out, will lead to drastic health consequences, including organ failure, poor skin and bone health and a huge decline in energy and strength. Quite simply, if you were to eat in a calorie deficit each and every day, eventually, you would die.

Everyone's calorific needs are completely different and various factors like your current weight, metabolism, age and activity level will affect daily calorie needs. Any advice that states specific calorie numbers followed by a bold claim such as 'eat 2500 calories per day to lose weight' or 'eat at least 3500 calories per day to gain weight' is best avoided! These blanket statements can't possibly make sense for everyone, as a 300lbs male is going to have completely different nutritional needs to a 125lbs female. In fact, the 300lbs male would likely lose weight at 3500 calories per day, whilst our 125lbs female would gain weight at 2500 calories, rendering both of these calorie diet claims utterly useless! All dietary needs are specific, and when it comes to calculating your own calories, you have to tailor it to your own individual starting point and end goal. I've seen some truly insane diet plans over the years, where people get carried away with copying their idols, in a bid to look like them. I once spoke to a client who was trying to emulate Ronnie Coleman's bulking plan from a previous off season. The problem is that Ronnie Coleman was about 280lbs, one of the most muscular people to ever grace the planet, and was taking a number of performance-enhancing drugs. This individual was around 180 lbs, had a fraction of the muscle and, to my knowledge, didn't take any PEDs. The 6000 calories per day that he was trying to ingest meant he gained huge amounts of fat, felt terrible and eventually gave up on the diet altogether, when he struggled with the sheer volume. Much, in the same way that overnight, you couldn't suddenly lift the weights that Ronnie Coleman could, you also can't expect your body to be able to tolerate the same food, calorie or macronutrient demand. From a social media context, you should be wary of emulating many of these 'celebrity body transformations,' and should even take a lot of the dieting and training plans with a pinch of salt. I've seen crazy numbers being banded around of late, stating caloric needs of around 8,000 calories per day for a 200 lbs male to get in shape for his latest movie.........when we go on to examine the type of calorie surplus you actually need to build muscle, you will see how ridiculous this claim really is.

Calculating your Maintenance Calories

When it comes to working out our daily caloric intake, researchers at Harvard Medical School and McCarty Weight Loss, point at the need for around 15 calories per pound for the moderately-active man and 13 calories per pound for the moderately-active female, to maintain their body weight[9], adding a calorie per pound for those who are more active (and/ or muscular) and subtracting a calorie for those who are less active or have a higher body fat % to start with. It's important to state that even an article in Harvard Health Publishing, refers to these numbers as 'rough'[10]. There are numerous calorie calculators online that are perfectly fine to use, some of them also take age, height, and body fat percentage into account, but I've always found that the 13 or 15 equation is a reasonable starting point. We're always using some guesswork in calculating our maintenance calories and even the best-designed calculators and methods can't allow for all metabolic considerations. So, using this method, a moderately active, 200lbs man should be able to maintain his current body weight at 3000 calories per day (200 x 15 = 3000). This is called your 'maintenance' calories. If you think that you fall into the 'very active' level, you could up this to 16 or 14 kcals per pound of bodyweight respectively, but as we all have different metabolisms, jobs, and our bodies change slightly with age, injury and illness, I would suggest that everyone starts with 15 or 13 and works forwards from there, using a trial-and-error basis over the first couple of weeks. On a personal level, I don't count added cardio into my maintenance equation up front (e.g. if I added my weekly cardio to the equation I'd likely fall into the 'very active' section) instead, I use it to add to the 'calories out' portion when I want to up my calorie deficit. This means that I could keep the 'calories in' portion the same and lose more weight by adding a few cardio sessions here and there. Mentally, this just works for me.

Having worked with hundreds of clients and friends over the years, and set up countless diets for myself, I've found this method to be extremely reliable for getting a ballpark figure for maintenance calories. Of course, everyone is different, and it's hard to legislate for differing genetics, NEAT (non-exercise activity thermogenesis) and metabolism. Finding out your maintenance calories can take a few stabs to get right and is an ever-evolving equation as you lose and gain weight over the years.

Setting up a Caloric Deficit

Once you've established your maintenance calories, you have two ways in which to ensure you find yourself in a calorie deficit:

1. Consume fewer calories (calories in)
2. Burn more calories (calories out)

For body composition and an aesthetic physique, when losing weight or building muscle, it's true to say that slower is better. The slower you can lose weight, the less muscle you should lose in the process, and the slower you gain weight (assuming a diligent training programme), the more of that should be muscle, and the less fat gained in the process. We want it to be slow and sustainable, but mentally, we also need to see the scales move and know that we're making (at least some) progress. After all, we live in an 'everything now' world and whilst we want this to be sustainable, it's also important for adherence and enjoyment that we see some kind of progress in the first couple of weeks. As a rough guide, we know that there are around 3500 calories in a pound of fat and so, putting yourself in a 3500 weekly calorie deficit (500 kcals per day), in an aim to lose around 1lb per week, is a good place to start[11]. For most people, this one-pound weight loss is more than enough, but if you want to see the scale move further, we can add some cardio to our usual training week and burn an extra 500 - 750 calories per session, 3 to 4 times per week. This can yield an extra 2000 calorie deficit, which should increase our weight loss to around 1.5 to 2 pounds per week from the off. With adequate rest and enough calories to keep you full and satiated, assuming you make sensible food choices, eating low-calorie dense foods in high volumes, this should see a tangible but sustainable weight loss.

So, using the above logic, our 200lbs man will use the following equation and programme to yield the following results:

Calories in portion:

200 x 15 = 3000 kcals maintenance

3000 – 500 = 2500 kcals per day

2500 x 7 days = 17,500 kcals in per week

Calories out portion:

3000 kcals burnt per day as a 200lbs man = 21000 kcal per week

500 extra calories burned at the gym 4 days per week = 2000 kcals

21000 + 2000 = 23000 Kcals out per week.

Result:

17500 – 23000 = 5500 calories deficit per week

5500 calories deficit per week will yield a 1.5 to 2 lbs weight loss

To count and record your calories, you can use an app like 'MyFitnessPal'. You can scan packaging or manually input meals and food to ensure you have accurately recorded your daily calorie and macronutrient profile. As your diet progresses, you can change and update the data to suit your new needs and track your weight, body composition and performance (strength, endurance) vs your diet, making it easier to know if you need to change your diet parameters.

Gaining Muscle – Setting up a calorie surplus

The same logic applies here to gaining weight as it does to losing weight. We have to set up a small and sustainable calorie surplus with the goal of fuelling our workouts and having some excess calories left over to ensure proper muscle growth and recovery. Our approach to a caloric surplus should be controlled and conservative, as increasing calories too quickly can lead to gaining excess fat, along with hard-earned muscle[12]. So, once we've worked out our 'maintenance' calories, again we work forward from here to calculate our daily caloric needs, to be in a surplus, and start to gain muscle and weight. But how much of a calorie surplus should we be in? It might be sensible to apply the same logic to a calorie surplus as we do to the calorie deficit, where 3500 calories seems to be the difference between gaining or losing a pound of body weight. So, our 200lbs man could sit at 500 kcals per day above maintenance at 3500 calories and expect to gain around 1lb per week. And this is certainly an option, but is there a better way to ensure we're gaining the right type of weight? After all, burning fat and building muscle must be different processes, using different mechanisms that require different raw materials, timescales and numbers. Specifically for bodybuilding and keeping an 'aesthetic physique', the idea here isn't to simply gain body weight; it's to gain muscle and not gain too much fat in the process. Most of the science seems to point to the need for a 2,700 to 2,800-calorie surplus (in the right weight training environment) to build a pound of muscle (not weight but specifically muscle), and therefore, if we do gain 1 lb of body weight in a weekly 3500kcals surplus, there is a good chance that a portion of this is going to be fat gain. So, would it be sounder advice to take a more cautionary approach to a calorie surplus, using a 2800 weekly surplus as a starting point (400 extra calories per day) and monitoring from there? Possibly, but we may need to go even further to ensure we're not piling on the fat. You also need to factor in the pace at which a 'natural' lifter can grow new muscle tissue. Studies[13] point at a natural ceiling of gaining around 0.5 pounds per week for the average lifter (with this number vastly reducing as the individual gets more experienced), meaning that we should probably half this caloric number, leaving us with a surplus of only 200 kcals per day, or 1400 kcals per week, as a starting point, since, if we need 2700 to 2800 surplus calories to build a pound of muscle but we can only build 0.5lbs a week, we need to space this 2800 kcals out over a 2-week period.

Using this more cautionary approach, our equation for setting up a small caloric surplus to gain muscle for the same 200lbs male would be:

Maintenance calories set at 3000 calories.

2800 calories to build a pound of muscle = 400 kcals per day.

However, as natural lifters are generally limited to building a max of 0.5lbs muscle per week, we should half this amount again leaving us with 200 kcals surplus per day.

3000 + 200 = 3200 kcals per day.

But is this small, 200 kcals surplus creating an optimal environment to build muscle? Will we see the scale move quickly enough for everyone's liking, and although we're limiting fat gain, should some fat gain be encouraged as, on the whole, weight gain could lead to quicker strength gains and therefore the possibility to grow even more new muscle through progressive overload in the gym? It really depends on a number of factors, including the lifter's main goals, experience and starting fat percentage.

Is a 200 kcals surplus enough?!

For week one of a 'bodybuilding'-style surplus, I would say that 200 is a great starting point, but it does have its drawbacks. Obviously, we know that calorie maintenance isn't an exact science and, when you're in a small surplus or deficit, it can be very hard to be sure you're hitting those numbers accurately. A bit more NEAT, a long walk to a meeting or a few of your calories being a little off when tracked, could easily put you at maintenance or even tip you into a deficit. I would argue that this approach is a good starting point and if you get it right, is fantastic for small, incremental weight and strength gains without gaining excess body fat. But is anything below a 500 kcals surplus more in line with a 'maingaining' or 'body recomp' approach than a traditional bulk/build/muscle-building phase? Whilst I think a 200 kcals surplus is a good starting point, you can definitely look to add to this and end up in a 500 kcals surplus, if your body is responding well. Using the mirror, how you feel, and your performance in the gym will dictate the surplus you want to be in. What I hope this does show, is that even if this approach is too conservative for some, these insane 8000 calorie diets, that you hear about online, are often nothing more than sensationalist marketing. On course, there are some elite sports people, endurance athletes and strength athletes, that need these types of numbers, but for the average person to put on muscle for a film, or to get in shape for a photoshoot, this is just crazy, and the truth is that, most of these people would likely need to be in a calorie deficit (not surplus) to get the kind of v-taper and 6 pack abs, that translates to the screen or stage. If you are training naturally, then being 4000 calories over maintenance, every day, will almost certainly lead to a lot of fat gain.

What is 'maingaining'?

Jeff Nippard describes maingaining as 'a type of body re-composition where your goal is to roughly maintain your body weight, whilst gaining strength in the gym and ideally gaining a little bit of muscle as well'.

It's a different approach to the classic bodybuilding 'phases' of cutting or bulking, that yield smaller and slower results in each field but allow you to maintain a more aesthetic physique all year round, and seems to be a healthy and sustainable choice for most gym-goers who aren't looking to don the stage. It's an approach that I've used quite successfully in between shows, when I want to stay at a lean (but not unhealthy) weight, have enough calories to sustain my workouts and (really importantly) have enough calories and food options to maintain a healthy mindset for work and socialising. Some of the big drawbacks of a big bulk or cut is that it can severely affect your ability to carry out normal tasks, often feeling weak, tired or anxious in a large deficit, or full, bloated and 'heavy' in a large surplus. This 'maingaining' approach could be the answer to maintaining a good physique and healthy mindset all year round. But what are the drawbacks and when might you be better off with the old-school approach?

Maingaining – The Good

- Seems to be a healthier and more sustainable approach
- Should gain minimal fat in the process with correct training and nutrition
- Should be able to gain a steady increase in muscle size and strength, albeit slower than a traditional bulk
- Promotes a healthier relationship with food/diet, where you're eating around the calories that your body needs, rather than force-feeding or being incredibly hungry

Maingaining – The Bad

- Takes a more precise approach to ensure you're not in too big a surplus or deficit
- Perceived progress is slower than a traditional bulk or cut
- For bodybuilding – It may not work as well for an off-season or contest prep 'bulk' phase as you don't leave yourself a lot of calories to cut/reduce when the show approaches, and you won't build as much mass as a traditional bulk phase

- At what fat % or weight should you actually maintain?
- Maingaining is really only an option if you are pretty happy with your current physique and strength levels. If you feel woefully short of your goal, then you aren't going to move the scale from 140lbs to 200lbs by maingaining or recomping; it's just too far a leap. Equally, you would struggle to radically change your weightlifting numbers by 30% - 40% in this small surplus.

Maingaining vs Cut/Bulk approach

I'm a huge fan of the thought process behind maingaining and I do think it's the way to go for a lot of individuals who aren't competing and don't put a huge emphasis on high-end strength. It should deliver the right number of calories and nutrients to stay healthy (both mentally and physically) and provide enough energy to fuel workouts and make modest improvements to strength. And if the individual is already lean enough, this can maintain a low (but healthy) fat percentage level. But when is 'maingaining' not the optimal choice and what are the other options? Is it optimal for someone who is very overweight, very underweight or is looking to compete in a bodybuilding show?

What is your starting point and what is your goal?

As always, to answer these questions, we have to look at your starting point (fat percentage, weight, training background) and at your overall goal. For someone who is vastly overweight, with a high fat percentage, and who is perhaps suffering with their health as a consequence, we should look to set them up with a slightly more aggressive deficit. I would still stick to the 500 kcals deficit from maintenance and look to create a further weight loss stimulus from the calories out portion if applicable. However, this deficit should be moderate enough to stay full (with good food choices) but low enough to lose 1-2lbs per week. Remember that even in the most severe cases, where a huge weight loss is needed from a health perspective, a weight loss of 1lb per week would yield a 52lbs weight loss over a year! So, although 1lb per week seems low, these numbers are not insignificant with the right sort of adherence, and it's the 'adherence' that diets live and die by. We could set up something more aggressive that will yield much quicker results, but in almost all cases, these aggressive weight loss diets have a track record of slowing, failing and often reversing! Many subjects actually end up putting on weight in the long run and a sustained and slower approach generally yields better adherence levels, and therefore, much better results. [14]

The same would apply to someone who is vastly underweight, or who has a very low body fat percentage (either due to their body type or perhaps a deeper relationship with food). I would still stay on the conservative side of a calorie surplus, limiting it at around 500 kcals surplus and aiming for better adherence and building a better relationship with food in the long term. Gaining weight or fat too quickly could have a negative effect on adherence and mindset and may see subjects resisting a calorie surplus altogether.

Equally, if my goal was to get as strong as possible, and aesthetics were not considered, I would be setting up a much bigger calorie surplus, creating an optimal environment to build muscle and gain weight (especially for strength athletes like powerlifters or 'strongmen/women' where it's generally accepted that 'weight moves weight'), and added 'bulk' can act like scaffolding for lifting huge poundages. But even considering this, the health consequences of the fat gain potential of being in more than a 500 kcals surplus for an extended amount of time are something I would seriously ask you to consider. And even for strength athletes, there does seem to be a sweet spot, where having too high a fat percentage will actually have a detrimental effect on muscle growth potential, hormonal profile and, of course, on your joints and cardiovascular system. To that end, it will be interesting to monitor the evolving sport of Strongman and see how newer athlete's, like rising star Mitchell Hooper, progress over the next few years. He's recently revealed that he consumes around 5,500 calories per day, and whilst that may sound massive, it's nothing compared to most of the world's elite who aim to consume anything from 8,000 – 12,000 per day. Early indications seem to suggest that Mitchell Hooper's more conservative approach to nutrition and scientific approach to his training, is worth monitoring............he may well be onto something.

Lastly, if I was way off from my size and strength goal, a natural, body recomp or maingaining approach probably isn't going to cut it. I think back to being a skinny teenager, sitting at around 140 lbs at 16 and being around 205 lbs by the time I finished university. Of course, a lot of this was down to natural growth as I got older and developed, but I also constantly ate in a 500 + calorie surplus, and whilst I gained more fat than I would have wanted, it gave me the foundation to put on a huge amount of weight and be much nearer to a level of strength and muscle mass where I'd be happy to 'maingain' or 'recomp'. Whilst 'maingaining' might be the answer down the line, if you need to make significant strides as a natural bodybuilder, you may need an extended calorie surplus and bulking phase in your earlier years of lifting.

So, there are my thoughts on calorie set-up, as far as the maths is concerned, but how do we get there, what foods should we eat, how do we update the diet as we lose or gain weight and how do we navigate special occasions, boozy nights out and turn a 'diet' into a sustainable and fulfilling lifestyle?

Setting up your Macros

Calories may be King/Queen for simply gaining or losing weight, but when it comes to aesthetics, building muscle and creating a strong, lean physique, setting up your macronutrients is key. There are 3 macronutrients that make up our diets, and, for optimal results, we want to ensure we are getting specific percentages of our calories from each of these groups. So, whilst the food we consume will determine our 'calories in' portion, the type of macronutrients we consume will actually affect our 'calories out' portion and affect things like food volume (dictating how full we might feel) and hormonal profile, affecting our mood and potentially the ability for us to build muscle or lose fat. Having said that, It's still important we don't overdo this section and start the whole 'paralysis by analysis' argument, and the three main takeaways from this should be:

1. Include enough protein for growth, repair and to gain the benefit of the 'thermal effect of protein'.

2. Eat enough fat to sustain healthy hormonal levels, organ health and brain function.

3. Take your remaining calories from the 'energy-yielding macros' of fat and carbohydrates. Most evidence points towards the fact that it doesn't really matter whether you choose to prioritise fat or carbs in terms of body composition. In terms of food volume and satiation, fats do yield 9 kcals per 1g and carbs only 4 kcals per 1g, so you tend to get more volume of food from prioritising carbohydrates and it does seem to be 'most people's preference for providing energy – specifically for creating a 'pump' feeling in the gym and a 'full' look in your muscles. However, many people are also very fat-adapted when it comes to energy and a high-fat and low-carbohydrate approach is perfectly fine, if that is your preference.

From my own findings and having worked with hundreds of clients over the years, the diet approach that I have seen work for fat loss, time and time again, is the following Macro Split:

Protein – 30%

Carb – 45%

Fat – 25%

So, if we assume our same 200lbs male wants to set himself up in a 500 kcals deficit of 2500 kcals per day, we would be using the following macros equation:

Calories – 2500

Protein – 194g

Carbs – 280g

Fats – 67g

Now you could accelerate the fat loss potential further by upping the protein % by 10% and lowering carbs, to utilise the thermic effect of protein, increasing your calories out but keeping the calories in the same. But generally speaking, around 1g of protein per pound of body weight is more than enough and it leaves a good amount for the energy-yielding macros to feel full and be sustained. If you prefer a lower carb and higher fat diet, then you can play around with those percentages, but just remember that this will likely lead to a lower food volume and may affect your levels of feeling full – thus potentially opening the door to cheating on your diet and failing over the long term.

If I was setting up a surplus, I would use a slightly higher fat % as I'm less concerned about food volume (I'll be in a calorie surplus and should be satiated), and the added fat percentage should have a positive effect for hormonal profile, normal cell and organ function, and therefore, muscle-building potential. I would maintain the 30% of calories coming from protein and lose 5% from the carbs portion. For this, I would use the following calculation for the same 200 lbs male:

Calories – 3200 (200 kcals daily surplus)

Protein 30% - 240g

Carbs 40% - 320g

Fats 30% - 107g

Food types and timings

In theory, as long as you stay within your macronutrient and calorie parameters, food timing and food choice should only matter from an adherence perspective. If it was possible to hit all your macro and calorie numbers and eat one pizza per day – this is perfectly fine. Of course, in reality, this is probably not possible and would likely lead to cravings, cheating and failure. Equally, how many pizzas realistically have a macro profile of 30% protein, 45% carbs and 25% fats?... I'd say none! As bodybuilders we'd also want to utilise 'protein synthesis' more than once per day, so eating in a few separate sittings, would be optimal. So, outside the lab and back in the real world, food choices and timings can be crucial to adhering to a calorie and macronutrient-controlled diet.

The post-workout 'anabolic window'

Another muscle-building myth that seems to have been debunked in the last decade is the idea of a post-workout 'anabolic window'. Even now, there are plenty of people who still cite a magical 20-minute window, post-training, when you should guzzle protein shakes or race to the fridge for your chicken and rice. Many studies now point to this being largely irrelevant and as long as adequate protein is eaten during the day, eating protein immediately after training is not necessary[15]. The real things to focus on from a food timing perspective are that you are getting adequate calories to fuel your workouts in the hours leading up to training and that your overall daily protein is adequate for recovery, growth and repair of muscles. Whether you eat within 2 minutes or 2 hours of training seems to be highly irrelevant, especially if you've eaten an adequate amount of food/calories before training. Perhaps the only circumstance when I would look to eat sooner rather than later is if I was doing some kind of fasted training protocol (which is unnecessary for optimal results but might be something you choose for adherence purposes) and then I would ideally eat pretty quickly post-workout, perhaps within an hour or so, to make sure I had adequate calories and nutrition for protein synthesis to occur.

The other consideration is that eating protein (or any other foods) directly after training certainly won't have a negative effect, and for many, drinking a quick-hit protein shake is incredibly convenient. Having used a high intensity training method for many years now, I can also say that eating pretty quickly after sessions like FST-7 or other drop sets, giant sets or super set finishers can be vital. This is not from an 'anabolic window' perspective, but from a general wellness perspective. Being drained, depleted, nauseous or light-headed can be a by-product of these sessions, and a hit of protein and/or carbs is generally a quick way to feel a bit better.

High Fat vs High Carbs

As long as you're adhering to a plan, hitting your protein numbers and calorie numbers, most research points towards the fact that whether you eat high carb or high fat, or an even combo of both, it has very little impact on body composition[16].

I reviewed dozens of research papers and the most common results are that a low carb approach yields a quicker 'weight' loss in the first 3 months, compared to low fat. Note I said weight loss, and not fat loss. This is most likely down to the fact that restricting carbs immediately depletes glycogen and water stores. Research between 6-12 months, seems to show no statistical differences between a low fat vs low carb approach, and nearly all health markers stayed the same.

However, when deciding which approach might be for you, these are the things I would urge you to consider:

1. Most people seem to be naturally carb or fat 'adapted'. I don't think this is as much biological as it is psychological but I would recommend you go with your instinct in the first instance for adherence purposes. It's easier to adhere to food that you like, so you must bear that in mind. For me, I know that I love to eat potatoes, rice, fruits and pasta as my staple energy-yielding foods. People like my mum or sister could take or leave starchy carbs and instead crave fatty meats, nuts and cheeses. It would be more sensible for me to prioritise a carb-based diet but for my mum to prioritise a fat-based diet. Within the proper calorie parameters, no one approach is better than the other.

2. If you struggle with overeating and being hungry, it may be best to prioritise a carb-based approach in the first instance. A gram of fat yields 9 calories, compared to 4 calories for a gram of carbs, so you can simply eat higher volumes of sensible carb options, as opposed to fat options. If you pair this with leaner cuts of meat and

low-sugar vegetables, this drastically increases the sheer volume of food on the plate for less of a calorie hit.

3. Fats are essential for normal hormone function, organ and brain activity. You should never completely exclude fat from your diet so even with a carb-dominated approach, I would still have 15%-25% of your calories coming from fats. This is paramount for natural lifters who need optimal growth hormone and testosterone levels.

4. If you go low carb as a bodybuilder, then you have to accept that your muscles will not be as 'full' or 'pumped'. Lower carbs will mean less water weight and whilst you may achieve levels of leanness and dryness, due to the lack of muscle glycogen and water in the muscle, the muscle belly will probably not look as round or big.

So, leading on from point 4, we'd ideally love to be big and full but also dry and lean! Could carb and calorie cycling hold the key?

Carb and Calorie Cycling – the best of both worlds?

Very simply put, this is the idea that you cycle carbohydrate and/or calorie numbers on a daily or weekly basis. For example, a week may consist of two low-carb days, two high-carb days and three medium-carb days. The weekly total of calories and carbohydrates should still be the same to reach the goal of your plan, but instead of a consistent daily number of calories and carbs, these numbers go up and down during the week. An example of how you might programme this is shown below:

Normal (linear) diet plan would consist of:
3000 calories per day = 21000 calories per week.
300 g of carbs per day = 2100g per week.

A carb and calorie cycling approach may look like this:
We still want to hit 21000 calories for the week and 2100g of carbs, but we will cycle the calories and carbs, up and down, so some days are high, some low and some medium.

2 x Low days = 2600 kcals and 200g carbs

3 x Med days = 3000 kcals and 300g carbs

2 x High days = 3400 kcals and 400g carbs

Overall, we are still hitting 21000 calories and 2100g carbs per week, but we've manipulated the carbs and calories per day, so each day is slightly different. Here is why we might choose to do this and what the possible benefits and drawbacks are:

The Good

1. This could help with adherence as we can use the higher days to factor in events like birthday parties, meals out and takeaways, whilst borrowing calories from the days earlier or later in the week.

2. We can use a lower carb approach with bigger 'refeeds' during the week so muscles stay full and hydrated.

3. This could help us 'peak' for a particular event as we use low days for leanness and dryness and add in high days

for the glycogen compensation, making the muscles look fuller and bigger for a set day or event.

4. We could use the same approach to peak for strength or endurance, to load up on carbs and calories in and around your heavy lifting days, but to go lower on rest days when the body doesn't need as much fuelling. You could even set it up so you have lower carb and calorie 'steady-state cardio days' aimed at burning calories, and higher carb/calorie 'weights days' aimed at building muscle and strength.

5. From a mindset approach, this could help us to stay strict on calories, knowing there is the carrot of a weekend 'feed' or high-calorie day around the corner. Psychologically, we sometimes just need that reward or milestone in the back of our minds to push harder.

6. From a simple scientific perspective, this makes sense to me. Imagine your muscle is a water balloon and the water is muscle glycogen (how carbs are stored in the muscle). The balloon is being filled with water. If the water is too low, the balloon looks saggy and soft and deflated. If the balloon is filled near to the top, it is big, inflated and hard. If the water keeps being poured in, at some point, the water is going to start to spill out. When we take on too many calories and carbohydrates for our muscles and liver to store, this can start to 'spill' and will end up being stored as fat. So, we constantly want to keep the muscle somewhere from halfway full to fully full! We can incorporate low days to help increase fat-burning, and, as muscle glycogen gets towards depletion, we can increase carbs/calories to

start to fill the balloon back up. Before the balloon gets too full and starts to spill, we pull back again... very simple! But there are some drawbacks to this approach:

The Bad:

1. Some people don't do well with fluctuations in their diets, calories and carbs and prefer to be 'dialled in' to something more consistent.

2. For people who don't love the numbers, data and calorie/carb-counting, this approach is definitely harder to plan and track up front, making it easier to go wrong. If you find this element of dieting and training particularly dry or dull, then the extra planning to cycle carbs/calories is an unnecessary complication that might affect adherence.

3. If not well-planned, performance may suffer, especially if you're looking to peak for sports or gym sessions around your lower calorie/carb days. More emphasis will be placed on getting the nutrition timing correct.

4. Lower or 'no carb' days may not work for some people's mood. If you struggle mentally, you're far more likely to cheat and fall off the plan.

5. Equally, people have the tendency to overdo high-carb or calorie days, finding it tough to start and stop when they're given more leeway to eat a wider variety of foods.

So, like any diet, there are positives and negatives and the key lies in an individual's ability to adhere to a plan and hit their calorie, macro and training goals. The more this diet plan is in sync with their strengths, weaknesses, food choices and general enjoyment, the bigger chance they have at achieving adherence.

Again, let's not overanalyse and try to focus on the key dieting points that can help us to overcome food cravings and hunger.

1. Focus on lean quality protein that will make you feel full. For example, you can eat a higher food volume of chicken breast than sausages, because sausages are more calorie-dense, containing more carbohydrates and fats along with protein. 100g of chicken will likely be more satiating than 100g of sausages and for half the calories.

2. When it comes to sauces, try to pick low-sugar and low-fat options. Sauces are not satiating in themselves and wasting 200 kcals on mayonnaise vs 50 kcals on a low-sugar ketchup (for example) would be crazy.

3. Don't waste calories on drinks. There are so many drink options that are low-calorie or calorie-free. Water, squash, diet soda, types of tea and coffee are much better options than high-sugar or high-alcohol beverages. Drinking calories rarely makes you feel full.

4. Take time to understand your cravings and adapt to your food timings adequately. Most research suggests that skipping meals leads to overeating later on, and therefore, a higher net calorie surplus in the long run. However, this doesn't ring true for everyone. There are people who see no tangible benefit from eating breakfast; it doesn't seem to affect calories or cravings for the rest of the day, and therefore, a sort of 'intermittent' fasting

approach might be used to save calories for later in the day. On the whole, I would advocate the spacing out of meals and nutrients throughout the day, but not everyone is wired the same and some people are more adapted to eating bigger in the mornings or the evenings. It's all about adherence!

Diet options

There are tons of different diet options to choose from that may help with adherence, enjoying your food and satisfying various moralistic or religious beliefs, as well as helping with things like allergic responses to food, health and well-being. No one diet is a magic bullet for health, and no one diet, in itself, will guarantee fat loss or muscle gain. These things lie in the calorie, macronutrient and micronutrient profile of the foods that you are choosing to eat and are mainly based on the volumes of such foods that you're consuming vs the amount of energy you are expending. Can you lose weight and be healthy on a vegan diet? Yes, of course. Can you also gain huge amounts of fat and be incredibly unhealthy on a vegan diet? Yes, most definitely. No one diet is particularly good or bad; instead, you have to look within that diet and examine the small print.

Diet Type vs Calories (weight, health and adherence)

Since I started paying attention to the complex world of dieting two decades ago, it feels like things have gone full circle when it comes to calories. Calories in vs calories out was the accepted method of weight control and, whilst neither the laws of thermodynamics nor the mechanisms for weight loss and gain were fully understood by the general public, the idea that we should eat a bit less and move a bit more seemed a sound approach to losing a bit of fat. Fast forward 20 years and things have certainly got a bit blurred. A plethora of diet alternatives is now on offer, all claiming to be the magic bullet for fat loss, and some of them rejecting the idea that calories make any difference to weight loss or gain whatsoever. 'Experts' from these different fields will tell us the different reasons that their diet is best. Intermittent fasting, low carb, low fat, carnivore, Atkins, Paleo, Dukan, Microbiome diets, Low GI diets, veggie or vegan all have their take on effective dieting for optimal weight management and health. Over the years, I have dabbled in most of these diets and still employ some of the strategies from diets like intermittent fasting and Low GI to contribute towards my diet goals at any given time.

I don't have anything overly negative to say about these differing diet options in themselves, but if you are mainly dieting to lose weight, and the vast majority are, then, no matter which of these diets you choose to follow, the equation of calories in vs calories out (CICO) will determine if you lose or gain actual weight. If you have a maintenance calorie level of 3,000 and you choose to do intermittent fasting, you complete your 16-hour fast but then proceed to eat 4000 calories in your 8-hour window, you will still put on weight. It doesn't matter that you went 16 hours without eating, because you have just eaten 1000 calories over your caloric limit. In itself, the diet type does not dictate weight loss or gain. No matter what diet you choose, the equation of CICO will still dictate weight loss.

A study published in the Oxford Academic, Journal of Public Health, named 'Weight Change During and After Ramadan Fasting', supports this claim[17]. Over 200 observers of Ramadan were studied, and during this period, the average weight loss was that of 0.84 kilos. Whilst it's a very modest total over a 4 week period, it does mean that the majority of people lost some weight. However, it was also reported that 38% of participants either lost no weight or put weight on. With the severity of the Ramadan fast (an average of 16 hours completely fasting, and much of the night time hours spent sleeping, rather than eating) you would have expected results to be a little more extreme, if fasting, in itself, was a magic bullet to weight loss. What these results suggest, is that the people who lost weight happened get themselves in a calorie deficit and the one's who put weight on, still found a way to pack enough surplus calories into their feeding hours, thus experiencing a net gain in body weight.

A caveat to my above statement: Just because a diet works from a CICO equation for weight loss, doesn't make it healthy. You could eat a pizza and chips once a day, be in a calorie deficit for the day and lose weight but be woefully short of your ideal protein amount and be lacking numerous micronutrients, fibre, vitamins and minerals. So, whilst you might be losing weight, your physical and mental health might be suffering and you'd likely perform horribly in an array of physical activities. On the other hand, some of the diets above, if done correctly, might be far more optimal from a health perspective, especially if you have certain health, gut, blood, allergen or micronutrient deficiencies, and whilst you may lose no weight on a specific diet, the food choices could make you feel much better and give you a full spectrum of healthy fats, vitamins, minerals and micronutrients. So, whilst CICO dictates weight, it doesn't guarantee optimal health, hormonal function or overall well-being.

The Carnivore diet is an example of this in action. Eating meat at the expense of all other food types may well have a benefit for weight loss, but it's also highly likely to leave you short of a variety of vitamins and minerals and the long-term effect on organ health is still unknown. It's also another diet that has attracted a 'cult' following, with many of it's fanatics stating that 'calories do not matter' when it comes to the carnivore diet. So to repeat myself (again), calories absolutely do matter, whichever diet you choose. The carnivore diet will likely be incredibly forgiving on the CICO equation because of the thermic effect of protein. If you are solely consuming meat, then the 'calories out' portion of the equation, is going to be far increased from the huge amounts of protein consumed. Whilst the Carnivore diet has had some positive reports for people with autoimmune diseases, for the general population, it's probably far from optimal. Limited food choices, the expense of meat and the ability to get enough 'energy' from the diet, are all hurdles that mean the Carnivore diet is going to be tough to follow, from a long-term adherence perspective.

Now, with so much choice out there, what should you do? Which diet is best for you? It's a very personal choice and one that needs to be made with an honest appraisal of your own relationship with food, mindset and preferences. For some people, intermittent fasting works great, especially if they prioritise a natural eating window. For example, some people are just not hungry at breakfast, and a fast through the night that continues to 1 pm isn't all that hard. But the trouble can start at 1 pm when excess hunger hormones lead the individual to overeat and still gain weight. You have to be honest with the realities of this approach and if you are someone who is prone to giving into cravings after long periods without eating, then a fasting approach might not be suited to you. Eating small and often, controlling cravings and keeping blood sugar stable throughout the day could be a better plan for these people.

Intermittent Fasting – how to set up an example protocol

Of all the current dieting trends, intermittent fasting is the one that's soared in popularity of late. Whilst I don't believe it's optimal for muscle gain or bodybuilding, and it's not a necessity for fat or weight loss, there are some tangible benefits that intermittent fasting enthusiasts and clinical researchers report[18]. Some speak of waking up to mental clarity and the 'reduced brain fog' that they often associate with periods of eating and processing meals, and some of the research would indicate that periods of fasting could lead to greater cellular repair, an increase in growth hormone and beneficial changes in gene expression related to longevity and disease protection. If you can make the CICO equation work for you, it may also be a handy tool in aiding fat or weight loss.

If you want to try the potential health benefits of intermittent fasting, but also want to lose some weight along the way, my advice would be to still start with the CICO equation and work backwards from there. In fact, if you want to do any of these diets with your weight in mind, you should always have an eye on the CICO equation.

So, if I was setting up an intermittent fasting diet plan, this is what I would do:

Keeping our 200lbs male as the example:

200 x 15 = 3000 calories for maintenance.

I want to lose around 1 pound per week so I'll put myself in a 500-calorie deficit for the day.

3000 – 500 = 2500 calories.

Of these 2500 calories, I want to get 40% from carbs, 35% from protein and 25% from fats =

Carbs – 250g

Pro – 220g

Fats – 69g

Final calories and macros:

2500 calories

Carb – 250g

Pro – 220g

Fats – 69g

Meal timings and considerations:
- I will set myself up on the standard 16-hour fast and 8-hour feeding window.
- Because I am weight training and trying to preserve as much muscle and strength as possible in a 'cut', I don't

want to train completely fasted. Therefore, I will aim to fast from 8 pm – 12 pm and eat between 12 pm and 8 pm. I will eat my first meal at noon and then train somewhere between 1 pm and 8 pm rather than pre-12 pm with no food. If I want to accelerate weight loss, I may choose to include some cardio along the way but will have to keep an eye on muscle mass and make sure this isn't promoting any lean mass loss whilst I'm eating in a deficit.

Food types:
- Given I am in a deficit, I have a big appetite and I am fasting for long periods, it's vital that I prioritise low-calorie, high-volume foods. A range of lean meats, grains, vegetables, low-fat yoghurts and berries will give me a much better chance of feeling full and satisfied, and therefore, adhering to the diet vs a diet that includes fast food and high-fat options, which are comparatively lower in volume and higher in calories. If you don't believe me, look at the amount of cheese you could eat for 500 calories vs a plate of chicken breast, rice and broccoli.

To help with fasting:
- I would prioritise a decent amount of liquids that yield little to no calories but may contribute to feeling full and satisfied. Water, squash/cordial, black coffee, tea and diet soda are all decent options to get you through that last couple of hours of fasting.

How I **actually** incorporate intermittent fasting into my diet:

- Whilst I don't run a strict intermittent fasting protocol, I do use the technique on occasions, to offset surplus calories when I know there is a big meal coming. If I know that I am going out for a big dinner or lunch, I will often choose to switch to an intermittent fasting protocol for that day. Missing breakfast and or lunch can buy me an extra 500 to 1000 calories that will be used during an 'eating window' and is a decent tool to help me stay within my calorie and macronutrient range. There's nothing magical about the process and I don't do it for long enough to feel the potential of the other health-related benefits, but I do find the odd fast to be mentally stimulating and a real battle of staving off cravings and hunger. If I'm trying to be really strict and ensure I don't overeat, I will make sure I break the fast with a pure protein snack, like biltong, chicken or a shake. Eating protein with plenty of fluids first will curb cravings for when I eat the main meal. You just have to make sure you stay within your calorie limit for that day and don't give in to growing hunger, which might see you binge for 8 hours and go way above maintenance.

Giving 'Experts' the Benefit of the Doubt

I've seen a lot of nutritional experts and sports scientists 'called out' for doubting the efficacy of the CICO equation. To give these people the benefit of the doubt, I don't think that truly qualified and clued-up individuals actually doubt that the CICO equation is what dictates weight loss or gain. I think what they are questioning is the efficacy of simply focusing all of your dieting attention on CICO at the expense of other factors like food choices, eating windows, macronutrient splits and micronutrient content. Some people just don't do well counting calories, having to constantly look at the numbers and record every bit of data, and focusing on specific eating windows or having specific foods or food groups that are included or excluded, works better from an adherence perspective. You would be taking a slight stab in the dark to start with, but you could easily diet in this way and use the scales, the mirror and how you feel to know if you're on the right track. If you're looking to lose weight and the scales have moved the right way after week one, you know you're doing something right. You don't necessarily need the CICO equation to confirm that for you. If the scales haven't moved the right way, you might have to cut down on your portions, train more or swap a fat/carb portion for an extra helping of protein.

Food Snobbery and nonsense

So, by now, we've identified that the equation of CICO is paramount for weight loss, macronutrients are essential for bodybuilding and aesthetics, and food choices can determine micronutrient content, and therefore, help to dictate whether a diet is healthy and optimal for performance. Given all of these factors, we'd be best placed to move away from thinking of foods as good or bad, and instead, take a holistic view of the whole diet. For example, whilst a big, cooked breakfast might contain a huge amount of your daily calories and a substantial amount of your daily fat intake, the point where it becomes 'unhealthy' can only be measured against the foods that you've chosen to eat for the rest of that day, week or month, and the exercise that makes up your CICO equation. If this meal has tipped you into a calorie surplus, led to you going way over your fat intake for the day and left you woefully short of protein and carbohydrates, then yes, this has been an unhealthy choice. However, if the rest of your day has included an adequate amount of exercise to balance the CICO equation and your other meals have included low-fat food choices and prioritised a selection of fruits and vegetables to satisfy macronutrient and micronutrient balance, then the cooked breakfast has been much less of a problem. I see this all the time, where specific food choices are thrown under the bus for being 'unhealthy', processed, or lambasted for their low nutrient content. Similarly, this often tells half the story, and the very same people who are prioritising organic, natural, grass-fed, locally sourced produce, are often getting it wrong from a macronutrient and CICO perspective. Whilst these choices might lead to improved micronutrient content and can garner other health benefits, we've also examined that the simple act of being overweight can have a catastrophic effect on long-term health and organ function and make you much more susceptible to heart disease, diabetes and a variety of other issues. So, when I see that these people are often demonising varieties of foods like bread, cow's milk, cereals, protein shakes, pasta or breakfast bars, I don't completely disagree with their sentiment, but they're often missing the point. Yes, I know that avocado, oily fish, organic eggs, nuts and pulses on the whole provide way more health benefits than the aforementioned foods, **but the problem lies in this**:

Person A wants to lose weight – they ate their cereal, with cow's milk, had a ham sandwich for lunch, a protein shake after training and some pasta with a tomato sauce, chicken and vegetables for dinner. Whilst the diet could have contained more protein and a better mix of micronutrients, they ended the day by eating around 2,200 calories, a 300-calorie deficit for the day.

Person B wants to lose weight – they ate their avocado on rye bread, with 2 free-range eggs and a probiotic yoghurt. They had fresh salmon for lunch, with some quinoa and a grass-fed steak with potatoes and vegetables for dinner. The diet contained a ton of good vitamins, minerals and fats but it contained 3000 calories, a 300-calorie surplus for the day.

Now, I'm taking some artistic licence here, but this example is prevalent in many of the people I've worked with over the years, and whilst Person A could be making changes to their diet for health and longevity, it's the super trendy, health-conscious Person B who's trying to do all the right things but getting the basics wrong. Even taking into account the extra thermic effect of protein, they're still in a calorie surplus, they're still going to gain weight and no matter how natural, organic or 'super' their food choices are, if they're in a consistent calorie surplus, they will gain weight week after week, month after month and year after year. In an ideal world, we'd want to be Person C, who understands the importance of healthier food choices for micronutrient content, but also takes a more holistic overview of their diet, picks foods that will help them to stay within a calorie goal and will contribute towards a sensible macronutrient split.

By all means, if you can afford the most organic, natural, fresh, local produce, then go for it, but don't think this is a magic bullet for health, fat loss or body composition.

All Roads Lead to Balance

Whether it's strength, cardio health, fat loss or many other things both in and outside the world of fitness, most roads seem to lead back to 'balance', and in my opinion, diets are no different. Diets that exclude whole food groups, prioritise extreme eating windows or see you eating in a huge calorie deficit or surplus, generally have a shelf life. I would always advocate using a diet that is well balanced from a macronutrient perspective, offers a wide selection of food choices and takes a conservative approach to calorie cutting or addition.

Whether you're in a cutting or bulking phase, things shouldn't need to change drastically. Foods and whole meals can often be kept very similar but by using slightly different ingredients, leaner cuts of meat and reduced fat or sugar versions of the same products, you can get very different results. As an example, here are two chilli con carne recipes from different parts of my prep. One I've used whilst bulking (calorie surplus), one I've used whilst cutting (calorie deficit). The thing to note here is that I've done nothing other than change a couple of ingredients. The food volume on the plate is still near identical, and therefore the ability to be full and satisfied is not compromised. Without using a specific 'eating windows' like you would for intermittent fasting, or cutting out whole food groups, like you would for keto, carnivore, or vegan diets, I've managed to cut out 294 calories from my day, using an incredibly simple hack. This could be the difference between a small calorie deficit or a small calorie surplus.

Whilst I don't want to 'demonise' any specific diet type, the diets that always seem to work, in the long term, seem to come back to using something that is incredibly simple, repeatable and balanced.

Bulking version of chilli con carne.

- 12% fat beef mince – 342 kcals
- Peppers – 45 kcals
- Onion – 28 kcals
- Kidney Beans – 55 kcals
- Sweetcorn – 52 kcals
- Tinned tomatoes – 60 kcals
- Chilli con carne seasoning mix – 90 kcals
- Cheddar cheese – 130 kcals
- Guacamole and sour cream – 100 kcals
- Basmati rice – 338 kcals

Total calories – 1,240

Cutting version of chilli con carne.

- 5% fat beef mince – 248 kcals
- Peppers – 45 kcals
- Onion – 28 kcals
- Reduced sugar tinned tomatoes – 40 kcals
- Kidney Beans – 55 kcals
- Chilli con carne seasoning mix – 90 kcals
- Sweetcorn – 52 kcals

- Tomato Salsa and low-fat yogurt – 50 kcals
- Basmati Rice – 338 kcals

Total Calories – 946

I could use remarkably similar examples for a variety of meals that I tweak very slightly, depending on my desired outcome. 4 whole eggs on toast can be swapped for 2 whole eggs and 3 egg whites, by swapping out chicken thighs for chicken breast, I can save 150 kcals from my Jerk Chicken, 0% fat yogurt and berries, being used instead of 5% fat yogurt and banana............the list could go on and on, but the big thing is that portion sizes, food volume and therefore satisfaction and adherence, are not overly compromised. And if you are dead set on using an approach like intermittent fasting, you can still use all these considerations, with in an eating window to make sure you are hitting your calorie and macronutrient goals.

Tackling Obesity – Tough Love or Kindness and Compassion

If you explore the data, there is no doubt that being severely overweight, in the obese or morbidly obese category, has a catastrophic effect on long term health. Despite the odd movement or sentiment to the contrary, numerous long term studies link obesity with a vastly increased risk of heart disease, cancer, and general, all-cause mortality. Given the facts, it's perfectly normal that we would worry about loved ones, friends, family and even some of our clients, if we work in the world of health and fitness. Anyone with half a brain will understand that eating yourself to a morbidly obese level, will be intertwined in a number of complex, mental considerations. So how should we tackle the issue of obesity, in an individual that clearly wants to change their habits, but doesn't know where to start? There's a school of thought that would suggest a 'tough love' approach. After all, most of us are armed with the facts, and in almost all cases, simply living a lifestyle that puts us in a small, daily, calorie deficit (eat less / move more) would see even the most obese of individuals, return to a 'healthier' body fat percentage in just a couple of years. I've seen various people who are fed up with a 'soft' approach and call for brutal honesty, advocating what's become known as 'fat shaming', calling out harsh truths about the health woes of obese individuals. The problem is though, forgoing my belief that this approach is just damn right cruel, this almost never actually works. For the few individuals that might be jolted into some sort of 'wakeup call' and respond well, the vast majority of morbidly obese individuals will react horribly to simply being told they are fat, overweight and they will die if they don't sort it out immediately. Like so many different subjects, the way that you approach and convey a message, is as important as the message itself. Your language, your tone, and your ability to exercise empathy and understanding, is absolutely crucial. And this isn't unique to the obesity epidemic. I've worked in the Projects industry for years and I've spoken to some incredibly talented and technical Project Managers. But what sets aside average from Great, is the ability to empathise, to bring people on the journey and to convey a message with compassion and understanding. And this is where so many of these channels and influencers, lose me. I often agree with their point of view, I often concur with the science, but if the language is instantly negative, hurtful, or aggressive, and the individual cares more about winning an argument or hurting the feelings of the 'apposing side' they've instantly lost 50% of the audience, who might feel stupid, offended or upset. 'Fat Shaming' just doesn't seem to be effective for an individual losing weight. What does seem to be effective is to start from a position of empathy, try and understand why this person might have got into this situation and start to slowly educate, putting subtle lifestyle changes into place, which will arm this person with the knowledge and know how, to start their weight loss journey. Try to work backwards, look at approaches or triggers that have halted progress in the past. Many people hate the scale. You don't have to use it. Many people hate counting calories, instead look at implementing lifestyle changes, educating them about making healthier food choices and different ways to burn more calories through exercise. Simply put, the vast majority of morbidly obese people, know that they are morbidly obese. They hate being that way and they're often stuck in a cycle, that's stopping them from getting well. Whether the factors around this are educational, economic, or mental health related, when an individual is reminded, they are fat, what the vast majority will hear is, you're disgusting, you're worthless, you're pathetic. Of course, a certain amount of honesty is needed but this is always present in education, which will show, in no uncertain terms, that being vastly overweight is hugely detrimental to health, wellbeing and longevity. And before I'm being accused of being soft or ultra-fluffy, I only suggest that we start from a beginning of love and compassion. It doesn't mean that all roads should finish there. I'm not suggesting that love, compassion or empathy alone, will make any dents into the morbid obesity of thousands of people worldwide, only that it's a great place to start. In fact, I think it's a great place to start for dozens of hot topics worldwide. Too often we see people from the far right or the far left, using harsh language, scare tactics, false data, and passive aggression, to use these 'hot topics' as tools to virtue signal, score political points or make the other side look stupid. Any time, we get these extreme views, it makes sensible people, who generally sit somewhere in the middle, with a healthy scepticism and large dose of common sense, retract from any debate, with an apathetic view that 'we'll leave it to the extremists on both sides to argue' rather than 'we'll listen to both sides, move the conversation forward and see if we can understand differing points of view'. Whether we're talking about obesity, identity politics, global warming, religious debate or a hundred different subjects and matters, just shouting the loudest, being passively cruel or dogmatic, will never serve the individual or the cause well. Unfortunately, Obesity has been politically hijacked. One side calling for 'tough love' and brutal honesty, taxes on fat people, higher travel ticket prices based on a person's weight, and a dramatic increase in vicious, online trolling. Whilst people from the other side claiming there to be no correlation between obesity and poor health, advocating for free extra seats for obese passengers and an ultimate 'live and let live' philosophy, where obesity is accepted and even encouraged. Ultimately, tough love doesn't seem to work and there's little merit in being deliberately cruel to someone who genuinely wants to lose weight. Equally, some people don't want to lose weight and may have accepted that the life they live will be full of enjoyment, even if it's not as long a life as they could have. There's something to be said for living a fulfilled and happy 60 years, compared to a more sanitised, watered down 80 years. As long as that person's mental health is good, what they choose their fat percentage to be, is largely inconsequential. If that's a cognizant choice then that's fine, as long as people are armed with the facts and the data around obesity. If that person gets into their 60's, they can't be shocked with the likelihood of health issues like heart disease, cancer, diabetes and the fact that their quality of life will potentially deteriorate very quickly.

Supplementation – the good, the bad and the unproven

Supplements are another minefield of sensationalist claims, false promises and unnecessary scaremongering. There are literally thousands of pre-workout, peri-workout, intra-workout and post-workout nutritional supplements, pills that promise to optimise your hormonal profile, kickstart metabolism and 'melt fat away'. You've probably guessed by now by the tone of this book that my apathy and scepticism extend well into the supplement market as, perhaps, the most charlatan area of all health and fitness. I'm not going to dwell for pages and pages on this subject because there are plenty of good YouTube channels and review websites that help to dismantle ineffective supplements and underdosed ingredients, and we simply don't have the time here to dive into a deep analysis of individual products, but I can say that as a general statement, the world of fitness, performance and health supplements seems poorly regulated and badly understood. Here is my take on some of the supplements that are in mainstream use and my experience with using them:

1. **Whey Protein**[19]. One of the most widely used and researched products for muscle and fitness and one of the most unnecessarily scrutinised and demonised supplements out there. I've heard a lot of nonsense about whey protein over the years, and even recently, I watched a video where it was claimed that whey is highly processed and not real food, and is, therefore, bad for you, as it stays in your system for over three years and will make you fat rather than muscular. Firstly, whey protein is processed, but it is real food. It's made during the process of making cheese (think little Miss Muffet, curds and whey). One of the biggest myths in the diet industry is that anything that's processed is bad for you, which, in itself, just isn't true. Yes, during many food processes, manufacturers might damage the nutritional integrity of a food or add fat, sugar and surplus calories to a product, but this is not always the case and is often no different to someone cooking at home, using a microwave at high temperatures, and adding a variety of seasonings, sugar, salt, fat or other ingredients to thicken sauces, soups and desserts. Secondly, whey protein is incredibly convenient and by far the easiest way to get a quick 40g of protein into your system if you are on the go, travelling or working and don't have the time or ingredients to make a full meal. Whey Protein is not a necessity if you are able to eat your daily protein

allowance in pure food, but this isn't always realistic for everyone and I know that on the days I am working away and going from the gym to the train station, it is a convenient way to get my protein in. Thirdly, it had been found in many studies that whey protein is the most 'bioavailable' source of protein, even compared to eggs and all meat varieties. This basically measures how 'useable' the protein source is in the body and it's found that whey protein delivers the most 'bang for your buck' per gram of protein from any tested food source. Finally, it's a great option for cutting as well as bulking. It's a fallacy that whey protein 'makes you fat'. Eating in too big a calorie surplus for an extended period makes you fat. If you eat in a calorie deficit and include whey protein in your diet, you will lose weight. Similarly, if you eat in a surplus and include whey, you will gain weight. Whey protein is not a necessity; if you can hit your protein numbers with other protein sources, then you don't need whey protein. But if you are struggling to hit daily protein, if you're a busy individual who might benefit from the convenience of a shake vs making another meal or you're perhaps on a high protein diet and you're struggling for food options that are high in protein but comparatively low in fat and carbs, this could be a great option for you. On a personal note, I use whey protein most days, sometimes for a post-workout shake if I'm on the go and often added to a natural yoghurt for taste. If I can get an extra 40g – 50g of protein from a couple of scoops, it tends to make hitting my macros that much easier for the day. On days when I'm less busy and have more time to prepare whole meals, I may not use it at all. Oh, and Whey Protein does NOT stay in your system for 3 years! It's incredibly fast acting and is absorbed and used in a 90-minute to 3-hour window.

2. **Creatine Monohydrate**[20]. Another one of the most researched and talked about supplements in the industry, Creatine is an organic compound that facilitates the recycling of Adenosine Triphosphate (ATP). You can think of ATP as the energy that drives muscle contractions, so recycling it quicker means we should be able to lift heavier weights, for more reps, more efficiently. It seems to have taken a while to get to this point, but I don't see many experts doubting the safety or efficacy of creatine these days. A few of the myths surrounding creatine included kidney damage, water retention and weight gain. Studies now point to the fact that in people with healthy kidneys, there are no short or long-term health considerations when taking creatine monohydrate at the recommended dose of 5g per day. And whilst it's true that creatine does cause water retention, this extra water is drawn into and stored in the muscle cell. If anything, this aids aesthetics, causing the muscle to look larger and rounder than before. As well as the obvious strength gain from simply building creatine stores, it's this extra hydration of muscle cells that may also contribute to the performance of the muscle. Put simply, a hydrated cell just works that much better than a dehydrated one. In my experience, those who are attributing creatine to

excess water or fat gain, are doing so whilst on a 'bulking' diet. In reality, these individuals are simply overeating, consuming huge amounts of calories that lead to fat gain and foods high in carbohydrates that lead to more water retention. There may also be the added likelihood that during a 'bulk' phase (especially a 'dirty bulk'), individuals are generally making food choices that might cause inflammation and lead to water retention. In my experience, people in a bulk phase tend to eat more fast foods, drink more alcohol and generally binge on calorific foods. We have to be careful in the cause that we are correlating to the outcome, and if you've had 6 pints of lager and a kebab the night before, it's unlikely that 'the creatine did it'.

There are also studies to suggest that creatine improves cognitive function and concentration as well as athletic performance. I've personally taken a very simple and inexpensive form of creatine monohydrate for well over a decade now. If I do have periods of coming off, most notably during lockdown when supply chains were struggling, I genuinely lose around 5% of strength and my muscles look flatter in comparison. I can't say I have noticed any specific cognitive changes but that's a pretty hard thing to measure. So, if strength, size, lean mass or general athletic performance is your goal, I would absolutely advocate the use of creatine monohydrate. There are also suggestions that research is pointing towards the efficacy of creatine monohydrate use for a much wider group of people outside of fitness or sport. I haven't dug deep enough into the research but if creatine is that safe, and improves strength, performance and mental cognition, it may well be a worthwhile supplement for the general population.

3. **Legal Fat Burners**. Many supplement companies sell a 'fat burner' product. Whilst I'll admit these are sometimes effective for fat loss, it's rarely for the reasons that you think. Most people seem to believe in a pill or set of ingredients that literally help to target 'stubborn fat' or 'melt fat away', as these are strap lines that are often used in various marketing campaigns. The truth is that the vast majority of these pills contain varying ingredients that contribute nothing more than caffeine to the pill. In return, this caffeine can help to give you focus and perceived energy, if taken pre-workout, may contribute to a slight and fleeting rise in metabolism through increased heart rate or body temperature, and may contribute to the suppression of appetite through feeling slightly nauseous or jittery. So, whilst these effects may aid weight loss, there is nothing magic about the pills themselves that will make you lose weight. For example, if you eat the same foods and do the same exercise, with or without the pills, you'll lose the same amount of weight. The efficacy of the pills will only play a part as a potential pre-workout aid or to make you eat less if the effects of the caffeine make you feel nauseous and jittery. It's hardly the dream you were sold on the bottle. In my opinion, there are better, more specific and cheaper pre-workout supplements out there, ones that may contain other efficacious ingredients that might help fuel a workout or facilitate a 'pump' better than

fat-burning pills. I also don't see the ability to suppress appetite through feelings of nausea as a healthy or sustainable factor for fat loss. Another ingredient that seems to be added to fat burners is L-Carnitine, an amino acid involved in the transport of fatty acid for metabolism, but most of us are not deficient in carnitine as it's present in meat, fish and dairy, and even those wishing to supplement it could do so outside of an expensive 'fat-burning pill'. The problem with the other usual suspects such as Yohimbe, Guar Gum, Capsicum or Raspberry Ketones is that there is comparatively little research into their effectiveness for fat loss. Even if some of these ingredients have been researched and are shown to have positive effects in some areas, the actual effect they have on someone to specifically burn fat is very limited. On the whole, I don't view fat burners as a necessary supplement for weight loss but if you do want to take them, I see their main efficacy as being taken pre-workout as a caffeine boost to aid your session. If you are doing this, I would look to train in the mornings. One fat-burning pill I looked into recommended taking 3 pills in one serving. Each pill contained 80mg of caffeine, so a 240mg hit of caffeine would be like drinking 3-4 cups of coffee in one hit. Not ideal if you train in the evening or if you take them on a non-training day. For someone who is not undertaking physical activity, it's likely that this hit of caffeine may result in feelings of nervousness, restlessness and anxiety. It would be like taking a strong pre-workout and then sitting at home or in the office. Not very pleasant.

4. **BCAA** – Branched Chain Amino Acids are made up of three of the nine essential amino acids and are lorded as the three most important amino acids for Protein Synthesis. Made up from Leucine, Valine and Isoleucine, BCAA claim to speed up and increase muscle protein synthesis and, therefore, lead to a greater potential for muscle gain. Given this statement, you would think that BCAA would be the perfect supplement to take post-workout and increase your potential to make lean muscle gains, but most recent literature points in a different direction[21]. Adding BCAA alone, in the absence of the other essential amino acids, doesn't actually contribute towards protein synthesis at all since we need all amino acids (a complete protein) to be present to elicit protein synthesis. Therefore, BCAA can only be useful if they are added to a complete protein, like protein powder. But again, topping up the grams of Leucine, Isoleucine and Valine don't seem to add to protein synthesis potential, in most of the studies conducted, and given that most individuals are already drinking protein powders, this extra expense to add 5gs of BCAA to 40g of quality protein seems pointless and expensive. If you are going to go down this road, you're better off getting EAAs (the 9 essential amino acids) but even then, if you're eating enough protein in the day, they're largely redundant. Some studies do point towards BCAAs reducing muscle soreness in the 12 to 36 hours post-training, but these don't seem to be conclusive enough to be spending an extra £20/£40 per month on. If you follow most of the good dietary advice for bodybuilding and athletic

performance, where you should be eating 0.8g to 1.2g of protein per one pound of bodyweight, you're already eating more than enough BCAAs from a variety of complete protein sources.

Body weight set points and the 'dual intervention theory'

Set Point theory, when in relation to human body weight, suggests that each individual has a 'set point' of weight or body fat that he or she will feel comfortable with[22]. If we get above this point, certain automatic regulations will occur that will aim to bring the weight and body fat percentage down in an individual. These regulations include the increase in NEAT (non-exercise activity thermogenesis), the decrease or increase in certain hunger-inhibiting hormones (more leptin produced and less ghrelin produced), and therefore, the rise in your basal metabolic rate, as your body aims to burn fat and return to a 'comfortable' set point. Similarly, getting below your set point, your body will naturally look to increase back towards your set point in the same way. Sleeping may become harder as the brain is constantly urging you to stay awake and look for food, your NEAT will be vastly reduced, and you may even notice that you blink less, find it hard to maintain a normal conversation and just fidget and move much less frequently. This time, your body will produce more ghrelin and less leptin in a bid to make you feel hungry and your BMR will decrease, aiming to put you in a sort of hibernation mode where you burn as few calories as possible. The more we move away from the 'set point', the more extreme these regulations become and the harder it is to sustain a particular diet or plan. It makes perfect sense and would help explain why certain individuals can stay 'naturally' lean with ease, and why certain people seem to really struggle. Our personal genetics are dictating our set point, and our set point is determining how easy it is, mentally and physically, to be a certain level of lean or muscular. I like the theory, but there is another theory that takes this a step further, and once understood in relation to your own body, I think it can provide an excellent basis for diet plans, goals and well-being. This is called the 'Dual Intervention Point Model'.

The Dual Intervention Point Model and applying it to your own training, diet plans and goals

Rather than a single set point, this model suggests that we have an upper set point and a lower set point of body weight and fat percentage that the body, and brain, will feel 'comfortable' with[23]. Like most things, these set points are largely driven by genetics and likely formed by evolutionary factors, namely that too low a body weight would have meant starvation, and too high a body weight would have meant risking being too slow to escape a predator, or too unfit to keep up with your group. The theory suggests that all individuals have slightly varying set points and getting too far above or below your specific set point will likely be incredibly uncomfortable for the mentality of the individual as the brain encourages the body to return to an 'acceptable' body weight range. So how should we use this in our own training? It's clearly not an exact science unless we have a range of lab equipment, but after we've dieted a few times, we can actually build a reasonably clear picture of what

our set points might be. I know myself that as I push towards
the 16 stone mark (224 lbs), I just don't feel good. My appetite
is vastly reduced, I feel sluggish and slow and my brain feels
'foggy'. My strength even starts to plateau and as I look at
my logbook, most of my best lifts have actually occurred at a
lower body weight nearer 15 stone or 210 lbs. This is probably
due to my lack of motivation and mindset and it's potentially
my body's way of saying 'we don't want to get any bigger, so
stop lifting heavy weights, eat a bit less and do some cardio'.
Equally, I don't feel particularly comfortable as I start to get
below 13.5 stone (189 lbs) and the last weeks of a show prep do
become increasingly uncomfortable to mentally and physically
complete. So, having visited these weights a number of times
over the years, I can put my low point around the 190 lbs
mark and my high point at around 215 lbs. Knowing that, if
I have a specific competition or show, I should be able to get
to 190lbs with little worry but I'll need to mentally prepare
myself for a nasty finish as I generally look to get to around
180lbs to compete. According to 'dual intervention theory',
those last 10lbs will be much harder than the 30lbs before…
and I would say that's absolutely accurate. So, if I don't need
to compete and get 'stage lean', I don't tend to diet to below
my 'low set point' and would aim to get to around the 190lbs
mark, then maintain this for a short period before deciding the
next dietary goal. Similarly, if I'm looking to build muscle and
enter a 'bulk' phase, I don't see the mileage in going beyond
the 215lbs mark. The other alternative is to find a true middle
ground and look at 'maingaining' within this sort of range. If
you find a real 'sweet spot', where you can get the energy to
fuel great workouts and mental cognition but not overdo the

calories to gain surplus fat, this can be a brilliant way to stay in good shape year-round without the extreme of a cut or bulk. So, to set up a cut, bulk or maintenance phase using your set points, you need to:

Find your low and high set points through some trial and error. This may take some time but most of us who have experimented with different diets over the years have some idea of how we feel, look and perform at various weights. I will use myself as an example of how we can set this up:

Set point ranges from 190 lbs – 215 lbs.

Cutting diet – aim for a slow cut, decreasing calories every week or two, aiming to lose around a pound of body weight per week until I reach 190 lbs as a cut-off point.

Bulking diet - aim for a slow build, increasing calories every week or two, aiming to gain around half a pound of body weight per week until I reach 215 lbs as a cut-off point.

Maintenance – Pick a middle sweet spot of 202 lbs. Aim to settle at around 202 lbs, living 200kcals either side of your 'maintenance calories' depending on how you're feeling that week. For example, depending on whether you're feeling full, flat, tired, big or small, you can set yourself up at exact maintenance or 200kcals either side in a small surplus or deficit in a bid to hover around your 'ideal' weight whilst making small improvements to your cardio, health, strength, endurance or physique.

Prepping for a show – Understanding that the last 10 lbs of fat and water weight will likely be the hardest of the whole prep, look to take yourself there mentally with the carrot of the competition but looking to get out of that place asap after the show. As soon as the show is over, the first goal is to get back towards maintenance and return to my 'low set point' of 190lbs. If the show wasn't happening, there would be little point in pushing to this level – your brain doesn't work very well, you look small in clothes, your strength is compromised and you always lose a small bit of muscle mass (even if you're trying to maintain as much as possible). Getting to a 'stage' level of leanness really has no perks, outside of the stage and competition.

To Note – Both this theory and much of the literature you read will often refer to specific body fat % rather than bodyweight. I tend to find this pretty useless and inaccurate for 90% of people. The tools and know how to accurately measure fat percentage are not present for most people and the adherence to accurately measuring body fat percentage is incredibly low, compared to stepping on the scales. If you have the equipment and know how, then feel free to swap your body weight for your body fat percentage, but be cognizant that equipment can be inaccurate and human error is common.

But should everyone count calories?

So, we've established that calories in vs calories out is the most important element when setting up a weight loss or weight gain programme. There are many different tools and protocols that we can use, but these are just different ways to achieve the energy balance that will make us lose or gain weight. Given this fact, does this mean that we should all be counting calories, all the time, and be constantly aware of what we're eating on a daily basis using a calorie tracker like MyFitnessPal? Well, no - for many, it's not necessary and it's just not realistic.

Most people don't want to constantly programme calories and macros as a matter of course. Some people are happy to do this for specific diet phases, or every once in a while, but living like this 'forever' just isn't conceivable for the masses. Equally, there are some people who should probably reject calorie counting altogether. Having worked with several clients over the years, I know that the visibility of calories can be incredibly triggering for those who suffer from eating disorders like anorexia or bulimia. Using apps like MyFitnessPal (even if the goal is to up calories) can have a devastating effect on someone's relationship with food, often becoming preoccupied or obsessed with calorie numbers, and craving the control to eat less and less. Even seeing calorie numbers on restaurant menus, whilst a fantastic tool for some, can be equally as triggering for people who have this relationship with food. It's hard enough for them to switch off and enjoy a meal out at a restaurant, without being reminded how many calories are in the cheesecake they wanted to order. So, no, I don't actually believe that calorie counting is for everyone; I just think we should acknowledge that it is the CICO equation that determines weight loss or gain. It doesn't mean that I advocate a life of calorie counting for the masses. I recently went to a 40th birthday party with over 25 of my best mates. I can safely say that I was the only one at this gathering who regularly counted calories, and clearly, my preoccupation with bodybuilding, aesthetics and physical performance was my main driver. But I didn't see a group of people who were morbidly obese! The group were in good health, prioritised sports or gym work and looked to eat a well-balanced and rounded diet. During the weekend, I had conversations about various approaches to health and fitness.

Some rowed, some swam, and others still played football or 5-aside with workmates. There were a couple of vegans and a vegetarian, some just ate intuitively, and others were dabbling with intermittent fasting and low carb. There were varying results, but by and large, this served to prove that there are many ways to be fit, healthy and happy. The main issue wasn't the outcome, or even the methods, it was that many of them were still attributing the outcome to the wrong thing, e.g. that there wasn't anything magic about low carb, intermittent fasting or veganism; when it comes to losing weight, it just worked to put you in a calorie deficit. Rowing, swimming, football or gym work are contributing further to the calories out part of the equation, and hopefully, helping to build or maintain muscle mass, having a positive effect on metabolism and body composition. The only problem here is that this gathering of 25 individuals doesn't accurately represent a cross-section of the population. Every single person had a background in some kind of sport – football, rugby, hockey, rowing or dance. Every person had an interest in health and fitness and paid some attention to dieting, training and their overall well-being. A combination of adherence through interest and enjoyment, favourable genetics that give a better chance of lower body weight/fat percentage set points, and sporting childhoods, meant that the chances of fitter, healthier, leaner and stronger people were almost guaranteed.

On the other hand, for those who have struggled time and time again to lose or gain weight, or who want to push to a new level for aesthetics, bodybuilding or performance, I would absolutely endorse a calorie-counting approach. But, if you're generally happy and healthy and seem to naturally maintain a healthy body fat percentage and are not bothered about gaining or losing weight or changing your body composition, you simply don't need to count calories or change what you're doing. And if you have a history of eating disorders, I recommend you seek specific, professional, medical advice for dieting. Also, if you want to take your health and fitness journey to the next level, try to focus on performance and well-being-related goals, which might be less triggering. Aiming to get a bigger squat or bench press might be a much healthier dopamine pursuit than a calorie or weight-specific goal.

CHAPTER 4

Mindset and Mental Health

The Legend of Big Mike

He's a monster of a man, 6 feet tall and just as wide! A former prop and powerlifter, you can find him in the gym at 5 am every weekday morning. I've seen Big Mike put up some insane numbers on the leg press, squat and shoulder press. He's also one of the most polite people you're likely to meet; always pleasant to talk to, even at 5 am. Big Mike spent more time wrapping up his knees, elbows and wrists than he did lifting weights, such was the punishment that his body had taken over the years. Spotting Big Mike was always a nervous task, firstly, because the weights he used were so heavy that the chance of effectively helping was minimal, and secondly, because he took each set so seriously, you dare not fuck up! Helping Big Mike on a rep that needed no help was a mortal sin! And it can be really hard to gauge if such enormous weights are going to go up for one more rep or come crashing down on his face! One such morning, I got the call-up. It was shoulders and Mike wanted to press the 65s... I looked down at the 65kg dumbbells and they looked like something that had been welded together by a blind man, using the sharpest metal he could find! They were wonky and misshapen and he wanted me to lift one into his left hand. I grasped it tight and just about cleaned the weight up, being careful not to cut my own finger off and almost certainly get Tetanus! I placed it in his hand and he was off. Now, the really impressive thing here, and my takeaway for my own training, was that Big Mike changed in an instant from the loveliest man in the world to a super-focused reptile. There was nothing else in his head; it was him vs the weight. His eyes changed and he looked like a man possessed. Three clean reps and the 4th just went up. I was sure he'd need help on the 5th so my hands just grazed his elbows in preparation to help - "my weight, my fucking weight, no touch, no touch…." He completed the 5th rep and threw the weights on the floor, unwrapped and almost immediately changed back to the kind, gentle giant. "Thank you, Sir, much appreciated; thank you for the spot." And that 5 minutes perfectly summed up Big Mike and so many of the great characters you find in the gym. That ability to 'get in the zone' for your set, block out all the noise and give everything for one more rep. In that moment, it feels like life or death, like your whole existence depends on that PB… 5 reps is fine but 4 is a complete disaster! And it highlights one of the reasons why we might train. That need to exercise some primal, raw part of yourself, where it's just you and the weight, just the sheer will and a bloody mindset to push through the feeling that your head might explode, like your whole family's lives depend on you raising that weight for that extra rep. Of course, nothing really happens if you fail, but in that moment, nothing matters more. A sick, mental game, that you play once a day. Sometimes you win, sometimes you lose, but some of us just crave that battle, that mental fight, and ultimately, that escape from the mundane.

It's Go Time

The ability to 'switch on' for sets or for key moments in sporting events is of huge value. That change in psyche from laid back, jovial or conversational, to an all-out intensity and focus on the task at hand, can be the difference between an average set and a great set, or success and failure on the sporting field. You can draw comparisons between a gym session and a sporting context such as golf or cricket. The use of cues or well-thought-out processes can really aid us to perform at our best when it matters most. In the above example, Big Mike manages to go from a lovely, chatty fella, to a super-hyped-up reptile in a matter of seconds, where he's overcome with an intense urgency and focus on the task at hand. The same process takes place for a golfer or batter, who can't possibly keep the same level of intensity or concentration for hours on end, and therefore, has to master 'switching on and off' between every shot played. This is a process that might include specific tapping of the bat/ club, breathing patterns, touching a particular area of their body, self-visualisation or 'trigger movements' that will all play a part in getting the sportsperson from relaxed to 'switched on' in a matter of seconds. In the gym, we can use similar hacks to make sure we maximise every set, and, when necessary, channel that inner aggression and intensity to push through strength plateaus and hit new PBs. Smelling salts, wrist or knee wraps, or audible queues like saying "my bar" can all be used as 'switches' as an aid to signify that now is the time to switch on. All the gym noise, the conversation you're having with your gym partner, the work email you've had to check between sets - these are all gone in that instant and replaced with nothing but an intense focus on you and the weight. It may sound silly but it's the sort of place to which you might have to mentally take yourself to keep making advancements, push through plateaus and reach the next level of training. And if you are someone who struggles with this, it's well worth experimenting with the use of headphones, wraps or straps. Even wearing a baseball cap (that you take off between sets but put on to lift) or physically saying "my bar" to use as that pre-set process to really amp yourself up and switch on can work. There is nothing magical in the use of any of these gimmicks, but in the same way that you're training your muscles to get bigger and stronger, you're also training your mindset to channel that extra focus, that extra bit of aggression, urgency or intensity at the vital time. From personal experience, I've often taken myself to some really dark places to push through heavy sets and gruelling finishers, taking myself back to horrible moments in my life and embracing the hurt, pain or embarrassment for some extra anger and aggression, or even imagining terrible things happening to friends and family. On a less morbid front, the use of good music and visualisation can also have the opposite effect, helping to take the focus away from the task in hand and making cardio a bit more bearable. These little hacks and tips to channel a training mindset are all very well, but for most people, the issue lies way before even stepping into a gym. What about the mindset to be consistent, to turn up and train, and to make an effective training and diet programme become a lifestyle?

The Experiencing Self vs The Narrating Self

"The experiencing self describes its feelings, needs, and desires, and reveals its own attitudes toward the situation and its circumstances. The narrating self aims to give a detailed account of the event, circumstances and its own actions, without saying much about its emotional state".[24]

We touched on this notion in the introduction, and I've always found this specific area of psychology fascinating and one that is incredibly applicable to training, fitness and all aspects of bodybuilding. Let us start with the narrating self from an aspect of building a diet and training programme. The narrating self can plan or imagine a series of well-intentioned plans, early training sessions, low calories, and a host of foods (like chocolate and alcohol) that they are going to abstain from. After all, the narrating self wants to be lean, strong, fit and healthy. However, when we consider the impact of the experiencing self and the part that this might play throughout the plan, you might start to see that you're in for a different set of behaviours and outcomes. Yes, the narrating self genuinely wants to train early, cut out chocolate and stop alcohol, but all of a sudden, the experiencing self is feeling lots of different emotions, desires and needs. It's all very well to plan a 5 am training session until you wake up feeling tired, groggy and cold. It's great to say you'll not drink for 3 months, until your best friend gets engaged and you want to celebrate with them. Not eating any chocolate is a great plan until your daughter buys you an Easter egg and she's so excited to eat it with you, in front of a film, that you just can't help yourself. There is very little planning, preparation or advice that I can give you for these random events. The impromptu night out, the takeaway your friend talks you into, the morning training session that you sleep through... these are all things that life throws at you, and these urges and temptations will always be there. You have to weigh up your life and happiness on the whole, to decide when, and if, you should stay strong, or if you want to come off plan for that moment. After all, I'd argue that celebrating certain moments with friends and family is infinitely more important than 6-pack abs. The advice that I would give you though, is that proper, realistic planning can avoid many of these types of pitfalls. If you programme properly, the odd night out or missed session shouldn't derail your whole plan. Put simply, you want to get your narrating self and experiencing self as well aligned and in sync as possible. To do that, you have to face some hard truths about yourself, your realistic goals, training timings, food types and nights out. Only if the experiencing self and narrating self are aligned will a plan work long-term. You might even say that true happiness can only be reached if the two selves are aligned. After all, it would save a lot of perceived failure, heartache and disappointment if our plans were really well aligned with our feelings, emotions, needs and desires... but taking it that far is way above my psychological pay grade. To align the two 'selves' from a training and diet perspective, ask yourself these questions before you decide on your training and diet plan:

- Taking other commitments into account, how many times per week will I realistically be able to train?

- What time of the day will I function at my best and actually want to train? If you are not a morning person, don't try to plan 6 am training sessions. On the off chance you manage to get out of bed, they'll probably be less effective than training later in the day anyway.
- Alcohol and cheating with food – can you plan your alcohol and cheat days around diary commitments like stag dos or weddings? Use these events like milestones in the programme, with hard weeks of training set either side and a 2-3-day 'downtime' in between. If you know you are the type of person who likes to go out every weekend, you need to plan your calories and sessions to account for alcohol calories. If you want to start drinking less, can you come up with an effective plan to slowly decrease 'nights out' per month? Whatever the situation is, you can include these in your plan. When you start to see cheat meals and alcohol as part of the programme, you won't have the emotional response that 'I have failed'. More often than not, this response leads to an abandonment of the programme altogether, instead of following a programme that includes this behaviour but leads to an overall improvement of mental health, body composition and training goals.
- Find a type of exercise that you enjoy. If your goal is to lose body fat, then think about different approaches to cardio that might work for you. If you enjoy football, CrossFit, climbing, golf or circuits more than the cross trainer or rower, then your experiencing self is much more likely to pair up with your narrating self and achieve your fat loss goals.

The Flipside:

But what about doing things that the narrating self wants but the experiencing self finds incredibly hard? After all, isn't overcoming the difficult things how we achieve growth? Can we hack our experiencing selves with enough grit, determination and belief? Well maybe, but my advice would be to prioritise one 'difficult thing' at a time and only push the important things. For example, you don't need to get up at 5 am and train before work if you can legitimately train after work at 5 pm... it's just not worth it if adherence, enjoyment and performance are compromised. However, once you are up and have trained, if you feel a sense of achievement, euphoria and pride from pushing yourself to train early, then look to do this on one day per week to start with and build from there if it's working for you. These things generally seem to fail when someone has tried to go from A to E instead of from A to B to C. I've lost count of the number of times I've done an induction with a new client and they say they'll train 6 times a week, count calories and give up alcohol, then, on investigation, I find out they've never once trained 6 times in a week, they drink every other day and have never counted a calorie in their lives. It's just setting yourself up for failure to go from one extreme to another. What this individual should do is slowly change behaviours, one step at a time, in a well-designed and realistic plan. Stage one would be to aim for 3 to 4 gym sessions per week, limit alcohol to weekends and prioritise whole foods that encompass a good amount of protein. Some people never need to get to stage 2 and are happy with the progress that gives them, but if you do want to build from there, you can then start to measure your sessions and ensure you're achieving progressive overload, reduce alcohol further if it's impacting training and body composition, and trial a week of calorie and macro-counting. If you want to further progress, we can then look at upping frequency, using more challenging exercises, looking at supplementation and manipulating calories and macros to achieve the set goal in a more precise manner over the course of a mesocycle. But simply going from nothing to everything in one go never seems to work out, and there is a startling lack of credibility in the 'experts' who tell you it does. Successful programmes and outcomes are based on chipping away at one goal at a time and changing behaviours slowly. Keep in mind that if you lost just half a pound a week, you'd be 26 lbs lighter in a year. If you started with a 3km jog and managed to run 1k further every month, you'd run 15km just 12 months later! In the same way that you need to slowly decrease calories for fat loss, you need to slowly introduce different stimuli and approaches to your lifestyle. Going from 'couch to 20km', getting 'ripped abs in 4 weeks' or '6 weeks to a superhero body', all sound like great tag lines, but they rarely work in the long run.

Mindset and Motivation

Cauda Equina Syndrome is a Medical Emergency

On the Friday evening, I went to the theatre with my family (if you get a chance to watch 'Book of Mormon' then take it, it's brilliant). Much of the chat was about whether my broken ankle would heal in time for the family ski trip and how predictable it was that I would injure myself at something so stupid as 'Ninja Warrior'! As we sat in our seats, I noticed that my sister was squirming around more than usual. Most of our family have had bad backs over the years, and these small theatre seats weren't ideal for any of us, but Amy's back was particularly bad. I asked her if she was planning to play hockey the next day, and she said that she was. Fast forward 24 hours, and I had a call to say that Amy's back had got worse. She had been rushed into A&E for surgery as she had a suspected Cauda Equina Syndrome, which, it turns out, is a medical emergency. One of Amy's discs had herniated and popped out of the spinal column with such force that it had compressed her Cauda Equine nerves, a collection of nerves at the base of the spine, that come together like a horse's tail. In the worst of cases, this will leave you with irreversible damage that will directly affect the nerves that control the legs, bladder and bowel function and even in the best of cases, this will be a long rehab, and can take up to two years for damaged nerves to regenerate and heal. As we frantically googled 'cauda equina' looking for some answers and advice, the overwhelming articles that came up were a selection of horror stories, talking of long-term nerve pain, complete loss of leg function and incontinence, accompanied by hundreds of adverts on how to seek legal advice for malpractice and slow diagnosis. You had to search very hard for any good news stories. Well, I am glad to say that this is a 'good news' story. At the time of writing this, Amy is nearly four years on from her initial surgery. She has given birth naturally to her daughter, been on two skiing holidays, returned to work and completed several long walks, such as Pen Y Fan. Whilst there are some long-term effects from the injury, she lives a happy and fulfilled life and has gotten used to her 'new normal'. For the six months following Amy's injury, I helped her to rehab nearly every single day. Like any good programme, we made a list of short-term advancements, long-term goals and a series of mental health-related tasks. She never missed a session, and whilst she had her down days, her grit, determination and resolve were incredible. We used a simple ethos around progressive overload to show that she was making steady progress, and, in the days, weeks and months that followed, Amy went from lying on her back, trying to move her toe a few inches, to performing weighted lunges and glute bridges, and from struggling to walk with crutches, to walking unaided for miles at a time. Amy knows she was fortunate. She knows that she was lucky to have the NHS, to have the help of family members and a partner who could be emotionally and physically supportive. How this would play out in a developing country, to a person with no family, living in a top floor flat, I do not know. But I do know that her recovery, rehab and continuing improvement in physical and mental health, is massively down to her own mindset and resolve. The power of thinking positively and the power of proper planning and goal setting can help you to move from point A to B and B to C, to feel a tangible progression and to know you are on the right track. Even the darkest of days, and there were some, were ended with a smile and an acknowledgement that, 'I will do this', 'I'll get better' and 'Tomorrow's another day'. And it's that mental toughness and resilience, the power to put your situation into context and chip away at a set goal, that can make all the difference, whether you're rehabbing from a serious injury or pushing towards a series of physical, mental and professional goals.

Applying Perspective, Context and Reason to 'Embrace Discomfort' (Warning, David Brent style Cringyness ahead)

I've been in enough offices and sporting changing rooms to know that being the most talented or genetically gifted gives you no guarantees of long-term success; nor is it a precursor to contentment or fulfilment in your professional, personal or social lives. Of course, the ones that generally 'make it' and rise to the top have the natural talent, but what divides success and failure, and what can make the process more enjoyable, less exhausting and more fulfilling is their mindset and motivation to stick to a plan, embrace continuous improvement, battle through times of discomfort, and find a way to ensure mental clarity in the big moments. Bodybuilding isn't a walk in the park. Whether you're looking to build new muscle or lose vast amounts of fat, we're going against millions of years of biological evolution. As we get further away from our natural body weight and fat set points, our brains and hormones will join forces to make us feel hungry or full, irritable and restless or sluggish and lethargic. The mirror will play tricks on you as you feel skinny, fat, watery, weak or bloated, at different parts of your programme. Even with the best laid plans, there will be numerous times during the months of prep, when you question everything, your motivation dips and things get tough. Whether it's the food or the training, the social sacrifices or the brain fog, some resilience and mental fortitude is needed to carry you through. This is where, I believe, the ability to apply context, perspective and reason to these situations can be an incredibly powerful tool.

Over the years, I've had countless friends and family ask me how and why I do it. How can I do the diets, the cardio, the weight training and the standing on stage, all tanned up, wearing little more than a pair of pants?! And the truth is, it's really hard. And that's just at my, very amateur, level. Juggling a body-building prep, with a full-time office job, personal relationships and a social life, is not easy. But it's also a choice of my own making; a choice I am incredibly fortunate to have. In fact, if you just read the previous line, this shows I have friends, a family, a job and a social life to consider. If we put this into perspective and context, I've already shown, in one line, that I'm probably more fortunate than 75% of the world's population. Whilst it might sound a little deep, over the top and almost on the verge of something David Brent-esque, here are a few of the hacks that I use to keep me motivated and grounded through difficult moments:

If I am anxious, nervous or worried about a situation, I try and imagine the enormity of the world, and the insignificance that this moment actually has on anyone outside my little bubble. I know this might sound morbid and maybe counter-intuitive to feelings of pride and motivation, but in the great scheme and context of the world, what I am doing is insignificant. I actually find this notion to be freeing. Overthinking business presentations, social interactions or standing on stage in my pants, is a far smaller deal, if you can master this mindset. There have been many times in my life when I have felt this feeling, and I try to take myself back to them. Being out at sea, in the middle of the ocean, looking across the expanse of the Alps, or gazing at New York City from one of their monstrous skyscrapers, gives me great imagery for this hack and affirmation that we are barely a tiny speck that exists in this universe for a limited amount of time. If I can harness the calm feeling that I felt from being awestruck at the vastness of the world, it can serve as a brilliant tool, to bring me back to the moment, rather than being stuck 'in my own head', overthinking and worrying.

I also use comparison, context and perspective, when I am deep into a bodybuilding cut. The early morning cardio is getting harder, weight training is exhausting, and I'm surviving on 1800 calories per day. Of course, these things feel tough, but, in the grand scheme of things, making the right comparisons, it's really not. I remember flying into Mumbai, over a huge shanty town, seeing what felt like millions of people lining the streets, and some sleeping head to toe on the pavement, and on the central reservation. The incredible poverty, and the contrast to the city's wealthier inhabitants, was a huge culture shock and a horrible sight to see. But no one needs to travel too far from their own home to see people who are genuinely suffering, who don't have a roof over their head, who are sleeping in freezing conditions and begging for food and water. Even in the depths of my prep, I can make a coffee in the morning, climb into my warm car, and drive to a brilliant gym with some of the best bodybuilding equipment in the UK. I eat 1800 calories, a number that many people the world over would kill for. At the end of the day, I get into my king-size bed, in my cosy house, equipped with clean water and heating, and I do it all out of choice. If you apply the right context, make the right comparisons and have the right perspective, none of this is really hard. It's a constructed version of hard. It's someone playing at being hard because they want to and because they have a choice to think past the simple act of surviving day to day. The fact I even have the choice to body build, train, and manipulate my diets is actually a privilege.

And if there's one thing I've learnt from 15 years of working in Sales, it' that, when things are hard, they're never as bad as they seem. If you can embrace the discomfort and ride the storm, things usually get better. Equally, in the great moments, they're never quite as good as they seem, and you're better to stay humble and grounded, keep working hard and don't get too carried away.

The truth is, though, however many (pretentious sounding) hacks you use, context, perspective and rationale you apply, you will feel incredible discomfort at various parts of your life. You can visualise, rationalise and tell yourself all the right things and sometimes, it just doesn't work. You have to **Embrace the discomfort**. You will not make dramatic physical changes without this discomfort. If you are cutting for a bodybuilding show, you will be hungry. You will ache from the training. You will feel like you have absolutely nothing left and somehow you have to find the energy to go for another 400 calories on the cross trainer or treadmill. Every fibre in your body will tell you to order a takeaway, to go to the fridge and eat that piece of cheese, or that you deserve a couple of beers as it's a Friday night. The fact is, you always have the choice to cheat, and that makes it hard! You have to embrace the discomfort and make it your friend. Crave that feeling, embrace it, take it on and win. Every single person who has ever stepped onto a bodybuilding stage, with an appropriate level of body fat, has been incredibly uncomfortable at some point during prep. Anyone who has done, and trained for, a marathon, has felt horrendous along the way. Crave discomfort to the point where you feel comfortable, and it will have an incredible carryover to other parts of your life.

Making the most of your competitive edge – Find Your Inner Warrior

I spoke in a previous chapter about the power of harnessing your competitive edge as a fantastic tool to aid fat loss, build muscle and apply progressive overload. As an individual, I've always been quietly competitive. I think back to my early days of sporting competition - a loss in a football or cricket game was devastating, coming second in an athletics meet was a disaster and even losing a game of FIFA on the PlayStation might have me bubbling inside. That's not to say I've ever been a bad loser, but my inner monologue was vastly different to the handshakes and smiles on the outside. In time, that same competitive edge translated to the gym, as a group of us started to lift weights in our local leisure centre. Every session became a competition between mates to see who could bench press, shoulder press, bicep curl the most weight, who could do the most pull-ups and who was going to flake out first on the most horrendous of drop and super sets. Progressive overload became an accident of competition, and, without really knowing it, along with our improving physiques and strength, we were building robust, durable and resilient mindsets. Our improving ability to turn up for sessions on freezing cold mornings, to overcome the muscular pain and lung-busting agony of horrible finishers and to stick to a diet and training programme, was translating to other parts of my life. Socially, I felt a different confidence and my performance, grit and determination carried over beautifully to an array of sports. But at some time in my early 20s, something changed. I always found it hard to put my finger on exactly what, but I was suppressing my ultra-competitive edge. All of a sudden, it felt like society was going the other way, that caring this much about winning and losing and bettering yourself was somehow uncool and undesirable. I was buying into a narrative that people didn't want that kind of warrior mentality as it was too brash, too aggressive, too much. I became aware that for many, lifting heavy weights and bodybuilding was synonymous with a 'meathead' culture, deemed unintelligent and all wrapped up in phrases like 'toxic masculinity'. I had about 18 months where my performance in the gym dipped and my mindset changed. The competitive, resilient, warrior mentality had become softer, and more docile and that mindset that carried over so well to my social life, academic or professional pursuits and sporting endeavours, struggled. What's more, my mental health deteriorated along with it. I felt on edge, unfulfilled and full of anxiety. I knew that I had to get back to that place where I could exercise my inner demons, train my competitive edge back and find that warrior mentality that would translate back into the other parts of my life.

If you've watched enough Joe Rogan, you'd be familiar with an old saying that's prevalent in Chinese and Japanese martial arts - 'It's better to be a warrior in a garden than a gardener in a war.' Jordan Peterson takes this saying and explains it slightly further by exclaiming, "You should be a monster. Everyone says you should be harmless, virtuous; you shouldn't do anyone any harm, you should sheath your competitive instinct. You shouldn't try to win. You don't want to be too aggressive. You don't want to be too assertive. No. Wrong. You should be a monster, an absolute monster, and then you should learn how to control it."

I don't know if I concur with all of Jordan Peterson's ideals and musings, but I absolutely love this quote, and what's more, I think the gym is the perfect place to find your inner monster, to push your boundaries of physical and mental fortitude in a safe and acceptable manner. The gym is one of the few places left where we can acceptably exercise huge amounts of aggression, and where we can channel this aggression, use all of life's pain, anger and frustrations to lift heavy weights, run faster, row further and become better. And if you can grow the mental fortitude to keep executing your plans, to keep applying progressive overload, week in, week out, month after month, year after year, in the face of life's growing responsibilities, pain, injuries, wear and tear, we may just have the chance of becoming what Jürgen Klopp describes as 'mentality monsters', to mentally go the extra mile when needed, to work that bit harder than the person next to you and be of more use to your loved ones, friends, families, parents and children.

Don't suppress your competitive edge... embrace it, use it to your advantage, become a warrior, a monster, and learn to control it. Really, in everyday normal speak, I think it's saying you should be the absolute best that you can be, try your hardest to achieve your goals, don't take any shit, don't accept unfair treatment, strive to hit your physical goals and develop a strong and healthy mindset to protect your mental health... **just don't be a dick**! We can all be helpful, polite and virtuous, accepting, loving and caring, but still have a monstrous desire to win, to be the best at the endeavours we choose to pursue and we shouldn't be apologetic about that. If we're drawn towards primal and physical pursuits like weight training, boxing or martial arts, then don't shy away from what could be an incredible outlet for your physical and mental health. Becoming a monster, and learning to control it, might be a much better alternative than rejecting competition altogether, and perhaps becoming a docile, frustrated and mentally weaker version of yourself. Or even worse, suppressing feelings of frustration, pain and anger, and finding that they come out in far more harmful ways than lifting a few weights on a Monday night. It's why gyms and boxing clubs are so prominent in disadvantaged areas. Those who have real reason to feel anger, pain and frustration, need an acceptable outlet to physically exercise and mentally process these feelings, hopefully leading to calmer, more fulfilled individuals and a skillset that can carry over to making better personal, professional and social decisions.

Supersonic

We were in the throes of the second lockdown, it was Friday evening and my Partner had gone to bed. It was about 10 pm but I was not particularly tired. Up to this point, I hadn't drunk any alcohol that day, after all, I was in the midst of some pretty serious training and had started to look into what comps might be running as we (hopefully) came out of Covid for the last time. I was surfing the channels to see what was on and I stumbled across 'Supersonic', the Oasis documentary.

I hovered over the channel, knowing what watching this documentary would mean for me. Should I just go to bed or shall I do this? Fuck it, I'm all in. It's lockdown and I'm bored and what's the worst that could happen? Without acknowledging it formally, in that second, I knew that I couldn't watch Oasis without a drink of some description. I opened a bottle of wine and started to drink as I enjoyed the brilliant music, hilarious stories and outrageous tales of drink and drugs. Some kind of edgy romanticism gripped me and I was whisked up in a frenzy of the 90's indie scene. Fast forward to three bottles of wine, three gin and tonics, a bottle of Prosecco and some vodka later, and I was sitting in the kitchen at 3 am, talking to the Bonsai tree... or so my wife tells me. Arguing with the tree, half wanting to fight it, half stroking and loving it, like a weird, demented moron, drinking on my own, seduced by the brilliance of Oasis, and a hedonistic pull towards the escapism of booze, I had pushed the dopamine button and the effects weren't going to be pretty. I woke up with very little memory of the evening. All the alcohol in the house had been drunk and I had that horrible feeling of fear, with the anxiety of not remembering, and the self-loathing from lacking the control to stop myself. I cringed at the thought of what I might have said to my Partner, how stupid I probably looked, and the fact that I would now lay in my pit of grief and despair for most of the day. My plans for cardio and training were out the window, I'd predictably eat crap all day, and I didn't want to look another human in the eye – well, luckily for me, it was lockdown, so that one was an easy win! What a fucking idiot! Why do I do it to myself?!

Young Men and the Suicide Epidemic

As I scroll through the business networking platform, LinkedIn, I come across two separate posts that are informing us that a young man has taken his own life. Up to this point, I'm lucky to say that I've not had any direct family or friends die by suicide, but half a dozen close friends of friends sadly have. Of course, everyone's mental battle is unique to them and I don't claim to even be a novice when it comes to the human brain, let alone an expert, but there are some startling similarities that seem to run through many of these horrible instances. Firstly, they all happen to be male. Death by suicide of course occurs in females, and is no less harrowing or important, but three to four times as many men take their lives every year[25]. There's often a recurring narrative of someone who is bright, socially active, fun, and, in many cases, professionally successful. And lastly, in many cases, none of their closest friends or family could have seen it coming. Even if life was sometimes hard, no one could have predicted that this would be the end, often labelling the individual as strong, confident, happy and 'fine'. The reason no one could see it coming was that these men never shared the burden of what they were living with. For one reason or another, they didn't open up about their genuine feelings, inner turmoil, feelings of anxiety, depression, despair or loneliness. I don't have any clever answers for this subject; all I can say is that if any young men are reading this paragraph, please go and talk to someone. Talk to a friend, a partner, a mum or a dad, talk to a counsellor, a work colleague or a bloke down the pub. A problem shared is often a problem halved, and in my experience of talking about mental health and personal demons, once you open up to someone, they are often compelled to share their truth with you. Your 'problem' probably isn't as unique as you think; others are struggling with similar issues and you can find comfort, sense and security in talking this through. Finally, if any of my close friends, family, colleagues or even the loosest of acquaintances are reading this and feel there is no way out, please reach out to me. Any mate would rather spend hours upon hours talking with their friend about their mental health than helping to plan their funeral.

Mental health, anxiety and depression and Pushing the Dopamine Button

It may seem odd for a book like this to focus on a niche like dopamine or even discuss topics like anxiety and depression. I'm certainly no neuroscientist and my high-level overview and simplistic outlook will likely butcher the subject for the well-informed. But if we're going to examine the efficacy of physical training and planning on mental well-being, then we should probably examine some of the factors that are in play in the modern world, where we see depression, anxiety and suicide at startling highs. We know the horrible facts surrounding suicide in young men, and sadly, these numbers seem to be growing rather than shrinking. In a world with advancing technology, unemployment at an all-time low, and fewer people going without food, water or shelter, and where huge factors like famine and homelessness are increasingly scarce, you would think that facts around suicide and mental health would be going in the right direction, but they're not. Every individual's mental health is unique to them. A CEO of a business is no more protected from depression and anxiety than the person that serves her morning coffee. Fame, fortune, security, friendships or marriages don't protect against mental health struggles, but there might be some specific pitfalls in the modern landscape that are contributing to our growing discontent, particularly the culture of 'everything now', with so many of our wishes and desires readily available at the touch of a button. If I so wished, I could listen to any song that I wanted, watch a hardcore porno and write an online message that could be seen by thousands of my 'online friends' within a couple of taps of a button. I could get an instant hit of nicotine with my £7 vape or call the right people and get any number of class-A drugs delivered to my house. I could go out and drink alcohol, or a hundred different types of coffee, order 9 different takeaways on the way home that would be delivered to me in one convenient drop-off and top it off with a plethora of performance-enhancing drugs to speed up my muscle growth and help to offset the calories from all the shit I've just eaten. All of these things give me an instant dopamine response, all without the necessity to really work, plan or think about how to get it. The more we seek instant pleasures, the more we want, and the quicker we want them. The laws of diminishing returns mean that we want a little bit more every time and our dopamine responses to these modern conveniences slowly get less and less intense. What effects are these modern advances having on our hardwiring, our ability to be properly satisfied, our long-term efficacy in producing dopamine, and our growing preoccupation with chasing the dopamine win, rather than the process of achieving the win?

Dopamine is a neuromodulatory molecule responsible for allowing you to feel pleasure, satisfaction and motivation[26]. Put simply, that great feeling of pleasure that you get when you've done something fun, enjoyable or satisfying, is caused by a surge of dopamine in the brain. Like most things to do with the brain, dopamine is a complicated beast. You might think that loads of dopamine really frequently = good, but that's not always the case, and like many other areas of mental health and pharmacology, it's true that you don't get anything for free, and for every action, there is often a reaction. You have to be careful in your pursuit of dopamine, which sources you come to seek a dopamine response from, and the sort of quick fix or hedonistic pursuits that might mess with long-term dopamine production or take your dopamine to under baseline once you crash from an extreme dopamine high. Things that might be considered to be 'pushing the dopamine button' for a quick hit of euphoria include alcohol, drugs, nicotine, masturbation, pornography or fast food - acts that elicit an extreme dopamine response but don't include any hard work or endeavour, and therefore, the lasting satisfaction that you might take from hard physical graft or academic achievement. Hitting the dopamine button too frequently might lead to feelings of emptiness, boredom or even depression, as dopamine highs diminish and the lows that follow those highs can take your dopamine to drastically low levels. Think of that horrible feeling you get that often accompanies a comedown or nasty hangover: The anxiety, weird feelings of shame, fear or discontent. In part, that may be your dopamine crashing past baseline (there are other factors at play like your pre-frontal cortex becoming overactive as you overthink the things you might have done or said the night before. When we drink, our pre-frontal cortex is the first area of the brain to be affected, the part of the brain responsible for judgement and reasoning and suppressing impulsive behaviour. This often wakes up with a bang as we cringe at the inappropriate joke we made or secret we told from the night before.)

'Pushing the dopamine button' often leads to a never-ending loop, a cycle that is out of our conscious control. As any cocaine connoisseur will tell you, a cocaine binge, (and I mean a proper binge, not a few lines on a night out, but the type of binge where your house door or hotel room is locked for 48 hours) is often accompanied by alcohol, other drugs, pornography and masturbation. This is a two-day cycle of eliciting as much dopamine as possible, until something has to give. Cocaine, alcohol, cigarettes, more cocaine, porn and masturbation, more cocaine, some more alcohol, some weed to take the edge off, some more cocaine to keep the party going, more porn and masturbation, more cocaine and finally some downers to end the binge and get you off to sleep. Twelve hours later, you wake up with your dopamine way below baseline levels, you've not eaten for 36 hours so the next 12 hours are spent shovelling 6000 calories into your mouth in the shape of fast food. Sure, it's because your body is genuinely starving, but binge eating is also another way to push the dopamine button one more time, in a bid to feel well and satisfied and offset some of the horrible feelings of anxiety, fear, depression and self-loathing.

Considering these basics around dopamine, what are some of the things we could do to limit these issues and keep your dopamine levels healthy and functional?

1. Try to limit 'quick wins' like masturbation, pornography, alcohol and drug use. Having reasonable gaps between

these pleasure-seeking activities will make them less habitual and feel like they are more earned. When I say 'limit', this is clearly different for different folk. If you're drinking, watching porn or using drugs every day, then having one day off per week is a good place to start. Like everything else, you should programme small, incremental gains that will add up over time. Of course, if you are an alcoholic or drug abuser, you should seek professional advice, and ideally, stop these pursuits immediately, but things aren't always this clear-cut.

2. Try and focus on the process rather than the win. The real satisfaction from winning a show or selling a business is the years of hard work and dedication that went into the process rather than the win itself. Wins last for a fleeting moment which will inevitably be followed by a dopamine crash and an obsession with the next win. The lasting and consistent satisfaction of enjoying the process as a succession of mini wins to achieve an overall victory is different altogether.

3. Try mental and physical tasks that will be a satisfying challenge to overcome. Sports, training in the gym, tests of endurance, writing, reading or studying can all be great outlets.

4. Try new things. The satisfaction of learning a new skill, fact or language can be incredibly rewarding.

5. Try planned breaks for your phone or technology, resisting the temptation to constantly check social media and the latest news and gossip. How often do you mindlessly scroll just praying for something to grab

your attention – you're looking for a cheap dopamine fix.

6. Train hard for a healthy dopamine fix. Endorphins released through physical training are generally guilt-free and longer-lasting. Of course, you have your off days, but generally speaking, the ability to get moving, sweating and active is a positive and even if you don't get the dopamine high of breaking a personal record every time, you generally feel good through any kind of physical exertion.

7. Where possible, I would look to make these pleasure-seeking activities as social as possible. There is something very different about drinking with friends vs drinking on your own. Equally, if you have the option to have sex with a willing partner rather than masturbate and watch porn, then I would take it! Pleasurable activities like drinking and sex are more rewarding and enjoyable when others are gaining pleasure from the activity. Logging onto XVideo is a low-effort dopamine pursuit vs the act of having sex with a loved one, putting the effort in so it's good for both parties and the accompanying feeling of love or companionship. Similarly, laughing and sharing stories with friends whilst getting drunk beats drinking three bottles of wine, on your own, in the lounge! Friends coming together to catch up is a worthwhile pursuit of dopamine, reinforced by positive feelings of friendship and joy.

8. Do things for other people. A dopamine spike that's elicited through genuinely helping friends, or things like

volunteering and charity work, can be just as rewarding and satisfying for you as it can be for them.

9. Get Outdoors. We touched on this in an earlier chapter, but there is no doubt that, for most people, being in nature is synonymous with feelings of wellness. There are numerous studies linking low levels of Vitamin D, with reduced levels of Dopamine.

Vaping – what I've witnessed so far

When 'vaping' came into existence, it was marketed as a healthier alternative to cigarettes. You get the nicotine hit, but without the horrible stuff that accompanies them. No tar, no gross smell and an absence of dozens of cancer-causing substances. Moving from 20 a day to 'vaping' in a bid to wean yourself off smoking seemed a logical and tangible step and one that may genuinely work. Now, assuming that studies 10 years down the line don't find something that's equally as horrendous for your health as smoking cigarettes, this can only be seen as a good thing. Anyone who's gone from smoking cigarettes to smoking vapes has taken a step in the right direction and should be applauded and encouraged. But there are a few issues that I've seen arising from smoking 'vapes' that may be incredibly worrying for addiction, and mental health, moving forward.

Firstly, the number of people who never smoked but now vape is startling. People who have always detested smoking have started to vape because it smells nice and it tastes good. Strawberries and cream is a nicer flavour than a standard Rothman or Benson and Hedges! Vaping is seen as socially acceptable and the same degree of embarrassment or shame isn't attached to someone who vapes. Secondly, vaping is so palatable that it's possible to continuously vape without taking much of a break. It's rare you'd see people smoke 2, 3 or 4 cigarettes on the bounce, but you see people vaping, constantly, inside, outside, at their desk, in the car. Not only is it socially acceptable to vape, but it's also even accepted that people might vape indoors. Of course it's discouraged, but the reality is, people vape in the office, in the car and in pubs. You wouldn't see the same laissez-faire attitude given to cigarettes, and rightly so. A few weeks ago, I went away for a mate's birthday and a bunch of people were vaping, myself included. For two days, barely 20 minutes went by without a vape being in someone's mouth. The sheer amount of nicotine that was consumed during this 48-hour period would have been startling. The temptation to push the dopamine button and get an instant hit of one of the most addictive substances known to mankind was overwhelming. You can see how it would become habitual very quickly, and how catastrophic this might be to a generation of otherwise non-smokers. To take in incredibly high doses of a potent and addictive stimulant, doses that we may have never seen or experienced before, what does that do to the hardwiring of the brain, to the dopamine reward mechanism that's firing every 15 minutes as you crave that extra nicotine hit? Well, we don't really know, but I do know that on that Sunday, through to about Wednesday, I felt horrible... slightly down, unfulfilled, reluctant to really get involved in conversation or get out of bed, and slightly on edge, with growing anxiety and general discontent. Maybe it was something else, but I couldn't help but think that consuming roughly 80 cigarettes' worth of nicotine in 48 hours, as a non-smoker, played its part! When

I dial into Teams calls and half the people are vaping, then I look around the office and colleagues are struggling to go 10 minutes without a sneaky drag at the desk, I can't help but think there could be some serious repercussions to come.

The Power of Training for coping with addiction, substance abuse and self-destructive behaviours

It's important to start this chapter with a disclaimer that weight training, cardio, dieting and bodybuilding are not magical, quick fixes for substance abuse, alcohol or drug addiction. The roots of these behaviours and illnesses are far more complex and often lie in one's past experiences, current mental state or DNA. However, I have worked with many clients and friends over the years (and can draw on some of my own experiences) and have found that the mental wellbeing from training, the order it creates, the absence of chaos with effective planning and programming, and the ability for a diet or goal to keep someone accountable, can all be incredibly powerful tools to help with self-destructive behaviours, positively channelling addictive personalities, and can have a short, and long-term, transformative effect on the brain, promoting feelings of well-being and self-worth.

Self-Destructive and Hedonistic Behaviours

There's something about my own personality that, every once in a while, pulls me towards hedonistic behaviours. It's reflected in most of my sporting heroes, who, as well as being world-class competitors, also have that self-destruct button.

Maybe it's because I identify with this personality or maybe it humanises them more, but it's always been the professional and personal sides of Ben Stokes, Shane Warne, John Daly and a whole host of 90's rugby players that I've always identified with. Since I was a kid, I've suffered panic attacks. It's something which the odd person would have been aware of, but it's taken me over 30 years to properly acknowledge and speak about. Whilst varying levels of anxiety have always been common, I'm glad to say that actual panic attacks were few and far between. The guilt, embarrassment and self-loathing that followed these moments of acute anxiety was far worse than the anxiety itself. I would feel like a fake or a fraud, portraying a strong front to my friends and family, whilst keeping my anxiety a secret. There were many times over the years, that I turned to alcohol and other forms of hedonism as a kind of self-destruct. The problem is that any feelings of anxiety, panic or self-loathing are exacerbated with various forms of eliciting a 'dopamine high'. There's no denying that in years gone by, this stuff has been way harder for men to talk about. Traditional masculinity is strong, it doesn't moan, or whine and it doesn't show weakness. Traditional masculinity protects its family, friends and loved ones and doesn't spend too much time, thinking about its own feelings. Truth is though, whatever your sex and however you identify, everyone is subject to the same feelings of fear, anxiety, grief, and despair. And the truth is, that men really do have a platform now. We know the realities around mental health and all the great work that's been done to break down the stigma attached to it. It's now on us, as Men, to use that platform, to be honest about our own struggles, and normalise these conversations so things can improve for the generations who come after us. No one will be surprised to hear that when I opened up to my Wife, I felt a weight had lifted off my shoulders. When I spoke to various friends and family, they opened up about the struggles that they had been keeping quiet about and (to my knowledge) no one I care about views me any differently. I know that when friends and family open up to me, or when I hear the mental health struggles of various celebrities, I have all the more respect and admiration for them. Overcoming adversity and pain, being scared of something and doing it any way, are things we should all look up to. Ultimately, it's clear to me that burying any kind of truth or struggle, can manifest in poor mental health. You have to be 'true to yourself', not in the Love Island way of giving yourself a pass to shag as many people as possible, but in the true sense of the phrase, to be authentic, honest and open, and it will rarely serve you badly in the long run. As I get older and more content with myself, my life, my friends, my family and my self-worth, these hedonistic 'pulls' seem to get less frequent, and, for the most part, these self-destructive tendencies with alcohol, binge eating and general 'pleasure-seeking' behaviours are far more controllable. However, it's been a long road to get to this place, and I know that a well-laid training plan, diet protocol and an eye on a long-term goal, are vital for keeping me on the straight and narrow. Having worked with others who suffer far more from self-destructive, and even addictive or obsessive behaviours, I've found the power of effective programming and goal setting to be incredibly important for these personality types. Hedonism is the pursuit of pleasure or pain, and, in many ways, the two things are very closely linked. Look at the relationship between pleasure and pain when it comes to drugs and alcohol. The immediate fix of a drink or a line of cocaine, that makes you feel great in that moment, followed by that feeling of shame, self-loathing, fear and anxiety. Training almost elicits the opposite feeling to this. The pain, discomfort and mental battle to get to the gym, complete hard sets and push your body through personal barriers; the self-discipline to reject certain foods, stick to calorie and macro goals, push through cravings and stay strong when others around you might be drinking or eating the wrong things; followed by the mental euphoria of hitting a PR, finishing a tough workout, the adaptation of your body to a certain diet or training stimulus, all have the ability to elicit that dopamine and serotonin response, make us proud, and contribute towards feelings of fulfilment and self-worth. Doing hard things that are well-planned, and in the absence of chaotic and impulsive behaviours, seems to do well for personality types like myself. The power of goal setting that encourages consistent behaviours, in addition to physical work, certainly has the ability to bring mental clarity. But these are all just words and big claims. Practically speaking, let's look at some of the physical and mental steps that one can take to get started on this journey, ones that I have seen, first-hand, can contribute to turning your life around:

1. **Do it for you**. If there is one thing I have learned over the years, when it comes to this sort of thing, it's that people have to be ready to change. They have to be ready to make this change because they want to for themselves. This may sound like a strange one and I didn't really understand it until recently, but those who are solely doing this for a partner, child or parent, will still have

the self-destruct button at the forefront of their mind. They'll be living a lie to themselves, where, as long as that partner, child or parent thinks they're doing well, this almost makes it true. You have to truly want to be better for yourself, find your self-worth, your pride in achieving a change and be accountable to you! In turn, you will be a better partner, parent or son/daughter as a by-product. But you just can't fake it for someone else. It doesn't seem to work in the long run.

2. **Realistic planning is key**. I speak in another chapter about the narrating self vs the experiencing self and how key it is to get these two things aligned. Of course, your narrating self may lie in bed and plan to get up at 5 am to train, but if your experiencing self keeps waking up and telling you you're too tired to train, it's too cold to get up and you can just train later on, this serves to do no one any good. You must plan realistically, and this includes a realistic plan for training timing, frequency, exercise selection, calorie and macro goals. Adherence is the most important factor in any training and diet plan. Adhering to 90% of a good plan is far better than adhering to 20% of the best plan ever!

3. **Plan your cheats**. It is completely unrealistic (and mentally unhealthy) to make a sustainable diet and training plan that includes no form of bad food, nights out, holidays or training breaks. We want this to be a lifestyle choice that is sustainable and mentally doable, not a 6-week fad to get over the line and let all the good behaviours fall apart. As part of any plan, I also plan my down time, cheat days and nights out where I'll

take a break from the plan for a set time and have a set
time to resume the plan. For me, it is best to take these
moments when they naturally occur and work in with
social moments with friends and family. Weddings,
birthdays, Christmas, anniversaries and holidays are all
examples of naturally occurring events that I factor into
effective programme breaks. I have two versions of these
programme breaks or cheats: The first version is lower
key, which might include a takeaway 'cheat meal' with
my Partner once a week or so, factoring the calories and
macros into my training week. The second version is a
much less frequent event that will generally mark the
end of a training cycle or specific goal and might be
a night out or weekend away with friends or family,
where drinking could be involved, there will be no
training, and food is not measured. For me, these serve
as a metaphorical carrot, where I'll push my training,
diet and goal setting incredibly hard, knowing I will
reach this great social event, and get a mental reset.
When this night out or weekend away is over, we start
a new training phase, with a new programme, and
push hard towards the next goal. For some, this more
extreme 'cheat' simply won't be on the table. You must
be realistic in your own assessment when it comes to
alcohol, bingeing and chaotic behaviours. This approach
of a weekly 'planned cheat' may work extremely well,
but the more extreme version of a boozy night out or
weekend away may not. If you do suffer from types of
substance abuse, in the same way, you need to limit
'pushing the dopamine button' too frequently, as these

big cheats and extended breaks from 'plan adherence' can set off a spiral of chaotic behaviour, and you must be accountable for your own mental strengths and weaknesses. I have worked with some clients and friends who simply do not feel the benefit of an extended 'plan break' and the ability to get back to the plan is just too hard once the chaos of the 'plan break' starts. For those people, I would factor in more frequent but less extreme 'plan breaks' where they may have a cheat meal or a day off from training/diet yet keep themselves accountable again within a 24-hour period.

4. **Find your passion**. Bodybuilding is not the only option when it comes to health and fitness. There are so many different ways that you can burn fat, build muscle, or work on your cardiovascular and mental health - CrossFit, circuit training, powerlifting, kettlebells, distance running, road cycling, peloton, mountain biking, and the list goes on and on. I know people who can't stand to be inside a gym for 45 minutes but as soon as you put them on a Peloton Bike and make it a competition, that 45 minutes doesn't even feel like training. Equally, I know folk who hate the idea of group circuits but thrive off of putting the earphones in and training alone, with their own thoughts. Whether team sport, group training or bodybuilding is for you, there are so many versions of fitness that you can effectively programme towards a planned outcome. I would urge you to try as many as you can and find your place. With some of these fitness communities, the friendships they forge and the extended adherence through simply

enjoying your workouts could make a huge difference to achieving your goals.

5. **Channel your addiction**. Consistency is incredibly important for the pursuit of strength, bodybuilding, fitness and generally excelling in the gym. If you can find a process that works for you and execute this day after day, week after week and month after month, then this consistency will bring results. Those of us who may have addictive or obsessive tendencies can yield great results by channelling this 'addictive' gene, finding solace and reward in measuring input and outcome, and putting this mindset towards a positive goal. Of course, you can go too far with this and anything that becomes too obsessive or all-consuming isn't healthy, but, by and large, channelling some of these compulsive behaviours towards the pursuit of health and fitness, and away from alcohol and drugs, can only be a good thing. For these personality types, having tangible goals and numbers, such as calorie and macro goals, and a training logbook, also serve to keep you accountable and focused. I've worked with countless people in the past who start to pass up on nights out because hitting a PR in the gym the next morning becomes more desirable and important than drinking 10 pints. Hitting their calorie and macro goals becomes a bigger focus than wasting 2000 calories on beer, and letting down their gym partner in the morning becomes unacceptable vs a night of sniffing cocaine. This is NOT any kind of quick fix and there is nothing magical about weight training

that is any different to yoga, golf, cold water therapy or whatever your chosen passion is – the key here is that this is something that keeps you accountable; you start to thrive off the self-development, goal setting and the overall process, and it provides a genuine high that rivals those provided by different varieties of substance abuse… hopefully, without any of the obvious downsides.

My relationship with Alcohol – How do I manage my drinking to work with bodybuilding

It took a long time to be honest about my relationship with alcohol, what 'type' of drinker I am and how to work out a strategy to best manage this for bodybuilding and general life. I am a classic binge drinker who grew up playing team sports, building friendships and getting to know teammates through socialising, nights out and a lot of alcohol. Training and playing hard followed by drinking until 4 am became the norm during my late teens and early 20s, whether that be rugby, football or cricket, and the drinking slowly became as important as the sports themselves. I thrived in this type of culture and have always gravitated towards a 'work hard, play hard' type of lifestyle, where nights out that include a lot of alcohol are the 'rewards' for a great team win or personal performance. In isolation, I don't think this culture is overly terrible, but there are clearly pitfalls to look out for, and if an individual starts to struggle mentally or physically, this type of binge drinking can compound problems and lead on to more serious issues. This type of living certainly has a shelf life, and, at some point, most people have to reduce the frequency of such events or reduce the intensity of such nights out before there's a problem. Like any good training programme, a 'drinking programme' (if that's what you want to call it) should also consider frequency, intensity and volume, and, like good 'exercise selection', it should also consider 'return on investment' and 'risk to reward'. How I deal with my own drinking habits is very specific to me and it's taken me a while to get to this point, but here is how I manage my binge-drinking tendencies, and make it work for me mentally and physically:

- I get nothing out of drinking one or two beers so the 'return on investment' of a couple of pints for a 450-calorie swing just doesn't work. If I go to the pub to watch a game or stay for a drink after golf, I just drink Diet Coke, and will not get 'persuaded' into a pint.
- If I have to go to an event but I have an important thing to do the next day, I can easily not have a beer, but when I do have a beer, I cannot easily stop! For my personality type, one beer can easily lead to 12 but no beers is not a problem. This is the 'risk to reward' element of the equation. Is it worth risking that pint when you consider where it might lead? This is particularly poignant when it's midweek and I have to consider going to work. Other people are capable of having 4 pints and going home at 11 pm, but I have proved over the years that I am not.
- My binge drinking is intense and high volume, and therefore, it cannot be too frequent. Bingeing every single weekend is something I cannot and do not want to do into my late thirties. The reality of feeling

physically terrible the next day and mentally terrible for 3 days is not acceptable. It's detrimental to work, training and my own mental health. I aim to only drink once per month at most (but usually once every couple of months) and these nights out are generally planned events like weddings, stag dos, and days away with friends and family.

- Nights out will be preceded by weeks of hard work in the gym and strict adherence to the diet. I want to get to a night out and feel like it's been physically earned and mentally needed. The golden rule is that I am back on the programme again within 48 hours, so the event has no significant impact on my training and hasn't derailed my progress. Done properly, these nights out should give me the mental break I need and the ability to refocus and go again for the next few weeks or months.

- Nights out, cheat meals, weekends away and holidays are all factored into the programme and considered in training and the diet. Alterations are made accordingly based on these factors. For example, knowing I will drink 3000 extra calories of alcohol on a Saturday night may mean that I reduce my calorie intake by 500 calories a day for the 6 days following the event.

Why do I drink at all?

Everyone's relationship with alcohol is incredibly personal to them. I sought to do nothing here other than share my own truths and experiences. If you resonate with them, that's great, but this section is not to copy, follow or even understand, and it's not about being a role model or saying that 'this is the right way'. Some people should not drink at all. If you want to give up alcohol, are happy to do that and it leads to a better and more fulfilled life, I would urge you to do that immediately. Why do I drink? What attracts me to drinking alcohol and that lifestyle? After all, it seems a strange contradiction to the health, fitness, sporting and 'gym'-dominated parts of my life.

I suppose I've always used alcohol as a kind of contrast to the 'healthy' bit of my life. For me, there's a kind of gritty edge or even romanticism attached to drinking in a bar, listening to Indie music, surrounded by your mates. It's just how my brain works, and to this point, I've not found anything to replace it. It's why I can't watch Supersonic (the Oasis documentary) without drinking everything in the cupboards. It's that self-destruct button that I often press as a kind of 'fuck you' to the wholesome, PG, world of clean eating, training and early nights. My friends, work colleagues and family would probably describe me as a walking contradiction and I'm ok with that. I'm not interested in being a brand or portraying something that I'm not. My biggest takeaway from this is that you're not defined by any one part of your life. When I drink and do something silly, it doesn't take away from the fact that I train and diet hard, day in, day out, week after week, month after month. But just because I body build, it doesn't mean that I don't also go out drinking with friends, have hangovers and make mistakes… I don't think we're defined by any one thing, but by a collection of interests, emotions and actions that shape us on the whole. Some of the most enjoyable, fun and hilarious memories have been shared with friends over a few drinks, nights out and weekends away. If you can work out your own approach to alcohol and nights out, they can certainly serve as useful mental breaks and contrasts to your training plans, but if you are stuck in a spiral of derailed plans, depression and anxiety, which is exacerbated by boozy nights out, you may need to think again.

Chapter 5

Bodybuilding, Competing and Staying Natural

I'm Going to Faint

We'd parked up at B&Q and my Partner drove as I was feeling 'tired'. She knows what this really means - it means I'm two weeks out from a show, my calories and carbs are incredibly low and I'm just feeling terrible! I open the door, get out of the car, and have to take a second as I get a head rush as if I'm inhaling one of those balloons at Glastonbury festival! "Are you ok?" she asks. "Fine, thank you..." I wasn't!

We go into B&Q and it's absolutely heaving. I'm boiling hot and shattered and my brain has this sort of 'fog' where I can't concentrate on the most menial of tasks. Everything seems to be magnified - the smallest of noises annoys me and I'm pushing through the crowd like a zombie. I bend down to pick up a tin of paint and as I rise back to my feet, it's the same head rush... but this time, it's not clearing. I'm seeing stars and flashes and I can feel my heart rate start to race. The anxiety comes over me and I just need to get out. "I'm just going to get some fresh air," I say to my Partner. I leave the store and walk straight across the road to Sainsbury's, trying my best to navigate one foot in front of the other before I pass out! I've overdone it; how stupid of me! I'm calculating the calorie deficit in my head like some kind of possessed maniac! I've already played golf this morning, then it was push day… what have I eaten? Very fucking little is the answer! I've overdone it, massively! I get into Sainsbury's and buy a jar of jam, walk back outside to the car park, sit on the floor and proceed to eat jam, with my hands, straight from the jar! What a sight to behold. I look like Lord Voldemort already, with extreme death face and sour milk 'prep breath'. God, I hope no one I know sees me. I walk back towards the car and my partner is coming out of B&Q. "Well, that was a nice afternoon out," she says sarcastically as we get into the car. "Sorry," I say, as I log half a jar of jam into my 'calorie tracker' as if it's a thing that any normal person does after they've nearly passed out in the local hardware store! Just two more weeks to go! I can do it!

Prepping, mindset and support – the reality of competing and should you do it?

The above tale typifies what the last few weeks of prep can look like. It's important to consider that most people who compete (like myself) aren't professional bodybuilders. This isn't their full-time job, and it's just not a reality that you can simply rest and recover between cardio and weight training. Most of us have full-time jobs away from the stage and even away from the fitness industry. You have to consider your work performance and the understanding of your employer, as you may physically, mentally and emotionally struggle towards the end of your prep. Bodybuilding is a largely selfish sport and it can easily take its toll on friendships and relationships. You can't easily eat out or socialise on prep and (as the above example can show) even completing the most mundane of tasks can sometimes seem like an uphill battle. Most wives or husbands, boyfriends or girlfriends don't body build, so it does take a particular level of understanding. I'm certainly lucky in that I have a very supportive wife and friendship circle. Don't get me wrong, she's not in the slightest bit interested in bodybuilding, but she knows how much I love it, and, for the most part, she leaves me to get on with it. We have a nice balance between understanding, support and merciless piss-taking – but that's what our relationship is built on and I wouldn't have it any other way. Similarly, I have a small group of mates who don't compete themselves but do train and they're always on hand to witness posing routines, give critique, encouragement and remind me how ridiculous the whole ritual is when I need a good laugh. But the reality is, that's where it stops. Expect 99% of people not to care, not to support and not to understand why you might put yourself through this excruciating exercise, to pay for the privilege, abstaining from nights out, alcohol and delicious foods and taking yourself to the brink of an eating disorder to do so. Not everyone respects the mindset and most people think that shaving your entire body, fake-tanning and stepping on stage in tiny pants is just weird. They'll also sometimes view it as highly arrogant, bordering on narcissistic, and won't see bodybuilding as a sport in its own right like football or golf.

So should you compete? The Why...

For 99% of people, competing is a terrible idea. The last few weeks of a prep are not healthy and you have to take your body and brain to a place they've never been before. Personally speaking, I look terrible towards the end of prep. I develop what my Partner calls a tiny shrew head and I get the classic death face. I once woke up to my wife staring at me in bed. 'You look so gaunt; you look like you're dead when you sleep.' Ha, ha! I genuinely lose most of the muscle from my glutes and my legs look skinny (many will say they do in any case). In clothes, I almost appear like I don't train at all. I could just be a lean/skinny guy. Of course, out of clothes, the veins, separation, absence of any visible body fat and dry abs, tell a different story, but who actually sees you out of clothes? And is it worth the reality of what it takes to get here?

Mentally, you can sometimes feel like there's a real fog clouding your thought process, and the ability to sustain conversation (especially a debate or presenting for work) can be incredibly tough. You have moments where you're very irritable and even moments of random anxiety, similar to getting the jitters when consuming too much coffee. This ultra-depleted state is not optimal for performance, well-being or mental cognition, and, done for longer periods, could also have a detrimental effect on major organs and cell function. Of course, we're clearly not made to be in big calorie deficits; our body thinks we're starving to death and it does everything it can to encourage you to eat. Your sleep will likely be affected as your brain likes to wake you up and encourage you to look for food throughout the night, and even your breath and urine can become rancid, as ketones get into wee and saliva.

So what about the positives - why would you compete? I can tell you why I compete, but it's deeply personal to me and I would urge you to find your own 'why' and be absolutely honest with yourself as to whether this is really for you.

Firstly, it's an examination of the knowledge that I've built up over the years. Do I have a sound enough, scientific approach to fat loss and muscle gain, that I can put together a correct and sustainable plan, to get me to peak for this date?

Secondly, it's the mental battle. I like being locked into this mental fight, doing something genuinely difficult that I know most other people couldn't start, let alone finish. It gives me a sense of achievement and I know that once the show is done, I will feel genuinely proud, which is a feeling I seldom get in other parts of my life.

Thirdly, I've always wanted to be a professional sportsman. I've lived and breathed sports my whole life and I just wasn't good enough to be a pro cricketer, rugby player or footballer. The self-imposed restrictions around diet and training are the closest I can get to locking myself into a routine, with a set sporting goal. I have to live like an athlete, prepare meticulously, go without certain foods and alcohol and be ultra-disciplined. I can plan my Mesocycles, look at the overall Macrocycle and aim to prepare, work, rest and peak at exactly the right time. I know there is a certain irony here, that when you look your best, you actually perform at your worst, but the mindset and discipline it takes to get to this point is the real challenge.

Fourthly, I love the actual process. I love it much more than stepping on stage. I often talk to a friend of mine who works in professional football and he always says, 'you have to enjoy the process'. Winning cups, leagues, trophies and even matches comes and goes in the blink of an eye. The final whistle goes and you're already planning for the next game. So, you must enjoy the process as a whole, and I genuinely do. I love the training and I love slowly reducing the calories and carbohydrates and seeing how my body reacts to the stimulus I'm putting on it. I love seeing the various body parts 'come in' as I go through the different stages of 'leanness'. When I get a few weeks out, I get a small line/dip that appears near my bottom abs, and I know I'm on the right track. It's a line that I had never seen before until my show in 2021 and I knew I had entered a level of lean. Learning to trust the process and the science and getting an outcome that you planned for 6 months previously is a great feeling and a validation that the knowledge you've built up is accurate and that you have the willpower, drive and skill to execute that plan.

Finally, competing is addictive. Every one of my last 4 shows has been 'my last show' and I find myself typing this 12 weeks out from competing again. Whilst the process of getting that lean can be horrible, once you're a few months down the line, you somehow crave to be back there. So, if you do choose to compete in just one show, you might be surprised to find you're still donning the trunks a decade down the line.

The Genetic Ceiling for Natural lifters

As a natural lifter, there seems to be a grim truth that we near the genetic ceiling for strength and muscle size reasonably quickly after we start training. As I type this, I'm 38 years old, and, if truth be told, whilst I have made some advancements in specific body parts, I haven't made **significant strength or size gains** for over a decade. That's not meant to be overly negative and I must qualify that due to better adherence, diet and the fact I no longer drink as much alcohol, I'm in better **overall** shape now than in my 20s. However, for pure strength and mass, I'm similar, if not a touch weaker, than I was 10 years ago. Whilst other factors around injuries, boredom, exercise selection and diets are at play, how much is this down to the natural genetic ceiling, and why are more and more people using PEDs in a bid to become bigger, stronger and leaner?

Natty vs PEDs and the startling difference

It's suggested that, depending on your genetics and how you respond to PEDs, you can expect to make strength, size and physique improvements between 2 and 8 times faster than that of a natural lifter, and of course, this lifts your genetic ceiling to a new level, allowing you to build more muscle and become stronger, quicker and bigger in the process. Using PEDs is no magic bullet to an immediately fantastic physique, many people respond horribly to PEDs and even with an array of extra supplements, the ones who get to the top, still work just as hard as those who are natural. There is an elephant in the room though, and one that we have to put out there for transparency. All things being equal, the same genetics, same work ethic and same diet, those taking PEDs will be streets ahead of someone who doesn't. It is just a fact. And the pill that may be hardest to swallow is that, as someone who has worked out naturally for 20 years, you can easily be overtaken (in size and strength) by someone who has a couple of years lifting under their belt. You just need to accept that is the case. A 1996 study by Shalender Bhasin supports this statement. In it, they assigned 43 men to 4 different groups. Group 1 was Testosterone and weight training, Group 2 Testosterone and no training, Group 3 Placebo and Weight Training and Group 4 Placebo and no training. Whilst the group who took steroids and did weights gained the most muscle size, it was also noted, that after 10 weeks of training, the group who took Testosterone injections but didn't train at all, reported a bigger increase in muscle mass, than those who had the placebo but trained 3 times per week, for a 10 week period. "*The men treated with testosterone but no exercise had an average increase of 3.2 kg in fat-free mass, and those in the placebo-plus-exercise group had an increase of 1.9 kg. The increase in the testosterone-plus-exercise group was substantially greater (averaging 6.1 kg).*" [27] I doubt whether this increase in lean mass would have a linear improvement as time goes on, if the individual continues not to train, but the initial response to PEDs and the pace in which an individual can elicit hypertrophy, is staggering.

In 2021, I competed in a classic bodybuilding show in the 2 Bros federation. The show wasn't billed as a natural show and there would be no testing, so I knew that I would be competing against other bodybuilders who would be using PEDs. Some people questioned why I would do this as I would have no real chance of winning and would probably look tiny on stage in comparison (against some, I did!). I've competed in a variety of natural shows (and other 'untested' shows) in the past and my answer is generally that the date of the show was the most practical and realistic in relation to my wider calendar.

I'm not a pro bodybuilder and I have to work around family commitments, birthdays, work and holidays and this show was on a fantastic date to peak before a summer break and then relax. I've always maintained that I compete to peak as my best self, to trial my knowledge of dieting and programming and for the personal, mental battle. So, winning would be nice, but if the show date doesn't allow me to realistically prep, the winning comes a distant second to other commitments. So, I entered the 'novice' category of the 2 Bros classic bodybuilding show. The overall line-up was pretty small in competitor numbers but the standard was fantastic, and specifically, this was a real eye-opener to the differences between natural and unnatural competitors. Of course, I knew this before and it's easy to see in the gym, but when you're there pumping up backstage, fully shredded, with little body fat, the difference in lean muscle mass is startling. Specifically, I got to see a well known social media personality up close. I won't name this person but I guess he'd be described as a YouTube influencer and certainly as an excellent bodybuilder, who has since gone on to earn a pro card. It was interesting to gauge his physique against mine, as he's a pretty good comparison, because, like me, he's around 6 foot to 6 foot 1. For this height, I was allowed to come in at a maximum weight of 230 lbs on stage... I actually weighed in at 178 lbs! It sounds absolutely ridiculous, doesn't it?! That is a full 52 lbs short of my maximum weight limit. For the record, most of the amateur competitors are a long way under the cap and I think this guy only weighed in at about 205 lbs himself, but to put that in perspective, it's 27 lbs heavier than me at the same height! Almost 2 stone. I was very lean for this show but definitely no leaner than him, and, assuming he may have used a proper dehydration protocol, he would have probably been further depleted than me. So, this chap would have a full 2 stone more muscle mass on his frame than I do. At the time of writing this, the person in question is 25 years old and I am 38. Assuming that he started lifting at a similar age to myself, I would have 13 years of additional weightlifting experience under my belt, 13 more years to build mass and grow muscle maturity and feed my muscles and physique with the right diet and nutrition, and 13 more years of potential knowledge and experience. And here I was, half the size of him (especially the bottom half and the upper back, where he was massive!). Even if his genetics are better than mine (which they probably are) it's still a stark size difference given the years of experience and effort. This does nothing to take away from his obvious talent, work ethic and genetics. I also know I'm comparing myself with a pro here, so it's probably not a like-for-like comparison, and against some of the other novice competitors I actually stacked up reasonably well, although I was giving size away to all of them. But it does serve to highlight some truths about natural vs unnatural and how far we can truly push things without PEDs. Namely, it's very hard, in my experience, to have both size and leanness as a natural competitor. If I'm very lean, I look so much smaller in clothes and lose so much strength and size. If I'm bigger and stronger, it's pretty quickly that the abs start to blur, fat gathers in the chest, lower stomach and subscapular and if I push it too far, I barely look like a bodybuilder at all! I believe that (for most people) PEDs move the parameters of how lean you can get whilst maintaining a good level of size and strength, and how strong and big you can get whilst maintaining a good level of leanness. Put simply, assuming average genetics and good adherence to training and diet, most naturals can be lean but not big or big but not lean, whilst the same people on PEDs find it much easier to achieve both.

But is the bar set too low for Naturals?

In researching for this book, I've watched hours of online footage that debates the 'natural status' of influencers, amateur and would-be bodybuilders. Channels like 'More Plates More Dates', 'Coach Greg' and 'Shredded Sports Science', among hundreds of others, have made a job out of calling out 'fake Nattys' and questioning the natural status of various celebrities and 'YouTubers' around the world. Having watched a number of these, I can see the good that this can do. Some of these 'natural claims' are clearly obscene, and it doesn't take much of a trained eye to see that people are playing hard and fast with the truth! Also, in a lot of cases, now it's become much more open and accepted, many of these ex-'fake nattys' have come clean. These channels help to normalise the truth around PEDs, help to educate the health pitfalls of PED use, and aim to give a realistic view of what is really achievable naturally. But is the bar set too low? And at what point do viewing numbers and controversial videos (e.g. picking an argument with someone for views) overtake a measured and reasonable argument? Is it always fair to 'call out' young men and women, who, for my money, could quite easily be natural? I've seen people be called out who have trained for a decade, weigh no more than 200lbs, and who are reasonably lean but nothing that could immediately step on stage. And then you scroll the comments and see hundreds of people calling them out for being 'obviously fake'. Now, I'm not talking about everyone here; anyone with eyes knows that it's a different kettle of fish when folks who are 280 lbs and have single-digit body fat, year-round, are claiming natural. It's very unlikely that they've never touched a banned substance. But I think about my own experience of being called out, even half-jokingly by friends and family, and it's not a very nice place to be. You do feel that your work ethic, knowledge and years of effort are being brought into question. But it's important to consider other people's genetic ceiling, effort levels and knowledge and acknowledge that I am probably veering towards the genetic elite when it comes to building muscle and getting lean. And if you're in this industry, you'll realise this is actually a humble statement (ironically) with most people preferring to say they have average genetics but have just worked 'so, so hard' to achieve what they have. And just to put one thing to bed right here and now... if you're an IFBB pro, and especially if you have won a pro show or stepped on stage at an Olympia, no one wants to hear how your genetics are average. You are in the genetic elite, you respond incredibly well to PEDs, but you also clearly have an excellent work ethic and adherence to a great training and diet protocol. You do not get there without all of these things! In this day and age, natural talent isn't enough without the work and the drugs, but if you don't have the genetics in the first place, all the drugs and hard work won't get you on an Olympia stage. And (drugs aside, hopefully,) the same goes for many sports these days. Such is the standard of professionalism, such is the size of the candidate pool, that you need natural talent, work ethic, top coaching and a bit of luck to be a top-level pro.

But back to the natural bar. I think the industry is getting dangerously close to setting the bar too low here. I can see how it happens. In the age of 'everyone's an expert', I can see how infuriated a lot of the legitimate experts are, including some of the aforementioned channels. These channels often do an incredible (and sometimes hilarious) job of calling out terrible form, poor advice, nonsense science and rubbish supplements, but even they seem to have moments where they're questioning the natural status of people who I think could very easily be natural. Whilst some of these influencers might annoy other experts in their presentation of 'fitness', and whilst these guys and girls are in excellent shape, to sit around the 200 lbs mark and be lean is not outrageous. If you have good genetics, good adherence, and training knowledge, and if your full-time job is to film yourself working out and prepping meals, then I see these physiques as absolutely obtainable naturally. Of course, there is every chance that they're not lifetime 'nattys' but this isn't as cut and dried as they might make out. In my opinion, this hypothesis of questioning someone's 'natty status' can serve to set the bar lower and lower, and suddenly, we're questioning every athlete and every person in a gym who dares to have good genetics and a reasonable work ethic. And perhaps, in some way, setting the bar this low may even encourage average gym-goers into PED use, as they perceive themselves to have hit a natural ceiling and can't see that anything much better is actually obtainable without drugs.

Why do I stay natural? Things you need to consider

This is a very personal decision for any gym and bodybuilding enthusiast and I don't expect everyone to agree with my outlook. I also don't judge people for using PEDs (as long as they're not competing in natural shows or other sports) and I can even understand why some people want to keep their PED use a secret, but if you are claiming 'natural' and then profiting from selling supplements, training and diet programmes, then I do believe this is highly unethical. Most people who have obsessed over training and bodybuilding for as long as I have, would have at least looked into certain substances, discussed PED use with friends and may have even considered steroid use, but my decision to stay natural is based on a number of factors:

Nurture

I see myself as coming from a 'sporting background'. I spent my whole childhood playing football, rugby, cricket and athletics. When I wasn't playing sport, I was watching it, discussing it, or studying it. From a young age, we're conditioned to believe that PEDs are bad, and in these sporting parameters, they are. Steroids and other PEDs equals cheating. Athletes know the substances they can't take and when they're found to have failed a drug test, they're rightly ostracised, banned from competition and labelled as a cheat. I remember numerous times when my parents would discuss athletes, cyclists or boxers and they would talk about 'drug cheats'. When I was growing up, I was conditioned into thinking that PED use always equalled Bad. Whilst I know now that this isn't always as cut and dried, my overriding feeling or thought when I hear PED use is still generally an override of bad... it just is. It's something I've become conditioned to think and feel. It's not to say that I judge open bodybuilders or influencers for using PEDs but I've always said - 'I don't judge you for using PEDs but it's not for me.'

Health

There are obvious health issues that anyone who chooses to use PEDs has to be aware of. Many people in the industry say, 'you get nothing for free' and the same can be applied to PED use. Organ health, heart problems, cholesterol, issues at the injection site, infections, skin problems and mental health issues around anxiety and anger, are all known side effects that could affect PED users[28]. There is enough literature out there that I won't go on about these health issues for too long, but broadly speaking, in my opinion, the risk to reward of using steroids just isn't there for most people. Of course, this will limit your ability to hit a certain size, conditioning or strength level, and if you really want to compete in open shows, it's something you will have to really consider. If you just want to look good on the beach or around the pool, it certainly isn't worth the risk, in my opinion. The things that are less talked about are the longer-term effects, not just on physical health but also on mental health and the things that you might have to go through for the long term. A lot of people who use PEDs for any length of time are likely to need TRT for a lengthy period and perhaps for the rest of their lives once they stop (as your body stops producing its own natural testosterone.) And for me, a real issue would be the mental side of stopping altogether.

The Mental Battle of 'coming off'

Something that is hugely underestimated and discussed less often is the mental battle of stopping steroids. If you use PEDs then you accept that some of your gains, size and strength have to be attributed to the drugs. This doesn't aim to take away from anyone's effort, dedication, knowledge or adherence to a training or diet protocol, but we know that, as the clue says in the name, PEDs 'enhance' this and increase your natural, genetic ceiling. Imagine knowing that stopping these drugs will almost certainly lead to a loss of size or strength and may lead to an increase in body fat. All the things that you've been training for, for X number of years, will be guaranteed to become worse in the coming weeks or months! Now, whilst I have first-hand experience of discussing this with clients and friends at the gym, I've not experienced this myself, but I can imagine it's pretty devastating. I've never bench-pressed 180kg, but if I had done, and 6 months later, I'm back to 140kg, I would imagine this is pretty soul-destroying. If I had got up to 17 stone, and a year later, I'm back to 14 stone and carrying more fat, this would be hard to take as a bodybuilder. Anyone who takes PEDs must do so while acknowledging there is a shelf life to this continuous improvement and the drop-off, for them, is going to be way more severe than for a 'natural.' This flies in the face of everything we want to achieve as gym-goers and bodybuilders. We're programmed to give the body a new stimulus, grow, repair, shed fat, adapt, improve, get stronger, leaner, bigger and quicker and everything in our planning and our psyche is set up for continuous improvement. It's not always linear improvement and often some areas stall, whilst other areas improve (e.g. a bulk vs a cut vs maintenance), but by and large, we're always trying to achieve some form of improvement. Coming off PEDs (for good) almost guarantees that you will see some form of regression over the coming weeks and months. Don't underestimate the effect this might have on your mental health and training. Especially if you're a big, strong guy or girl and some of your identity is wrapped up in this persona and image, the potential of losing 50 lbs of weight and a ton of strength may be harder than you think.

Professional Bodybuilding and PEDs

Outside the largely amateur world of natural bodybuilding is professional bodybuilding, where the prize money is bigger, sponsorships can be worth thousands and worldwide fame and recognition is more common. The crazy thing to consider about professional bodybuilding, with events like The Olympia and The Arnold as their pinnacle, is that in terms of PEDs, it's the exact opposite to every other sport. In contrast to other sports, where tested athletes are banned for misuse of PEDs and other banned substances, it's literally impossible to compete as one of the top 20 bodybuilders in the world unless you're using a plethora of PEDs. No one competing at this year's Olympia would claim to be natural, and no one would be expected to be. Although some people have claimed to attain a pro card naturally (and I believe a lot of these claims are genuine), it would be very close to 100% of professional bodybuilders who use PEDs. Also, the ones who earn a pro card as natty and stay natty can expect to be placed dead last in every contest from there on in.

From a personal perspective, my view has always been that, although I wouldn't want the health risks for myself, those who choose to use PEDs as a grown adult can do so, providing they adhere to the following criteria:

- They don't compete in sports. And for me, this includes sports of all levels. As well as professional sports, I also don't think someone should be playing division 6, Saturday club rugby if compounds like testosterone or growth hormone are helping them to get unnaturally bigger, stronger and quicker. It's unfair and potentially dangerous.
- They don't compete in natural bodybuilding. This seems an obvious one, but you'd be amazed how many bodybuilders, who do use PEDs, compete in 'natural' shows.
- They are honest about their PED use and don't seek to attribute their physique to certain supplements that they then sell to make money, if, in reality, their physique should be attributed, in part, to the use of PEDs.

Outside of that, I've never been judgemental about people who use PEDs. A lot of the physiques I admire and people I like in the industry, like bodybuilders, powerlifters and strength athletes, have often used PEDs and been honest about it. Many of the people who train in my local gym use PEDs; they're decent people, it's not the end of the world.

But is there more we need to consider here? Given the abundance of 'fake naturals' selling useless supplements, the number of bodybuilders pushing the envelope towards (and past) 300lbs-physiques to win professional events, and the simple fact that in the last decade, PEDs seem to have moved from a bodybuilding and strength subculture into the mainstream of social media and fitness influencing, should I be changing my stance from an ethical, moral and health perspective?

In the UK, sports like rugby and football have attracted bad press from ex-players and regulatory bodies for their past practices around concussion. We're now seeing potential lawsuits being brought against some of these governing bodies, because ex-players are experiencing terrible symptoms down the line that may have been caused by things like heading the football, high tackles, playing on with head injuries and questionable training protocols that may have contributed to things like dementia further down the line. These are incredibly complex issues and talking through the minefield of duty of care vs personal choice vs rule changes vs other contributing factors to injuries is far beyond the reach of this book or my own knowledge. But it's very easy to look at these other governing bodies, which are coming under scrutiny from current and past competitors, and examine whether some of these questions should be asked about Professional Bodybuilding. Yes, of course, these are consenting adults who choose to take PEDs in the name of the sport they love. By and large, they know the potential pitfalls and believe they can take these substances whilst working with a medical professional and limit the potential for adverse health factors. But should a sport or governing body actually be condoning and encouraging the use of PEDs as an actual barrier to entry? It's easy for them to say that they don't condone or encourage PED use, but in reality, you can't compete in the highest echelons of the sport without them. So, in real life, you have a sport where to reach the pinnacle, you have to be taking a plethora of steroids, growth hormones, fat burners and dehydration aids to compete. It sounds like an absolute moral and legal minefield. I could guarantee if you asked a cross-section of the general public their opinion on this, they would think it's complete madness - every competitor, juiced up to the eyeballs, trying to reach impossible levels of big and shredded, in the name of winning a trophy that's judged by a governing body that seems to ignore, condone and quietly encourage the use of PEDs. If this is the elite, the pinnacle of the sport of bodybuilding, surely this is condoning, normalising and glamorising steroid use. After all, natural bodybuilding is barely a sport at all; it has no airtime, very little exposure and the prize money is non-existent. I could name lots of 'bodybuilders' but perhaps only 5 or 6 'natural bodybuilders', and I love the sport! I would imagine the average person could name a handful of bodybuilders past and present and absolutely no nattys.

I guess, to that end, the problem lies in simple supply and demand. There is no real demand to watch a bunch of natural bodybuilders on stage because it's a largely unimpressive sight compared to professional bodybuilders who use gear. People want to see freaks. They want to see people pushing 300lbs, with super-striated glutes, dug-out hamstrings and delts like cannon balls. In the main, there is very little demand for people to watch smaller natural bodybuilders, who look more comparable to themselves. And I would be lying if I said I was any different from a consumer perspective. I'm intrigued to see who looks more freaky out of Big Ramy and Nick Walker at the next Olympia. I can't wait to see if Urs or Breon can push Chris Bumstead, with insane V-tapers and waist-to-shoulder ratios. But if you take a holistic view of the industry and look at the competitors that we've lost over the last few years, you can't say that super physiological amounts of PEDs aren't playing their part. In the last few years, we've lost some legends of the sport. John Meadows, Shawn Rhoden, George Peterson, Paul Poloczek, Rich Piana, Dallas McCarver, Cedric McMillan and Andreas Frey to name but a few, have all passed away as reasonably young men, mainly in their 30s, 40s and 50s. Whilst it's never as black and white as to simply attribute their deaths to PED use, you can't get away from the fact that this is a disproportionate number of young deaths and all of these men used large amounts of PEDs and were unnaturally massive. It's not for me to judge whether any of these guys would have swapped their bodybuilding careers and impressive physiques for more time on earth. Some will say that they lived the lives they wanted to, excelled in their passion and entered professional bodybuilding and PED use with eyes wide open. But if the pinnacle of the sport didn't tolerate gear use, and the bar was set much lower for natural competitors to compete at sensible and achievable weights, there's very little doubt that longevity and health would be improved overall. In reality, I can never see us getting to that point, as the pendulum has swung so far the other way; it's all about 'mass monsters', ultra-dry and shredded physiques. People want to see freaks, not impressive but attainable bodies. There simply isn't enough interest in natty bodybuilding to ever commercialise or monetise it as a sport.

The Balance – It's not all bad but if you are going to use... consider this...

As someone who drinks alcohol, eats junk food and occasionally smokes (when he's drunk enough), there is a level of hypocrisy to simply call out PEDs with no balance or counter. I am in no way condoning alcohol, cigarettes or any other kind of drug, and there will be many people in the world who use PEDs at the expense of other drugs and may be healthier because of it. Someone who is smug about their natural status but drinks every weekend and smokes 20 a day should probably think again. Some of the more sinister side effects of PED use can also be attributed to alcohol, recreational drugs, poor diet choices and cigarettes. The potential for increased cholesterol, damaged organs, cardiovascular disease, weight gain or weight loss, are all increased with the use of PEDs but are also more prevalent with people who have bad diets, drink, smoke or use recreational drugs. If you are going to use PEDs, I would seriously urge you to look at these other factors and come up with a sensible approach to your wider diet and lifestyle. Someone who is using varieties of PEDs and continues to drink alcohol, smoke and eat badly, may well have the perfect storm to contribute towards some of these serious issues. But someone who has decided to use PEDs and does it at the expense of alcohol, cigarettes, or recreational drugs, may well be in a better boat. This is generally a personal thing, with individuals reacting very differently to PEDs and, on the whole, anything above a standard TRT dose, prescribed by a doctor, probably won't contribute to longevity of life and overall health. What I am sure of though, is that whatever legal, moral or health issues we discuss, people will still use PEDs. We can't bury our heads in the sand and just hope this goes away or pray that our Youngsters 'respond well' to their first cycle. Education, knowledge and transparency is the always the best way forward. It's up to people in the fitness industry to be honest and transparent about steroids and it's up to professionals, Doctors, Pharmacists and many of these other experts, to give sound and real advice, facts and figures. Whatever you choose to do, make sure you do your research, consult a proper medical professional, and really weigh up the pros and cons of PED use.

Chapter 6

My Contest Bulk, Cut and Prep Diet and Training Plans

He has a Smooth Leg...

It's August 2018 and the morning of my show. I've barely slept a wink and I wake up to find most of my tan on the bed. Luckily, my Partner's away on holiday or it wouldn't land particularly well.

I'm woefully underprepared as I notice there's still some hair on my shins... I better shave again before the final layer of tan goes on! My mate comes over and helps with the final coat... let's be honest - this is really weird! We're in hysterics as he helps tan those hard-to-reach areas with a sort of mini roller that you'd use to paint your house. I slide my ballbag to the side and tan all around the inner thighs and he's rolling on the floor in tears! It's another reminder that whilst I love the process of bodybuilding, the actual show day isn't as enjoyable. It's the complete opposite to every other sport where you'd generally moan at the training and preparation but love the game... for me, the comp day is just a means to an end. It's all about the science behind effective programming, dieting and the sheer will and fortitude to get through it. It's a mental battle to overcome, a process that takes planning, knowledge and a whole host of willpower. Even getting on stage should make you proud – it's one of the hardest things I've done and a process that 99% of people just can't put themselves through and probably shouldn't! That being said, this time around, it's rushed, it feels very last minute and I'm not convinced I've pushed the diet nearly enough, but the show is a day before I join my wife on holiday and it was just too perfect a date to turn down. Now the tan is on, I feel better. More striations show through and I feel big and full, if not as lean as I wanted. Off we go to the NIA in Birmingham!

It's 'pump time' backstage and it becomes apparent who my competition will be. It's a really supportive environment backstage because we all know what each other has been through and sacrificed to be here. We're chatting and pumping and scoffing down sweets, rice cakes and jam and I'm feeling ok. One of the lads comments, 'How have you kept that size on your shoulders?' Another says, 'You're massive for a natural, mate'… and I start to think that maybe I have a chance! Have I been overly negative and actually I'm looking great and big and full and yes, I'm going to win?! Looking around, would I swap my physique with anyone here? The answer is... probably not. An air of confidence comes over me and I can't wait to get on stage. But when we do get on stage, and I see everyone else under those lights, I start to realise why I have kept the broadness in my shoulders and size in my arms… it's because I'm at least 10 lbs overweight, and, in the years since, with a few more shows behind me, I now realise I was nowhere near an acceptable level of 'lean' to be on that stage. Unfortunately for me, the judges also knew it.

It was an unusually stacked comp, with around 18 people in my class, so the judges would call about 6 people on at once to do the mandatories. I was first up and the poses actually went ok. Posing has never been a strong point and I was hardly fluid, but I felt positive and completed all the required poses to a reasonable standard. I felt tired and sweaty but I did ok. Unfortunately, that wasn't the end of it. Everyone else went to the back whilst another group came to the front of the stage for their turn. But not me. "And number 4, please stay at the front." It was me, again. So, I stayed at the front and did another full round of the mandatory poses. My tan was running, I was sweating hard and my lats and quads had just started to cramp. I got through it, and thank God, I could finally rest, or so I thought. We all went to the back of the stage and the next group were called… "and number 4, please come back to the front." I couldn't believe it. Me again! I didn't have it in me. My tan was running down my face, all my muscles were cramping and I barely even flexed. I assumed they were punishing me for coming in overweight and for having a poor tan and being badly shaved! Either way, it was a humbling experience and one that I never wanted to repeat.

I walked off stage and my mate had taken a few pics for me… they weren't good. And even with his kind words and positivity, I could tell that he knew I didn't do well. I left the arena and walked outside and the same chap who commented on my big shoulders before the show was on the phone. "Yeah, I reckon I did well. Yeah, at least top 3. Ah, yeah, the lad with big shoulders… nah, not really… nah, I don't think so… well, he was carrying a bit more fat than I first thought and he had a pretty smooth leg." My mate and I looked at each other and started to laugh. It was a very polite way of saying that I had small, shit, soft legs, carrying too much fat and I was absolutely no threat to anyone! We went straight to McDonald's, ate £30 of burgers and drove straight home. There was no point in putting myself through the humiliation of the evening show and, even if I wanted to, all my tan had sweated off! Whilst I laughed it off and didn't dwell on the failure for too long, I vowed that I would come back stronger and not make the same mistakes again!

My actual contest bulk, cut and prep diet and training for 2021 (the good one!)

I'll start this chapter by admitting that I am rubbish at bodybuilding. I can do the training bit, I can do the science bit and I've got the mental fortitude to do the diet, but the actual sport of bodybuilding, on that stage… I am woeful. People think that bodybuilding is about lifting heavy weights and eating chicken and rice, but it's not. You have to be well presented, groomed and tanned – I am not. The posing is an art form; you need poise, stage presence and the fitness and conditioning to be able to show your physique in a range of poses. The poses themselves are incredibly technical - feet placement, breathing patterns, body angles and timing all need to be considered. The simple act of continuously tensing for minutes at a time is exhausting. All of the chat below is about my contest training and diet, because those bits are my passion, but if you are looking to compete, don't underestimate the time and effort it takes to learn about the actual sport of bodybuilding, the mandatory poses, posing routines, tanning, shaving and music! You can tell, very quickly, those who (like me) are here as a means to an end, for the training and diet and the challenge, and those who are proper 'bodybuilders' in the true sense of the word.

During the lockdown of 2020, I decided that I would make 2021 the year that I competed again and really push the boundaries. I aimed to prioritise bodybuilding (not just 'the gym' but actual bodybuilding), live and breathe the training and the diet, practise the posing more than before and try to present the best physique that I have ever had on stage. I picked a show date and would aim to plan out a full 9 months of training, diet, bulking, cutting and peaking for that date. Below is my account of the whole affair - training methods, macros, calories, supplements and an account of my weight and appearance at different stages. You have to consider that this is personal for me, but this does serve to give a completely truthful and realistic account of what I did, how it worked and how I felt. I wouldn't recommend copying the exact plan, but it could serve as a skeleton to help you get started and how to slowly taper calories, set up macronutrients and look at exercise and diet choices to peak for a specific date.

Whilst I've spoken about the perks of 'maingaining' for general health, fitness and performance, I would absolutely advocate using a three-phase approach when it comes to preparing for a bodybuilding show. Phase one will see me slowly adding calories and progressing weight and reps in the gym in the bid to build extra muscle mass and improve the weak points of years gone by. This is known as the 'off season' or 'bulking phase' and will run for 4.5 months as the first phase of the prep. Phase two will be a similar length 'cutting' phase, where I will aim to slowly reduce calories, add cardio and burn as much fat as possible, whilst maintaining as much muscle mass as I can. Phase 3 is a (very bodybuilding-specific) final push for the show. Some call it 'peak week' but it's basically to get me primed for that specific date. It involves manipulating muscle glycogen and water to come in at my very best. This phase is completely unnecessary unless you are competing. It's not all that healthy and incredibly taxing both physically and mentally.

Phase 1 – The Bulk - 18 weeks

Goals – Build muscular size and strength. Raise metabolism. Increase weight and therefore 'maintenance calorie' starting point for cutting.

Calories – Starting at maintenance calories of 3,100 and slowly adding every 1 to 3 weeks as required to end up at around 4,100 calories to finish.

Macros – I will maintain a 40% carb, 30% protein and 30% fat macro ratio throughout phase one.

This means a starting point of:

Carbs – 305g, Pro 240g, Fat 100g. Calories = 3100.

And a finishing point of:

Carbs – 420g, Pro 300g, Fat 135g. Calories = 4100.

Adding calories slowly - It's vital to note that I did not simply jump from the starting point to the finishing point in a matter of days or weeks. Just as the process of getting stronger in the gym is a slow grind of adding small weights to the bar every week, month, or year, dieting is exactly the same. Your body can't handle a random surge in calories. If I jumped from 3100 straight to 4100 in a matter of weeks, my body would simply gain a lot of fat quickly. This addition in calories happened slowly over the course of 18 weeks. As I started to get used to the surplus calories, I would add 100 - 200 calories every one to three weeks depending on how I was feeling. If the scales were moving fast enough, I didn't need to up the calories, but if I had stalled, I needed to increase them. If I felt like I was gaining too much fat vs muscle, I would cut back, but if I was adding mass and not gaining excess fat, I could push again. This was a constant game with the mirror, the scales and how my body was feeling, performing and responding. As I was gaining weight and muscle, my 'maintenance calories' were constantly evolving and rising.

The Training – For the training, I went for my favoured 4-day 'bro split' with 1 day off. So, every 10 days, I would train 8 times and have 2 rest days. The split was as follows:

1. Legs
2. Chest and Triceps
3. Shoulders
4. Back and Biceps

The Formula – Each session would be around 12-15 working sets and one or two 'finishers' that would work the muscle through a variety of angles and rep ranges, always prioritising a heavy compound with the aim of getting stronger as the programme goes on in the rep range of 5-8. This would be followed by a couple of assistance movements in a classic hypertrophy 8-15 range and would always end with a 'finisher'. For this phase, I did a tweaked variation on Hany Rambod's FST-7 training where I would pick an exercise and complete 4 sets of 8-15 reps with only 30 seconds of rest between them. The aim is to keep the weight as high as possible but go to failure each time. I then do 3 additional sets as a straight drop set, with 1 set of partials to finish.

Here is a sample of my programme, though it's important to add that you can swap out exercises for any similar ones, especially if you connect with those better:

Legs
Hack Squat - 4 x 5/8
Leg Press - 4 x 8/15
Lunges - 4 x 8/15
Calf raises - 4 x 25
Ham Curl finisher (7 set finisher)

Shoulders
Dumbbell shoulder press - 4 x 5/8
Lateral raise - 4 x 8/15
Rear delt flye - 4 x 8/15
Shrugs (7-set finisher)

Chest and Triceps
Flat Bench press - 4 x 5/8
Incline dumbbell press - 4 x 8/15
Triceps overhead - 4 x 8/15

Chest flye (7-set finisher)

Triceps pushdown (7-set finisher)

Back and Biceps

Pull-ups - 2 x failure (one wide grip; one pronated)

Lat pull-down - 4 x 8/15

Dumbbell bicep curl - 4 x 8/15 (2 sets standard, 2 sets hammer grip)

Bent-over row - 4 x 8/15

Machine preacher curl (7-set finisher)

Any row machine (7-set finisher)

Cardio – For health and digestion reasons, cardio was kept in 2 or 3 times per week in the shape of walks, golf or the odd cross-training session, but I didn't do anything measurable or intense during this phase.

Phase 1 results:

Weight – I started at a weight of 209lbs and ended up at 226lbs so I gained 17lbs of weight along the way and, whilst I definitely put on some fat, it wasn't until right at the end when I pushed the calories up to the 4000 mark and started sitting above 224lbs (16 stone) that I felt all that heavy or cumbersome. In all honesty, I ended up gaining more fat than I needed to, and the photo I've used for this phase is a kind one! There is obviously no way that I've put on 17lbs of muscle in an 18 week period. I've accumulated some fat along the way and the water weight / full glycogen stores will also account for some added mass.

Strength – There were some reasonable strength gains along the way, but interestingly, my strength seemed to peak about 3 weeks before finishing phase 1 and didn't improve in a linear fashion with an extra few pounds. Perhaps I had hit a performance 'sweet spot' where, from a cardio and hormonal perspective, I started to suffer with that extra weight and body fat. Some of my lifting improvements are below:

Hack squat – starting 3 plates x 5 reps. Finishing 4 plates x 5 reps.

Bench Press – Starting 120kg x 4 reps. Finishing 130kg x 5 reps.

DB shoulder Press – starting 46kd db x 5 reps. Finishing 50kg db x 5 reps.

Plate loaded lat pull – starting 4 plates x 8 reps. Finishing 5 plates x 6 reps.

To Conclude Phase 1

So, I was bigger and I was stronger and I didn't feel horrendous. I made the advancements that I wanted to make, I was the heaviest I had ever been, and I had made some good strength gains in the lat pull and hack squat. My legs will never be a good point, but they had grown and they had got stronger, so you can't ask for much more than that. The last few weeks at over 4000 calories had become more of a drag. I've never struggled with eating volume before but it's obvious to me that once my body gets to around 16 stone, it really doesn't want to get much heavier. At this point, my appetite had started to suffer and I assume my leptin levels (the appetite suppressant) were elevated and my ghrelin (the hunger hormone) was far suppressed. If we're to buy into the dual intervention theory, then I have found my high-end weight and fat % for sure.

I definitely put on more weight and fat than I actually needed to, but I left myself a decent amount of time to slowly cut. The really pleasing thing is that I was ready for a change. I was craving more cardio, reduced calories and the feeling of being lean again. Well, thank God for that, because I was about to get more of that feeling than I've ever experienced in my life before! Be careful what you wish for!

I know what you're thinking 'Did you even train legs?' It's not the best of photo's, if I'd have known that 18 months later, I'd be writing a book, I would have taken more! I guess this shows that when you don't feel or look your best, you're reluctant to take shirtless pics. This is probably quite flattering given the angle and the shadows. At 226lbs, I had plenty of work to do over the next 18 weeks.

Phase 2 – The Cut – 18 Weeks

Goals – Slowly strip off body fat whilst maintaining as much muscle mass as possible.

Calories – Starting by cutting straight back to a new maintenance calorie level of 3,400 and slowly tapering and cutting down to 2,000 calories to finish.

Macros – The new macro ratio is 40% protein, 35% carb and 25% fat with a starting point of:

Carbs 340g, Pro 300g, Fat 94g. Calories = 3,400

And a finishing point of:

Carbs 200g, Pro 178g, Fat 55g. Calories = 2,000

Tapering Calories Slowly- In the same way that we increased calories gradually in phase 1, we're going to apply the same principle for reducing calories. Whilst we might see general weight fall off us if we were to go straight to 2000 calories, we would also see devastating amounts of muscle and strength loss, not to mention the mental element of cutting your calories in half overnight. To preserve as much hard-earned muscle as possible, we want this process to be as slow and meticulous as the bulk and we'll look to slowly decrease by 100-200 calories every 1-3 weeks as we see fit. Using exactly the same methods of using the scales, mirror and performance in the gym as indicators to keep calories the same or decrease them, our first port of call is to come straight back to maintenance and further cut from there. There's little point in slowly cutting from 4100 as this is already a surplus of around 400 - 600 calories and we don't need to be gaining even more weight. From a macros perspective, I've changed the ratio to prioritise higher amounts of protein to help sustain muscle mass and give an increased thermogenic effect to fat-burning. Carbs stay at 35% to help fuel workouts and maintain muscle glycogen levels. I'm wary of dropping carbs too low in a calorie deficit and getting 'flat'. Once you lose that pop in the muscle or muscle roundness, it can be very hard to get it back on a prep without going back into a calorie surplus. I've dropped fats, but only ever as low as 25% which is considered towards the acceptable low end for a good hormonal profile. Especially as a natural bodybuilder, you have to accept that your testosterone will likely be in the bin after this prep and you must at least get this amount of fat in your diet on a daily basis.

The Training – I changed the training to a 3-day split, completed back-to-back with 1 day per week rest. Rather than a traditional push/pull/legs, I work better with specific body parts, so whilst the split is similar, I chose a slight variation with a chest/shoulders/triceps, legs, and back/traps/biceps split.

The Formula – I still wanted to work the muscle through a range of angles and a variety of rep ranges. However, the really heavy sets of 5 were out the window after the first month or so. I know that some will say you should keep the heavy stuff in to encourage muscle retention and density, but I was already pushing the frequency and volume and didn't want to tempt fate by keeping the intensity super-high. I had started to lose strength by about week 3 and I wasn't going to be setting any PBs any time soon. Heavy sets of 5 just seemed like a dare to get injured, so these were parked. I also chose to move to a multiple-day split rather than a classic bro split because I was no longer eating the required calories to sustain one muscle for a whole session. Eating in a deficit and expecting your chest or back to eat up 20 sets, recover and be ready to go again in a few days just isn't realistic. I could tangibly feel when a muscle was done, and it was way short of the volume and intensity that I was putting into each muscle split during phase 1. I would still train hard and generally to failure, or at least form failure, but my emphasis was far more on mind-muscle connection, feeling the contraction, and controlling the tempo. Whilst I would still start with the big compounds, I would also favour the use of machines during this phase as a way to limit the risk of injury and keep things simple. I would look to complete a couple of compound movements in an 8-15 rep range and finish with some super sets and drop sets across a variety of machine and isolation exercises. A sample of the sessions is below:

Chest / Triceps / Shoulders
Dumbbell shoulder press - 4 x 8/15
Incline Machine Chest Press - 4 x 8/15
Lateral Raise - 4 x 12/15
Triceps Overhead - 3 x 8/15
Pec Deck flye superset rear delt flye - 3 x 12/12
Dips superset press-up finisher - 20/20, 15/15, 10/10, 5/5

Legs
Hack Squat - 4 x 8/15
Lunges - 4 x 10/12
Leg Press - 4 x 12/15
Leg ext. superset ham curls - 3 x 12/12
Calf raises - 3 x 25

Back, Traps and Biceps

Pull-ups - 2 x failure (one wide grip, one pronated)

Lat pull - 4 x 8/15

DB bicep curls - 4 x 8/15 (2 sets of standard grip and 2 hammer grip)

Seated row - 3 x 12/15

Bicep Preacher machine drop set - 5 x 10 drop sets no rest

Shrugs – 100 shrugs with as little rest as possible. Don't let go of the bar.

Cardio – Would be done twice per week in the first 3 weeks, 3 times per week in weeks 4-8, 4 times per week in weeks 8-12 and every day in the last 4 weeks of prep. My cardio sessions can be picked from the options below:

1. 500-calorie cross trainer. This tended to take anything from 40 mins to an hour depending on the intensity, which, in turn, depended on how tired or depleted I was.

2. 500-calorie stair master or stepper. I found calories were burned slightly quicker but this was way more taxing and I couldn't do this in the last 4 weeks or so.

3. A round of golf. This might sound weird but it was fantastic for my mentality. It didn't even feel like cardio but I was in the fresh air and walking for up to 4 hours at a time. What's more, I rarely thought about food and could just pack what I wanted to eat into that 4-hour window. Whilst a round would burn 1100-1400 calories depending on the course, only 500-700 of these calories are 'active calories' so this satisfied me from a numbers perspective. There will be some who will say that this

isn't precise or scientific enough for a prep, but I'm not a pro and I stand by the fact that golfing during this cutting phase gave me the momentary escape that I needed from the mental battle and a way to burn calories and still have fun.

4. Walking was also an option that I enjoyed but it would take more like 90 minutes to burn 500 calories and as I was walking whilst golfing a couple of times per week, I favoured the first two options of a gym-based session.

To Conclude Phase 2

I finished Phase 2 having lost over 40 lbs in weight. Whilst I had lost some muscle mass and significant amounts of strength, there is no doubt I had achieved the aim of this phase - to burn as much fat as possible whilst retaining as much muscle. In an ideal world, I wouldn't have come down this light, but it was only at around this weight that the separation in the quads and hamstrings really came in and I even got a bit (really tiny bit) of feathering in the glutes and lower back, which is rare for me. The order in which you lose fat and the appearance of different body parts is all down to genetics. If you were to just look at my abdominals, you may have said I was dialled in and ready to go about 10 lbs ago, but the lower half and posterior muscles weren't there yet; it took longer to see that detail come through. From a mental perspective, this was up there with the hardest things I've done. I ended up weighing in at 178 lbs for the comp, and even if we allow a few pounds for dehydration (I didn't run a particularly savage protocol), I was a genuine 182lbs or so, which equalled a weight loss of 44 lbs in just over four months from the start of Phase 2. If my high set point for body weight is around 16 stone or 224 lbs, then my low end is definitely around 190lbs or 13Stone 5lbs, and the accompanying body fat, which I would guess to be anything from 6%-8%. Once I hit that last 3 weeks and dipped below the 190lbs mark, it was tough! That last 10lbs was 10 times harder than the 30 lbs that went before it, which makes perfect sense given the dual intervention theory.

By 10 weeks out, things had moved quite considerably. I was down to 205lbs, which shows that a large amount of water weight had come off. I still felt pretty good in myself as the calories were reasonable at 2800 per day. If I wasn't competing, I would stop dieting and maintain at around this weight. Strength hadn't diminished too far and I was feeling much leaner and fitter than 8 weeks previous. Amazingly, I still had about 20 lbs to lose to be stage ready!

At 3 weeks out I was down to 187lbs and was probably happiest with my physique here. In hindsight, I may have overdone the last few weeks. Whilst the photo's looked good for bodybuilding and under this specific lighting, my actual appearance on a day to day basis, did not look healthy. I was incredibly gaunt, weak and way below my 'low set point' for body fat.

Phase 3 – Pre-Show run up – The Final Push – 12 days out

This is the phase that you do not need to put yourself through unless you are competing. This isn't healthy and, unless you need to be super shredded under lights for one day, this will negatively impact your physique, hormonal profile and mental health in the short, and perhaps, long run. Dropping calories and carbohydrates this low and manipulating water is not necessary in general life.

Goals – Manipulate glycogen stores and water retention to come into the show as ripped and dry, but as full, pumped and muscular as possible.

Calories & Macros: Week one (depleting). Calories = 1800. Carbs under 100g, Protein 220g, Fat 60g. During this phase, I will be over-drinking, forcing my body into 'flushing mode' by drinking around 8 litres of water per day.

5 days out (the carb up) Days 1 & 2. Calories = 2500, Carbs 300g, protein 220g, fat 50g.

Day 3 Calories = 3000, carbs 400g, protein 220g, fat 50g. Reduce water to 2 litres.

Day before the show = Here we have two choices based on whether I was feeling flat or full and whether I felt dry and lean or fluffy and watery.

1. Repeat Day 3 and potentially add to the carbs if feeling really flat.
2. Pull back and repeat days 1&2 with fewer calories and carbs.

Based on the fact I was feeling really lean and dry but a little flat and small, I repeated Day 3 and kept carbing up. I only sipped water and would drink around a litre that day at most. I stopped eating at around 6 pm as I didn't want to wake up with a bloated stomach full of food.

On Show Day: Calories and macros were just a by-product of how I felt. I didn't want any substantial food as I wanted my stomach to be flat and empty, but I needed to prioritise simple sugars to achieve a 'pumped' and vascular appearance. I also didn't want to radically change my diet all of a sudden and risk an upset stomach or feeling generally unwell on show day.

I ended up having the usual breakfast of porridge but with some added jam, made quite dry with half the usual water. Forty-five minutes before the show, I had 5 rice cakes with jam and some Haribo sweets before going on stage. I was flatter and less pumped than I could have been but versus the idea of coming in watery, bloated or soft, it was the better play. I knew my mid-section was going to be a strong point so I would rather showcase that to the best of my ability, even if I'm slightly flatter in other parts.

The Training – Week one, during the carb depletion, my training remained the same. During the last 5 days, I would stop training legs completely. After such a gruelling phase, the legs are a body part that tends to look better when rested and fully recovered and you don't want to be going into a show knowing you may have to tense your legs for 10 minutes of stage if they're tired. My last 4 sessions were just a push/pull training split, done in a 'pump' style straining with nothing to complete failure. The idea in that first week when depleting carbs is just to get the muscle as empty as possible of glycogen, allowing for the super compensation of the carb refeed pre-show. My very last session was an all-over upper body session, where I did 3-4 sets per upper body part. I put a specific emphasis on the delts and lats, as these are body parts that I really want pumped and emphasised on stage to try and create that imposing silhouette.

Week one (depleting) - Same split as before but training legs early in the week so they rest for a full week pre-show.

4 days out – 2 upper body push/pull sessions of around 16 sets, stopping short of failure to get a pump but not exhausting the muscle. With two days out, a short pump-style session for lats and delts with a variety of pulls, rows, lat raises and rear delt flyes.

Cardio – In the last week, I did two 30-minute walks and two 30-minute cross-training sessions at a very low intensity. At this point, it's not about burning calories as much as keeping the same process that my body has become used to and not changing too much at the last minute.

To Conclude Phase 3

All in all, it had been a savage 9 months for different reasons, but I was pleased with the outcome and happy that the science had stood up. I spent the first three days post-show eating what I wanted and feeling glad it was over but once that initial relief had passed, I missed it. I missed being locked into a plan and a goal, day in, day out, and I craved being back in the midst of working towards something. Within a week, I had signed up for another show and the work began again. Whilst I would never recommend the sport of bodybuilding for 99% of people,

I would absolutely recommend a tangible competition or event of some description, for anyone who wants to get in serious shape and hold themselves accountable to a training and diet plan. To devise and execute that plan successfully might be one of the most rewarding things you will ever do.

Here I am the day before the show, looking like an emaciated chicken wing! I was down to 182lbs here, although I would officially weight in at 178lbs on show day.

Show Day! All the hard work and sacrifice into 3 carefully chosen pics......I say 'carefully chosen' because you'll notice I've included none of the back shots, which were awful by comparison. I couldn't have done much more in terms of application and hard work, especially diet adherence and cardio. Although my 'weak points' and posing were still poor, I am definitely proud of what I presented, the work and effort that went into it. I was looking forward to getting back towards a healthy weight, and starting to plan the next challenge.

To Wrap It Up

The biggest goal of this book was to try and simplify the world of fitness, health and bodybuilding. It seems slightly disappointing that I can summarise 25 years of training, bodybuilding, researching and studying into one paragraph, but I think I can.

If you don't know where to start on your health and fitness journey, just go into a gym, ask for some help and advice, and get started. Everyone, at some point, has felt anxious, embarrassed or unsure of where to start. Don't overthink it, just turn up. Whatever level you are at, your aim is to always do a little more, each time, each day, each week, month and year. Chip away at the training, the diet and the mindset, and make small improvements, one step at a time.

From a training perspective, understand that there are so many options available to you, and no one approach is 'the best' or the 'only way'. Your training goal should dictate your training methods. Whether you want to do weight training, bodybuilding, CrossFit, powerlifting, running, cycling or a dozen other approaches, try and pick something that you enjoy, you can measure and you can improve at. Of course, this choice may affect body composition, aesthetics and performance. You won't be able to build lots of muscle if prioritising cycling, but most people don't want to look like a bodybuilder. Whatever approach you choose, try and do some kind of weight-bearing exercise, especially into older age.

From a diet perspective, understand that there is no magic diet. Calories in vs Calories out will dictate weight loss and gain, your macronutrient choices will contribute to body composition, and food types and timings will affect health and adherence. You can choose from a hundred different diets like intermittent fasting, vegan, low carb, high carb, paleo or 4 square meals a day. As long as you adhere to the above principles, they can all be successful.

For bodybuilding, understand that proximity to failure is the most important factor, and most rep ranges, from sets of 5 to sets of 25, can elicit a hypertrophic response as long as they are at, or very near to, muscular failure. Try to pick exercises that are worth the risk to reward and return of investment, and prioritise two aspects of intensity, volume and frequency, but not all three. Gaining or losing weight, in a slow and controlled manner and over a longer dieting phase, will give you the best opportunity for preserving muscle in a cut, and limiting fat gain in a bulk.

From a mindset perspective, find your passion, something that drives you and makes you want to focus and improve. If you're the competitive type, then don't shy away from that. Keep a logbook, and aim to get stronger, quicker or go further, time and time again. If you're someone who has obsessive or addictive tendencies, then use that, and channel it into your health and fitness journey, but keep yourself accountable with realistic plans and goals. And if you have been pulled towards hedonistic behaviours in the past, you have to acknowledge the realities around them, evaluate your dopamine pursuits, and plan accordingly. Effective programming and training can be transformative for these personalities.

Most of all, be yourself and enjoy your life. Your health and fitness pursuit should contribute to a better, happier life, but it doesn't need to define you. With excellent programming, applying the basics and having some set rules, you don't have to live like a monk. On a personal level, of course there are occasions when you have to make sacrifices, but outside of the last few weeks pre-show, I would never miss a friend's stag do, a golfing weekend away, dinner with the family or a takeaway with my wife. These things are too important to me, as they're things that build relationships and create memories. With the right knowledge, a good plan and by applying the basics around calories, macros and training, you can do all of these things, and still have the health and fitness journey that you want.

Notes

1. 'Homo Deus'. Yuval Noah Harari. 2015. Dvir Publishing.
2. 'Daily Energy Expenditure through the human Life Course'. Speakman and Pontzer et al. 2021.
3. 'Role of Sleep and Sleep loss in hormonal release and metabolism'. National Library of Medicine. Rachel leproult and Eve Van Couter. 2009.
4. The Priory Group. www.priorygroup.com/eating-disorders/eating-disorder-statistics.
5. Barbara Spinjers. Center For Discovery, Eating Disorder Treatment. www.Centerfordiscovery.com/blog/get-the-facts-eating-disorder-statistics
6. 'Loading Recommendations for Muscle Strength, Hypertrophy, and Local Endurance. A re-examination of the repetition continuum'. Schoenfield, Grgic, Van Every, Plotkin. 2021.
7. Journal of Internal Medicine. 'Health Consequences of Androgenic Anabolic Steroid Use.' H. Horwitz, J.T Andersen, K.P Dalhoff. 2018.
8. 'Effect of the shoulder position on the bicep branchii EMG in different dumbbell curls'. Journal of sports science medicine. Liliam F. Oliveira, Thiago T. Matta, Daniel S. Alves, Marco A.C. Garcia, and Taian M.M. Vieira. 2009.
9. 'How Many Calories Should You Eat to Lose Weight?'. www.totalwellnessandbariatrics.com/how-many-calories-should-you-eat-to-lose-weight.com. 2022.

10. 'Calorie Counting Made Easy'. Harvard Health Publishing. July 11th 2020.

11. 'Caloric Equivalents of gained or lost weight'.. The American Journal of Clinical Nutrition. Max Wishnofsky. 1958.

12. 'Effects of Different Dietary Energy Intake Following Resistance Training on Muscle Mass and Body Fat in Bodybuilders: A Pilot Study'. Journal of Human Kinetics. J Hum Kinet et al. Sciendo, 2019.

13. 'The influence of frequency, intensity, volume and mode of strength training on whole muscle cross-sectional area in humans.' Sports Med. Wernbom M, Augustsson J, Thomee R. 2007.

14. 'Maintanance of Lost Weight and Long Term Management of Obesity.' National Library of Medicine. Keven Hall and Scott Kahan. 2019.

15. 'Nutrient Timing Revisited: is there a post-exercise anabolic window?' Journal of International Sports Nutrition. Brad Jon Schoenfeld & Alan Albert Aragon. 2013.

16. 'Effects of Low-Carbohydrate vs Low-Fat Diets on Weight Loss and Cardiovascular Risk Factors A Meta-analysis of Randomized Controlled Trials'. Alain J. Nordmann, MD, MSc; Abigail Nordmann, BS; Matthias Briel, MD; et al. 2006.

17. 'Weight Change During and After Ramadan Fasting' Journal of Public Health. Peter Hajek, Katie Myers, et al. 2012.

18. 'Intermittent and periodic fasting, longevity and disease.' National Library of Medicine. Valter D. Longo, Maira Di Tano, Mark P. Mattson,[3] and Novella Guidi· 2021.

19. 'A systematic review, meta-analysis and meta-regression of the effect of protein supplementation on resistance training-induced gains in muscle mass and strength in healthy adults'. British Journal of Sports Medicine. Robert W Morton, Kevin T Murphy, Sean R McKellar, Brad J Schoenfeld, Menno

Henselman, Eric Helms, Alan A Aragon, Michaela C Devries, Laura Banfield, James W Krieger, Stuart M Phillips. Oct 2020.

20. 'International Society of Sports Nutrition position stand: safety and efficacy of creatine supplementation in exercise, sport, and medicine.' Journal of the International Society of Sports Nutrition.Richard B. Kreider, Douglas S. Kalman, Jose Antonio, Tim N. Ziegenfuss, Robert Wildman, Rick Collins, Darren G. Candow, Susan M. Kleiner, Anthony L. Almada & Hector L. Lopez. June 2017.

21. 'Branched-chain amino acids and muscle protein synthesis in humans: myth or reality?'. Journal of the International Society of Sports Nutrition. Robert R. Wolfe. 2017.

22. 'Set points, settling points and some alternative models: theoretical options to understand how genes and environments combine to regulate body adiposity'. National Library of Medicine. John R. Speakman, David A. Levitsky, David B. Allison, Molly S. Bray, John M. de Castro, Deborah J. Clegg, John C. Clapham, Abdul G. Dulloo, Laurence Gruer, Sally Haw, Johannes Hebebrand, Marion M. Hetherington, Susanne Higgs, Susan A. Jebb, Ruth J. F. Loos, Simon Luckman, Amy Luke Vidya Mohammed-Ali, Stephen O'Rahilly, Mark Pereira, Louis Perusse, Tom N. Robinson, Barbara Rolls, Michael E. Symonds,and Margriet S. Westerterp-Plantenga. Nov 2011.

23. 'Set points, settling points and some alternative models: theoretical options to understand how genes and environments combine to regulate body adiposity'. National Library of Medicine. John R. Speakman, David A. Levitsky, David B. Allison, Molly S. Bray, John M. de Castro, Deborah J. Clegg, John C. Clapham, Abdul G. Dulloo, Laurence Gruer, Sally Haw, Johannes Hebebrand, Marion M. Hetherington, Susanne Higgs, Susan A. Jebb, Ruth J. F. Loos, Simon Luckman, Amy Luke Vidya Mohammed-Ali, Stephen O'Rahilly, Mark Pereira,

Louis Perusse, Tom N. Robinson, Barbara Rolls, Michael E. Symonds,and Margriet S. Westerterp-Plantenga. Nov 2011.

24. 'Homo Deus'. Yuval Noah Harari. 2015. Dvir Publishing.

25. Office of National Statistics. 2019. www.ons.gov.uk/peoplepopulationandcommunity/birthsdeathsandmarriages/deaths/bulletins/suicidesintheunitedkingdom/2019registrations

26. WebMD. Hope Cristol. 2021. Webmd.com/mental-health/what-is-dopamine.

27. 'The Effects of Supraphysiologic Doses of Testosterone on Muscle Size and Strength in Normal Men.' The New England Journal of Medicine. Shalender Bhasin, M.D. 1996.

28. 'Health Consequences of Androgenic Anabolic Steroid Use.' Journal of Internal Medicine. H. Horwitz, J.T Andersen, K.P Dalhoff. 2018.

Printed in Great Britain
by Amazon

54326343R00165